IF HITLER COMES

" It seems a pity to discourage them too much—they mightn't come."

Cartoon by 'Pont' published in *Punch* on 23 October 1940.

IF HITLER COMES

Preparing for Invasion:
Scotland 1940

GORDON BARCLAY

BIRLINN

First published in Great Britain in 2013 by
Birlinn Ltd
West Newington House
10 Newington Road
Edinburgh
EH9 1QS

www.birlinn.co.uk

ISBN: 978 1 84341 062 1

British Library Cataloguing-in-Publication Data
A catalogue record for this book is available on
request from the British Library

Typeset by Mark Blackadder

Printed and bound by T J International, Padstow

Dedicated
to the memory of

J. Colvin Greig
(21 October 1928 – 11 May 2006)

and

Ian A.G. Shepherd
(22 March 1951 – 15 May 2009)

The title 'If Hitler comes' was first used in the 1941 reprint of a novel, originally published in 1940 as *Loss of Eden*, by Douglas Brown and Chistopher Semple, which described all too believably the decline and fall of Britain after a weak government made an 'accommodation' with Nazi Germany in May 1940.

CONTENTS

LIST OF ILLUSTRATIONS

ACKNOWLEDGEMENTS

Many people and organisations have helped in the writing of this book, directly and indirectly.

The book is dedicated to two friends, who were very influential in my life. First, Colvin Greig, who gave me my first chance to go on an archaeological excavation, at Cullykhan in 1968, and gave me a firm grounding in archaeological fieldwork. He and his wife Moira became like a second set of parents. Second, Ian Shepherd, Scotland's first Regional Archaeologist, for Grampian, who died prematurely, as county archaeologist for Aberdeenshire. He and I worked together for many years and he started off my interest in Second World War defences; he was a kind, generous, knowledgeable man. Both Colvin and Ian were great fun, and I feel privileged to have known them.

Other workers in anti-invasion defences in Scotland have generously shared their knowledge with me: Mike Craib, for sites in eastern Scotland; David Easton, then of RCAHMS; Gavin Lindsay for sites in Orkney; Andrew Guttridge for sites in Caithness, and his plans of pillboxes in the area. Allan Carswell, Professor Peter Stachura and Robert Ostrycharz have kindly shared with me their great knowledge of the Polish forces in Scotland.

Forestry Commission Scotland, through their archaeologist Matthew Ritchie, provided invaluable information and support for my work on the defences on the forest estate in Fife and Moray. Matthew's wife, Dr Monika Maleska-Ritchie kindly translated part of the 'Kronika' of the 1/11th Polish Engineer Company in Lossiemouth in the summer of 1940. Scottish Water kindly provided a plan of the gun-house at Carnoustie, which has been adapted to modern use as a pumping station. Stewart Angus of Scottish Natural Heritage facilitated access to original Aberdeen University beach survey photographs from the 1970s. Tom Cunningham, SNH's reserve manager for Tentsmuir, has provided much useful information, and Colin R. McLeod, also of SNH, has shared with me his truly encyclopaedic knowledge of the Barry peninsula.

Adam Barclay, David Hogg, David Easton and Hugh Andrew have all helped with fieldwork; Gordon Corbet of Scottish Wildlife Trust not only facilitated access to one of the Trust's pillboxes at Largo, but helped me clear out all the rubbish prior to my making a plan. My thanks for their company.

I am particularly grateful for the considerable help of Colonel W.H. Clements, Dr Jeremy Crang and John Graham in reading a draft text and providing very helpful comments. Dr Mike Osborne not only commented on the draft but also generously gave of his time and expertise to help me with pillbox and other defence-related questions. The remaining mistakes are of course my own.

A small number of organisations look after important documents, photographs and maps about the defence of Scotland in 1940–41, and their staff have been unfailingly helpful and kind over the years. These include the National Archives at Kew, Scotland's National Records, Edinburgh, the National Library of Scotland, Edinburgh, and the Polish Institute & Sikorski Museum in London; the last operates without any public subsidy and I am particularly grateful to the staff of that archive for their assistance.

My thanks also to the staff of the Royal Commission on the Ancient and Historical Monuments of Scotland, particularly Kevin McLaren of the National Collection of Aerial Photography (aerial.rcahms.gov.uk), the Imperial War Museum and Fife Council Museums, who provided a great deal of useful illustrative material.

The Environmental Programme of ESRI, publisher of the leading Geographical Information System software, ArcMap, provided an inexpensive copy of the program to aid my mapping of the anti-invasion defences of Scotland; without this the data collation would have been a nightmare.

Finally, my thanks to Hugh Andrew of Birlinn for his encouragement to write the book, and to my wife, Elizabeth Goring, and our son, Adam, for their forbearance in the face of the demands the project made on me and on them.

PROLOGUE: MAY 1940

*Warning message from G1 9th (H[ighland]) Div[ision] re notice
from Admiralty of concentration of flat bottomed ships in* NORWAY.

(War Diary of 28th Infantry Brigade, 10 May 1940)[1]

Troop carrying aircraft assembling STAVANGER.
Possible attack Orkney and Shetland.

(HQ of 26th Infantry Brigade: urgent message to 5th Battalion
Queen's Own Cameron Highlanders, Tain (the northernmost
infantry unit on the British mainland), 17 May 1940)[2]

In that week in 1940 the long sandy beaches of Caithness lay open and undefended. The four military aerodromes, operational or under construction, within the county, had small, if any, garrisons. In Scotland north of the Tay there were fewer than 40 modern single-wing fighter aircraft: two squadrons of Hurricanes at Wick (a third had left on 13 May and its replacement did not arrive until the 22nd) and ten Spitfires 140km away at Dyce, Aberdeen, with a detachment further south at Montrose. The next possible reinforcements to the south were at Turnhouse and Drem, 280km away.[3]

Detachments of nine bomber squadrons were based at Lossiemouth and Kinloss, with elements of one also at Wick. A squadron of Blenheim bombers moved from Hatston in Orkney to Sumburgh in Shetland on 16 May.[4] Radar cover in the far north was provided by the Chain Home stations at Thrumster in Caithness and Caitnip in Orkney and the Chain Home Low station at Nether Button. Wick lay only 10 minutes flying time away from the main base of the Home Fleet at Scapa Flow, and only 480km (2 hours flying time) from the aerodrome at Sola, south of Stavanger, already, by mid-May, securely in German hands.

The only front-line infantry north of Tain were in Orkney (7th Battalion Gordon Highlanders) and Shetland (7th Black Watch, supported by machine guns of 8th Gordon Highlanders). What if . . .?

. . . *during the night of 17–18 May 1940, a force of long-range bombers, Ju 88*

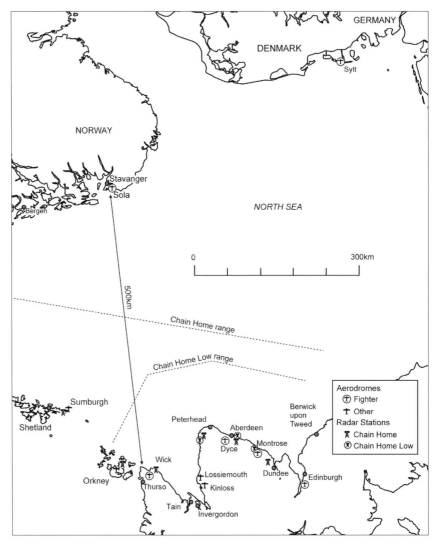

Figure 0.1.
The North Sea, May 1940.
Aerodromes under
construction or not relevant
to the hypothetical attack
on Caithness are not shown.
The ranges of the Chain
Home and Chain Home Low
systems are approximate.

fighter-bombers and Ju 52 transport planes (each of the last capable of carrying 18 parachutists) are armed and fuelled at Stavanger Sola aerodrome, and far to the south, at the northernmost aerodrome in Germany, on the island of Sylt, a diversionary force of bombers and fighter-bombers is simultaneously prepared? Early in the morning of the 18th most of the fighters at Dyce and Wick are drawn off by the Sylt-based diversion towards Peterhead (threatening Invergordon or Dyce), and the main force from Stavanger flies below the Chain Home system's operational minimum height to achieve surprise at first light over the Caithness aerodrome (as was really done by a German aircraft attacking Wick on 1 July 1940).[5]

Out of the early morning sun the limited air defences of the operational aerodromes at Wick and Castletown are overwhelmed by the bombs and machine guns of the low-level attack. The majority of the reserve fighters are destroyed on the ground and the few Hurricanes in the air over Wick if not damaged or shot down, flee, their ammunition expended, to Hatston in Orkney, from where the only fighters in the islands, obsolete Gladiator biplanes, had already flown to their doom against the German force. Even before the bombing attack on Wick is over, the first of the 300+ parachutists carried in the first 20 Ju 52s land at Wick to suppress the anti-aircraft fire, destroy the remaining aircraft, and secure the aviation spirit tanks. Smaller teams seize the other aerodromes in Caithness. As the Hurricanes that had been attacking the diversionary force return to Wick, running low on fuel and out of ammunition, their base is already falling into German hands and further Ju 52s, carrying troops and light anti-aircraft and artillery, are preparing to land.

A second wave of bombers and escorts is approaching. The remaining Dyce Spitfires return to base and are refuelling and rearming, preparing to head north. All the Caithness aerodromes are now in German hands or severely damaged, and the next flight of German bombers diverts to bomb Hatston aerodrome in Orkney, while the escorts prepare to fight off the unescorted British bombers approaching from Lossiemouth and Kinloss. The aviation spirit on the Caithness aerodromes has been secured. The success of the first assault triggers the order for a force of Me 109 fighters to make the flight from Sola – which can only be one way as they do not carry enough fuel for a return trip – to form the defence of the new Luftwaffe base at Wick. Further Ju 52 aircraft, each towing two or three DFS 230 assault gliders, carrying Luftwaffe ground crew, bombs and ammunition leave from airfields in Denmark and north Germany. A shuttle of Ju 52s flies non-stop between Sola and Wick and by the end of 20 May Caithness and the ports of Thurso and, most importantly, Wick are in German hands. The road bridge at Helmsdale has been blown to stop a British counter-attack from the south and a cycle of savage Luftwaffe bombing raids from Wick begins on Scapa Flow (only 10 minutes flight away); the Home Fleet has scattered into the teeth of waiting U-boats and is in retreat to its western bases and is no position to intercept a fast convoy from Norway to Wick, which has further reinforced the German garrison of Caithness, giving it self-sufficiency for a month. Orkney and Shetland will soon become untenable. Far to the south, two days later, on 20 May, the German forces reach the sea at Abbeville, the evacuation of the BEF (British Expeditionary Force) from Dunkirk is about to begin, and on 26–28 May the British War Cabinet meets to decide whether to continue the fight.

Would that discussion have reached the same conclusion? Would the reality of the invasion of mainland Britain have galvanised British resistance, albeit weakened by the loss of Scapa Flow? Or with a portion of the British mainland in enemy hands and apparently secure for the foreseeable future from counter-attack by land, and British prestige irrevocably damaged, would a German approach for a peace settlement – preserving the Empire while leaving Germany a free hand in mainland Europe – have been accepted as the only prudent course of action? As Stephen Bungay has written: 'If Britain had given up in 1940, the war could have had one of two possible outcomes: Nazi or Soviet domination of Europe'[6] and the course of world history would have been changed.

ADMIRAL DRAX'S PAPER

Just such a German scheme was envisaged by Admiral Sir Reginald Plunket Ernle-Erle Drax, C-in-C at the Nore, in a paper put to the Chiefs of Staff Committee (CSC) on 25 July 1940.[7] He suggested that the Germans could put 50,000 troops into northern Scotland and within a few days concentrate on the aerodromes near Wick such a force that Scapa Flow would become untenable. Once the Home Fleet had been driven off, Orkney and Shetland could have been taken and Scapa captured. The Joint Intelligence Committee's (JIC) self-satisfied dismissal of the paper on the basis, first, that the aerodrome guards could be made strong enough to resist assaults by up to 500 parachutists and, second, that 17 aerodromes in Scotland north of the Tay would allow the diversion of sufficient bombers and fighters to operate against the invaders, does not convince. But even if true in July 1940, that view was not true in May and would not be true again once the Battle of Britain was in full swing. By August JIC had changed their view after representations by the Naval Commander in Shetland, Lord Cork and Orrery,[8] and, fortunately, the Germans had been as surprised as anyone else by their success. And, contrary to universal belief at the time, they were not making long-term strategic plans and were not ready to use the opportunities their success in April and May 1940 had opened up. It is just as well.

PART 1: HISTORY

Dieses Haus darf nur mit Genehmigung des Befehlshabers der Sicherheitspolizei für Grossbritannien betreten werden.

———

No entrance without permission of the Chief-in Command of the German Secret Police for Great Britain.

1. INTRODUCTION

Between May 1940 and the summer of 1941 the United Kingdom faced the threat of an invasion that, had it succeeded, would have meant the enslavement of Britain's population and the redirection of its whole society to further the Nazis' nightmare racist war. That period saw an unparalleled effort to prepare the defence of the UK against such an invasion. Although southern England was always likely to have been the main target, Scotland's nationally important heavy industries, vital Royal Navy bases and key convoy ports were seen as very vulnerable to the sort of airborne attack that had devastated the defences of Belgium or, perhaps more worryingly, the combined operations that had overwhelmed Norway.

The threat of invasion did not really pass until it was clear that Germany and her allies were bogged down on the Eastern Front in 1941, but by then the anti-invasion preparations had developed a life of their own, and for a further two years or more absorbed *matériel*, energy and training time that could in most cases have been directed more productively.

It is debatable whether Hitler ever intended to invade, and it is widely believed that his preparations were intended only to put pressure on the British government to negotiate; but it seemed certain to the British people and most of their political and military leaders in the summer of 1940 that he could and would launch an invasion. Indeed, it was believed certain that plans for an invasion had long been prepared.[1] And it seemed certain to most people that within Britain a Fifth Column of Nazi sympathisers and agents was working actively to spread rumours, confusion and despair, to sabotage military sites and civilian industry and installations, and to aid the invasion forces.[2] While Churchill, the armed forces, the men who joined the Home Guard and much of the population believed that they should and could stand firm and worked hard to prepare, some – keen supporters of fascism and Germany during the 1930s – would have welcomed Hitler.[3] Others could foresee only disaster in standing up to the apparently unstoppable German forces and believed that the British Empire could only be preserved by making peace from a position of weakness, effectively leaving Germany with a free hand in mainland Europe and Scandinavia.[4] Yet others (with, it must be said, rather

Opposite.
A bilingual notice prepared by the Germans for use after the occupation of Britain.

3

limited imagination) thought that the rationing of tea and the imposition of petty restrictions meant that they would be 'as well off under Hitler'.[5] The fate of the peoples of mainland Europe, especially vulnerable minorities, was a matter of indifference to many on both right and left of the British political spectrum. With the Germans and Russians allied, many Communists in politics and the trades union movement opposed the war effort and significant parts of the pacifist lobby were 'strikingly equivocal' about or apologists for Nazi Germany in the 1930s.[6]

In the last days of May 1940, facing the imminent fall of France, with Belgium suddenly capitulating on the 28th, and uncertain as to how many men could be saved by evacuation from Dunkirk and other French ports, the British Cabinet debated whether to fight on or to seek terms with Germany.[7] In those days a bold stroke, of the kind described in the Prologue, could have changed the course of the war. This book is about what was done in the summer of 1940 and the first half of 1941 to ensure that such a bold stroke could not succeed.

WHY THIS BOOK?

My interest in anti-invasion defences grew out of a request by the late Ian Shepherd (local authority archaeologist for Grampian Regional Council and then Aberdeen-shire Council) that I, as area Inspector of Ancient Monuments for Historic Scotland, consider for legal protection as scheduled monuments, a group of pillboxes in Kincardineshire (Fig. 1.1). Some of these had been noted by Wills in his pioneering 1985 book on pillboxes.[8] Background research, with input from Ian and the local Forestry Commission manager, Graham Tuley, led to a fuller recognition of the extraordinarily well-preserved 'Cowie Line' – an anti-tank stop-line – running inland from Stonehaven, of which the pillboxes were only the most visible part.[9]

Many hundreds of Second World War structures have been recorded in Scotland and the rest of the UK in the last two decades. Historic Scotland funded a rapid survey of the whole country by John Guy in the 1990s, to provide a basic dataset of twentieth-century defences. The Defence of Britain Project, organised by the Council for British Archaeology (CBA) between 1995 and 2002, encouraged local volunteers throughout the UK to submit information; CBA then arranged for the collation of that information into a usable form and the database of the Project has been made available online.[10] The CBA also co-ordinated, with funding by government heritage agencies, a series of surveys of War Office files to record references to defence-related structures built mainly during the Second World War. The database of Scotland's national body of survey and record for the historic

Figure 1.1.
The late Ian Shepherd, county archaeologist of Aberdeenshire, at the granite pillbox at Findlaystone Bridge on the Cowie anti-tank stop-line, inland from Stonehaven (Author).

environment, the Royal Commission on the Ancient and Historical Monuments of Scotland (RCAHMS), has not only incorporated most of this information, but has added hugely to it through the efforts of its own staff (notably David Easton), particularly in the examination of wartime and post-war aerial photographs.[11] Individuals in Scotland with a particular interest in defensive sites, or who have perhaps simply photographed them in passing, have made knowledge about sites, both surviving and lost, available in a number of ways, either through traditional publishing (for example in pamphlets or books about particular areas or places) or through photographic or other websites. Much of the information on the web and in personal collections, has, unfortunately, not been lodged with RCAHMS, probably the only place where its long-term survival is reasonably certain.

While there is a huge amount of information available, little has been done to give it meaning or to describe groups of sites and structures as coherent parts of a wider pattern of construction and activity, or in a historical context. While historical sources have been used to locate sites, they have not been used to tell the story of how, why and by whom they were built, and how they were intended to be used. As a consequence, accounts of the defences can be rather generalised, both chronologically and geographically. The defences may be presented as a homogeneous mass that appeared 'in 1940' and as reflecting a single coherent purpose, rather than the accumulation of structures intended to meet changing perceptions of threat, often reflecting changing or even conflicting priorities. Individual sites or small groups of sites – perhaps surviving fragments of what was there, maybe reflecting a number of phases of work, and possibly surviving in a radically changed landscape – may be given an interpretation that seems to make sense to the observer, but which may bear little relation to what was built, why and when.

Simplistic views of the defences add to the accumulation of inaccurate popular narratives or even 'myths' that surround the Second World War (as discussed in the next section). The perception of the anti-invasion defences as 'simple' or as 'much the same' wherever one encounters them in Scotland or indeed throughout the UK, as they were *supposed* to be built to an identical pattern, also undermines efforts to protect this part of our built heritage. The protection of a sample, say of a complex of anti-tank cubes and pillboxes, in one part of Scotland will not actually preserve a representative cross-section of what was built in different parts of the country. It is now clearly understood that, at least in Scotland's more distant past, study and preservation should take account of regional differences as well as changes over time.[12] This book demonstrates, I hope, that regional variation and chronological depth are equally important concepts in the study and preservation for our wartime heritage.

Consideration of the defences built in Scotland has also to some extent been overshadowed by what we have found out since the war about German intentions and capabilities. We now know, for example, that no plans were made for an assault anywhere but on the south-eastern tip of this island; defences built elsewhere can, as a consequence, be retrospectively categorised, consciously or unconsciously, as 'unnecessary' or 'wasteful'. The next step is to place what is thought of as unnecessary or wasteful in a lower category of value. I have tried in this book to look at the defences as they were considered when they were built, as (generally) reasonable precautions against possible actions by the enemy, although I have made it clear where I think that the response was out of proportion to the real risk, especially after the summer of 1941.

Considerable efforts have been made in other parts of the UK, especially in England, to provide consistent regional surveys (through Mike Osborne's still-developing county-based *20th Century Defences* series) and to convey variety and chronological depth (as in William Foot's *Beaches, Fields, Streets and Hills*[13]). This volume, however, is the first attempt to provide a reasonably comprehensive account of the anti-invasion defences built in Scotland, in the context of contemporary military and political concerns and priorities. I hope that this book both provides an informative and readable account of what was built, and why, and provides a reasonably sound basis for decision-making in the conservation of this part of Britain's past.

SOURCES

As an archaeologist I have a particular distrust of secondary sources. Calder,[14] among others, has explored the reshaping of the contours of memory by wartime and post-war representations of the time – in other words, people end up remembering what is accepted as the collective memory, especially after 50 or 60 years have passed. Oral history tends to be unspecific as to times and even precise places, and contemporary or later accounts from the lower end of the chain of command tend to have limited awareness of the wider picture, and as a consequence seem to overemphasise apparent chaos at a local or detailed level and individual stupidity and inefficiency. The accounts of people higher in politics or military command are also unreliable; they cannot avoid (especially if prepared for publication) being at best centred on the self, at the worst, disingenuous and self-serving.

My intention has been to write a historical and archaeological account based as far as is possible on the evidence of sites and original documents. These include: British and Polish military files; minutes and papers of the War Cabinet and its subsidiary committees; Scottish Office and other government department files; modern and historical maps, both published and unpublished; and wartime, post-war and modern aerial photographs. Even these primary sources have their problems. Military files were kept for a variety of purposes unrelated to historical research, and different units and formations took strikingly different approaches to filling out the key record of what they did: their War Diaries. Work on Polish documents and maps, often much fuller than British equivalents, is made more difficult by their quirk of not consistently dating things, especially as the papers were not always filed in such a way as to maintain their original relationship. Military and government records also seem to reflect narrow and immediate concerns and, especially in 1940, the often hasty and incomplete collation of information.

One secondary source has, however, been very helpful in writing this book: David Newbold's 1988 PhD thesis, 'British Planning and Preparations to Resist Invasion on Land, September 1939 – September 1940', is a readable and authoritative account of high-level military policy based on a detailed study of government records, published sources such as diaries, private papers and even interviews with senior commanders still living in 1981. It inevitably concentrates, where it covers the disposition of troops and the intentions of commanders, on the east and south of England, but it is an unrivalled account of the wider picture against which the defence of Scotland has to be seen. No book derived from the thesis seems to have been published, but it is accessible online and free of charge from the British Library.[15] Redfern's survey of War Office files at the National Archives at Kew is a further invaluable starting point for anyone interested in Scotland's defences – he extracted every reference to defence structures he could find.[16] The lists are, however, overwhelming in their quantity and detail, and compound the risk of seeing the defences as an aggregated mass.

MAPS AND DIMENSIONS

The maps in this book are based on out-of-copyright one-inch and quarter-inch Ordnance Survey maps, generally those overprinted in 1939–40 with the military grid for Army use, and show the coastline, boundaries of towns, roads and railways largely as they were at the time of the invasion scare. North lies at the top of all maps, except where indicated. On pillbox plans the seaward or 'enemy' side, where that can be identified, also lies at the top of the page.

All distances and dimensions in contemporary documents were given in imperial units. Where quoting or using distances from these documents, imperial measurement (still widely used as the standard measurement in the UK) are used; distances established by the author are given in kilometres. Smaller dimensions are given in imperial (if an original document is the source) with a metric conversion; measurements established by the author are given only in metric units.

APOLOGIA

Clausewitz, the Prussian philosopher of war, who himself was commissioned into the 34th Prussian Infantry Regiment at the age of 12,[17] wrote that if one had never personally experienced war, one could not understand how difficult it was to organise or achieve anything, nor why a commander should need any brilliance and exceptional ability – 'Everything in war is very simple, but the simplest thing is difficult'.[18] His concept of 'friction' – the way in which the actions or omissions of individuals and events or circumstances conspire to make everything slower, less certain, less efficient – 'is the force that makes the apparently easy so difficult'. I am conscious that I have no military experience but I have tried in this book to take account of the 'friction' faced by the soldiers defending Britain, having to catch up on decades of political penny-pinching and unimaginative military doctrine, using imperfect people and institutions, in the teeth of the German gale. I believe they achieved miracles and I hope that I have been fair to them.

No book of this kind can ever hope to be complete. Not only has much detail had to be omitted for reasons of space, but defence sites from the war are still coming to light. As noted above, many are also known of by local people but have not as yet been incorporated into national or local authority archaeological records. Inevitably, therefore, many people reading this book will be able to say, 'but he's missed out . . .'[19] The most complete and easily accessible record of defence sites in Scotland is available online at www.pastmap.org.uk, which displays the contents of the national archaeological record, some local authority archaeology records and information on whether sites are scheduled monuments or listed buildings. New discoveries can be reported through Archaeology Scotland's annual publication, *Discovery and Excavation in Scotland*.

The story of Scotland's war is complex and as yet is only partly written. To maintain focus I have not ventured far from the planning and construction of the anti-invasion defences into related areas that are of equal interest: the legislative powers taken by government that included the powers to build defences on private land; the impact on the lives, livelihoods and civil liberties of civilians in towns and in the country; or the relationship between the War Office and other government departments, especially the Scottish Office. These are subjects worthy of books of their own.

2. COMPLACENCY: TO MAY 1940

HIGH COMMAND

In the summer of 1940 the key decisions about the war, and especially about the defence of the United Kingdom, were being taken in the Chiefs of Staff Committee (CSC), a subcommittee of the War Cabinet, comprising the professional heads of the three armed services (the First Sea Lord, the Chief of the Imperial General Staff and the Chief of the Air Staff). The Committee had two important subcommittees, which often provided the papers for discussion: the Joint Planning Staff and the Joint Intelligence Committee (JIC). At the height of the invasion crisis CSC was meeting twice a day, with meetings often into the night.

This book is largely concerned with the Army. During the period under review there were three Commanders-in-Chief, Home Forces, one after the other. The three men's different approaches, methods and achievements will be examined as they appear in the story. They had to deal with very different circumstances, and had different powers to tackle the problems they faced. Some problems they had in common: competing priorities driven by the War Office and politicians; where were the Germans capable of landing? With what sort of force would they try to land? Could they reinforce and resupply their forces? Were British troops best placed close to the vulnerable places, or held back for strong counter-attacks? All three had to react to circumstances that sometimes changed rapidly, adapt to the new forms of warfare being developed by the enemy, and cope with the knee-jerk and, on occasion, panicky reactions of politicians and senior commanders in the three services to these changing circumstances and new forms of warfare.

Beneath C-in-C Home Forces was a varying number of Army Commands: Scottish Command concerns us most, but Scottish Command at one time included Northern Ireland, and excluded Orkney & Shetland; to the south was Northern Command, and beyond it Eastern and Western. The Commands were subdivided in different ways throughout the war, and these subdivisions had changing functions. Scotland's subdivisions are dealt with below.

COMMAND STRUCTURE IN SCOTLAND

During the invasion crisis Scottish Command was led by Lt General Sir Robert Harold Carrington, KCB, DSO (1940 to May 1941) and Lt General Sir Andrew Thorne, KCB, CMG, DSO (May 1941 to 1945) (Fig. 2.1). Thorne in particular was an active soldier who, with better luck, might have expected to command a Corps or Army in the field.[1]

After a short-lived arrangement of 'Sub-areas' and 'sectors' in 1939–40,[2] the Army Areas in Scotland were reorganised in July 1940 into North Highland, South Highland, Edinburgh and Glasgow.[3] In the months after October 1940 the four Army Areas in mainland Scotland were split into Sub-areas, an arrangement that lasted through the period covered in this book: The four mainland Areas and their Sub-areas in 1940 are shown on Figure 2.2. The use of county names is at one's first encounter, rather misleading, as 'Sutherland' included also Caithness,

Figure 2.1.
Generals Carrington and Thorne on manoeuvres in Aberdeenshire, 6 May 1941, around the time of the handover of Scottish Command from the former to the latter (Imperial War Museum H9416).

ORKNEY & SHETLAND

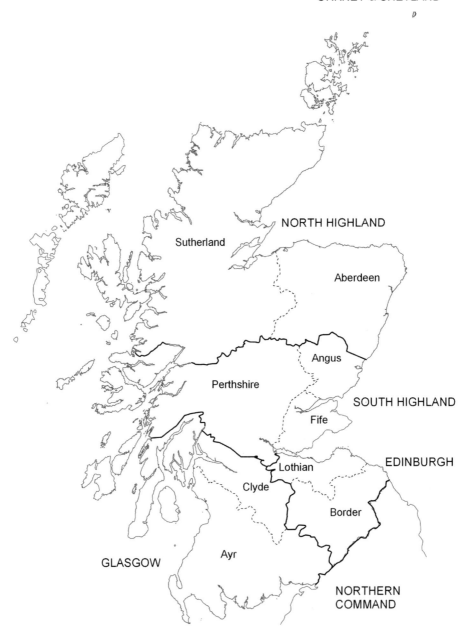

NORTH HIGHLAND

Sutherland

Aberdeen

Angus

Perthshire

SOUTH HIGHLAND

Fife

EDINBURGH

Lothian

Clyde

Border

Ayr

GLASGOW

NORTHERN
COMMAND

0   150km

Ross & Cromarty, Inverness-shire and Nairn, while 'Aberdeen' included Kincardineshire, Banffshire and Moray.

The command arrangements for Orkney and Shetland, where the local Army commander was subordinate to the Naval commander of 'Orkneys and Shetlands Command',[4] varied during the period described – even moving outside Scottish Command at one time; and the county of Caithness was moved from the Sutherland Sub-area to Orkney and Shetland in 1941.

The establishment of the Sub-areas reflected a need to separate the roles of the Field Force, or 'Field Army' (higher quality units of infantry, artillery and engineers, better trained and equipped, and capable of movement to counter-attack across Scotland) and 'static' units (locally based units with limited mobility, for example, lower-grade infantry battalions, Pioneers, searchlight troops, anti-aircraft gunners, Home Defence and Young Soldier battalions), which could fight only close to their bases. The nature of the British Army in May 1940 is described in the next chapter.

The duties of the Sub-areas were formally: the command and training of all troops apart from Field Forces; the defence and 'immobilisation'[5] of open spaces and ports; the defence of aerodromes, 'immobilisation' of petrol, transport, public utilities, Post Office and food; administration as delegated by Area commanders; and all liaison with RAF, RN and civil powers as appropriate. During the period under study responsibility passed to the Areas and their Sub-areas for the construction and maintenance of defence works and the provision of 'static' defence (guarding Vulnerable Points (see Chapter 6), aerodromes and the beaches). In the face of a German attack their role was to delay it as much as possible while the Field Force manoeuvred to counter-attack. The Areas relied increasingly on Home Guard and non-front-line troops based in the areas to fulfil their varied roles. The Sub-areas could also count on the men based at and being trained in the depots (Infantry Training Centres) of the major Scottish regiments, in Inverness, Aberdeen, Perth, Edinburgh, Stirling, Glasgow, Hamilton, Ayr and at Fort George (and the King's Own Scottish Borderers in Berwick-upon-Tweed), which could each contain over 1,000 or even 2,000 men at various stages of training, although very few might be considered fully effective.

Of course, the units and larger formations of the Field Force (brigades and divisions) were located within the boundaries of Areas, and Operation Instructions for Field Force formations and Areas made explicit who was responsible for commanding whom in a particular geographical area, in different circumstances, especially when action was imminent.

Although roles and boundaries changed over time, the 1940 Sub-area boundaries have been used to provide a structure within which to describe the defended beaches, the stop-lines and the important sites whose defence was a priority, such as ports and aerodromes.

Figure 2.2.
The boundaries of Army Areas and Sub-areas established during 1940.

THE ARMY IN SCOTLAND

At first sight it can be difficult to understand why the Army was worried about the possible arrival of 25,000 or more German troops in the summer of 1940. After all, at the height of the invasion threat in 1940, there were 181,000 British troops and 169,000 Home Guard in Scottish Command,[6] based on the quarterly Army returns for July–September 1940.[7] The preceding quarterly return, for April–June 1940, showed the total Army personnel as 157,000, of whom about 66,000 were infantry, 43,000 Royal Artillery and 11,000 Royal Engineers.[8]

In contrast, during the same quarter, on 27 May 1940 (albeit when the Home Guard was only a few days old), Lt General Carrington, GOC Scotland, wrote a rather bad-tempered note to GHQ Home Forces about the overstretch Scottish Command was suffering. He noted that he had only one infantry division (9th (Highland) Division,[9] a second-line Territorial Army formation) in the Command: the division had only nine battalions of infantry (7,813 officers and men)[10] of which one was in Orkney, one was on its way to Shetland, three were in the Cromarty–Invergordon area guarding the fleet oiling base, one was split up guarding Vulnerable Points, and three were in Fife and Kinross protecting Rosyth naval base. In addition 8th Gordon Highlanders, the machine gun battalion of the division, had 710 officers and men (and 48 medium machine guns). The 9th Division also had three regiments of field artillery and an anti-tank gun regiment and at this point two instead of its normal three companies of Royal Engineers (another 500 or so men). As noted in Chapter 3, below, 9th Division was one of the 'duplicate' Territorial divisions formed in the summer of 1939 and its equipment and training was inevitably far behind the first-line Territorial divisions, which were either in France or ready to go there.

The April–June 1940 return actually showed the presence of 30 infantry battalions in Scotland, but some of these were clearly shattered remnants after Dunkirk (there were three battalions without any officers and one had about 50 officers and men) and/or units without equipment, and General Carrington noted, for example, that the re-forming remnants of 46th Division in the Scottish Borders could muster only the equivalent of two battalions of infantry. The contrast between the raw totals for the two quarters (157,000 or 181,000) and Carrington's figure for his single division (fewer than 10,000) is in the difference in capabilities, equipment, training and mobility, in other words, *effectiveness*.

It is clear from what is written in the files that few units at this time had a reasonable level of equipment, enough transport and enough of the necessary training to act offensively in the field. Because of the almost complete lack of military vehicles, even key reserve formations had to hire a proportion of their transport when an invasion risk was believed to be imminent, and prolonged requisition of buses, delivery vans and so on had a very damaging effect on civilian life.[11] As noted above, the rest of the troops were 'static' – with specific local responsibilities and limited capacity to act beyond a very limited distance. They might arguably be able to hit the enemy hard but only if the enemy came within reach. Thus, starting with the total of 66,000 infantry in the April–June return, we are left with effective numbers of 10,000 or so, and those very much scattered across the country – the difficulty faced by the defender is always that he must defend many places, while the enemy may choose to attack only one.

If we do the same with the Royal Artillery, and take off coast defence batteries and anti-aircraft artillery, there were, in June 1940, 19 field and anti-tank regiments in Scotland, with 10,326 officers and men. It is clear that some of these units were, like the infantry, in a poor state: one regiment had one officer and 57 men (field regiments usually had around 30 officers and over 500 men), and few units had anything like their full complement of modern guns.

A year later, however, at the end of May 1941, the 'Field Force' in Scotland had been transformed. In addition to the static battalions and other troops, 51st Division, in North Highland Area, had its full nine battalions of infantry, relieved of beach defence duties to allow them to train, three field regiments of Royal Artillery, an anti-tank regiment and four Royal Engineer companies. Attached to it were a machine gun battalion and a reinforced regiment of medium artillery, and three companies of the Reconnaissance Corps (and a mobile bath unit). The 52nd Division in Perthshire and south of the Forth had almost exactly the same complement. There was, in addition, the four-battalion 227th Independent Brigade in Caithness, an infantry battalion in Orkney and three first-line battalions in Shetland (plus a Home Defence battalion). And of course the Polish Army – the equivalent of over a division in strength (10–12 battalions), with artillery, field artillery, engineers and even a fledgling tank regiment – garrisoned Angus and Fife. And finally, the Norwegian contingent, organised as a brigade from March 1941, was positioned to defend the Invergordon area.[12]

PLANNING FOR HOME DEFENCE IN THE RUN-UP TO WAR

The resurgence of Germany as a military force had begun before the Nazis came to power,[13] but from 1933 the rebuilding of the German armed forces accelerated rapidly. British reactions were in the main directed to countering the perceived threat from Germany's air force, and the (exaggerated) impact of bombing. The Chiefs of Staff Committee reported in February 1937 that there was 'no danger of invasion' and that it was not necessary for land forces to be positioned with any regard to dealing with an invasion – the Navy and Air Force could deal with anything likely to happen, other than a limited raid in one or two ships, or sabotage parties landed from submarines. Airborne assault was then considered a negligible risk.[14]

In February 1939 it was still believed that the scale of mainland forces necessary in the UK was 'to man the anti-aircraft defences and to maintain order . . .'[15] As the threat to peace increased in March, with the occupation of the rump of Czechoslovakia, and Britain joined in the French guarantee to Poland, defence measures included bringing the 12 Territorial divisions up to full strength, and the doubling of their number (as noted in Chapter 3 below), introducing conscription, and making preparations to arm and equip these men. The Regular divisions were to go to France if war broke out, to be followed by the Territorial divisions as they were ready for service.[16] The Army in Britain was (apart from the fixed coast defences) to be reduced to a small force of partly-trained troops, whose main function was to provide trained men to the BEF, which was also given absolute priority for arms, transport and officers.[17]

The German Army

The real capabilities of the German army, against which the British Army was to be pitted, is scarcely relevant in our story; what is important is how it was perceived by the defending forces, as it was that 'idea', the picture painted by German propaganda, the shocking victories of 1939–40 and British prejudices, that Britain was preparing to defend itself against. The British managed to believe quite contradictory things about the German Army. First, they believed in a stereotype of unimaginative, unenterprising Germans, unable to act without orders. As a consequence, they believed that the Germans had to plan their battles to the last degree and, when, as was inevitable, such plans did not survive contact with the enemy, were incapable of improvisation.[18] At the same time, the British recognised that the German Army was extraordinarily efficient and capable of rapid opportunistic shifts in forces, allowing the exploitation of opportunities. The British seemed, however, incapable of recognising how they achieved this; the study of foreign armies was not encouraged at the Staff College between the wars, and British exercises were conducted on the assumption that enemy forces would be organised and, crucially, would operate and react, in the same way as the British forces.[19] The reality of the German Army was very different. The German command structure, perfected during the First World War, allowed the man on the spot to use his initiative as how to achieve general objectives set by his superiors, and allowed the German Army to reap the full benefit of mechanisation and mobility. The British Army, in contrast, remained committed to the sort of rigid command and control structure that impeded the fullest development of the necessary 'mobility, activity and quickness' and was 'a recipe for delay and lethargy'.[20] As Hutchison wrote perceptively in 1938, 'Reference back for authority [as in the British system of command] is neither the easiest nor the most certain way of attaining [success]'.[21]

In the opening phase of the war the world had grown accustomed to German forces being boldly and ruthlessly handled, exploiting the capacities of new weapons and types of troops, finding ways of throwing their enemies off balance through the application of force and the undermining effects of a 'Fifth Column' of traitors. Hitler was widely believed to be 'infallible' and every German move was believed to be planned to the last detail, long in advance. For example, it was noted with considerable concern in the Ministry of Information reports on public opinion, on 15 June 1940, that, 'Hitler's "prophecies" are getting a wide currency and the tendency to discuss his phenomenal powers needs immediate discouragement. Such phrases as "He's a genius", "What's the date for London?", "He's uncanny", are frequent in overheard conversations.'[22]

Therefore, in the summer and autumn of 1940 Britain was expecting a bold assault or series of assaults, which had been long-prepared, possibly using unexpected types of attack, and accompanied by a devastating and perhaps irresistible air attack.

THE JULIUS CAESAR PLAN: SEPTEMBER 1939 TO MAY 1940

On the outbreak of war in September 1939, four of the five Regular Army divisions – the bulk of the trained men of the British Army in Britain – departed for France. The C-in-C Home Forces, General Kirke, was not expected to have to organise resistance to an invasion and had only a small staff and headquarters, and relatively limited powers. Kirke saw his main role as completing the training of units for early departure overseas and converting the large numbers of new recruits into soldiers as quickly as possible,[23] both tasks that were aided by units being concentrated in one place. Any task that required the dispersal of units, such as guarding Vulnerable Points or undertaking an anti-invasion role near the east coast (away from the better training areas in the west), was an unwelcome obstacle. As the need for anti-invasion forces grew, Kirke's plans were frequently derailed by the War Office, for example by taking trained units at short notice from his strategic reserve for posting overseas.

Before October 1939 the only German troops expected to land on British soil had been small parties of parachutists. However, fears were raised on 25 September 1939 about the possibility of 'a large scale landing in England [sic]',[24] in a letter from the Air Ministry to Brigadier Kennedy of Home Forces, referring to a conversation the author had had with Goering 'some time ago'.[25] In October Churchill, then First Lord of the Admiralty, raised the possibility of a combination of the weakness of the Navy in the North Sea and longer winter nights allowing a German seaborne landing on the east coast. A few days later, on 27 October 1939, this fear was given more substance by reports from the British embassy in Belgrade of intelligence from various sources that a large-scale invasion – 12,000 parachutists and 80,000 troops landed by sea and protected by a flotilla of submarines and motor launches, and by 5,200 aircraft (more planes than the Germans possessed) – was planned.[26] General Kirke believed that news of this improbable venture was 'obviously put about by the enemy'.[27] Churchill, however, argued strongly in the War Cabinet that the risk was real, a task aided by the pessimism of Sir Dudley Pound (for the Navy) and Sir Cyril Newall (RAF).[28] Kirke and Hore-Belisha (Secretary of State for War) both tried to keep things in perspective, pointing to the known unreliability of the sources, but Churchill would not be diverted and the outcome was that anti-invasion preparations were to be made, and it was even suggested that divisions be brought back from France. Newbold is sure that this particular invasion scare was a deliberate piece of misinformation by the Germans, and that others over the next few months were also German-inspired, intended to do what they did in fact achieve – create uncertainty and slow down the commitment of troops from the UK to France.[29] By the end of the month the War Cabinet had calmed down somewhat, but decided that the preparations set in train should continue. The main consequence of the discussion was that Kirke was required to prepare plans to deal with a large-scale invasion: this was to appear as the Julius Caesar Plan (usually known as the 'J.C. Plan') on 15 November.[30] It was inevitably a hastily put-together document that would be amended 18 times by the end of May 1940. The name came from the two code words, JULIUS (indicating that an attack was contemplated) and CAESAR (that an invasion was imminent).

Newbold notes that 'the major weaknesses in the "Julius Caesar" Plan in November 1939 were not in General Kirke's assumptions . . . nor . . . his general plan of operations' but in the poor state of training ('often in the basic rudiments of modern warfare'), equipment, weapons and of the troops he had available.[31] Six first-line Territorial divisions had key roles in the J.C. Plan in England, with elements of two more in Scotland, and the GHQ reserve of three more. The second-line Territorial divisions (including the 9th in Scotland) were more widely scattered for training and had only local roles in the J.C. Plan. All formations were short of light machine guns, Vickers medium machine guns and 3-inch mortars.[32] In Scotland, 15th Division had the lead role, with support if necessary from the 9th (in northern Scotland) and the 52nd (based near Glasgow). There was, however, only enough transport to equip one division, and there was not a single 2-pounder anti-tank gun in the Command.[33] The situation was little better in the other UK Commands.[34] Indeed, most transport throughout the UK still had to be provided by voluntary hiring from private companies as late as May 1940.[35]

The J.C. Plan was based on certain assumptions about German capacity and capabilities: that there could be 4,000 trained parachutists who might seize one or more aerodromes; that there were 1,000 civil aircraft with the necessary range, each capable of carrying 15 men; that there might be 6,000 air-landing troops; that a division could embark in 20 transport ships and make a crossing at 15 knots, taking 20 hours to the nearest point on the British coast; that the invasion force would be escorted by 25–30 modern destroyers; and that a landing on a beach was hardly possible during winter and therefore the enemy would more likely attempt to enter a port with transports, the port having previously been captured by parachute troops. The Humber and the port of Harwich were considered the most likely targets, but four other possible landing places were identified, two of which were in Scotland: Aberdeen and Dundee. It was also expected that an invasion force would be accompanied by a heavy air offensive against the fleet, air force and other objectives.

Because of the importance of defending the landward side of fixed coast defences (which could fight off a seaward landing) and ports themselves, Scottish, Northern and Eastern Commands were ordered to provide a strong infantry defence for the coast guns, and 18-pounders were provided to reinforce the defences of four ports, including Aberdeen and Dundee in Scottish Command.[36]

While the Plan had certain weaknesses – mainly in the state of equipment and training of the divisions it relied upon – it was a basically sound contingency plan against a fairly risky and unlikely endeavour for the Germans in the winter months. Although the J.C. Plan was amended frequently, its underlying principle remained the same – to protect the ports.

The appendices of the J.C. Plan document as amended over the months helpfully set out the main Field Force formations in Scotland, and charted their strength in artillery and anti-tank guns (Table 2.1): 18-pounder guns and 4.5-inch howitzers were obsolescent First World War weapons; the 25-pounder was the standard modern gun.

While the BEF was busily erecting over 400 pillboxes in France, few static defences were erected at home. Instead, the defence planners were obsessed with the new problem of parachutists 'almost to the exclusion of everything else'.[37] There was constant unease about a deluge of airborne troops, aided by a strong Fifth Column, that the Germans worked hard to stir up, in a not unsuccessful attempt to delay the reinforcement of the BEF.[38]

By 3 May 1940, Kirke had only eight weak or inexperienced divisions, plus elements of two more, to carry out the J.C. Plan, of which one was earmarked to be moved overseas.[39] The forces in Scotland had been reduced to the 9th Division

Table 2.1. Artillery strengths of the infantry divisions in Scotland, as recorded in the J.C. Plan over the winter of 1939–40. Each division should have been equipped with 72 25-pounders and 48 anti-tank guns

		18-pounder	4.5in howitzer	25-pounder	2-pounder anti-tank guns
November 1939	9 Division	8	–	–	–
	15 Division	–	8	–	–
	52 Division	16	24	–	–
January 1940	9 Division	8	–	–	–
	15 Division	8	16	–	–
	52 Division	8	16	–	–
3 May 1940	9 Division	6	12	6	8
	15 Division	6	6	6	4
22 May 1940	9 Division	4	11	–	8*

* The table notes that these few guns were provided by an anti-tank training regiment.

north of the Forth, with elements of the 15th Division near the border with England. Kirke still considered East Anglia to be the most vulnerable invasion area, and the J.C. Plan still reflected the likely risks of an invasion launched from the ports of north Germany. His priority was still the reinforcing of the BEF, and Home Forces came a distant second in priority for equipment and men.

Amendment 14 to the J.C. Plan was issued on 3 May 1940, showing two infantry divisions (still the 9th and 15th) in Scotland, but on the same day the CSC discussed the problem that the 15th was about to move out of Scottish Command, and the recall of 5th Division from the BEF in France was considered.[40] The J.C. Plan amendments also show that the 9th Division, the only one left in Scotland had – between 3 May and 22 May – been stripped of its six 25-pounder guns and three of its other field guns, leaving it with only 15 obsolescent artillery pieces (down from 24 on 3 May). Its eight anti-tank guns had to be provided by 53rd Anti-tank Training Regiment, Royal Artillery (RA).

Comfortable assumptions about British naval control of the North Sea had been badly shaken by the successful German invasion of Norway in April 1940, which 'made the North Sea and the Navy seem far less formidable barriers'.[41] On 2 May 1940, the CSC considered a report on plans to meet the risk of invasion, and discussed German capabilities, their possible plans and aspects of defence (such as the defence of aerodromes) almost every day during May. The threat of parachute and airborne troops was uppermost in their minds: the German invasion of Norway had involved the capture of Fornebu aerodrome at Oslo by airborne troops landed in Ju 52 transports in the face of ground fire, and Sola aerodrome at Stavanger had been captured by 131 paratroopers, supported quickly by two air-transported battalions of infantry which moved rapidly off to capture the port.[42] As early as 3 May 1940 the CSC was discussing the defence of aerodromes against troop-carrying aircraft.[43]

On 5 May, CSC saw the presentation and discussion of further key papers about invasion risks. First, a JIC paper on German capabilities was discussed: 'Germany still has the merchant shipping and landing craft necessary for landing operations on a large scale', but German naval losses in Norway were felt to preclude an imminent seaborne invasion.[44] The effect of parachute troops in Norway was noted, but their vulnerability if not reinforced was understood, although it was considered possible that airborne troops could be used for large-scale diversions and attacks on isolated Vulnerable Points. 'Organised sabotage' of British aerodromes at crucial junctures was also felt to be a major risk. These discussions were carried out against yet further, presumably German-inspired, reports of imminent invasion, this time via the British embassy in Ankara, which again almost succeeded in precipitating the withdrawal of a division from France.[45]

On 29 April, the CSC had instructed the Joint Planning subcommittee to prepare a paper on the possible seaborne and airborne invasion of Britain, in the context of possibly bringing troops back from France to strengthen the defences of the UK. A draft of it was also discussed on 5 May.[46] This, of course, was before the coast of the Netherlands, Belgium and France had become available for launching a German attack, although a German violation of Dutch neutrality was considered possible. The risk of raids on Shetland from occupied Norway was, however, a new feature of discussion. Yet the JP draft reveals a number of misconceptions, not least about the supposed lack of success of airborne troops in Norway – they had, of course, been very effective for the small numbers used – and the importance of Fifth Column activities in Norway (which were in fact almost non-existent). JP considered that Britain faced a danger from small airborne or seaborne raids (to destroy radar stations or other key installations) but could wheel out a piece of rank (and utterly inaccurate) prejudice, that such raids would demand 'a high degree of individual initiative for which the Germans are not conspicuous'. It was, of course, this very characteristic of German infantry – the ability to improvise and take the initiative without waiting for orders, especially in junior officers and NCOs – that made the German Army 'the most professionally skilful army of modern times'.[47]

The third important paper discussed on 5 May was a more detailed JIC appreciation of German capabilities in the use of airborne troops, particularly in seizing a bridgehead for an invasion that would also involve a major bombing campaign against Britain's air and sea defences.[48] This paper had a crucial role in influencing the scale of defensive preparations made in 1940, and in the following years. The possible seizure of Shetland as a forward base was discussed and the paper went on to describe Germany's (supposed) forces: 5,500 parachutists (in ten battalions with light artillery, mortars and machine guns) and a single airlift capacity of 11,500 infantry in support (with more and heavier artillery).[49] The paper provided inaccurate and rather frightening figures of 800 available transport aircraft, including 670 Ju 52s. British intelligence routinely exaggerated the size of German forces – for example, reporting a likely German tank strength of 7,000–7,500 in the invasion of the Low Countries and France, whereas in reality they had 2,574.[50]

This consideration of the capabilities of parachutists and air-landed troops, and the size of the landing areas they needed, had an important impact on instructions to 'immobilise' possible landing grounds near certain ports, aerodromes and beaches. The immediate response to the risk of airborne attack was also the issuing of Amendment 15 to the J.C. Plan on 9 May, which instructed Commands to establish mobile columns to deal with airborne troops.[51]

On 7 May, Kirke told CSC that he was planning to meet three kinds of attack: widespread air bombardment (in which troops would be needed to help the civil authorities deal with the consequences); airborne attack on aerodromes; and a combined air attack and seaborne invasion, in which it was essential that ports be defended from enemy seizure.[52] Kirke complained that 6,000 men of the Field Force were guarding Vulnerable Points, a number he planned to reduce to 4,500. He was particularly concerned by the possibility of German raids on the east coast, and now in Shetland, and the Committee agreed to a reinforcement of the small garrison there if Kirke, on his planned visit to Shetland later in the month, found it was necessary.[53] The potential loss of Shetland was considered a major issue as 'The effects on our prestige of enemy troops in occupation of British soil would be serious and far-reaching'.[54]

On 10 May, Germany attacked the Netherlands and Belgium, both neutrals, and France. As Newbold has put it, 'The chickens of the period of disarmament and unpreparedness during the inter-war period were truly coming home to roost'.[55]

3. THE MAY PANIC

In a radio discussion programme broadcast while this book was being written, Dame Vera Lynn, one of the participants, piped up, about the wartime British Army, 'The finest in the world'. It was not. As David French has written, 'In September 1939 the British Army appeared to be a formidable force of 53,287 officers and 839,410 other ranks. The reality was that it was neither a homogeneous nor a fully trained fighting force.' Nor were its separate arms adequately prepared to work together.[1] The limitations of its doctrine, in particular the rigid command and control structure that were 'a recipe for delay and lethargy', was mentioned in Chapter 2. In 1939–40 (indeed, until late 1941), it was equipped neither physically nor psychologically to fight the German Army in a continental war.

Britain's Field Army comprised a full-time professional core (325,000 in April 1939, scattered across the Empire) with a larger part-time Territorial Field Force (325,000).[2] In the summer of 1939 the Territorial Army was doubled in size and 12 'duplicate' divisions were formed, with a cadre of men from their parent Territorial formation: for example, 9th (Highland) Division was formed as the 'duplicate' of 51st (Highland) Division. Inevitably, the duplicates were less effective than their longer-serving parent formations and were referred to as 'second line Territorial divisions', marking their inferiority. The duplicates 'lacked all but the barest minimum of equipment required for training' and consisted virtually of 'semi-trained riflemen . . . straight off the street'.[3]

Divisions and Brigades

In Scotland during the period under review, the fighting units deployed were primarily infantry, artillery and engineers. Alongside them were units not primarily or initially intended to fight, such as the Pioneer Corps and support units. Infantry *battalions* were normally formed into *brigades* of three battalions (although sometimes only two, or up to four) and three brigades would form a *division*, along with Royal Signals, Royal Engineers (RE) companies, Royal Artillery (RA) regiments and batteries, Royal Army Medical Corps and Royal Army Service Corps (RASC). A division might be accompanied by non-divisional troops, into which category its machine gun battalion (see opposite) or additional Royal Artillery batteries might fall. Divisions were, until Dunkirk, the main self-sufficient fighting formations – where infantry, artillery and engineers, with their supporting departments, moved and fought together. After Dunkirk 'Brigade Groups' were tried, to create flexible multi-arm formations below the divisional level, with an integral anti-tank battery, field artillery regiment, machine gun company and an anti-aircraft platoon with heavy machine guns.[4] Independent brigades, often with similar all-arm structures, were also created, particularly in more isolated areas; a good example is 227th Independent Infantry Brigade in Caithness from February 1941, which had three or four battalions at different times, field artillery, engineers, pioneers, etc. Infantry battalions could also operate 'unbrigaded', for example, under the command of an Army Area.

Infantry Battalion

The backbone of the infantry was the battalion, the 1938 establishment being 769 officers and men; of these some were designated as first reinforcements to its companies, and the strength into action was therefore, ideally, 21 officers and 637 other ranks. In 1940–41 actual numbers recorded for battalions in service in the quarterly returns could range from 500 or so to over 1,000. Each battalion had four rifle companies (most men armed with the Short Magazine Lee Enfield .303-inch bolt action rifle), each 100 strong, and an HQ company. Each rifle company had three platoons and an HQ; each platoon (30 strong) had three sections (the smallest sub-unit, with eight men) and its own small HQ. A rifle platoon would be equipped with three Bren light machine guns, a 2-inch mortar (a not very powerful weapon, with an effective range of 500 yards), and a Boys anti-tank rifle; this was a cumbersome 0.55-inch calibre gun, losing its already limited anti-tank capability in the face of growing thickness of tank armour. The HQ company of the battalion had six platoons, undertaking specialist functions: signals; assault pioneers; four Bren guns in an anti-aircraft role; two 3-inch mortars (a far more powerful weapon, with a range of 2,800 yards (2.56km)); ten Universal/Bren carriers, each with a driver, Bren-gunner and two further crew; administrative staff; the band, and so on. The Bren light machine gun was a key infantry weapon, capable of around 500 rounds per minute but its fire limited by its use of a 30-round magazine, or a 100-round pan (for anti-aircraft fire), with an effective range of about 600 yards. It was much more portable but far less powerful than the Vickers machine gun, see below. The British Army was far more thoroughly mechanised than the German, but while the battalion should have had 65 tracked or four-wheel vehicles and 14 motorcycles, in the summer of 1940 virtually no unit had anything like its proper allocation of vehicles.

Machine Gun Battalions

Before the Second World War four regiments of infantry were converted to machine gun battalions, armed with the Vickers .303-inch medium machine gun, and individual battalions of regiments (e.g. 8th Battalion Gordon Highlanders) were also converted to this role. A machine gun battalion in 1940 comprised an HQ company and four machine gun companies, each of three platoons of two sections; a section had two guns, a platoon 12 and the whole battalion 48 Vickers guns.[5] These sturdy and reliable guns could keep up a devastating fire of 450–500 rounds a minute at a range up to 3,000 yards for hours on end, in defence or as part of an attack: 'the backbone of the defence, the deadly scythe which sweeps aside resistance in the attack'.[6] A single Vickers, taking up the space of two riflemen, could have the firepower, far better directed and controlled, of 50–100 riflemen. Machine gun battalions might be split into widely flung detachments, as 8th Gordons were in the summer of 1940.

Royal Artillery

Field artillery – the maid of all work – was organised after 1938 in regiments of 24 guns, in two 12-gun batteries, each with three 4-gun troops. This organisation was found to be a problem in divisional artillery in the BEF, where the even number of batteries could not be easily divided to support the three infantry battalions of each brigade. Thereafter, regiments were reorganised into three 8-gun batteries.[7] The modern gun for these units was the 25-pounder, a good all-round field gun, but with a lighter weight of shell than its German counterpart.[8] During the period under consideration, however, many units were equipped with the older 18-pounder and 4.5-inch howitzer, and later, with 75-mm French guns supplied from the USA, or after Dunkirk, with no guns at all, until they could be re-equipped. In June 1940, 9th Division in Scotland had three field regiments, RA, but these were recorded as mustering only 15 guns between them in May 1940 instead of their establishment of 72.[9]

Medium artillery, normally part of a corps (made up of a number of divisions and further supporting arms), was equipped with 5.5-inch gun/howitzers or the older 6-inch howitzer; there were 16 guns per regiment. There was no corps-sized formation in Scotland during 1940–41 and medium regiments and batteries appear below in the account of the defence of Scotland mainly as providing artillery support to beach defence.

Anti-tank regiments (with four 12-gun batteries at this stage) were, in Scotland at this time, normally attached to infantry divisions and were armed mainly with the 2-pounder gun, which was becoming less effective as tank armour became thicker. Each brigade also had an anti-tank company, usually armed less well than the anti-tank regiments.[10]

In Scotland in 1939–41 the only heavy regiments and batteries manned coast artillery, for example 178th Heavy Battery, RA at Cromarty, Invergordon. The coast defence batteries of the Fixed Defences (Forth, Clyde, Cromarty and Scapa Flow) and the Emergency Battery Programme batteries were armed with a range of naval-surplus 6-inch and smaller-calibre guns and are described at various points in the text. In 1940 additional batteries known as Defence Batteries (Mobile) were established, at first armed (in Scotland) with ex-naval 4-inch guns, to provide additional fire onto vulnerable beaches.

The Royal Artillery also included Scotland's anti-aircraft defence – guns, searchlights and other types of defence. Their men were generally under the command of the Air Defence of Great Britain rather than any local field formation or Army Area, although their men often had local defence responsibilities, for example, dealing with parachutists close to their sites.

Royal Engineer Field Companies

An infantry division would normally have three (or occasionally two or four) Royal Engineer field companies, ready to undertake any RE work needed, from laying and clearing mines, to the construction of accommodation or pillboxes and the demolition or building of bridges. Fully trained and equipped RE companies (with anything from 150 to 270 men) would be expected to make a good showing in combat, if required, but in 1939–40 many were raw recruits with no military experience. The division would also have a Royal Engineer field park company, responsible for storing, moving and supplying equipment for the field companies. Other specialist RE units built roads and aerodromes, or operated military railways, but their fighting capacity in 1940 would have been even more limited, owing to lack of training, weapons and experience.

Pioneer Corps

The Auxiliary Military Pioneer Corps (later the Pioneer Corps, and the Royal Pioneer Corps) was re-established in 1939. Initially composed of reservists, elderly First World War veterans, men of low medical category and 'aliens', many of whom were refugees from the countries of the enemy, their broad role included providing labour for Royal Engineers and assisting civil authorities in clearing bomb damage. In Scotland, Pioneer companies (around 275 men) played an important role in building and manning the defences on the coast and inland, and their War Diaries show that some of them had a decidedly military style, with intensive small arms and combat training.

Home Defence and Young Soldier Battalions

These units were established within the existing regiments (often being numbered 10th and 70th battalions respectively) to employ, on the one hand, older men (mainly ex-servicemen of 35 to 50), or men of a low medical category, and on the other, young men below 18. The Young Soldier battalions were made up of young men from very varied backgrounds – from public school to reform school; these very mixed units needed first-class officers and NCOs, but usually had to make do with 'aged First World War subalterns' and low medical category NCOs. In some battalions 'this nearly ruined what was otherwise a first class venture'.[11] For a very jaundiced opinion of the Young Soldier battalions, see p. 71. The HD and YS battalions were generally larger than front-line infantry: a figure of 1,200 men was not uncommonly recorded in the quarterly Army returns.

The Home Guard

On 14 May 1940, recruitment began for the auxiliary military force, at first called the Local Defence Volunteers, rapidly renamed the Home Guard, and by 4 June GHQ could report that 300,000 men had already been recruited in Britain, and 94,000 rifles had been issued, with a further 80,000 on their way from Canada.[12] The number of men taken on vastly exceeded the expected numbers and, by August 1940, a ceiling (not adhered to) of 135,000 had been set for Home Guard numbers in Scotland alone.[13] During 1941 the arming and training of the Home Guard improved and by the time of the stand-down in 1944 it was a highly efficient and well-armed body. But in the summer and autumn of 1940 the units were poorly armed and, while committed and enthusiastic, were largely untrained. To an even greater extent than most of the army, the Home Guard units could only operate close to their base, and Home Guard numbers reflected the density of population rather than invasion risk. The numbers available in rural areas vulnerable to landings in the east and in the north were thus relatively low. Their main practical value in the period of the invasion crisis was to free other soldiers from guarding Vulnerable Points, and to provide internal security – for example, dealing with crashed enemy aeroplanes and capturing their crews.

Empire and Allied Units

Britain hosted a wide range of Empire forces and also soldiers, sailors and airmen from defeated allies, but no troops from the Empire were based in Scotland (apart from the Canadian Forestry Corps). The largest military contingent was from the Polish Army (about a division strong), with a brigade-sized force of Norwegians (undergoing training for most of the period under consideration) and a detachment of unknown size of Free Yugoslavs, who seem to have been stationed alongside the Poles, but who are mentioned only once in the available files, in December 1941.[14]

Armoured Units

Throughout most of the period under discussion no tanks were stationed in Scotland. The Polish Army was very keen to develop an armoured capability and had the beginnings of an armoured unit in Blairgowrie, Perthshire by February 1941.[15] For a few weeks in the summer of 1940, in July and August, 7th Battalion Royal Tank Regiment was briefly based in Perthshire. While it was in Scotland it had a wide-ranging counter-attacking role in support of 5th Division, from as far north as Aberdeen to Belhaven Bay and Gullane in the south-east. The tanks could plan to work in this enormous area because of the creation of a 'tactical train': three tank squadrons and the HQ squadron of the regiment (18 'I' tanks, 2 light tanks and 4 Bren carriers) with 120 officers and men could be conveyed in 31 railway coaches, ramp waggons, flat waggons and vans anywhere the rail system went and where suitable de-training points existed.[16]

PUBLIC OPINION

We are fortunate to have, from 18 May to 27 September 1940, the daily reports of the Home Intelligence Department of the Ministry of Information (MoI).[17] The reports were compiled from Mass-Observation reports and the Wartime Social Survey, supplemented from informal conversations, even overheard remarks, the contents of letters seen by the postal censor, Special Branch reports and so on. The reports have been edited for publication and accompanied by a full scholarly apparatus by Addison and Crang.[18] Some of the themes identified were: the prevailing levels of anxiety about the likelihood of invasion; the preparedness (or lack) of the government and people's role in the war effort; Fifth Columnists/pacifists/was the Duke of Windsor a fascist?; the possibility of a German invasion of Eire and the risk to Wales and the west; Hitler's 'infallibility' and the date he would launch the invasion.

Anxiety was fuelled by attention-seeking fools, as MoI reported on 6 June 1940 with a scarcely concealed frustration and contempt, 'Stellar Bulletin. An eminent astrologer and his publisher, both capable of spreading alarmist reports, have predicted that Monday and Tuesday, 10 and 11 June, are "fatal days". Large-scale invasion is indicated and danger to the Royal Family to whom it would be hazardous to "cross water".'[19]

FRIGHTENING THE NAVY . . . THE RAF AND THE 'BOMBER WILL ALWAYS GET THROUGH'

Although not directly affecting the construction of the anti-invasion defences by the Army, the defence posture of the other two services provided a context for the land defence. The mythology of 1940, created while the Battle of Britain was raging, and reinforced since, credits the RAF's victory as preventing an invasion; the official history of the war at sea[20] and more recent accounts have, however, sought to get across a more nuanced account about the relationship between the air battle and the failure of any attempt to launch an invasion.[21] It is clear that the Navy was always going to play the key role in deterring an invasion or in defeating a flotilla, but in 1940 the Navy's actions were constrained by its perception of its vulnerability to aerial attack.

The RAF entered the war in 1939, having won a struggle for survival as an independent air force after the First World War, with a quasi-religious belief in the effectiveness of strategic bombing as a way of winning wars, and a strong aversion to being used as 'flying artillery' for the Army. Between the wars, visionaries and propagandists for aerial warfare promoted the view that aerial defence could not be effective. In 1939–40, although the Navy's anti-aircraft defence was not strong, the Luftwaffe's capacity for bombing of ships was limited: only the slow-moving Ju 87 dive-bomber was particularly effective, and it was vulnerable to anti-aircraft fire. German bombs were at this stage of insufficient weight to do the task effectively, and destroyers had a great capacity to manoeuvre to avoid bombs. However, in the spring and summer of 1940 the Royal Navy suffered losses to air attack in the Norwegian campaign and the evacuation of the British Expeditionary Force from French ports. While these were in waters where manoeuvre was difficult, they strengthened an already acute naval belief that most of their ships were very vulnerable to air attack. It would have been too much to expect the senior command of the Royal Air Force, committed as it was to stressing the value of air power, and committed to a belief in the effect of bombing, to help the Navy develop a more balanced view of the risks to their ships from aerial attack.[22]

As a consequence, the Chiefs of Staff could take a very pessimistic view of the chances of fending off a German invasion. They reported on 26 May 1940 that 'while our Air Force is in being our Navy and Air Force together should be able to prevent . . . a serious seaborne invasion of this country' but that if 'Germany gained complete air superiority . . . the Navy could hold up invasion for a time but not for an indefinite period'. Even the Admiralty reported (First Sea Lord to the prime minister) that 100,000 men might be landed without interruption.[23]

It has been argued by Dildy that, as a primarily continental power, Germany did not handle its surface fleet effectively, nor fully understand the possibilities offered by maritime power.[24] They certainly understood the disruptive capacity of surface raiders loose in the Atlantic, and the capacity of the U-boat fleet to strangle Britain, but, unlike the British and the USA, they were not 'expeditionary minded' in the sense of being able to project force long distances by sea. In making preparations for defence, the British may well have overestimated German capabilities in this area, in seeing potential threats of expeditions landed in any part of Britain and Ireland. Britain's successful assault on the Lofoten Islands in March 1941 showed the sort of imaginative large-scale raid that could be mounted by a maritime power,[25] and perhaps Britain's greatest error in considering the defence needs of the UK was planning for this sort of large-scale raid by the Germans, who seem in fact to have had neither the psychological or physical capacity to undertake similar raids. The invasion of Norway had, after all, been of a small, unprepared, lightly-armed neutral.

THE FIFTH COLUMN . . . EXCUSES AND FEARS

A feature of the first half of 1940 was self-exculpation in the face of defeat, British and Allied. It was widely believed that Fifth Column activities by people of German origin or Nazi sympathisers had played a major part in the defeat of Belgium, the Netherlands, Norway and Denmark, incidentally relieving their governments and armed forces of some blame for poor political decisions and military unpreparedness. The Fifth Column panic in Britain in 1940 was fuelled by the highly coloured reports of exiled politicians (such as the Vice President of Czechoslovakia and the Dutch Minister of Justice) or British diplomats (for example, Sir Neville Bland, Minister Plenipotentiary to the Netherlands).[26] And military officers who had been overwhelmed by the Germans were anxious to show that they were not at fault; rather it was the great capabilities of the enemy, the implication of course being that no one could have beaten the Germans. In Britain the effect of the first was to raise fears that a Fifth Column here was readying itself to aid an invader; the effect of the second was to increase the myth of German (and especially Hitlerian) invulnerability and infallibility (Fig. 3.1).

A Ministry of Information 'Fifth Column' pamphlet issued in June 1940 sets out the fears and the supposed lessons learned from the fall of other countries.[27] German subversion had been aimed at centres of communication, transport and other Vulnerable Points, to do everything possible to help the German forces occupy the country, to carry out sabotage and to demoralise and confuse public opinion.

The strength of Fifth Column fears rose and fell through the summer and a constant feature of the summer was rumours of 'hypothetical nuns, bombs and parachutists'.[28] By 5 June, MoI reported that 'There are signs that Fifth Column hysteria is reaching dangerous proportions in some towns and villages: there are fewer rumours but more accusations'; in other words, a 'witch-hunt'.[29] By 14 June, worrying signs of vigilantism were evident as 'Edinburgh attempts to form "Sixth Column" to discover Fifth Columnists. This is not regarded favourably by police'.[30]

While some of the excesses of the Fifth Column panic seem absurd in retrospect, the fear that the higher levels of government and society were riddled with potential traitors is comprehensible. A brief survey shows just how many Scottish MPs, peers (from dukes downwards), lords lieutenant of counties, former senior Army and Navy officers, and businessmen, were vocal in the late 1930s in support of Germany – as a natural ally of Britain, as a victim of French vindictiveness through

Figure 3.1.
The classic idea of the Fifth Columnist: a middle-aged governess (or is it a man pretending to be one?) draws a concealed pistol from her pram and shoots a Home Guardsman; an exercise in Tain, Ross-shire, August 1941 (Imperial War Museum H12502).

the terms of the Treaty of Versailles, as a country showing a new way forward through Nazism, or as a bulwark against a 'Judaeo-Bolshevik plot'.[31] After all, the Duke of Windsor – the former king – was widely suspected of being pro-Nazi and a potential traitor.[32]

In this atmosphere the arrest of many prominent fascists in May 1940 was widely welcomed, as was recorded in the MoI daily reports: 'The arrest of Mosley and other Fascists has overwhelming approval'.[33]

The Montrose Fifth Column

Montrose's MP, Lieutenant Colonel C.I. Kerr, was a member of the Right Club, a secret society founded by Captain Maule Ramsay, MP for Peeblesshire and South Midlothian (whose home was in Kerr's constituency). The sons of the Duke of Montrose were also active in extreme right-wing politics. The *Montrose Standard* had welcomed a violently pro-Nazi lecture in the town in January 1939 as 'one of the most stimulating addresses heard here recently'.[34] Whether anxiety about the loyalty of local landowners and politicians made this part of the Angus coast peculiarly jumpy, there was a particularly intense outbreak of Fifth Column hysteria there for a month in the summer of 1940. The garrison of Montrose that summer was 128th (Highland) Field Regiment, RA, with a company of 8th Gordon Highlanders' machine guns, 307th Heavy Battery, RA (manning the battery of two 6-inch former naval guns guarding the coast) and a Royal Engineer detachment.[35] The first signs of concern were summarised in an Intelligence Report in June 1940, in the War Diary of 128th Field Regiment, RA in which activities over two weeks between 8 and 20 June were recorded:

> Suspicions were first aroused in this unit that certain activities were going on in the neighbourhood which might be of a Fifth Column nature [in] which five windows in FERRYDEN 2271 [the military grid reference, actually wrong, as this point is at sea in the middle of Lunan Bay] were observed to be flashing signals at about 2200 hours by means of pulling blinds up and down thus exposing and screening lights in the rooms. These signals were acknowledged from the direction of MILTON NESS 2885 . . . it is still day light at 2200 and powerful lights must have been used . . . Activity, it will be observed is particularly marked round the area of FERRYDEN. The police investigated but could not catch anyone at it.[36]

On 14 June at 23.00 hrs, 'A man was observed looking through Field Glasses at Defensive Works along the beach and links. He was observing from FERRYDEN . . . The man made off and was not seen again'.

On the 15th, 'A light on the south bank of the River S ESK observed . . . coming from road junction . . . This light came from the head lamps of a car and sent the message "D.F.". This was answered by "T" from a house at 231785 which is a double house of the semi detached type [on the north side of the river, facing the sea]. The owner is Miss Mitchell who is reported by the police as being trustworthy.' At 00.30 hrs on the 20th, 'Signals appeared to come from a house situated in BENTS ROAD near the MARINE HOTEL [close to Miss Mitchell's house] . . . operated by means of an ordinary table lamp' during and after an air raid warning. At the same time, nearby, more signals were being passed by a window blind being raised and lowered. Two hours later, 'A light was reported sending Morse signals, which could not be read by the signaller who observed them' on the beach below St Cyrus. 'This was answered, again unintelligibly, from FERRYDEN'.[37]

Reporting of 'signals' resumed on 26 July and for the next five nights, but the area under suspicion had moved to the north of the town: flickering lights near Rock Hall, north of Montrose; a light appearing 'every time a plane goes over' in the Warburton Farm area; lights signalling from an old manse near North Esk Road; flashing lights across Montrose Basin; a Naval trawler reporting a light near Rock Hall; a light flickering beyond St Cyrus – no bearing could be taken but it was later checked and found to go through Rock Hall. It resembled rapid visual signalling.[38]

What were these crude signals meant to be? To whom were they directed? No one seems to have given any thought to just how much security-sensitive information might be transmitted by a table lamp being switched on and off six times. What is certain is that fears of the Fifth Column necessitated the guarding of many Vulnerable Points, at first by Regular troops, and increasingly by lower-quality units and by Home Guard, and also prompted a level of internal security and control in Britain that many found frustrating, demoralising, exhausting and occasionally, at the hands of over-enthusiastic Home Guard, fatal.[39]

MAY 1940

The defeat of the forces of France, Britain, Belgium and the Netherlands by Nazi Germany began on 10 May 1940 and was over well before the French signed the armistice with Germany on 22 June. The 'long retreat' of the Allied forces from Belgium and eastern France began on 16 May and the evacuation of British, French and Polish troops from Dunkirk and other Atlantic ports began ten days later. Newbold coined the term 'the May Panic' for the British response to unfolding events,[40] and unfortunately, during the 'panic', critical judgement was often lacking in considering when, how and with what the Germans might arrive in Britain.

But the contingency plans for dealing with the possible invasion of the UK had to be reassessed drastically. Parachutists, already the chief fear after their role in the fall of Norway, now, after their spectacular success in the Low Countries, became the focus of what in retrospect seems an unreasonable level of concern.

As early as 10 May 1940 the CSC had determined that the coast between the Wash and Sussex was most vulnerable to invasion. However, the events of the next few days, especially the German occupation of the coast of the Netherlands as a potential base for an air assault, would begin to change this view. One possibility, which any rational assessment of risk, practicality and value would have shown was unlikely, to say the least, occupied a disproportionate amount of attention during the summer of 1940. This was the idea that the Germans would invade and occupy the Republic of Ireland, in conjunction with Fifth Column and anti-British groups such as the IRA, in part to interdict Britain's supply routes from the west, and in part to act as a springboard to invade western England, Wales or south-west Scotland. This was first discussed in the War Cabinet on 14 May. While it was recognised that rumours of this kind might be intended to draw Britain into violating Irish neutrality by a pre-emptive invasion, the idea would not go away, and over the summer and beyond succeeded in drawing off significant military resources to Northern Ireland.

Meanwhile, on 13 May 1940 – the day the Dutch government and royal family fled to Britain – Kirke reported that he had recommended the creation of Young Soldier battalions to mobilise 20,000 men below military age to defend aerodromes, allowing older men in Home Defence battalions to concentrate on defending other Vulnerable Points, and continuing the freeing of Field Army troops for more active warfare.[41] He also reported that he had asked the War Office to consider the formation of a voluntary corps made up of ex-soldiers, members of rifle clubs and so on, who could guard their localities. The creation of the Local Defence Volunteers was announced the following day (14 May 1940) at 9 p.m. by Anthony Eden, but very much driven forward by Kirke, who had discussed the matter at the War Office on the 11th.[42] Churchill had, of course, put forward the idea of a 'Home Guard' in October the previous year.[43] Kirke also promoted the idea of rapid immobilisation of transport and reported on the deliberations of a subcommittee of the Home Defence Executive on the destruction of ports, roads and railways in advance of German forces. This 'scorched earth' policy was moderated on 22 May, when plans to immobilise the ports for 7–10 days, rather than utterly destroy everything, were prudently put in place.[44] On 12 May 1940 the War Cabinet discussed an unrealistically extensive scheme of immobilisation of open spaces and main roads that could be used for landings, but Home Forces managed to apply some realism in the approach to what would otherwise be an enormous job, the plan being modified to reconnoitring areas within 3 miles of an aerodrome or a port near or on the east coast that might require immobilisation.[45]

Further concerns were raised on 16 May at the CSC about the strength of the garrison of Shetland, and indeed the weakness of the forces defending Scotland as a whole – at this date about one infantry division – in the face of concerns about the movement of airborne troops in Norway.[46] Kirke was unhappy about any further commitments for his already overstretched Home Forces, dismissed Admiralty concerns as 'panicking' and felt that he had already reinforced Shetland adequately.[47]

Discussions on the same day included consideration of a JIC paper on security measures against air invasion, based on lessons learned from the German campaigns so far in the war, from Poland to France. JIC wished to 'stress the completeness of the German plans for such an invasion, of their effectiveness in sabotaging all attempts at resistance, and the secrecy with which the German preparations are carried out'[48] and included some highly coloured accounts of parachute and Fifth Column activities in the Netherlands, such as reports of resident German nationals firing guns from their windows.

As noted in the Prologue above, on 17 May 1940 troops in the north of Scotland were put on 2 hours' notice to move because of reports of troop-carrying aircraft assembling at Stavanger.[49] On 19 May the C-in-C Home Forces minuted the CSC about the defence of Scotland – a machine gun company (12 guns) was being moved from Aberdeen to Shetland and three 4-inch guns were being mounted to protect Lerwick harbour.[50] 'As regards the rest of Scotland I have only a certain number of troops and I consider it preferable to maintain a preponderance in the East Anglian and Home Counties and for the defence of London.' His statement that 'In the Orkneys there are over 7,000 men' is disingenuous; within the recorded Army strength in Orkney (5,400) there were only two units, a single infantry battalion (7th Battalion Gordon Highlanders, 700 men, raised in September 1939) and one Royal Engineer field company (200 men), who could realistically be counted upon to make a good showing in offensive, mobile combat. The defence of important places, like the Island of Hoy and the key naval installations on the island at Lyness, were left to the men of 95th Heavy Anti-Aircraft Regiment and other balloon and anti-aircraft troops.[51]

The unfolding disaster in May 1940 for the Allied armies in Belgium and France led to a rapid reappraisal of the invasion risk: the Germans were not only close to controlling the entire coastline facing mainland Britain, but could now also mount air and possibly seaborne assaults from French, Belgian and Dutch soil.

On 20 May 1940, JIC could report to CSC that it believed (true to British apprehensions of German efficiency) that 'The planning [for a combined airborne and seaborne invasion] may be assumed to be generally complete'. Invasion was expected from ports from north-west France to Norway, with invasion from or via Spain or Ireland also considered possible. It was, furthermore, to be expected as soon as the German air force was no longer needed for day-to-day support of German forces in northern France.[52]

On 21 May General Ismay wrote to the prime minister (the letter being discussed the following day at the War Cabinet) noting that unfolding events on the continent showed that home defence plans, based on dealing with parachutists and defending the landward side of ports (that is, the principles of the J.C. Plan), were no longer adequate.

> . . . our Home Defence preparations at the present time are mainly directed towards dealing with . . . parachute troops and with the protection of ports from the landward side. I think the events of the last few days and the grim possibilities of the next must cause us to modify our views.

> In view of past experience in Norway, Holland and France, it can be taken for granted that the Germans have the plan for the invasion of this country worked out to the last detail, and have provided all necessary special equipment, such as motor landing craft, &c.[53]

This assumption that the Germans could only proceed on the basis of exact and detailed planning reflects the complete misunderstanding of the German way of war, already discussed in Chapter 2.

The imminent loss of the near continental coast meant that much of the south coast of England would be within range of both fighters and bombers, and short sea routes would extend the risk of invasion from the east coast, already feared, to the south coast. Despite doubting the possibility or imminence, CSC saw the possibility of an invasion on the south coast as a new threat for which plans had to be prepared.

The panic during this period is perhaps best illustrated by a JIC paper about the invasion considered by CSC on 24 May 1940,[54] which opened with the memorable phrase 'Germany's aim is to conquer England [*sic*]'. In this document, the rather unlikely idea that the Germans would first invade Ireland as a base to invade 'England' really took root. The German people's 'psychosis of ruthless certainty' had to be broken; they had to be made aware that German forces landing on British soil and Fifth Columnists would be 'exterminated'. Fears of new German weapons to be used in the invasion were raised: the spreading of anthrax and foot and mouth disease; liquid oxygen bombs; radium, thorium or uranium bombs; fire-raising liquid; gliding bombs; pilotless radio-controlled aircraft; crewless tanks controlled by radio from aircraft; and long-range rockets. While some of these were indeed achieved by the end of the war or even long after it, by one side or another, asserting them as realistic threats in the summer of 1940 was certainly unbalanced and probably detrimental to the development of practical responses to real threats. The document talked of the Germans having 600 seaplanes which could land on lochs and reservoirs supported by 6,000 fast motor-boats each carrying 40 men across the Channel – a supposition that led to a colossal amount of wasted effort 'immobilising' bodies of water (both inland and in coast wetlands – see below); parachutists dropping from Zeppelins; the appearance of 'cobwebs' of unknown use that had been spread over parts of France from two German balloons in 1939; and guns capable of firing 150 miles. It is comforting to note that CSC was on the same day discussing the rather more practical matter of the immobilisation of port facilities.

On 22 May Kirke had only 14 infantry divisions available for the J.C. Plan in Britain; 6 more than had been available on 3 May, but only 5 of the 12 Territorial divisions included in this total were first-line formations and their training and equipment was still patchy. As noted already, the 9th (Highland) Infantry Division, forming the garrison of Scotland, was a poorly-trained and inadequately-equipped second-line Territorial formation (Fig. 3.2).

On 23 May, CSC drew attention to a possibility that had not been given much attention hitherto: invading forces landing on beaches. As the forces inland had little or no anti-tank capacity, it was argued that the best chance of repelling an armoured force was to prevent it leaving the beach.[55] Kirke objected, however, to the scale of beach defences implied, and especially to the implications of manning such defences, to the detriment of the partly mobile Field Force inland. Although he had already attended a meeting that day at which it had been agreed that beaches between Wick and Swanage would be reconnoitred, 'Kirke remained sceptical of defending the beaches with extensive obstacles.'[56] His strong preference was still to have mobile columns ready to counter-attack, and to protect the ports (which the enemy would still need to capture to supply his expedition), but the Defence Committee wanted to consider the proposal urgently. The next day, Scottish Command received a request for information on vulnerable beaches, to which they responded by the 31st. Construction work began almost at once and thus began the process that would see the beaches of the south and east coasts, as far north as Caithness, blocked by hundreds of pillboxes, thousands of concrete cubes, hundreds of thousands of mines and uncountable miles of barbed and Dannert wire. As noted above (p. 14), on 24 May the weak defences of Scotland had been highlighted in C-in-C Scottish Command's letter to Kirke, complaining about his inability to defend everything that he was expected to defend – beaches, ports, aerodromes, Vulnerable Points – with 9th Division, his only fighting formation.

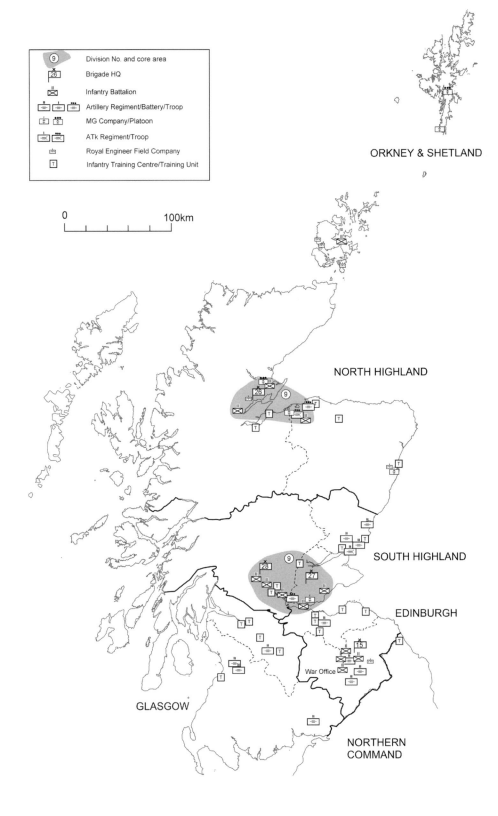

Legend:

⑨	Division No. and core area
26	Brigade HQ
	Infantry Battalion
	Artillery Regiment/Battery/Troop
	MG Company/Platoon
	ATk Regiment/Troop
	Royal Engineer Field Company
T	Infantry Training Centre/Training Unit

0   100km

ORKNEY & SHETLAND

NORTH HIGHLAND

SOUTH HIGHLAND

EDINBURGH

GLASGOW

War Office

NORTHERN
COMMAND

By 25 May 1940 the War Cabinet and CSC were discussing British strategy 'in a Certain Eventuality', which was code for France falling out of the war, most of the BEF being lost and the British Commonwealth fighting on alone.[57] The report stated baldly that, 'Germany has ample forces to invade and occupy this country. Should the enemy succeed in establishing a force, with its vehicles, firmly ashore – the Army in the United Kingdom, which is very short of equipment, has not got the offensive power to drive it out'. The authors of the report overestimated German naval strength at this stage, believing that Germany had 9–15 destroyers, an aircraft carrier (she had none at any stage in the war), 6 cruisers and 2 capital ships; in fact, at the end of the Norwegian campaign, over half of the German surface fleet had been lost, and only seven ships (including 4 destroyers) returned of the 22 that had set off.[58]

On 25 May 1940 Scottish Command was allocated £100,000 (present value over £5 million) to pay for the construction of anti-invasion defences.[59]

Kirke Leaves; Ironside Arrives

On the same day General Ironside made a 'spirited and selfless offer' to relinquish his post as Chief of the Imperial General Staff (CIGS) (a job he had hated and for which he was widely considered unsuited) to take over the command of Home Forces.[60] The move was actually part of a high-level reshuffle reflecting unhappiness with Ironside's role as CIGS, and the desire to promote his Vice Chief to the top job, but Kirke 'behaved with dignity like the good professional soldier he undoubtedly was'.[61] Newbold's opinion is that, after the Dutch coastline fell into German hands:

> General Kirke ... displayed drive and energy in adapting to the new situation ... and fought a running battle to moderate the more exaggerated demands of a Government obsessed by fears of sabotage, fifth columnists, and enemy paratroopers raining from the skies. His insistence that only a thin force should cover the beaches and that the emphasis should be on well-defended ports, backed by strong mobile columns in reserve, combined with his opposition to tying up large numbers of troops in the static defence of airfields and other vulnerable points, beach obstacles and pillboxes, was to prove a superior approach to that of his successor ... General Ironside, and was more akin to that of the highly competent General Brooke, who took over the post later on.[62]

Newbold was anxious that it be recognised that Kirke 'laid the foundations of Britain's planning and efforts to resist invasion on land in the Second World

Figure 3.2.
Troop dispositions in May 1940. The only Field Force formation in Scotland was 9th Division, split between the areas round Stirling and Inverness. 15th Brigade was in the Border Training Area, with a further battalion under direct War Office control. Home Defence battalions were split up guarding Vulnerable Points and their location is not shown.

War'.[63] Ironside's tenure (25 May to 19 July) can be considered a brief step into the past, to the 'Maginot mentality' of fixed defences, between two commanders – Kirke and Brooke – who understood that *this* war was not to be won by the methods of the last. It was, however, largely that brief period that saw the decisions made, and much of the actual work done, that led to the construction of concrete barriers on the beaches and, inland, the building of anti-tank stop-lines, described below. Ironside, although he had an excellent reputation, had not commanded troops in the field for 20 years, and had not had the recent hard-won experience of the 'new' kind of warfare that some of his younger colleagues had gained in France, Belgium and Norway.[64] It is interesting, though, that the MoI daily report of public opinion for 27 May reports 'Satisfaction at Ironside's appointment'.[65]

On 28 May 1940 JIC reported to CSC on the strength of German forces in Norway, which might possibly be used to launch an invasion.[66] The force reported – 10 destroyers, up to 5 submarines, 16 motor torpedo boats, 100 long-range bombers, 39 dive-bombers, 40 fighters, the equivalent of a division of infantry, with artillery and perhaps with tanks – appeared suitable for limited operations against outlying parts of the UK mainland, Shetland or the Faroe Islands, possibly as part of a larger invasion plan. On 30 May CSC reported to the War Cabinet that 'in our view . . . it is highly probable that Germany is now setting the stage for delivering a full-scale attack on England [*sic*]'.

In retrospect, we know that Germany had no plans to attack Britain in May–June 1940, first, because the speed of victory in the West surprised even them, and second, the Germans were not the hyper-efficient planners that they were perceived to be. But an attack launched then against an unprepared and confused country would certainly have succeeded in a way that no later plan could have.

The defence measures put into effect in such haste from May 1940 were in some cases misguided. At first informal, and then more structured, roadblocks sprang up, manned by over-enthusiastic, newly-recruited Local Defence Volunteers trying to catch Fifth Columnists, the main effect being to hamper the movement of troops and supplies for the J.C. Plan.[67] However, the efforts seemed necessary at the time and 'He would have been a very foolish man who allowed his reasoning, however clean-cut and seemingly sure, to blot out any possibility against which provision could be made'.[68]

In the meantime, public morale at the end of the month was good. 'There is no defeatism and a general confidence in ultimate victory'. The same day's 'rumour summary' reported, wearily, 'Nuns, parachutists, paralysing gases, bombings, etc. are widely reported today'.[69]

4. CRISIS: JUNE TO OCTOBER 1940

JUNE 1940

Ironside was lucky to be taking over the job of Commander-in-Chief, Home Forces at a time when no-one doubted the importance of the task, and, from early June, he was granted greater powers to co-ordinate and compel than Kirke had had, including complete operational control over all military forces in the United Kingdom except air defence/anti-aircraft troops. In particular, he was allowed to use the sometimes very large numbers of men in training units in his defence plans, so long as this role did not impede training until an emergency arose – in the area descriptions below, the Infantry Training Centres, Officer Training Units and Royal Engineer and Royal Artillery training establishments will be mentioned frequently in relation to their role in defending towns, beaches and stop-lines.

The replacement for the J.C. Plan was promulgated on 5 June 1940,[1] to deal with an invasion across the shortest possible stretch of water and in an area where fighters and bombers could both operate, but with diversionary or subsidiary operations in Shetland, Ireland or the north of Scotland.[2] The document included the instruction to immobilise landing grounds within 5 miles of listed ports and landing beaches (in hand since May, with aerodromes added on the 11th), and instructed the blocking of beaches on a large scale. Despite some added elements, notably the introduction of improvised armoured cars armed with Bren guns or Boys anti-tank rifles ('Ironsides') to try to compensate for the critical lack of British tanks, the new plan made no major changes from the J.C. Plan.[3]

CSC's concerns about German capacities and intentions were predicated upon the assumption that, 'The invasion of this Country will be for Germany her culminating effort of the War. She may be expected, therefore, to press it with the utmost intensity, regardless of loss, and to throw into the balance all her available resources.'[4]

Neither Churchill nor Ironside seem to have shared the widespread feeling in early June 1940 that an invasion was imminent, but what were seen as prudent preparations were pushed forward with considerable energy. On 4 June 1940 (the day that Churchill made his 'We shall fight on the beaches' speech) Ironside reported on preparations for defence, 'In all Commands, preparations for defence against air-borne and sea-borne attack are proceeding as rapidly as possible . . . Defensive measures cover the immobilisation of facilities at ports on the East and South Coasts from Peterhead to Newhaven, as well as the blocking of port areas from landward attack and the immobilisation of possible landing ground for enemy aircraft.'[5]

The Commander Royal Engineers of Scottish Command issued a series of instructions about beach defences and immobilisation in the week or so after 4 June: setting out the order of priority in which beaches were to be tackled (those at Wick and in East Lothian first); defining how they were to be blocked (lines of 3ft 6in [1.06m] cubes 5ft [1.5m] apart, to herd tanks into killing lanes and minefields); instructing that the beaches were also to be obstructed to block the landing of gliders and aircraft; and naming the civilian contractors who were to do most of the work.[6] Work was to be contracted for where possible through local authorities, but where 'local authorities do not pull their weight they should be short-circuited'. Divisions and their RE were also encouraged to report civil engineering companies who were being 'deliberately slow'. In all, 'The essential thing is to use common sense and get on with the job as quickly as possible.'[7]

In mid-June 1940 Scottish Command received permission to take forward the largest anti-tank stop-line in Scotland, the Command Line, described in Chapter 15, and on the 13th prepared its first progress report on the defences: beach reconnaissance was completed and work had begun on the priority beaches; aerodrome immobilisation was being held up by lack of clarity in policy and a shortage of digging machines; roadblocks were in place leading to all major ports; 100,000 Molotov cocktails had been made; 50,000 LDV (Home Guard) had been enrolled in Scotland (but only 8,800 rifles and 1,300 private guns had so far been issued); and arrangements had been made for the destruction of petrol supplies if necessary. Good progress was being made on siting 6-inch gun batteries.[8]

On 9 June 1940 General Carrington, the C-in-C Scottish Command, wrote what is a key document in understanding the concerns in Scotland about the limited troops available and the risks the country faced.[9] In it he described his concerns about a German invasion of Scotland north of the River Tay, comparing the level of risk faced before and after the fall of Norway. Before, he might have had to deal with large- or small-scale raiding by a force of up to 2,000 men landed from ships, or a smaller body of parachutists might have attempted the seizure or destruction of a major installation, or to cause a diversion. Hitherto, the three most important areas to defend had been the fleet base at Invergordon; Rosyth Naval Base and Edinburgh; and Glasgow and the Clyde, and an infantry brigade had been allocated to each. As troops had been withdrawn, he said, Glasgow–

Clyde and the area south of the Forth had become the responsibility of training units, while Invergordon and Rosyth still had a minimum of two battalions each for their protection. The extent and use of parachute troops in Norway and Belgium and the availability of airbases in Norway, Denmark and the Netherlands had, in his view, made Scotland more vulnerable to airborne assault. To deal with this problem, he reported, he had strengthened 9th Division's mobile infantry columns with artillery, engineers and medium machine gun troops, and made other provisions to deal with what he called, 'minor attempts . . . to create "sore points" by means of seaborne landings or sporadic attacks on aerodromes or other vulnerable points by parachutists'. However, 'The possibility of the enemy landing by air a powerful force and seizing a port through which to maintain [a force landed by sea] cannot be altogether dismissed.' He went on to identify six parts of mainland Scotland in which the enemy might attempt such an operation, and this usefully summarises suppositions that steered defence policy in Scotland in 1940 (with the author's comments in square brackets):

A. *Caithness.* Flat country suitable for air landings, but 'no very suitable port for maintaining a force so landed'. [In other contexts, Wick *was* considered a major risk.]

B. *Tain–Invergordon.* 'A few suitable landing places for aircraft, but again no suitable port for maintenance' [presumably as Invergordon naval base lacked the cargo-handling facilities of a commercial dock].

C. *Coast of Moray Firth from Inverness to Aberdeen.* Many aerodromes and open spaces suitable for landing aircraft. 'Aberdeen, if captured, would be capable of maintaining a large force, and there are several auxiliary ports such as Peterhead'.

D. *From Aberdeen to Dundee.* Many suitable places for landing aircraft, and a large force could be maintained through Dundee.

E. *Fife and Kinross.* Many places suitable for landing aircraft and many small ports through which a force could be maintained. [The harbours on the north-east, east and south-east faces of Fife are actually tiny; other than Rosyth, which is well up the river behind heavy defences, only Methil and to a lesser extent Kirkcaldy are harbours of any size.]

F. *Coast between Edinburgh and Berwick-upon-Tweed.* 'Many suitable places for landing aircraft, but no port for maintenance unless the Forth Fixed Defences were overpowered and Leith captured'.

He believed that the most probable aim of such attacks (especially in areas A and C) would be to gain bases for air attacks on other parts of the UK and his view was that the forces 'at present in Scotland are unavoidably dispersed and would be insufficient to prevent a determined attack of the nature envisaged'. His statement that 'Reinforcements from elsewhere will be required' is marked, in the copy in the GHQ Home Forces file, with a question mark. One role of the troops in Scotland would be to delay the enemy to allow counter-attacking forces to gather, and to this end, the next part of the paper discussed the creation of 'demolition belts' to help slow the enemy advance (see p. 90). The section in the conclusions reiterating the 'demolition belts' is annotated ominously in the margin 'This spells withdrawal'. GHQ, however, responded positively to the proposals for demolition belts.[10]

It would be beyond the purpose of this book to go into detail about the slight shifts in emphasis in GHQ, CSC and War Cabinet perceptions of the invasion threat through the rest of June 1940, in particular the rather arcane discussions about how the enemy might phase an attack, but a constant feature was the expectation of diversions or raids away from the main invasion site in the south-east, up the east coast or in the far north, mainly to draw off naval and air forces, but capable of being expanded opportunistically into larger-scale invasions. The invasion of Eire, with its tiny army, as a diversion or to provide an invasion base was a constant nagging concern.[11] In the end some 31,000 troops (a figure comparable at the same stage to the forces in Scotland), backed by 15,000 Home Defence troops, were stationed in Northern Ireland to secure Ireland from a possible invasion by up to 15,000 German troops.[12]

Scottish Command's second progress report on defence works on 21 June 1940 showed that defence measures on two of the three high-priority beaches were making good progress, while eight other beaches were up to a third finished. Glasgow Area's open spaces were largely immobilised, while Edinburgh's and Highland's were a third complete.[13] LDV numbers were up to 70,000, while 11,900 government and privately owned firearms had been issued. Work had begun on the largest of the inland anti-tank stop-lines, the Command Line across Fife and Perthshire, and mention was made of a reconnaissance by GHQ officers of the northernmost section of the GHQ Reserve Line, the main UK anti-tank stop-line.[14]

After the evacuation of Allied forces from Norway and from Dunkirk and the other Atlantic ports, the Field Force in Scotland (reduced to 9th Division) was strengthened by 148th Infantry Brigade (returning from Norway) on 6 May,[15] the Regular 5th Infantry Division (its 15th Brigade was one of the few fully-equipped formations in Britain) and the battered remnants of the 51st Division in the south-west (a first-line Territorial formation) – the latter reduced to 154th Infantry Brigade, engineers and support units after the surrender of the rest of the division at St Valery.[16] All needed to re-form and re-equip after the evacuation. The BEF as a whole had lost over 2,300 guns (including 432 2-pounder anti-tank guns and 837 modern 25-pounder or 18/25-pounder artillery pieces), 90,000 rifles, 8,200 Bren guns and almost 64,000 vehicles, including 600 tanks.[17] The effect of the losses and shortages on Home Forces was exacerbated by the decisions to equip and send a second BEF to western France in the early days of June; even though it returned quickly to the UK further equipment was lost. On the retreat to Dunkirk, Lieutenant Colonel G.P. Rose-Miller had instructed his Cameron Highlanders to collect any abandoned rifles they came across, as they would be needed at home,[18] but this foresight was rare.

It is telling, in relation to 9th Division's capabilities, that Carrington wrote on 27 June 1940, 'I would point out that the 148th Brigade and the 5th Division are the only troops at present in SCOTLAND which, quite frankly, are capable of carrying out mobile operations and the 148th Brigade must at the moment of necessity be put down for the local defence of the FIRTH of FORTH, for which no other troops are available.' The 5th Infantry Division was left in central Scotland until September/October 1940 as Scottish Command's reserve,[19] but 148th Brigade was moved to Northern Ireland in July 1940.[20]

On 25 June 1940 Ironside introduced key parts of his defence plan to CSC that would cause controversy in the short term and then fatally undermine confidence in him as Commander-in-Chief.[21] There were to be three elements in the defences: the coastal crust; a line of anti-tank obstacles down the centre of England (the GHQ Reserve Line); and mobile reserves behind this line.

The defences of Scotland were described thus, 'The defensive organisation in Scotland was less well advanced than in England, though the area south of the Forth and Clyde was already well defended. North of this line defences were weak and consisted mainly of isolated battalions in strong points. In the Shetlands there was one battalion with some guns. The battalion was 950 strong and should be able to deal with any raid on the islands'. CSC was, of course, much more worried about the defence of England.[22]

The anti-tank 'stops' (stop-lines) envisaged by Ironside (in a GHQ document dated 15 June) were intended to slow down German mobile columns and 'prevent the enemy from running riot and tearing the guts out of the country as has happened in France and Belgium'[23] and were to be built using wire, anti-tank obstacles, pillboxes, anti-tank guns and mines, making the fullest use of natural barriers such as waterways. In the hierarchy of importance of the lines the GHQ Line was considered the most important, but although planned to, it was not extended into Scotland; the Scottish Command Line was the most important in Scotland. Although Ironside continued to emphasise the importance of mobile counter-attacking formations, and was concerned about a 'Maginot' mentality infecting the troops building and manning beach and stop-line defences,[24] the apparently static nature of his defensive scheme was to cause trouble for him.

On 26 June 1940 the Vice-Chiefs of Staff expressed the 'gravest concerns' about Ironside's scheme, in particular that, after the coast crust, the main resistance might only be offered after the enemy had overrun nearly half of the country.[25] Their view was that 'the only policy was to resist the enemy with the utmost resolution from the moment he set foot on the shore'. Ironside's plan 'was completely unsound and needed immediate and drastic revisions'. Although the plans received a more positive reception at another meeting later that day the positioning of the reserves, perhaps 12 hours away from the coast, was still problematic. Churchill intervened in a letter to the Chiefs of Staff arguing that while it was 'prudent to block off likely sections of the beaches with a good defence' the advantage of fighting on the beaches where the enemy landed could not be 'purchased by trying to guard all the beaches'.[26] Instead, mobile brigade groups were to be ready to 'spring' on the enemy's lodgement(s), with 'four or five good divisions' in reserve, should the enemy capture a port. He did not explain, however, where such formations were to be found.

Further discussion took place on 29 June, when Ironside attended the CSC to clarify his defensive posture. First, the few troops in the beach divisions had been instructed that there was to be no withdrawal from beach positions and they were to fight it out where they stood. Second, the troops available were only partly trained and had very little artillery: 'Formations in this condition were unsuitable for counter attacks on a large scale . . .'[27] The beach defences were, within a short time, to be much more than a crust, as they were completed and strengthened.

On the same day the MoI daily reports of public opinion noted, 'There is a strong rumour that Hitler's efforts against this country will begin on Monday and his prediction that "all will be over by August 15th" is widely repeated. People do not "believe" the prediction but it is freely passed from mouth to mouth and evidence shows that the "inevitability of Hitler" is an important factor in public morale.'[28]

Some considerations of the risks of invasion were highly speculative and alarmist. Denis Wheatley, the novelist, was a member of an organisation, the London Controlling Section, which co-ordinated military deception and cover plans, and wrote two memoranda on German capabilities.[29] His first (25 June 1940) included greatly exaggerated numbers of German aeroplanes and ships available for an invasion (2–3 capital ships, 2–3 cruisers, 30–34 destroyers) and the second (1 July) promoted a very alarmist view of the Fifth Column threat, based on the reports of the former Vice President of Czechoslovakia, Dr Treviranus. He passed on Treviranus's suggestion that Britain dress 3,000 Poles, Austrians and Czechs in German officers' uniforms and place them in likely invasion areas 'to mingle with the Germans, issue false orders and delay the advance'. Wheatley's certainty that there was 'no doubt whatever that volunteers could be found for this extremely dangerous service' was perhaps misplaced.[30]

Meanwhile, on 27 June 1940 Carrington, as C-in-C Scottish Command, sent to GHQ his 'Appreciation of Situation' in relation to the sole object of the defending troops, 'To destroy any hostile troops which may arrive in SCOTLAND from the air or from the sea'. He started with a withering appreciation of the troops available (which he listed in an annex; see Table 4.1): the training units had been stripped of trained men and could be relied upon to produce only about 50 men each;

Table 4.1. Summary of the garrison of Scotland on 27 June 1940, as set out by General Carrington, with his comments on the state of some of the key units.

Unit or formation	Carrington's comments	Guns
5th Division	now reforming; fit for employment in bde [brigade] groups as soon as weapons are available	16 x 2-pounder anti-tank guns 6 x 25-pounders
9th Division	has not progressed beyond individual training.	8 x 2-pounder anti-tank guns 4 x 18-pounders 20 x 4.5 in howitzers
51st Division	amounts to one weak Inf. Bde at 50% of strength, at present reforming	
148th Infantry Brigade	now reformed and for the most part is re-equipped in infantry weapons (except anti-tank guns)	
51st Field Regiment, RA		18 x 25-pounders
Highland Area	10 Training Units 6 Home Defence Battalions	
Edinburgh Area	5 Training Units 1 Home Defence Battalion	
Glasgow Area	6 Training Units 6 Home Defence Battalions	
Training Units		8 x 2-pounder anti-tank guns (until 15 July) 14 x 18-pounders 28 x 4.5-inch howitzers

51st Division was 'at present not fit for fighting'; 9th Division was 'not fit for use as a Mobile Formation'; this left only 5th Division and 148th Brigade fit for mobile operations, but they too were deficient in artillery and anti-tank weapons.[31]

He believed that the courses open to an enemy in an 'attempt' against Scotland were, first, a landing in Orkney to capture Scapa Flow (where reinforcements from the mainland could not be landed easily); second, the capture of the Firth of Forth, via the beaches either north or south of the estuary, thus turning the flank of the Forth Fixed Defences and laying open the strategically vital port and manufacturing area around Glasgow and the Clyde; and third, an attempt to land airborne forces anywhere between Dundee and Caithness, but most probably near Aberdeen or Dundee, from where an attack on the Clyde area might be developed. Carrington's conclusion that any attack on Scotland would 'probably' have to be met entirely from local resources was annotated 'Certainly' in the copy on the GHQ file.

Carrington further developed his theme by emphasising his inability to defend Caithness and most of the Scottish beaches, and a statement at this point in the document, stressing that only the most dangerous beaches should be guarded, and as large as possible a mobile force organised for counter-attack, is annotated 'Yes' (underlined) in the margin in the GHQ copy. Carrington concluded that his mobile force had to be based to cover central Scotland and the Firth of Forth, either concentrated round Crieff–Stirling–Perth, or split between northern and southern Scotland; he preferred the former. The 148th Brigade was to cover the Lothian coast, with a brigade from 5th Division covering the Fife coast. Ninth Division (less two battalions in Orkney) would be responsible for local defence between Wick and Dundee, with its three brigades based in Dundee–Aberdeen, Aberdeen–Inverness, and in Inverness with a detachment at Wick. The remainder of 5th Division would concentrate round Crieff–Perth–Stirling, either to occupy the Command Line or operate offensively to defend the Forth area.[32] The remnants of 51st Division, recovering in south-west Scotland from the events in France, were given no operational role. The planned dispositions were agreed to the following day by GHQ Home Forces. The commander of the Army forces in Orkney and Shetland, Brigadier Kemp, had, however, written over the head of Scottish Command to GHQ, also on the 27th, seeking reinforcements to counter an attack on Scapa Flow, which Carrington had refused him.[33] This is dealt with in Chapter 10.

Late June 1940 saw growing concern in senior circles about perceptions of Ironside's supposedly 'static' approach, although the lack of suitably trained troops, transport and equipment made any other approach difficult to conceive of. Commanders in individual areas did not help by taking a rather local view of defence needs, trying to maximise the resources in their area without considering the overall picture, which only GHQ could really see. As noted above, they were also capable of going over the heads of their superiors to try to grab greater resources. In defence of Ironside, and his predecessor and successor, it must be said that CSC at times seemed to want or expect everything at once: beaches obstructed and manned, aerodromes and other Vulnerable Points securely guarded against parachutists; while also deploying mobile, trained and aggressively offensive formations ready to strike back, which did not actually exist at this stage, and the creation of which was hampered by guard duties.

JULY 1940

July saw a renewed spate of invasion rumours. On 2 July the MoI daily reports of public opinion noted, 'There is an increase in rumour, and yesterday (the day before Hitler's threatened invasion date) there were many reports of parachute landings and invading troops . . . In spite of this atmosphere of tension people are not depressed. Many people say they think our defence preparations are inadequate but at the same time they say "We shall beat them off", "We'll teach them a lesson", "Let them come".'[34]

More officially, in the days between 7 and 10 July 1940 there were 'indications that a sea and airborne expedition is in an advanced stage of preparation'.[35] German dispositions in Norway gave particular concern, although we now know that it was not until 2 July that Hitler gave even the preliminary orders for the planning of what was to become Operation Sealion. On that day an insightful JIC paper about Germany's next moves was discussed at CSC: (a) a move towards peace coupled with proposals to reorganise Europe; (b) operations against the UK; (c) operations against Russia; (d) an advance into south-east Europe; and (e) an attack on Africa.[36] They correctly believed that Germany's superiority was such that more than one of these might be profitably pursued at once but that a move against Britain was the most probable.

Despite reports of shipping and troop concentrations in Norway and the Low Countries and the absence of such indications in France,[37] CSC and Ironside 'steadfastly, and correctly, in view of the severely limited resources available to Home Forces, maintained that it was England that should receive total priority for defence'.[38] On 5 July Ironside could write, 'Everything seems to point to the Germans starting something from Norway and the Baltic against Iceland, the Shetlands or perhaps Scotland. I have only the troops necessary for the barest defence there and cannot send any of my reserves up to the north, for that will be the thing that the Germans will want me to do. I shall have screams from Scotland to go and save them, but I shall have to try to resist that, or I shall not have the people ready in the south for the main thrust . . .'[39]

On the day before (4 July 1940) a memo from the Director of Combined Operations, putting a very pessimistic view of German preparations in Norway, had been discussed at CSC,[40] 'He [the enemy] has had years to plan and construct material for this attack and just as he was able to surprise the French with thousands of efficient tanks he is likely to have planned surprising equipment to force a landing on these shores'. On 10 July the Naval Staff concluded that in calm and misty weather the enemy might put 100,000 men ashore without interference by the Navy.[41]

As reports from Norway persisted,[42] Ironside realised that Scotland's defences had after all to be strengthened. To support 9th Division (a 'semi-trained, ill-equipped, second line Territorial formation'), 5th Division and the re-forming remnants of the 51st Division, the 7th Battalion Royal Tank Regiment was moved north on 13 July, with 35 Matilda Mk II infantry tanks. Despite this, CSC still considered Scotland's defences were 'very light'.[43]

Scottish Command weekly Intelligence Summaries dated 6 and 12 July 1940 made rather misleading assumptions about the types of tank that the Germans could transport against Scotland in the Ju 90 transport aircraft and the Do 26 flying boat.[44] These included three types of Polish light tank (around 2.5 tons), the obsolescent PzKW I (5.7 tons), armoured cars and a supposed new specially designed light metal tank at 1.5 tons. Even the PzKW II (9 tons), the Czech TNHP (8.5 tons) or LTL (7 tons) were thought to be light enough to be carried by the Ju 90. Indeed they were, but this aeroplane never went beyond the prototype stage. The Do 26 flying boat could in fact carry only 500kg of cargo and only six were built, and three of these had been lost in the Norwegian campaign.

At about this time we find the first mentions of a force that was to play a major part in the defence of Scotland from later in the year: the approximately 17,000 Poles evacuated from France in June who were now re-forming in southern Scotland. By 14 July, two battalions of Poles had been organised using French rifles and the rest were at first proposed by Scottish Command as a useful labour force, building defence works and cutting wood. The local Polish Commander, General Bukacki, had, however, insisted that his troops must be reorganised, equipped and trained as a separate force. Carrington reacted badly to this, claiming that the Poles would consequently be nothing but a drain for months to come and that priority should be given to arming British units.[45] Carrington did not receive a reply from the War Office until mid-September, only to be told that the Polish leader, General Sikorski, was determined that his men be equipped and used as a unit. This was surely the right decision: maintaining morale and motivation in this refugee army would have been even more difficult had the Polish Forces been scattered widely and limited to menial tasks.[46] Their value was recognised in time: on 25 June 1941 the Inspector of Allied Contingents, General Sir George Cory, could write to the Vice Chief of the Imperial Staff on his five-day inspection of the Polish forces, 'The manner to which exercises were carried out, the quick grasp of the tactical features of the ground by senior officers, and the aggressive movements of the troops themselves make them . . . very suitable for use as "Storm Troopers".'[47]

On 16 July 1940, Colonel Everleigh, Deputy Commander Royal Engineers for Scottish Command, wrote a heartfelt note to Carrington about the shortages he faced, in trying to fulfil the defence construction programme, of infantry officers to decide on the siting of defences; of RE officers to translate military requirements into instructions comprehensible to contractors; of labourers, troops and volunteers to build the defences; of suitable civil contractors, equipment and materials; and of military and civilian labour. The Royal Engineer units in 9th Division had been employed on defence works continuously since they were formed and consequently had had almost no military training: 'Many have hardly handled a rifle'. The only RE officers with military experience were the senior officers; apart from a few reservists the rest of them were 'civilians with no military knowledge who have been put into uniform by the stroke of the pen'. He concluded, 'It is seldom realised that [the Command's] area is three-fifths of that of England, its length from end to end is 450 miles i.e. further than from Berwick to Land's End, and its maximum width is 220 miles. Its great extent, its sparse population and relatively meagre communications add greatly to difficulties . . .'[48] He noted in his War Diary, 'It was noteworthy that civilian firms contracting to supply pill-boxes, etc. completely failed to fulfil their promises.'

In July 1940 (Fig. 4.1) Scotland's garrison comprised 5th and 9th Divisions and 148th Brigade; the remnants of 46th and 51st Divisions were also in the Command, but were re-forming after the evacuation from France.

The MoI daily summary of public opinion noted on Wednesday 17 July 1940, 'Invasion date (Friday). This prediction largely spread by means of prominent press publicity is a dominant topic of conversation. Evidence shows that many people are seriously alarmed (evidence that domestic and commercial plans have been changed) . . . The legend of Hitler's "invincibility" is a continuous factor in popular psychology'.[49]

On 19 July 1940 Hitler made a speech to the Reichstag at the Kroll Opera House containing his final 'peace offer' to Britain and the 'offer' was refused in a broadcast by Lord Halifax on 22 July. Transcripts of the speech were dropped by German air force planes, and the Chief Constable of Aberdeen was criticised for rather too assiduously seeing to their gathering up before people could read them.[50]

Newbold is not alone in taking a very negative view of the likely effectiveness

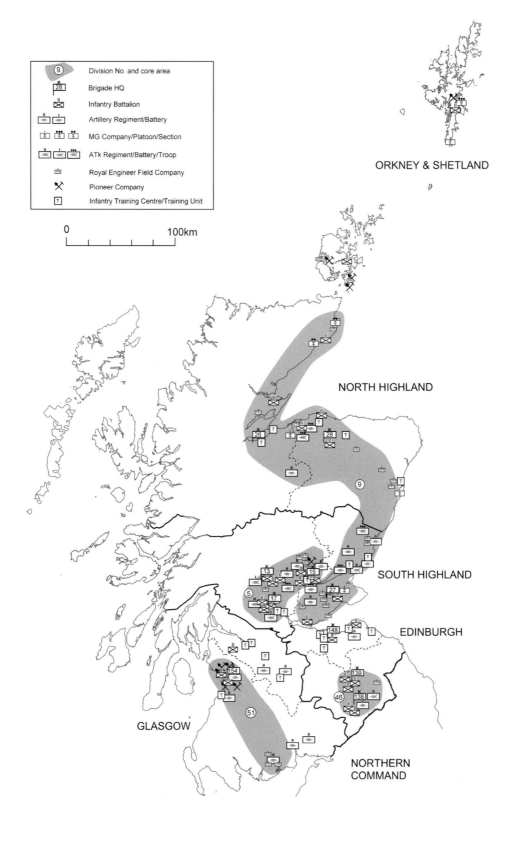

Division No. and core area

Brigade HQ

Infantry Battalion

Artillery Regiment/Battery

MG Company/Platoon/Section

ATk Regiment/Battery/Troop

Royal Engineer Field Company

Pioneer Company

Infantry Training Centre/Training Unit

0   100km

ORKNEY & SHETLAND

NORTH HIGHLAND

SOUTH HIGHLAND

EDINBURGH

GLASGOW

NORTHERN
COMMAND

of Britain's land defences in the latter half of July 1940. He believed that the main GHQ Line was the greatest 'white elephant', along with the other Command, Corps and Divisional stop-lines, although he dealt only with the southern English lines.[51] He believed that the lack of depth in most of the defences would have given them only a brief delaying effect on advancing armoured forces (although some, like the Scottish Command Line, described below, were in fact built in some depth) but conceded that 'the system of "stop-lines" seemed the best solution that General Ironside could devise in the circumstances'.[52] Significant concerns about the possibility of German landings in the north of Scotland (although not mentioned by Newbold) were discussed in the days following 25 July 1940, as a consequence of the paper by Admiral Drax (C-in-C at the Nore) already described in the Prologue.

By this stage, however, Ironside's reign was almost over. Concerns about the 'static' nature of his defence proposals set out at the end of June had matured into a widespread lack of confidence in his leadership among his superiors and his subordinates. The final straw appeared to be Ironside's support for the War Office and naval view that the east coast was still the likeliest landing point; Churchill led those who held the opposite view, that 'the sovereign importance of London and the narrowness of the seas in this quarter make the South theatre where the greatest precautions must be taken'.[53] In this he was supported by General Sir Alan Brooke, commander of Southern Command.

Concerns about the security of Eire led, at this time, to instructions to press on with the construction of defences in the west of Britain, which infuriated the prime minister, '... is it really to be supposed that the enemy could sail an unescorted expedition from the western shores of France some 600 miles, and make a landing, not only in the face of our Naval forces, but in the very jaws of our air defences?'[54] In his view the west coast had to rely on the Navy, air force and mobile infantry columns for its defence.

Brooke, with recent experience in France of the Germans' 'new' forms of warfare, was a vocal opponent of the view that the east coast was the likeliest invasion target, and believed that the equipment situation now allowed a greater number of units to be withdrawn to a more mobile, active role, and for training, and opposed the 'stop-line' approach.[54] On a visit by Churchill to Southern Command on 17 July the two men found that they were on the same wavelength, and two days later Brooke replaced Ironside, who was created field marshal and retired. The appointment of the new C-in-C was, however, read by some of the public as crystallising 'suspicion voiced recently that all is not well with Home Forces and more vigour is required'.[56]

On the same day, an ULTRA decrypt of a message from Göring to his Luftwaffe generals, passing on Hitler's intention to prepare and if necessary carry out an

Figure 4.1.
Troop dispositions in July 1940. The remnants of 51st and 46th Divisions were reforming after Dunkirk. 46th Division moved to Fife a few days after this, and guarded that area until the Poles took over in October. 9th Division, scattered along the east coast, was a poorly-trained and ill-equipped second-line Territorial division. The only two capable formations in the Command at this stage were reckoned to be 5th Division (the Command reserve) and 148th Brigade. Artillery and engineer units of 49th Division (whose infantry had gone alone to the BEF) were in place on the Command Line, in East Lothian and in the Borders but no divisional area is marked. Home Defence and Young Soldier battalions are not shown, as their men were usually split up to guard Vulnerable Points.

invasion, gave the first firm indication of the development of German plans, although no information as to where the blow(s) might fall.[57] On the 22nd the MoI daily summary of public opinion reported that 'People cheerful and optimistic at weekend when Hitler failed to invade Britain on Friday [19 July] as threatened'. This saw the beginning of 'a drift in opinion towards disbelief in invasion'.[58]

Brooke inherited beaches that were significantly better defended than they had been a few weeks before,[59] but the GHQ Line did not meet with his approval, even had he the troops to man it. His approach was to depend on a light line of defence on the beaches, with highly mobile and aggressive forces behind the beaches: 'The idea of linear defence must be stamped out'.[60] Equipment, training and transport were still deficient and meant that the supposedly mobile forces were far from well-prepared for their role. Brooke found the standard of training in some formations very low: 46th Division in the Border Training Area in Scotland was found, on his flying visit to Scotland on 27 July, to be 'in a lamentably backward state of training' and 9th Division (about to be merged with the remnants of 51st Division) was in much the same state.[61]

During the month the equipment shortage was ameliorated to some extent by the arrival of the first shipments of arms from the USA, including in the first convoy, on 8 July, 250,000 rifles and 300 field guns, mainly French-design 75-mm 1897 pattern guns. These guns appear frequently in the descriptions of the defences of Scotland below, and, despite their age, were first-rate guns, most of which had been re-equipped with split trails and pneumatic tyres for motor traction, rather than the poles and spoked wheels with which they had been drawn into battle by horses in the First World War. At least one unit, however, 152nd Field Regiment, RA in Orkney and Shetland, was supplied with guns with the old steel-tyred spoked wheels which could be towed no faster than 6 m.p.h.[62] They came along with 1,000 rounds per gun, albeit old ammunition requiring reconditioning (although the dropping of 152nd Field Regiment's ammunition into the sea at Stromness will not have helped).[63] A further 200,000 rifles and more field guns arrived on 31 July.[64] Churchill would hear no criticism of the total of 820 75-mm field guns which, in 1940 and 1941, were 'a great addition to our military strength for Home defence'.[65] The number of field guns in the Army had grown from 600 at the beginning of June to over 1,600 by early August (excluding the 75-mm guns, which were issued at the end of the month,[66] but apparently including the one o'clock guns from Edinburgh Castle, without firing sights, issued to 151st and 152nd Field Regiments, RA).[67] Anti-tank gun numbers improved from 120 at the beginning of June to 580 by mid-August (albeit still only being 22 per cent of establishment of Home Force units) and 3-inch mortars were still in short supply.[68]

Public opinion in Edinburgh, on 24 July, sounded a rather concerned note, 'A rumour in Edinburgh last night said that the best guns had been transferred to England, and as a result faith in our defences is becoming undermined.' As the statistics show, however, the modern guns had indeed gone.[69]

AUGUST–SEPTEMBER 1940

Reflecting Brooke's priorities, GHQ Home Forces issued an order on 7 August stating that 'the absolute priority now enjoyed by defence works can no longer be maintained.'[70] What is clear, however, is that defence construction *was* to continue, that hundreds of miles of barbed and Dannert wire were to be allocated to Commands for defence works, and that increasing the wall thickness of pillboxes to shellproof standard was to continue, where materials were available.[71] Commander Royal Engineers Scottish Command issued a note on 18 August 1940 informing all units that cement was rationed, and discretion was to be exercised in blocking beaches – only a single row of cubes was to be erected, or only the most dangerous sectors were to be blocked. Barbed wire was rationed from the 20th.[72]

By August 1940 the guarding of Vulnerable Points had become an issue again, absorbing too many soldiers from the Field Army and significantly disrupting their training, as they were widely dispersed on guard duty. Despite a great improvement in the situation in the spring, as a result of General Kirke's efforts, the invasion scare in May and June and the growing number of new military and civilian facilities needing a military guard (at least in the eyes of the bodies responsible for them), had driven the numbers of troops guarding Vulnerable Points across the UK up to 58,000, of which no fewer than 17,000 were from the Field Army. The 375 RAF stations, radar stations and fuel depots absorbed 25,000 alone, of which 10,000 were Field Army.[73] Brooke described GHQ as 'swamped with demands for troops to protect Vulnerable Points'.[74] The thorny issue of the responsibilities of the RAF and the Army in providing and commanding defence forces for the growing number of aerodromes would not be resolved for some months.

From mid-August ULTRA decipers of German air force signals began to give GHQ a much clearer idea of the development of plans for invasion (although no clear idea yet of where it might arrive) and, coupled with intense aerial reconnaissance, revealed that Germany's plans could not be matured for some weeks. It was therefore considered possible to send reinforcements to the Western Desert at the end of August. The most significant loss abroad was a regiment of 48 anti-tank guns, difficult to replace at home. Meanwhile, in the public's mind the passing of yet another of Hitler's 'prophesied' invasion dates (15 August) was reported as 'having a tonic effect'.[75]

During August, CSC and Brooke became concerned again about the risk to the north, in particular Orkney and Shetland (because of Scapa Flow), and sent a small reinforcement. Around the middle of the month Brooke also had to face the possibility of an attack from Norway, from where troops were confidently reported as having embarked on the 11th.[76]

In the absence of any clear indication of an invasion site, debate continued about where the Germans might land, with East Anglia (good tank country) still the preferred candidate, although Brooke held to his view that the south coast was where the blow would fall. Newbold suggests that the planners were influenced by youthful reading of such fictional invasion stories as Erskine Childers's *Riddle of the Sands* (1903), in which a flotilla of German barges filled with infantrymen was to fall without warning on the east coast.[77]

However, the Chiefs of Staff, by early September, given the growing weight of evidence in the form of barge numbers in the Channel ports, were coming round to Brooke's view that the south-east corner of England was the German target. But Brooke was worried enough by the overstretch in Scottish Command (particularly the shift of 15th Brigade from southern Scotland to the north-east of Scotland on the 16th) that he spent two days, 27 and 28 August, inspecting beach defences north of the border (Shetland and Orkney had been removed from his responsibility as C-in-C Home Forces to direct War Office control on 8 August).

By September Home Forces were still not in a good state to resist an enemy invasion. Of the 27 infantry divisions available, only four were fully equipped and only half had adequate transport. Artillery was still 25 per cent below complement, and anti-tank guns around 75 per cent below complement.[78] Training for mobile counter-attacking operations was still incomplete and Sir Aukland Geddes, Regional Commissioner for south-east England, believed that the Army would not be ready to fight competently until 1943 and that the second-line Territorial Divisions were 'quite pathetic in their incompetence'.[79]

Public opinion was being prepared in September for a possible invasion, but most people seemed to be confident that it would be defeated, or even believed an attempt had been made, and had failed.[80] Different strands of intelligence now suggested strongly that an invasion was imminent; a 'striking increase' in the number of barges from the Texel to Cherbourg; the movement of motor boats and larger vessels towards the same area; the movement of two German air force groups to the Low Countries and of dive-bombers to the Straits of Dover; and the capture of four German spies landing on the south-east coast, who confessed that their task was to be able to report on the movement of British reserve formations over the next two weeks. The moon and tides were also favourable for a landing between the 8th and 10th.[81] Naval forces had readied themselves for combat, short of moving the Home Fleet south. At seven minutes past eight on the evening of 7 September GHQ Home Forces issued the codeword 'Cromwell' to Eastern and Southern Commands – the signal for 'immediate action' (unfortunately the code system did not provide for a state of readiness between 'intermediate' and 'immediate action'). Although other Commands received the signal for information only, the code was acted upon in many other parts of the country.

Scottish Command sent 'Cromwell' to its constituent formations, the order being recorded in 5th Division's War Diary at 21.05,[82] with the order cascaded to the brigades and individual units, most of which 'stood to' through the night. Others were more active: HQ 46th Division, in Stirling, alerted its 137th Infantry Brigade to reports of enemy landings by parachute and small boats at 01.15 on the morning of the 8th.[83] The codeword reached 153rd Brigade in Aberdeenshire at 22.10 and the brigade was ordered to 5 minutes' readiness to move. Church bells were rung in Stonehaven, indicating (supposedly) that German troops had already been sighted; by 01.30 on the 8th all units of 153rd Brigade were ready to move, and roadblocks and defence posts were manned.[84]

Early in the morning of the 8th, Lieutenant Colonel Nutt, CRE in charge of the construction of the Command Line, sought instructions from 5th Division as to whether the roadblocks on the line should be closed; they referred him to South Highland Area; South Highland Area referred him to 46th Division, who told him to man the roadblocks.[85] Nutt had already passed 'Cromwell' on to the units building the line, and 110th Edinburgh Army Troops, RE began to prepare its various detachments for action, including the party ready to blow up Burntisland dock, and had all its roadblocks manned by 03.45.[86] 276th Field Company, RE in Aberdeen moved to prepare the agreed demolitions on the Cowie Line, and at 04.00 2nd/Lt Cooper and seven sappers left in a truck to attend to the demolition of the road over the Devil's Elbow, south of Braemar.

'Cromwell' was cancelled by Scottish Command at 11.25 on the morning of 8 September.[87] The feeling of anti-climax must have been very great, and the MoI daily summary of public opinion noted, in the west of Scotland, considerable discussion in the Home Guard about the call-out and 'some say they will refuse to "turn out on a fool's errand again"'.[88]

The first long-term postponement of Germany's Operation Sealion on 17 September 1940 spelled the real end of the invasion risk, but of course no one in Britain knew that and planning continued, albeit with a recognition that the risk of seaborne invasion at least had diminished. Scottish Command's *Forecast of Defence Policy for Winter*, dated 23 September 1940, noted, 'Weather conditions are likely to hamper severely any enemy attempt to invade SCOTLAND this winter. In spite of this, reasonable precautions against an attempt must be maintained'. Field formations were to be concentrated inland to focus on training but would be available as a mobile striking force. Forty-Sixth Division was to move to southern Scotland but have no operational responsibilities.[89] The greatest change in the situation in Scotland was the arrival of the Poles, to guard Fife and most of the Angus coast in mid-October 1940. General Kukiel, GOC Polish Forces, and some of his staff officers, arrived in the Command on 6 September to reconnoitre the area before his men took over.[90]

5. CONSOLIDATION AND (OVER-) ELABORATION: OCTOBER 1940 TO JULY 1941

By October work on the Scottish beaches was reported to be about 70 per cent complete.[1] After September CSC's discussions of the invasion risk became less intense, as winter weather seemed likely to restrict German opportunities. By 10 October, when CSC considered possible Axis intentions, Britain had had three months to increase its strength and many German aircraft had been destroyed in the Battle of Britain: any failed attempt by Germany to invade would, in the words of the Joint Intelligence Committee, 'prove disastrous to Germany'.[2] However, CSC discussed the possible imminence of invasion on the 18th, the period being favourable for a number of reasons: the tides, the moon and, extraordinarily, Hitler's horoscope.[3]

For Scotland the key document of this period was the *Scottish Command Defence Scheme* of 2 October 1940, which consolidated all the arrangements made during the summer: general defence policy; command and organisation; location of static defence troops, coast, beach and stop-line defences; aerodromes and ports to be defended or immobilised; civil organisation; and the destruction of food and fuel.[4] Over the winter, the threat to be faced was likely to be 'hit-and-run' raids that might be carried out by air or sea on Vulnerable Points and which might 'take as little as an hour in which to complete the whole operation'.[5] By the middle of the month the Polish Forces moved to take over the defence of Fife and the Angus coast to just south of Lunan Bay.

On 27 November 1940 GHQ set out its requirements for the defence of the UK in 1941,[6] balancing the needs of Home Defence to deal with a range of possible attacks against the needs of the Middle East. The expected scale of attack on Scottish Command was one to two German divisions conveyed by fast convoy from Bergen or Stavanger. Northern and Southern Commands were expected to face two to three seaborne and one to three airborne divisions, while Eastern Command was still expected to bear the brunt of the assault: 20 seaborne divisions and one to three airborne.

The year closed with Scottish Command instructing its Areas and the Polish Forces to strengthen defensive works in Caithness, Angus, Fife and East Lothian on beaches also mentioned in the October Scottish Command Defence Plan, and to bring existing defences up to a new, higher standard set in *Military Training Pamphlet No 30, Pt III* published on 8 October 1940.[7] There was also a complaint by Carrington about his prospective loss of the 216th Infantry Brigade from north-east Scotland to Northumberland; these troops had been intended as reliefs for Orkney and Shetland and he suggested, quite rightly, that the defence of Scapa Flow was more important strategically than that of Northumberland.[8] Figure 5.1 shows troop dispositions in late December. The key formations were 51st Division, covering North Highland Area between Invergordon and south of Aberdeen; 216th Brigade was still covering the north-east coastline; the Polish Forces covering Fife and Angus to just south of Montrose; and 52nd Division in reserve, with one of its brigades guarding the coast of East Lothian. The 46th Division had moved back to the Borders Training Area after its stint in Fife in the summer and autumn. Unbrigaded battalions defended Orkney, Shetland and Caithness, with one also at Lossiemouth.

On 14 January 1941 Scottish Command reported to GHQ that defence works completed or in hand were to cost £2,580,000 (in modern terms over £130 million, and a colossal rise since May), of which only £2,153,000 had been budgeted by GHQ. Additional costs had been incurred because work originally to be done by military labour had had to be done by contractors. Anti-tank obstacles had been brought up to the higher standard set out in *Military Training Pamphlet 30* on the more important beaches and further pillboxes had been built. The additional £427,000 was needed to build 47 pillboxes (£30,000); anti-tank obstacles other than anti-tank ditches (£175,000); alterations to roadblocks (£100,000); flame fougasses (a type of petroleum warfare, described on p. 104) (£2,000); dummy [coast] batteries (£20,000); alterations to beach guns (£5,000); provision of four additional river crossings (£40,000); and miscellaneous works, dugouts, contingencies (£18,000).[9]

On 4 January 1941 CSC discussed a paper looking at options for Germany, written from the German point of view. It was noted that, 'German victory necessitates the defeat of the British Empire. This necessitates the defeat of the United Kingdom – England [*sic*]. England can be defeated in two ways, invasion or starvation'; of these, invasion seemed to offer the more certain route, and the paper concluded that it appeared certain that every possible effort would be made to bring off a successful invasion.[10] The Vice-Chiefs of Staff reported to CSC on 26 February 1941 that, 'Everything points to the most strenuous endeavours by Germany to win the war in 1941 . . . Successful invasion of this country would end the war . . .' They recognised, however, that an invasion would be a 'gambler's throw', and that all other methods to subdue Britain would be tried first. A state of uncertainty might thus have to be suffered throughout 1941, as the Germans considered their plans and Britain gained strength. The Vice-Chiefs believed that the weather would prevent any invasion before 1 April 1941, and that thereafter Kent would be the primary invasion site, even if attacked through its flanks in East Anglia and Sussex, with possible diversions of up to six divisions against Orkney and Shetland, northern Scotland, northern England, the Faeroes, Iceland or Northern Ireland, or a major diversion or even invasion by up to five divisions against Eire.[11]

Meanwhile, in the continuing 'fiddling' with the command structure for the defence of Orkney and Shetland, responsibility for the islands had been passed back from the War Office to GHQ Home Forces, and thus to Scottish Command, on 14 January 1941.[12]

During February 1941 the Commander Royal Engineers of Scottish Command promulgated the GHQ order that no further pillboxes were to be built and in April he signed the contract for the construction of the Innes Links (Lossiemouth) emergency naval gun battery,[13] the last of these to be built on the Scottish mainland.

In the same month the Poles extended their area of responsibility to the north, to the northern boundary of Angus Sub-area, to take in Montrose and Lunan Bay as part of a larger-scale reorganisation, to deal with the consequences of 216th Brigade (less 15th Argyll & Sutherland Highlanders) moving from northeast Scotland to Northern Command and the creation of 227th Independent Brigade (comprising three infantry battalions in Caithness and one at Tain); the locations are summarised on Figure 5.1.[14]

Scottish Command issued an updated situation report on possible invasion risks on 1 March 1941.[15] The expected scale of attack was two infantry divisions (supported by up to 200 light tanks), with an airborne brigade directed against Orkney and Shetland. Most of the force would arrive by sea, and 'Interference of enemy convoys by our naval forces will be small during the first 48 hours, gradually increasing, until after four days reinforcements by sea will be strictly limited and be subject to casualties'. It was considered probable that this attack would take place while the main attack was directed against England. The main threats were seen as being to Caithness (threatening Scapa Flow and difficult to retake from the south), the port of Aberdeen and the approach to central Scotland across Fife, Angus and Perthshire, or via the beaches of East Lothian. To counter this, Scottish Command had two infantry divisions, the Polish Forces (equivalent to a division), a four-battalion brigade in Caithness, one battalion of Norwegian troops (barely trained), Home Defence and Young Soldier battalions, Home Guard and training units. But no tanks. The east coast of Scotland was stated to be 450 miles long, of which 90 miles was vulnerable, with 78 existing or projected aerodromes.[16]

On 5 March 1941 CSC recommended that every effort be made to complete beach scaffolding by 1 April 1941, the notional beginning of the invasion season.[17]

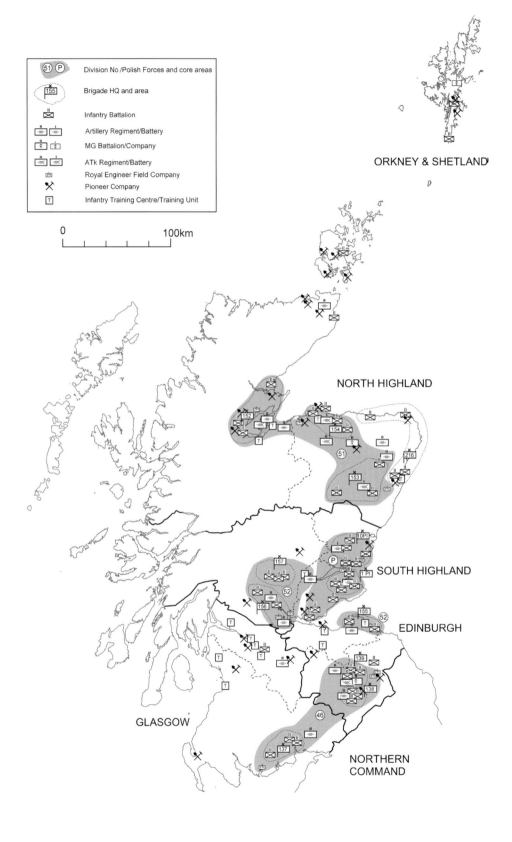

ORKNEY & SHETLAND

NORTH HIGHLAND

51

SOUTH HIGHLAND

EDINBURGH

GLASGOW

NORTHERN
COMMAND

Legend:

51 / P	Division No./Polish Forces and core areas
155	Brigade HQ and area
	Infantry Battalion
	Artillery Regiment/Battery
	MG Battalion/Company
	ATk Regiment/Battery
	Royal Engineer Field Company
	Pioneer Company
T	Infantry Training Centre/Training Unit

0   100km

152
154
153
216
157
156
155
139
138
137
46
52
52
10Pl
P

The matter of beach scaffolding is described in more detail below (p. 100). During the month further efforts were discussed to reduce the number of troops being used to guard Vulnerable Points, which were to be classified in order of importance.[18]

It was considered by CSC on 27 March 1941 that 'The forces in Britain are none too big to deal with a determined attempt at invasion. A large percentage of the available manpower of the army is allocated to tasks which are not directly related to measures for dealing with invasion.'[19] On 1 March 1941 the Army had stood at 2,133,000 personnel, less 158,000 in garrisons in India, Burma, Iceland and Africa and 340,000 in the Middle East. Within the UK was the Imperial Reserve of ten divisions (which while in Britain could aid the Field Army for Home Defence). Fixed commitments took up 935,000 (including air and coast defence 46,300; defence of aerodromes and Vulnerable Points 113,000; recruits under training 100,000). The 'Home Army' in the UK stood at 519,000, of which 324,000 were equipped at a higher scale while the remainder (195,000) were equipped at a lower level, and could form the basis of county divisions, not expected to be particularly mobile.

Scottish Command Standing Operation Instructions 1941, an update of the *Scottish Command Defence Plan* of October 1940, was published on 18 March 1941. The roles of mobile and static forces were set out clearly and specific defensive arrangements were listed or their character described: beaches defended; lochs to be patrolled or immobilised; the Command Line; port immobilisation; road and rail-blocks; minefields; immobilisation of petrol, food and communication centres; demolitions; and air co-operation.

Figure 5.2 shows the location of Field Force formations (51st Division, 52nd Division; the Polish Forces; 227th Infantry Brigade and the as yet unbrigaded units in Orkney and Shetland) in late May 1941, with Pioneer and training units/centres also shown. The 46th Division had by then moved from its training grounds in southern Scotland to East Anglia.[20] The success of German misinformation in relation to the possible invasion of Ireland is demonstrated by, at the same time, the Field Force in Ulster being comparable to that of Scotland: three divisions and three independent brigades.[21]

The successful German invasion of Crete in May 1941, through the capture of Maleme aerodrome, exposed fatal weaknesses in aerodrome defence. The key lessons drawn in a lecture by the Commander-in-Chief Scottish Command on 12 June 1941 were that: aerodromes were the enemy's main objectives; artillery cover had to be provided in depth; all ranks on aerodromes had to be provided with rifles and grenades and a high proportion of Tommy Guns to defend themselves; and artillerymen had to have the same, to defend their guns against parachutists.[22] An immediate consequence was the moving of many of the beach

Figure 5.1.
Troop dispositions in December 1940. 51st Division had been re-formed in August by the merger of 154th Brigade of the old 51st, and the duplicate 9th Division. 46th Division had spent July–October in Fife. The Poles had taken over responsibility for Fife Sub-area, most of Angus and part of Perthshire in October. 52nd Division was split between central Scotland (the Command reserve) and garrisoning East Lothian (155th Brigade). Home Defence and Young Soldier battalions are not shown, as their men were usually split up to guard Vulnerable Points.

defence guns (now 18-pounder and 75-mm guns) from the beaches to provide artillery cover for nearby aerodromes, and a change in the emphasis of defence plans, back towards dealing with airborne assault, stressing the role of mobile troops in providing counter-attacking forces against enemy troops assaulting aerodromes.[23] Caithness, with its aerodromes close to Scapa Flow was also placed under command of the Orkney and Shetland Defences, to co-ordinate the defence of the north better.[24]

On 21 June 1941 Germany invaded the Soviet Union: Britain and the western front suddenly stopped being the focus of the war and the defeat of 'England' ceased to be Germany's primary war aim, although realisation of this fact in Britain was slow in coming. Although it was feared until the autumn that Germany might win a rapid victory and then turn back towards Britain, the risk of invasion, limited in the summer of 1940 and highly unlikely in the spring of 1941, became an impossibility in the summer of 1941. From being prudent precautions against an identifiable risk, defence preparations and the numbers of men making them became an impediment to the successful prosecution of the war, wasting materials and time better spent training for offensive warfare.

(OVER-) ELABORATION

By the summer of 1941 Scotland was heavily fortified: many miles of beaches had been obstructed by concrete blocks of different designs, with pillboxes among and behind them; significant structures had been built on a series of inland anti-tank stop-lines, in particular, the Scottish Command Line, the Cowie Line and the Bonar Bridge defended locality. The defence works in Scotland had cost over £2.5 million (over £130 million in modern value).

Figure 5.2.
Troop dispositions in May 1941. The Norwegian Brigade was posted to the Tain area, its first operational posting, in July 1941, but at this stage its artillery battery was posted with 51st Division for training. The extension of the Polish area to the north boundary of Angus Sub-area is indicated. Home Defence and Young Soldier battalions are not shown, as their men were usually split up to guard Vulnerable Points.

Even without the benefit of hindsight it is difficult to justify the effort that went into defence construction from the summer of 1941 onwards, even to face the possibility that rapid raids might be made 'which may take as little as an hour in which to complete the whole operation'.[25] What can one make of instructions on 26 July 1941 to increase the thickness of pillboxes in Scottish Command from bullet- to shellproof (albeit only on the 'enemy' side – but what was the 'enemy' side if the assailants dropped from the air?)? Why issue new pillbox designs in August 1941, when pillbox construction (except on aerodromes) had been suspended months earlier?[26] And why install flame projectors in 16 minor harbours on the Scottish coast (including 'harbours' scarcely worth the name, like Helmsdale) in 1942–43, to be manned by specially trained teams of naval ratings?[27] It seems reasonable to describe the efforts as ill-directed in the context of the prevailing situation of competition for resources and manpower.

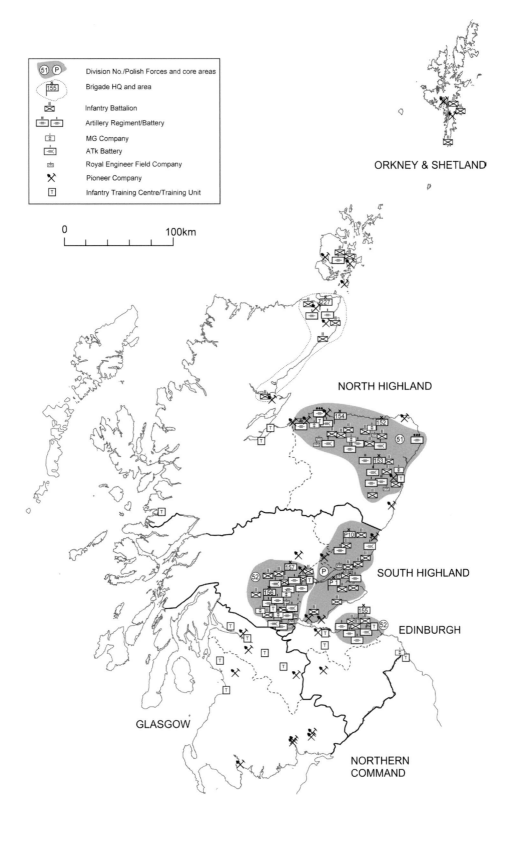

ORKNEY & SHETLAND

Division No./Polish Forces and core areas
Brigade HQ and area
Infantry Battalion
Artillery Regiment/Battery
MG Company
ATk Battery
Royal Engineer Field Company
Pioneer Company
Infantry Training Centre/Training Unit

0   100km

NORTH HIGHLAND

SOUTH HIGHLAND

EDINBURGH

GLASGOW

NORTHERN
COMMAND

PART II:
THE DEFENCES: 1939–41

'SPOT AT SIGHT' CHART Nº 1
ENEMY UNIFORMS

GERMAN PARACHUTIST

GERMAN SOLDIER

6. TRAINS AND BOATS AND PLANES

T he next four chapters will consider the sorts of defences that were built or prepared from the outbreak of war to the summer of 1941, and look briefly at what was done later, after the risk invasion had really passed.

AERODROMES

The capture of aerodromes in Norway in April 1940 by German airborne troops was the first practical demonstration of the great risk posed by this new form of warfare, which had been identified in the J.C. Plan of November 1939. Enemy troops could be landed on or near them by parachute, and, once they had taken control, further men could be landed by glider and aeroplane to consolidate their hold, followed (as at Stavanger) by the capture of the nearby port. German action in Norway and then in Belgium showed that the concerns were real. But it was not until May 1941, with the loss of the island of Crete through the capture of Maleme aerodrome, that anything very effective was done to deal with the risk,[1] which was finally dealt with by the formation of the RAF Regiment in January 1942.[2]

The various lists of vulnerable aerodromes and their guards, issued during 1940 and 1941, were not consistent: names, roles and categories of importance were changed, aerodromes were closed, and in one case the RAF seemed unaware of the existence of at least one of its own emergency landing/flying training grounds (at Perth Racecourse), which the Army was guarding in November 1941. Also, aerodromes did not have to be complete to pose a risk, and because of the prolonged construction process, they might have to be guarded for months before they were in active use (Fig. 6.1).

Responsibility for defending aerodromes, preparing them for immobilisation, and for immobilising the countryside and beaches around, was a complicated matter. From mid-1940, arrangements were in place for elements of the Field Force or other Army units in a reasonable state of arms and training to be ready to counter-attack against any aerodrome under attack by the enemy, in support

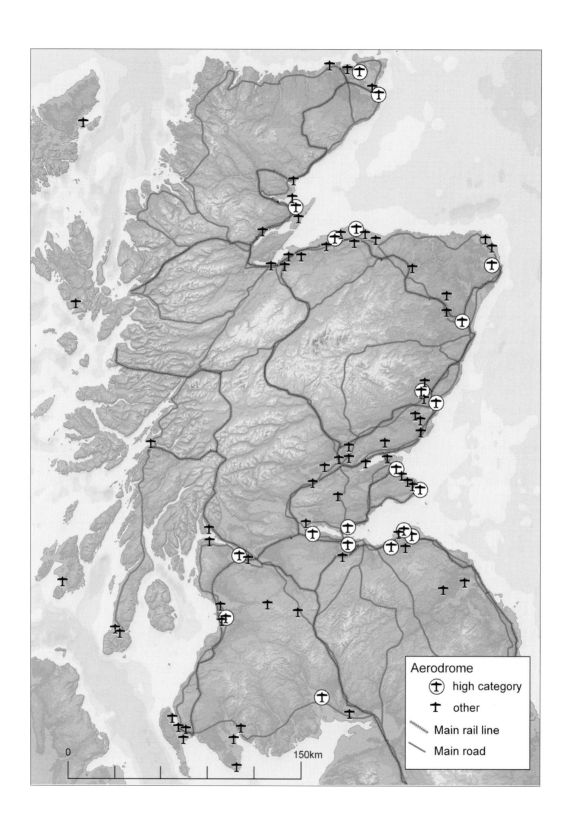

Aerodrome

(T) high category

T other

Main rail line

Main road

0   150km

of the aerodrome's garrison, if it had one.[3] But in May 1940 the Field Army was being drained to provide static guards for aerodromes. Eight of the nine fighter aerodromes in Scotland (Prestwick was unguarded) at that date were together absorbing a total of 16 officers and 560 men (getting on for a battalion of infantry).

An unseemly struggle between the Army and RAF over responsibility and resources for aerodrome defence continued throughout 1940 with the Army emerging temporarily victorious (as being in overall charge of aerodrome defence) but looking pretty dog-in-the-manger about it. Young Soldier battalions were set up in 1940 to provide guards for aerodromes, but their ineffectiveness is described below, and, as had been expected, competing needs led to the numbers of guards being reduced.

To prioritise ground defence measures, aerodromes were categorised in different ways: the complex categories established by the Taylor Report in July 1940[4] seem not to have been applied in practice by the Army to Scottish aerodromes. Instead a simpler categorisation into A, B and C, based not only on location but on function, was used until September 1941 (see below). The scale of garrison actually on the aerodrome according to this prioritisation was set out in December 1940: Class A – aerodromes (likely to face attack in direct assistance to invasion; landing grounds within 20 miles of Edinburgh; all fighter stations) were to be guarded by a company of a Young Soldier battalion, 219 men. Class B – Aircraft Storage Units, by a Pioneer company, say 250 men, and factories by half a company; Class C had reduced manning (unspecified) and were to be guarded by armed RAF station personnel.[5] The Young Soldier battalions were, however, a cause for concern: on 29 May 1941 Air Marshall Sir William Mitchell wrote, '*Poor discipline of "young soldier" battalions. At DREM this poor state of affairs was forcibly represented to me by the Station Commander. Their discipline is bad and their behaviour even worse, recent escapades being to steal an RAF lorry and to jab a Hurricane's wing with a bayonet . . . The officers are not of the same regiment so do not take much interest in their men and, in short, the so-called guard would be of little use against a German airborne attack, I am afraid.*'[6]

On 31 May 1940 the Air Ministry had become responsible for destroying all aerodromes and landing grounds not required for use by the RAF, and for the destruction or immobilisation of all spaces suitable for landing aeroplanes within 5 miles of those that were retained.[7]

Proposals to defend aerodromes could be overambitious. In August 1941 General Sikorski was very keen on a Polish defence scheme for Dunino aerodrome in Fife. Scottish Command responded in November 1941 with scarcely veiled sarcasm, 'While the scheme submitted reflected the greatest possible credit on the Poles for thoroughness and ingenuity of design, incorporating as it did many of the best features of the MAGINOT and SIEGFRIED LINES – not to mention

Figure 6.1.
Military and civilian aerodromes in Scotland, other than Orkney and Shetland, in mid-1940. The northern isles at this stage could muster only one operational military aerodrome each, at Hatston, in Orkney, and Sumburgh in Shetland. Higher-category aerodromes were those that housed fighters, or were vulnerable or otherwise required a larger guard.

TORRES VEDRAS [Wellington's defence lines round Lisbon in 1809–10] – unfortunately it could not be accepted or approved . . .'[8]

PORTS AND COAST ARTILLERY

In the period between the wars coast defence was seen as a very low priority. While proposals for the defence of naval bases and major ports had been put forward as early as 1934, shortage of money had prevented most of them being implemented by the outbreak of war. Fortunately, it was the practice of the Royal Navy to store surplus medium-calibre guns removed from warships. Many had been fired only a few times. In the spring of 1940 the Navy made available over 600 guns, especially 6-inch and 4-inch guns, for the 'Emergency Battery Programme' for the defence of vulnerable ports, and to provide fixed artillery to cover vulnerable beaches. Batteries of 6-inch and 4-inch guns are mentioned in various places in the area-based descriptions below.

The tables (6.1 and 6.2) and map (Fig. 6.2) show the situation in November 1940 with additional information from the *History of the Coast Artillery*, showing the gun strength at its greatest extent, in autumn 1941, at 'Major' and 'Minor Defended Ports' (Fig. 6.3).[9] By 13 June 1940, rapid progress had been made in Scotland and 6-inch guns were already in place at the emergency batteries at Aberdeen, Montrose, Dundee and North Berwick, with those at Wick, Cromarty, Peterhead and Dundee close to completion.[10]

In addition there were two 'Beach batteries' in Scotland of the same nature as the port batteries but not positioned to protect a port directly: Fidra (not on the island of that name, but on the adjacent coast, and effectively part of the Forth Fixed Defences) and Innes Links, at Lossiemouth, both armed with a pair of 6-inch guns.

The role of emergency batteries was primarily to prevent capture of the port and to prevent troopships, transports and landing craft from approaching the beaches.[11] If matters went badly, the guns could engage troops in boats or landing craft or tanks attempting to gain a footing on beach or, if there were no ships or landing craft left to engage, to engage landward targets. The batteries were not normally to open fire at a range greater than 6,000 yards. Regulations stated that no merchant vessel was to approach within 3 miles of the coast between sunset and sunrise, except in convoy, unless arrival had been notified in advance. Coast batteries would bring any errant vessel to a halt by a single round across its bows – a not infrequent occurrence that must have relieved the boredom of the crews.[12]

Many ports were nominated at various times during the war for immobilisation. On 24 May 1940 CSC earmarked a number, many of which were not formally

Table 6.1. 'Major Defended Ports' in Scotland

	Allocation 1937–39	In position May 1940	In position November 1940	Approved scale February 1941	'History of Coast Artillery' figures for autumn 1941
Orkney (Scapa Flow)	4 × 6-inch 1 × 4.7-inch	6 × 6-inch 3 × 4.7-inch 12 × 12-pounder	6 × 6-inch 3 × 6-inch (naval) 3 × 4.7-inch 18 × 12-pounder 3 × 6-pounder	6 × 6-inch 3 × 4.7-inch 18 × 12-pounder 9 × 6-pounder	11 × 6-inch 3 × 4.7-inch 17 × 12-pounder 9 × 6-pounder
Invergordon	4 × 6-inch	4 × 6-inch	4 × 6-inch 2 × 6-inch (naval)	4 × 6-inch	4 × 6-inch
Firth of Forth	4 × 9.2-inch 22 × 6-pounder	3 × 7.2-inch 14 × 6-inch 4 × 12-pounder	3 × 9.2-inch 14 × 6-inch 2 × 6-inch (naval) 4 × 12-pounder 6 × 6-pounder	4 × 9.2-pounder 16 × 6-inch 4 × 12-pounder 6 × 6-pounder	3 × 9.2-inch 16 × 6-inch 4 × 12-pounder 6 × 6-pounder
Aberdeen	–	–	2 × 6-inch 2 × 6-inch (naval)	2 × 6-inch	4 × 6-inch
Dundee	–	2 × 6-inch	2 × 6-inch 2 × 6-inch (naval)	2 × 6-inch	4 × 6-inch
Clyde			4 × 6-inch 2 × 4.7-inch 2 × 4-inch 2 × 12-pounder		4 × 6-inch 2 × 4.7-inch 1 × 12-pounder

'defended' at this time. In Scotland, these included Peterhead, Aberdeen, Montrose, Dundee, Methil, Burntisland, Leith and Granton.[13] The Taylor Report on aerodrome defence (see above) also set out a list of 27 ports in Scotland; any aerodrome within 20 miles of one of these was categorised as 'Class I'.

In 1940 block-ships, or drifters or barges to act as block-ships, were provided at a dozen Scottish ports: Granton, Leith, Peterhead, Methil, Burntisland, Aberdeen, Buckie, Macduff, Lossiemouth, Wick, Fraserburgh and Cullen.[14] 'Immobilisation' of a port extended to the removal of working parts and cables from dock cranes, moving bridges and machinery, rolling stock from railways, the blocking of lock gates and the removal of pipes from oil and water tanks. It was also made clear that the defences of ports had to be arranged so that they could also prevent the egress of the enemy from a captured port.[15] Local arrangements were also made

Table 6.2. 'Minor Defended Ports' in Scotland

Minor	Armament November 1940	History of Coast Artillery figures for Autumn 1941
Sullom Voe	2 × naval 4-inch	'Shetland' 2 × 6-inch; 4 × 4-inch
Lerwick	2 × naval 4-inch 2 × naval 6-inch	
Wick	2 × naval 6-inch	2 × 6-inch
Peterhead	2 × naval 6-inch	2 × 6-inch (described as 'beach battery')
Fraserburgh	–	–
Montrose	2 × naval 6-inch	2 × 6-inch
Inverness (Fort George)	2 × naval 6-inch	2 × 4-inch
Buckie	–	–
Stranraer	2 × naval 4-inch	2 × 4-inch
Ardrossan	–	–
Campbeltown	–	–
Oban	–	–
Loch Ewe	–	2 × 6-inch
Stornoway	2 × 4-inch (manned by RN)	2 × 4-inch
Lamlash	–	
Kyles of Lochalsh	–	

Figure 6.2. (opposite) 'Major' and 'Minor Defended Ports' and other ports in mid 1940, excluding Orkney (Major – Scapa Flow) and Shetland (Minor – Sullom Voe and Lerwick).

for drawing hawsers across harbour mouths, or jamming lock gates and so on.

The Army was responsible for the immobilisation of all spaces suitable for landing within 5 miles of 16 ports in Scotland listed in May 1940. The first priority were Peterhead, Aberdeen, Montrose, Dundee, Methil, Burntisland, Granton and Leith; second priority were Scrabster, Wick, Invergordon, Inverness, Buckie, Macduff, Fraserburgh and Arbroath.[16]

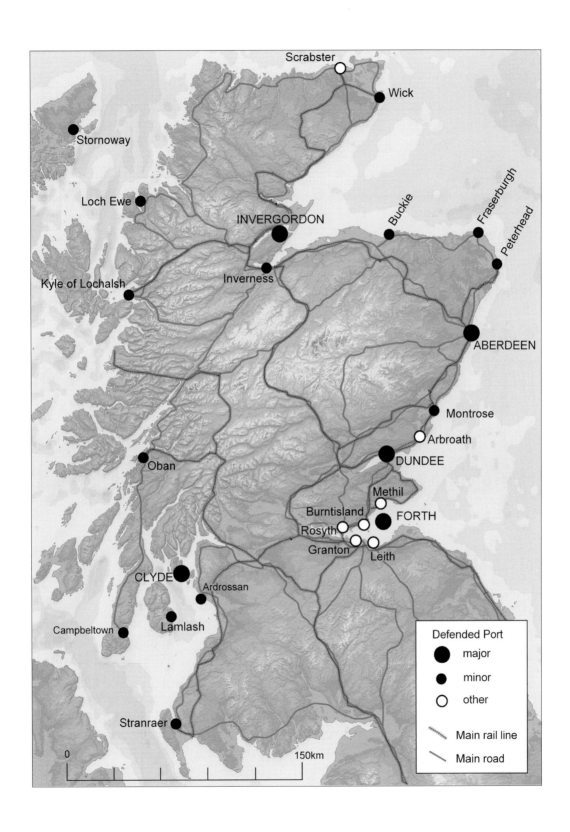

Scrabster

Wick

Stornoway

Loch Ewe

INVERGORDON

Buckie

Fraserburgh

Peterhead

Inverness

Kyle of Lochalsh

ABERDEEN

Montrose

Arbroath

Oban

DUNDEE

Methil

Burntisland

FORTH

Rosyth

Granton

Leith

CLYDE

Ardrossan

Campbeltown

Lamlash

Stranraer

Defended Port

● major

● minor

○ other

Main rail line

Main road

0   150km

An Admiralty list of October 1941 recorded 'Observed [or 'Controlled'] Minefields', which consisted of tethered mines, usually on the approach to a port, which could be set off remotely from a control station on shore. At Aberdeen there were three lines of such mines, of seven, eight and eight mines respectively, outside the harbour entrance, and five groups of five mines each covering the approach from due east of the entrance. The control tower was noted as 'Type E – strong'. There were also three fixed torpedo tubes at the entrance to the harbour.[17] There seem to have been further controlled minefields at Buddon, at the mouth of the Tay, where the control tower was listed as a Vulnerable Point, and at the entrance to Montrose harbour, where the tower was being guarded in November 1940.[18]

Port areas were normally sealed off by barbed wire fences and were often defended by pillboxes (Fig. 6.4) – see the maps of Wick, Aberdeen and Dundee.

IMMOBILISATION

Within 5 miles of designated ports or aerodromes and close to vulnerable beaches, any possible landing ground large enough to allow a glider, aeroplane or parachutists to land was obstructed: that is, 'any reasonably even open space area not less than 600 yds [548m] by 150 yds [137m] with a slope not greater than 15 degrees' and bumps less than 3ft (0.9m) high were not to be considered 'obstructions'.[19] At first, vehicles, farm carts and scrap metal were strewn over open spaces, but soon timber posts were being erected in patterns on beaches and more rarely on fields and golf courses, while patterns of ditches became the norm on land. A War Office letter of 27 May 1940 set out the pattern – a continuous ditch with the spoil piled in non-continuous dumps on either side of the ditch. These ditches were to be arranged in squares with a 150-yard (137m) side.[20] In 1941 the policy was modified because of the impact on food production.[21]

LOCHS AND RESERVOIRS

On 12 July 1940 a telegram was sent to the War Office (unfortunately the name of the sender is not known, but the tone suggests that he was well-connected) suggesting that a company of infantry, an anti-aircraft detachment and the arming of a local steamer were needed to protect Loch Tay as it had been, 'systematically reconnoitred by air during last fortnight . . . German planes over west end of loch each of last three nights . . . have reported this and suspicious incidents round shore to military authorities Scottish Command but could you expedite arrangements to deny use

Figure 6.3. (opposite top) Torry Point Battery, Aberdeen, with two 6-inch naval guns (ringed), battery control tower, accommodation and other buildings, including a pillbox, at bottom right (RAF/ National Collection of Aerial Photography).

Figure 6.4. (opposite below) The harbour perimeter and a guarding pillbox at Aberdeen (Aberdeen Journals).

Figure 6.5.
Patrol launches on Loch
Lomond. August 1940.

of loch as hostile seaplane base . . . local defence utterly inadequate.'[22]

The perceived impact of airborne troops in the invasion of the Low Countries in 1940 extended to a great fear of assault troops landed by seaplane on lochs or reservoirs, especially those near a Vulnerable Point. A minute of November 1940 stated as fact that, 'The enemy has 24 squadrons of flying boats or float planes (288 aircraft)', although it was recognised that 192 of these were small planes unable to carry troops. While 'the enemy is not . . . in a position to land any large body of troops on inland waters . . . It would . . . be quite possible for the enemy to land a small party near some vulnerable point.'[23] As a consequence, lochs and reservoirs were either blocked in various ways (wire ropes, moored logs, steel drums or rafts) or patrolled. The Loch of Strathbeg in north-east Scotland, for example, was blocked by floating log obstacles placed in north-east to south-west rows anchored with galvanised cable attached to concrete-filled sandbags (see pp. 193–6 to see how this fitted into the local anti-invasion defences). By May 1941 a month's work and the expenditure of £350 was needed for repair.[24] Patrolling was confined to lochs too big to obstruct: the first inland water patrols were set up in July 1940 when the two-boat patrol in Loch Leven and the five-boat patrol in Loch Lomond were established.[25] The boats were normally manned by two naval ratings and two Home Defence battalion privates, with total armament of a Bren gun and three rifles.[26] By September 1940 boats of the 940th Inland Water Transport Operating Company, RE were patrolling three further lochs in Scotland: the Lake of Menteith, Loch Ard and Loch Rannoch (two boats).[27] By comparison, there were 37 boats on six of the Cumbrian lakes and 38 boats on the Norfolk Broads. While it was at first felt better to keep the existence of the boats a surprise for any enemy landing on them, there was widespread press coverage at the end of August 1940, with images of four of the five boats patrolling Loch Lomond (Fig. 6.5).[28]

ARMOURED TRAINS

The story of the armoured trains in Britain has already been told in detail.[29] They were intended to provide a way of rushing heavier support to isolated and vulnerable places, especially on beaches, and after Lieutenant Colonel Alan Mount, RE, Chief Inspector of Railways at the Ministry of Transport, suggested that armoured trains could be of considerable value, a design was worked out quickly in late May 1940. By 10 June six trains were already in hand in the UK and material for another 14 was available. Their role at first was to patrol the coast to locate enemy detachments and parachutists, to reinforce threatened points, and to protect railway gangs.[30]

On 7 June 1940 Scottish Command had independently seen the advantage of being able to move a unit (albeit more lightly armed than those that were built) rapidly to far-flung and lightly defended beaches: 'Approval is requested for the use of small Armoured Trains consisting of [a] small tank engine with cattle truck in front and rear, trucks being sandbagged and loop-holed with an L.M.G. and Anti-Tank rifle in each truck. Approximate number of trains required 20. Trains required for rapid reinforcement of threatened points in lonely districts where communications are poor'.[31]

Lieutenant Colonel R. Briggs of the Royal Armoured Corps, however, took a contrary view later in the year: 'We do not consider they [armoured trains] are of real value against a well trained and disciplined enemy'.[32] It is not clear who 'we' were, or on what basis the opinion rested.

The first trains built were to comprise a 2–4–2 tank engine (in Scotland, 30-year-old LNER Class F4s); two low-sided waggons, placed between the engine and the armoured waggons to improve sight-lines; two armoured 20-ton coal waggons (one behind and one ahead of the engine and split into two parts, with the guns in the sections away from the engine); 6-pounder Hotchkiss guns, one at either end, with wrap-around shield (this short-barrelled First World War naval gun, of the kind used to arm the first tanks in that war, was ideally suited to the trains). The crew also had six Bren guns provided for anti-personnel fire and two Boys anti-tank rifles. Through the life of the trains, their armament and equipment was improved, and early modifications included the provision of an anti-aircraft mounting for a Bren gun and lining of the armoured trucks with wood to prevent ricochets (Fig. 6.6).[33]

The numbering/lettering of the 12 trains and the four Train Groups (numbered 1 to 4) each with between two and four trains, seemed designed to confuse: the trains were known both by numbers 1 to 12, and by letters A to L (later A to M, as 'I' was renamed M), but not in any sensible way (Train letter B was also known as Train number 6).

At first, in July 1940, Scotland was allocated six trains: numbers 3, 5 and 7

were supposed to go to Inverness, Aberdeen and Forfar; while 11, 12 and 14 were supposed to go to Stirling, Edinburgh and Glasgow.[34] In the end a different set of trains seems to have been allocated.[35] Their stay was brief. Competition from other Commands and the ceiling of a total of 12 trains for the whole of Britain imposed by GHQ led to Scotland retaining only three trains: J[10], K[12] and L [11] at Stirling, Longniddry/Edinburgh and Aberdeen (Fig. 6.7).

The key roles envisaged for the armoured trains were set out on 13 July 1940:[36] patrolling of coast rail-lines to locate enemy detachments and gain information; reinforcing threatened points with firepower; dealing with tank attacks; and acting as an armed roadblock or pillbox. The dependence of the train on its rails made 'the choice of a fighting position with a covered line [of] retirement of the greatest importance'.[37]

Running on the public railway network was always a problem because of normal civilian traffic, the movement of military personnel and equipment, and the supply of raw materials to industry. The armoured trains ordinarily took their turn with civilian traffic but had increased priority 'during unexpected hostile action in the vicinity' and during 'active operation'.[38]

At first the trains were manned by a Royal Engineer train crew with a Royal Armoured Corps fighting crew, made up of tank men who at that stage, after the fall of France, had no tanks.[39] The RE sergeant accompanying the RAC officer commanding the train, in one of the armoured waggons, sent commands to the engine crew using bell signals.[40]

In the summer of 1940 Colonel Mikołaj Kolanowski of the Polish Army, who had commanded a Polish military railway regiment in the 1920s, suggested that some of the surplus Polish officers could man the armoured trains. The suggestion was accepted and the first to be taken over were the three in Scotland from November 1940 onwards. The legendary 'dash' of the Poles was apparently reflected in their driving style: 'Polish Engineer personnel must be restrained when driving the train from excessive speed and the limit of 25 mph must be impressed upon them.'[41]

VULNERABLE POINTS

Vulnerable Points were usually installations of strategic value that required protection from sabotage, hit-and-run raids or larger-scale enemy assault. Lists of Vulnerable Points turn up on many military files and include such obvious sites as radar stations, key installations on the telephone network, BBC transmitters and so on. They might or might not include military installations, as these would often be self-protecting (thus aerodromes did not always appear). The lists included

Figure 6.6.
The forward waggon of one of the armoured trains, showing one of the pair of Hotchkiss 6-pounder guns and the Bren guns in the rear compartment (Imperial War Museum 7034).

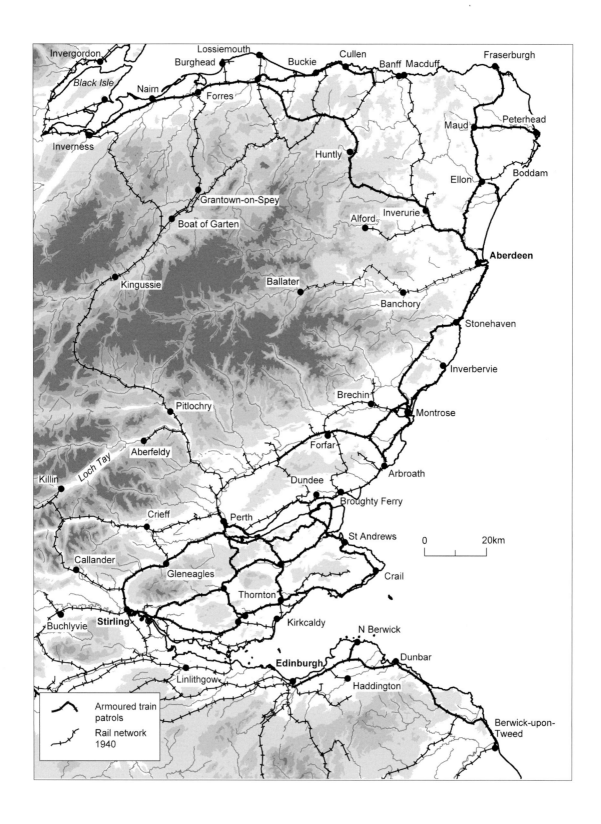

Invergordon

Black Isle

Nairn

Inverness

Forres

Burghead

Lossiemouth

Buckie

Cullen

Banff Macduff

Fraserburgh

Maud

Peterhead

Ellon

Boddam

Huntly

Alford

Inverurie

Aberdeen

Grantown-on-Spey

Boat of Garten

Kingussie

Ballater

Banchory

Stonehaven

Inverbervie

Pitlochry

Aberfeldy

Loch Tay

Killin

Crieff

Brechin

Montrose

Forfar

Arbroath

Dundee

Broughty Ferry

Perth

St Andrews

Callander

Gleneagles

Crail

Buchlyvie

Stirling

Thornton

Kirkcaldy

N Berwick

Dunbar

Linlithgow

Edinburgh

Haddington

Berwick-upon-Tweed

0   20km

Armoured train
patrols

Rail network
1940

infrastructure, such as water treatment plants, electricity generators and gasworks, as well as major tunnels and bridges on the rail network, food, petrol and ammunition storage depots, key shipbuilders and factories. It is certain that in the early stages of the war, guarding many hundreds of Vulnerable Points drained thousands of regular infantry away from training or more active defence measures. That said, public opinion reacted with 'Satisfaction at more soldiers on guard at key points'[42] and in Edinburgh with 'Complaints about unguarded points of importance'.[43]

General Kirke, the first C-in-C Home Forces, had a constant struggle against demands from other parts of the armed forces (particularly the Air Ministry and RAF) and government departments for guards for installations. In November 1939, 34,000 men were employed guarding Vulnerable Points, of which no fewer than 20,000 were from the Field Force.[44] By January 1940 the total number of Field Force troops being used was still 15,600 and by March it was 13,500, out of a total number of 37,000 guards.[45] Strenuous efforts by Kirke reduced the Field Army commitment to 4,500 of the Field Force by April.[46]

Kirke complained again to CSC on 20 May (the day German tanks reached the sea at Abbeville) that his Field Force was being eroded by demands 'to increase static guards in all directions' especially by the Air Ministry.[47] The equivalent of over seven battalions were guarding aircraft factories between Glasgow and Bristol, and even greater demands were being made for the protection of aerodromes (including 22 not in use) against a possible attack by up to 500 parachutists – a demand that, if satisfied, would immobilise the majority of the anti-invasion Field Army.

During 1940–41 the job of guarding Vulnerable Points was increasingly taken over by Home Defence and Young Soldier battalions, and by the Home Guard. This freed better quality troops for more useful occupations, although the view was expressed in July 1941, after Crete, by the Commander of Aberdeen Sub-area that 'aerodromes are such vital points that they should be guarded by the very best troops available'. This view was confirmed by 'the [exercise] "attacks" on KINLOSS and LOSSIEMOUTH this week by No. 6 Commando . . . the inadequacy of the infantry defence was quite clearly brought out'.[48]

Figure 6.7.
Map of the rail network in 1940, showing the principal patrol routes of the three armoured trains, based in Aberdeen, Stirling and Edinburgh.

7. BEACHES AND STOP-LINES

The first line of land defence, should the invaders have evaded or disabled the Royal Navy and Royal Air Force, was on the beaches, particularly on the coast facing mainland Europe and Scandinavia.

In the summer of 1940 Rear-Admiral F.C. Dreyer was commissioned to survey the coast of Britain (excluding the east coast of Scotland from Berwick-upon-Tweed to Lossiemouth, which was undertaken by Scottish Command). He did this at a ferocious pace: his report on the coast from Carlisle to Ardrossan was submitted on 12 August, and he had reached Inverness and the Moray Firth (via the Caledonian Canal) by the 20th. He highlighted many risks to factories and towns on the west coast but seems to have had an unrealistic idea of what could be done. For example, he recommended that Oban needed one and a half battalions of troops to guard it. But he also reported a widespread popular belief that Scotland was to be abandoned undefended to the Germans, as there were so few men and anti-tank guns in the country.[1]

For the more vulnerable east coast of Scotland, the list of possible invasion beaches had been put together at a Scottish Command conference on 27 May 1940 and was sent to GHQ Home Forces on the 31st.[2] General Carrington noted that these 13 beaches, from Sinclair's Bay to Dunbar, totalled 80 miles in length, mostly with unimpeded access inland, and thus required complete blocking, not just the obstruction of exits. The beaches at Tentsmuir and Dunbar were reckoned to be the most 'dangerous'.[3]

Further lists of vulnerable beaches were issued or amended at various stages over the next year or two. The *Scottish Command Defence Scheme* of October 1940 included 92 miles.[4] This document's replacement, *Scottish Command Standing Operation Instructions 1941*, of March 1941,[5] listed the beaches in more detail (for example, by breaking up Lossiemouth into 'east' and 'west' beaches). The length of defended beach had now reached over 125 miles, although some beaches were to be blocked by 'mine only'. The October 1941 amendment to this list included almost 140 miles of beach and this maximum extent is what is illustrated on the map (Fig. 7.1).

The first beach obstacles to be erected were concrete cubes, either 3ft 6in/4ft

Figure 7.1.
Vulnerable beaches as included in the most comprehensive list, of October 1941.

84

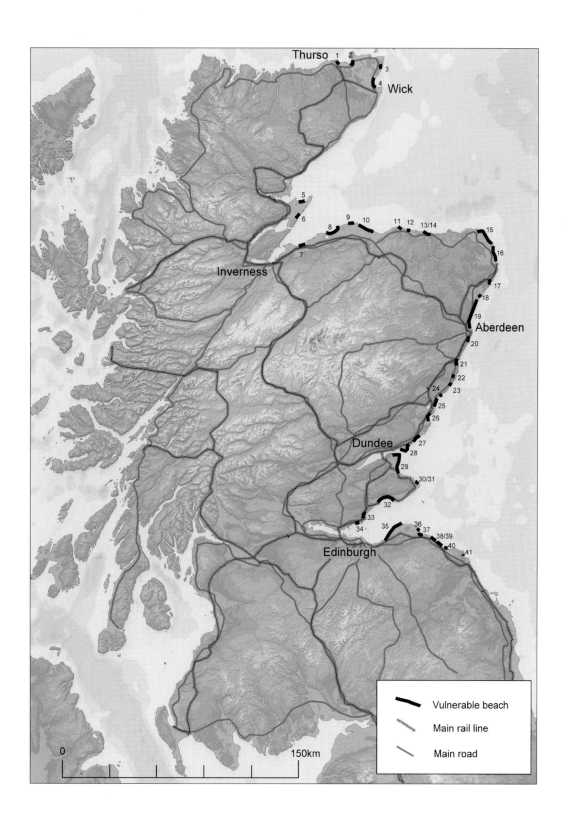

high or 5ft high (1.06/1.2m or 1.5m), in single or, less often, staggered double and, in places, triple lines, usually accompanied by wire fences, the obstacles usually being covered by firing positions, including pillboxes, either within, behind (or more rarely) in front of the line of cubes. Cubes could cover the whole length or a significant part of a beach or, where the dunes were high, could block only possible exits such as access tracks, dune blow-outs or stream-beds. Single lines of cubes were often reinforced by additional lines of dragon's teeth after December 1940 and by beach scaffolding from the spring of 1941 until February 1942. Anti-tank mines were used to block beach exits, easy routes from beaches, or even, with barbed wire, as the only barriers on a beach. In a few cases anti-tank ditches were dug behind the beaches.

Where a beach was within 5 miles of a port or aerodrome it was 'immobilised', usually by the erection of anti-glider poles.

Table 7.1. October 1941 beach list (x = mentioned also on the May 1940 and/or the March 1941 lists). The text description of a beach's defences is not always accurate, e.g. Sands of Forvie was actually blocked with cubes.

Number on map	Name	Documented length & character	May 1940	March 1941
North Highland Area				
1	Thurso Bay	2.5 miles		x
2	Dunnet Bay	2.5 miles		x
3	Freswick Bay	0.5 mile		
4	Sinclair's Bay	5.5 miles	x	x
5	Portmahomack	1 mile	x	
6	Shandwick Bay	1 mile	x	
7	Nairn	4.5 miles. 'Minefield & wire only'	x	x
8	Burghead Bay	7 miles	x	x
9	Lossiemouth West	2 miles		x
10	Lossiemouth East	9 miles	x	x
11	Cullen Bay	1 mile		x
12	Sandend Bay	0.5 mile		x
13	Boyndie Bay	0.75 mile		x
14	Banff	0.5 mile. 'Minefield only'		x
15	Fraserburgh Bay – Rattray Head	9 miles	x	x
16	Rattray Head – Peterhead	8 miles	x	x
17	Cruden Bay	2 miles		x
18	Sands of Forvie	1 mile. 'Minefield only'		x
19	Newburgh Bar – Aberdeen	12 miles	x	x
20	Nigg Bay [Aberdeen]	0.5 mile		x

Number on map	Name	Documented length & character	May 1940	March 1941
21	Stonehaven	0.75 mile		x
22	Braidon Bay	0.5 mile. 'anti-tank ditch only'		
23	Bervie Bay	0.5 mile		x
24	Milton Ness	1 mile		
South Highland Area				
25	St Cyrus – Montrose	4 miles	x	x
26	Lunan Bay	3.5 miles	x	x
27	Arbroath	4 miles		x
28	Carnoustie – Monifieth [Barry]	5.5 miles	x	x
29	Tayport – St Andrews [Tentsmuir]	10 miles	x	x
30	Cambo Ness	200 yds. 'Minefield only'		x
31	Tullybothy	1 mile. 'Minefield only'		
32	Largo Bay (including Elie)	8 miles	(only Elie)	x
33	Kirkcaldy (& Dysart)	3 miles		x
34	Burntisland	0.5 mile		x
Edinburgh Area				
35	Port Seton – North Berwick	12 miles	Aberlady only	x
36	Ravensheugh Sands	1 mile. 'Minefield only'		x
37	Belhaven Bay	4 miles	x	x
38	Whitesands	'Minefield & wire'		x
39	Thorntonloch	0.5 mile		x
38/39	Whitesands to Thorntonloch	4 miles. 'Wire only'		
40	Pease Bay	0.75 mile. 'Wire only'		
41	Coldingham Bay	0.75 mile. 'Wire only'		

DEFENCE BATTERIES (MOBILE), ROYAL ARTILLERY

Artillery batteries positioned specifically to fire directly onto vulnerable beaches and their approaches were established in at least three parts of eastern Scotland, equipped until the spring of 1941 with 4-inch naval guns. One battery (942nd Defence Battery (Mobile), RA), of six guns, operated round the mouth of the Tay, from Carnoustie to St Andrews. The second (943rd Battery), of ten guns, provided cover on the beaches north of Aberdeen (a pair of guns at each of Balmedie, Newburgh and Peterhead, and four guns at Sinclair's Bay in Caithness).

These guns were not absorbed into the coast defence structure and, on the withdrawal of the 4-inch guns in spring 1941, to arm merchant vessels, they were replaced by 18-pounder field guns and shortly after by 75-mm guns (these batteries are described in more detail under the areas, below). Mention of a further battery of this kind in East Lothian[6] probably refers to a pair of 6-inch naval guns on First World War field carriages, absorbed into 943rd Battery in 1941 (see p. 277).

STOP-LINES, DEFENDED LOCALITIES AND CHECK-LINES

In what follows a difference is drawn between, on the one hand, anti-tank 'stop-lines' and defended localities (built largely in 1940), intended to hold up the advance of enemy forces, and, on the other, 'check-lines', listed in documents from 1941 onwards. These seem to have had more of the character of internal security lines, where the identity of vehicle passengers could be checked.

As the official history of the defence of the United Kingdom put it, the forces available to General Ironside in May 1940 were, 'not only ill-equipped; they also lacked mobility . . . In the absence of strong mobile forces deeply imbued with the offensive spirit, Ironside came to the conclusion that his best chance lay in combining his few mobile columns with static defences deployed over a wide area'.[7] Behind the defended beaches this meant the creation of anti-tank stop-lines and defended localities.

The anti-tank defensive systems seem to fall into four broad categories: (a) anti-tank stop-lines almost wholly formed by a largely unmodified natural feature, such as a major river; (b) stop-lines almost wholly formed by constructed or dug features, or where a natural feature had to be enhanced considerably to form a barrier; (c) stop-lines formed by a line of roadblocks, for example blocking all north-east to south-west trending roads between the sea and the mountains, where the open country between was not obstructed; (d) 'defended localities' where natural constraints on lines of communication meant that large areas of the country could be isolated by one road or bridge being blocked and heavily defended. Additionally, some lines listed in 1940–41 may be characterised as the product of desk- and map-based assessment, as they seem to take little account of the real landscape, and others seem to have been ephemeral, in that nothing is recorded as having been built or prepared. Redfern, after his trawl through the War Office files, identified a total of 33 linear defence systems (stop-lines and check-lines) but some of these appeared relatively late in the war as part of Home Guard schemes of defence or internal security. One of the more complex, formal anti-tank stop-lines, the Cowie Line, had dwindled into this sort of 'check-line' by 1943.[8]

Figure 7.2.
Stop-lines and check-lines in mainland Scotland, mainly those determined by Scottish Command. See Table 7.2.

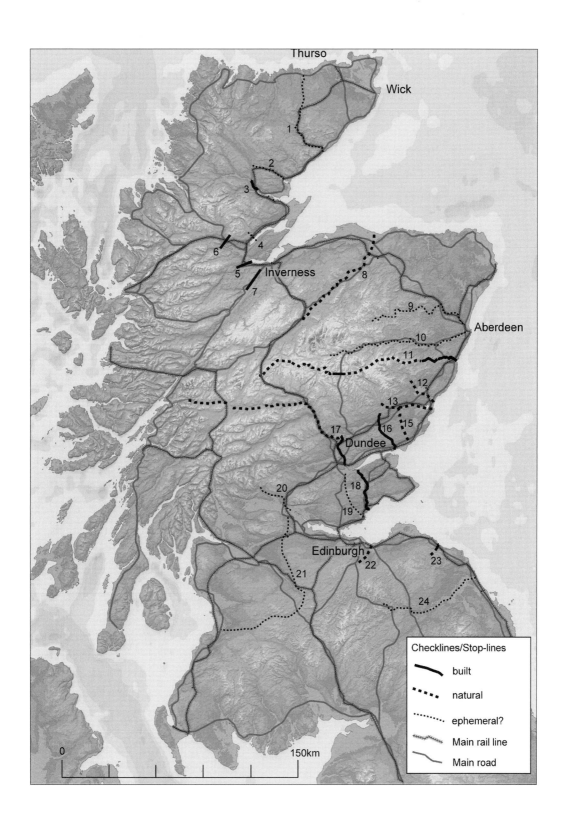

Thurso

Wick

1

2

3

6

5 Inverness

4

7

8

9

Aberdeen

10

11

12

13

15

16

17

Dundee

18

19

20

21

22

Edinburgh

23

24

Checklines/Stop-lines	
▬▬▬	built
▪▪▪▪	natural
⋯⋯⋯	ephemeral?
∿∿∿	Main rail line
────	Main road

0   150km

An intention to reconnoitre six 'demolition belts' had been announced by Carrington on 9 June 1940,[9] and two formal lists of stop-lines, developing the 'belts', were promulgated for Scotland in July 1940[10] and in June 1941.[11] Some of the lines had appeared in Carrington's 9 June memorandum and in both lists; others were effectively the same, or had much the same effect, although the way they were named or described might be slightly different; others vanished after the first list, never to be mentioned again, while new ones appeared. Additionally, locally designed stop-lines also emerged. Defensive doctrine began to change late in 1940, however, when linear defence gave way to the defence of what became known as 'focal points' (see below). Roadblocks established as part of a stop-line would often continue in use, but as part of a wider pattern of roadblocks across an area.

Each stop-line, its purpose, the structures associated with it and the units that were to man it, are described in more detail in the account of each Sub-area of Scotland. The total 'set' of those promulgated by Scottish Command (and others known to have been built on the mainland) is shown on the accompanying map (Fig. 7.2) and in Table 7.2 below. The table does not include the route of the GHQ Line from the border to the Firth of Forth, as Scottish Command seems to have had no intention of building this, but it does refer to the Scottish Command list of check-lines promulgated in 1943.[12] Redfern included the following as separate lines: Broughton to Biggar in Peeblesshire and Lanark to Peebles but these seem to have been part of the larger Tweed Line, as described in 1943 (no. 22 below), and have the character of internal security check-lines only. Peebles to Leadburn seems to have been a security check-line only.[13] One line, no. 23 below, does not appear on any list of lines, but was probably built. The many anti-tank lines in Orkney and Shetland were not included in Scottish Command lists and are dealt with in Part III.

NODAL/FOCAL POINTS

In January 1941 Eastern Command claimed that the expression 'nodal point' had originated there.[14] It had been noted, first, that German armoured vehicles tended to keep to the roads as much as possible and, second, that English roads tended to converge on towns and villages, where the Home Guard was most numerous. By defending these strongly, German advances could be halted or slowed. However, it was quickly realised that this approach to defence could have very serious consequences for the resident civilian population if any battle for a town was prolonged, and major efforts were recorded on file to try to find ways of mitigating these effects.

Table 7.2. Stop-lines promulgated by Scottish Command

Number on map	When recorded	Name	Nature
1	Only July 1940	Helmsdale–Melvich	Poorly conceived and ephemeral.
2	Only July 1940	Loch Fleet to Lairg	Effect achieved by blocking only two roads. Pillboxes at Lairg end.
3	June 1940/July 1940/ June 1941/1943	Bonar Bridge defended locality	Over 20 pillboxes covering bridge and approaches.
4	June 1940/July 1940	Dingwall	Ephemeral? Given effect by lines 5 and 6/7.
5	[June 1940] July 1940	[Beauly Firth–River Beauly] Kessock–Kilmorack	Narrow bridges blocked and three pillboxes erected.
6	First mentioned December 1940	Loch Garve defended locality	Road and rail blocked at narrow point, covered by four pillboxes.
7	July 1940/1943	Caledonian Canal	Limited number of crossings of Great Glen; canal provides barrier at north-east end.
8	June 1941/1943	River Spey	All crossings provided with roadblocks.
9	June 1941/1943	River Don	Almost no evidence of construction. Ephemeral?
10	June 1941/1943	River Dee	Crossings to be disputed by Home Guard and other units. Few structures.
11	June 1940/ July 1940/1943	Cowie Line	Modified river bank, natural features, mountains, demolitions, pillboxes and roadblocks halfway across Scottish mainland.
12	November 1940/ April 1941	North Esk (Angus)	Concrete blocks at coast (east end). Otherwise river forms barrier. Roadblocks on all crossings.
13	November 1940/ April 1941	South Esk (Angus)	River forms barrier. Roadblocks on all crossings.
14 (Not on map)	July 1940	Unnamed	Ephemeral combination of rivers North and South Esk. Superseded by 12 and 13.
15	November 1940	Carnoustie–Finavon	Roadblocks on roads across coastal plain.
16	July 1940/ November 1940	Kirriemuir Line	Roadblocks on roads across coastal plain.

Number on map	When recorded	Name	Nature
17	June 1940/July 1940/ June 1941/1943	Command Line North	Modified river bank; up to two lines of anti-tank ditch on both sides of River Tay. Pillboxes. Line continued north and west by demolitions and mountains.
18	July 1940/June 1941/ 1943	Command Line South	Double line of anti-tank ditch across Fife with many roadblocks and pillboxes.
19 (Not on map)	1943	Burntisland– Kinross–Perth	Ephemeral? One pillbox north-east of Kinross?
20	June 1940/July 1940/ June 1941/1943	R. Forth–R. Teith– Callander–L. Lubnaig	Effectively the northernmost sector of the GHQ Line. Limited number of crossings. Later spigot mortar emplacements at Doune. Otherwise no constructions.
21	June 1941/1943	Ayr–Lanark–Airdrie– Stirling	Ephemeral? No structures recorded.
22	June 1941/1943	River Esk (Midlothian) [1943 – Musselburgh– Penicuick–Pentland Hills]	A series of bridge demolitions and road cratering by Canadian Pipe Mines, along the Esk.
23	Not listed, but originated June 1941	Dunglass to Elmscleugh	Modified river bank, roadblocks, rail blocks, demolitions, minefields and wire.
24	June 1941/1943	River Tweed [1943 extends to Lanark]	Ephemeral? One pillbox at Kelso and later spigot mortar positions. Otherwise check-points.

8. BARRIERS

*'Within economic limits it is not possible
to guarantee more than a few minutes delay
against fast medium or heavy tanks.'*[1]

CONCRETE

There was a great variety of anti-tank barriers made of concrete and other materials; experience, trials, concerns over quantities of material, changes in policy and local preferences all determined what sort of barrier was used, where and when. Pre-war Royal Engineer manuals did not provide designs for the sort of concrete obstacles erected on the beaches, and it is likely that the designs for the cubes was promulgated in May 1940 alongside the designs for pill-boxes emerging from the Department of Fortifications and Works, but have not yet come to light in the files.[2] Designs were tested and evaluated from August 1940 onwards and standards for the construction of concrete obstacles were codified in *Military Training Pamphlet 30, Part III*, issued in October 1940.[3]

Of the types of concrete barrier described in official publications and in advisory notes issued by various authorities from the middle of 1940 and 1941, only two seem to have been used in Scotland: cubes, 3ft 6in–4ft (1.06m/1.21m) and 5ft (1.5m), and dragon's teeth, also known as tetrahedra or 'pimples', with a 3ft or 4ft (0.91m or 1.22m) base, particularly useful on soft ground.

CUBES

The rectilinear lumps of concrete placed on beaches and in other places were most often called 'cubes' in official documents. They were the most common concrete barrier and were cast on site (Fig. 8.1), within wooden or corrugated iron shuttering. An unknown proportion incorporated steel reinforcement. Some were made of fine, well-made concrete (Fig. 8.2) and show no signs of their 60

Figure 8.1. (above)
Polish engineers erecting
cubes near Lossiemouth;
note the steel reinforcement
awaiting shuttering in the
background (Polish Institute
& Sikorski Museum, London).

Figure 8.2. (opposite)
A single line of anti-tank
cubes at Lossiemouth, with
steel loops to anchor barbed
wire (Author).

years on the beaches; others were made of poorly-mixed concrete incorporating a high proportion of beach pebbles and probably salty beach sand, and have not survived well. Some were set on reasonably deep foundations to aid stability; others had 'foundations' only about 30cm across and 15cm deep. Some had already been tumbled by the sea within months of being built. Some show signs of the smaller height of cube being raised by 30cm or so (Fig. 12.6).

In some areas, large sewer pipes filled with concrete and placed on rough concrete bases cast onto the beach took the place of cubes (Fig. 8.3). In Orkney small circular steel drums filled with concrete were used alongside dragon's teeth to block beaches (Chapter 10). In many areas pieces of local rock (e.g. Caithness slab and granite) were set into the tops of the cubes, perhaps to make them more likely to catch the bottom of a tank. Many cubes had steel rings in the centre of their tops, to anchor the complex pattern of barbed wire that covered them (Fig. 8.4). In Angus, in particular, rounded cement tops were added to some cubes to support upright steel posts to hold barbed wire (Fig. 13.11). The distribution of this feature suggests it was a Polish refinement.

Dragon's teeth were also known as pimples, or less commonly as tetrahedra or 'German pattern "teeth"'. They were made in two sizes, with a 3ft and 4ft square base – most in Scotland are the smaller size. They were cast on site in removable wooden shutters, often straight onto bare rock, and sometimes in sets of two,

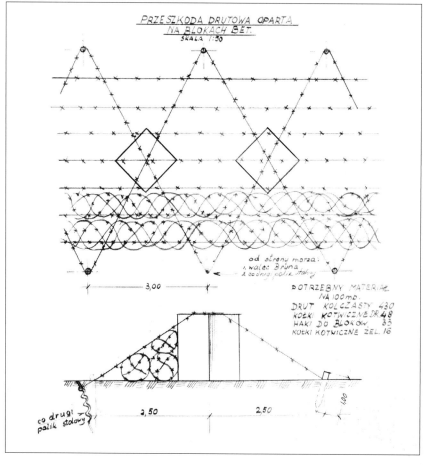

PRZESZKODA DRUTOWA OPARTA
NA BLOKACH BET.
SKALA 1:50

od strony morza:
1. walec Bruna
2. codnie: palik stalowy

3,00

POTRZEBNY MATERIAL
NA 100mb.
DRUT KOLCZASTY 430
KOŁKI KOTWICZNE DR. 48
HAKI DO BLOKÓW 33
KOŁKI KOTWICZNE ŻEL. 16

co drugi
palik stalowy

2,50   2,50   1,00

three or more, sharing a single base. Where they were set in sand, to ensure stability, their bases could dwarf the tops (Fig. 8.6). They appeared not only on beaches but flanking roadblocks on the Command Line, and in 350m-long stretches in two places on the line, where the anti-tank ditch could not be dug (Fig. 15.8).

On 19 December 1940 Scottish Command wrote to the Army Areas in Scotland, and to the Polish Forces, noting that defences built up to that date were often not to the standard set out in *Military Training Pamphlet 30*, and were to be strengthened.[4] The standard barrier to be provided in new work was five rows of dragon's teeth. Where there was an existing single row of cubes, or a row of cubes with a single row of pimples, this was to be brought up to two rows of pimples in front of the cubes (this can probably be seen at Freswick Bay in Caithness (Fig. 11.6) and at Tentsmuir, in Fife (Fig. 14.12)). Two rows of cubes would not require strengthening, but three rows of pimples (which had been set as the standard as recently as December 1940)[5] would be brought up to five.[6]

The most comprehensive tests of the effectiveness of these barriers were undertaken in May 1941[7] to establish the length of delay that six different types of barrier (excluding an anti-tank ditch) would impose on enemy tanks. The various types of defence lasted only between 70 and 90 seconds, most requiring just a few successful hits from the tanks' guns.[8] It was only in May 1942 that in

Figure 8.3. (opposite top) A mixed line of cubes and concrete-filled sewer pipes, tumbled in the surf, south of Newburgh, Aberdeenshire. (Author)

Figure 8.4. (opposite below) A Polish Army diagram of the wiring up of a line of anti-tank cubes (Polish Institute & Sikorski Museum, London).

Figure 8.5. Polish troops constructing dragon's teeth in front of pre-existing cubes at Carnoustie, 1941. The car of a small railway to carry materials is visible at top left. (Polish Institute & Sikorski Museum, London)

Figure 8.6.
Dragon's teeth with massive foundations at Freswick Bay, Caithness (Author).

some places instructions were given to stop building concrete beach defences: at Tentsmuir in Fife scaffolding was henceforth to be erected instead of the ephemeral protection given by pimples 'under local conditions', probably the loss of cubes to drifting sand and storm erosion.[9]

One-metre-thick concrete walls were occasionally used as anti-tank barriers, especially beside roadblocks – the longest known is a 325m length in Kettlebridge, on the Command Line.[10]

ANTI-TANK DITCHES

Anti-tank ditches formed a well-established part of the repertoire of anti-tank obstruction. The classic ditch built in the early part of the war, and illustrated in the 1940 *Military Training Pamphlet*, was 18ft across, with a slope leading down to a flat bottom a maximum of 6ft 6in (1.98m) broad, to a near-vertical face at least 5ft deep (1.52m), facing the enemy tank and usually revetted with wooden poles and brushwood (Fig. 8.7). The spoil was piled up on both sides and flattened to be no more than 2ft high. Tests of the value and cost of different types of anti-tank barrier showed that the anti-tank ditch was one of the most effective forms and also the cheapest. Fifty yards (about 45m) of traditional ditch would cost £30 (£1540 at modern value), while pimples and cubes cost almost £200 and scaffolding

Figure 8.7.
A textbook anti-tank ditch
(Imperial War Museum 2473).

(see below) was an eye-watering £519 (£26,655 at modern values) for the same length.[11]

An equivalent barrier could be provided by adapting a natural feature, for example, by raising or steepening the bank of a river. The Cowie Line in Aberdeenshire is one of the best-preserved examples (Fig. 12.40). Also, a ditch could be created quickly by use of a Canadian pipe mine – a pipe drilled into the ground at a shallow angle, filled with explosives and detonated (p. 105).

WIRE

Barbed wire was the ubiquitous defence material. In the vast majority of cases any other kind of defence – roadblock, anti-tank ditch, scaffolding, anti-tank cubes – would have been accompanied or festooned by barbed wire. It was supplied in two types: plain barbed wire in rolls, and concertina or 'Dannert' wire. Dannert wire (named after its inventor) was manufactured in such a way that, when it was strung out, it retained its shape as a sprung coil. Plain barbed wire was used as 'cattle fences' – four stands of wire held on steel posts – or double apron fences, where the basic cattle fence had aprons of wire spread out on both sides (Fig. 8.8). Dannert wire was deployed in single or multiple coils, one of the most commonly mentioned in the files being a triple Dannert fence, where two coils

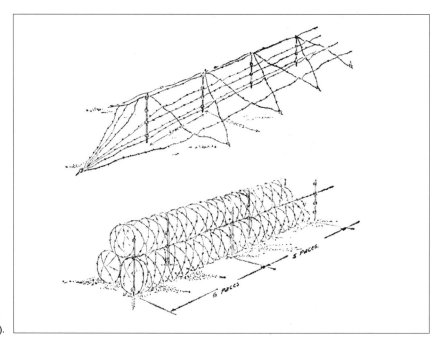

Figure 8.8.
The 'double apron' pattern of barbed wire obstruction and a 'triple concertina' of Dannert wire. *Military Training Pamphlet No. 30, Part III* (1940).

were pinned side by side and a third laid and pinned along the top. The wiring up of beach defences would often use a mixture of the two. Rolls of Dannert wire could also form a roadblock (see below).

SCAFFOLDING

Scaffolding, in the form of vertical frameworks of steel scaffolding tubes, braced by angled tubes to the rear, was used in Scotland on beaches and inland from early 1941. Scaffolding seems to have first been put forward as a defence measure in October 1940, 'as some compensation' for the reduced anti-invasion naval forces to be based at Plymouth and Rosyth (to allow ships to return to convoy duties);[12] it was seen as a way of delaying the first waves of an enemy invasion until more distantly located naval forces could intervene. On 5 March 1941, the Chiefs of Staff Committee of the War Cabinet recommended that every effort be made to complete beach scaffolding, if possible by 1 April 1941 – the rather arbitrary working date for the beginning of the 1941 'invasion season'.

The results of trials of anti-tank scaffolding were rather mixed. In trials in October 1940, March 1941 and finally in March 1942, tanks were sometimes held, but more often managed to drive through the barrier, with or without firing at it first (Fig. 8.9).[13] An annotated Polish Army engineering drawing for D Type Defence Scaffolding[14] allows the amount of steel used to be calculated: a fraction under 13 tonnes of steel would be needed to obstruct 100m of beach; 129.6 tonnes for 1km. Admiralty Z1 scaffolding – the kind used most often and for which there is more evidence – provided an even higher barrier, and thus consumed even more steel per 100m. The Polish archives also contain an excellent photograph of beach scaffolding (of the common, higher, Type Z1) being erected at Lunan Bay in April or May 1941 (Fig. 8.10). Unfortunately the scaffolding, erected by 143rd Pioneer Company and/or Polish troops, managed to obstruct the firing lines of the Polish beach artillery.[15]

It was decided in early September 1941 – that is, at or beyond the end of the 'invasion season' and surely after any possibility of invasion by sea had passed –

Figure 8.9.
Tests of beach scaffolding on 24 October 1940, in Southern Command; '14 ton Cruiser Tank still held by defence – 7th run' (The National Archives, WO199/1422).

Figure 8.10.
Scaffolding being erected at Lunan Bay, 1941 (Polish Institute & Sikorski Museum, London).

to erect scaffolding along Sinclair's Bay in Caithness, where it was erected behind the sand dunes, both to protect it from shelling from the sea and to reduce the speed of tanks attempting to charge it.[16] Ambitious plans for scaffolding on the beaches between Aberdeen and Fraserburgh resulted in only about 6–7 miles being erected of a planned 25 by 14 February 1942. In the Kingston–Findhorn sector, while almost all the material necessary had been dumped on the beaches, no scaffolding, out of a planned 15 miles, had been completed. The decision was promulgated on 12 March 1942 that no more scaffolding was to be erected and the dumps of material were left to rot or to be taken for salvage by local salvage committees.[17]

Scaffolding was used to complete the Inganess–Scapa anti-tank line, east of Kirkwall in Orkney, the northern part of the Kirkwall West anti-tank obstacle from the coast to Wideford Hill[18] and some of the anti-tank stop-lines in Shetland.

The scaffolding was an idea, not a very good one even in October 1940, to deal with a problem (the need to reinforce or replace existing anti-tank obstacles) that did not, by the summer of 1941, need a solution. The waste of steel and the diversion of troops from more productive tasks was absurd. Admiral Sir Tom Phillips suggested to CSC in September 1941 that Britain's allies, the Russians, should perhaps be told about the 'value of scaffolding as an anti-tank obstacle'; it is not known what the Russian reaction to this was.[19]

ROADBLOCKS

Roadblocks were one kind of obstacle to the enemy's advance, intended to stop a tank to allow an opportunity to attack it.[20] While improvised roadblocks could be made of any materials or vehicles to hand, or even barbed wire, four types of formally constructed roadblock were used or survive in Scotland. The first type of permanent movable roadblock that most commonly survives today – horizontal-rail blocks – were best suited to narrow, minor roads, where the post-war effort of removal might not have been considered worthwhile, and their massive structure made removal a not inconsiderable job. The features that survive are the massive concrete cube (cast in timber or brick shuttering) at either side of the road; these cubes would have sockets, a single vertical slot with internal steps, or three vertical slots, the intention of which was to hold three lengths of steel tram-line at different levels (Fig. 8.11).

Vertical-rail blocks were used on larger roads, usually over 18 feet (5.5m) across, and required sockets to be let into the road surface (and where necessary the pavement) in two or, after May 1941, five lines, to hold the bent steel girders

or rails that would form the barrier. Each socket had a cover plate rebated into the road surface so that normal traffic could use the road unhindered. Very few of this kind of roadblock survive, or at least are now visible.[21]

In the linked-cylinder type of roadblock, four or five cylinders of stone or concrete were linked end to end by chain or wire and could be rolled into position across a road with both ends secured. On East Lothian beaches some of these were combined with a horizontal-rail block (Fig. 8.12). A simple roadblock could also be achieved by stringing a strong chain or wire rope between two concrete blocks or even wrapped round trees. These rarely survive now although a broken length of chain is attached to a dragon's tooth at Lunan Bay. A form of roadblock could be made by placing a number of U-shaped lines of Dannert wire across and along a road, strongly anchored to roadside features, with the top of the 'U' towards the enemy.

The simplest form of block to delay traffic, which might be used in conjunction with any of these roadblocks, was a simple sheet of cloth hung across the road to block the view of a vehicle driver to cause uncertainty and hesitation – there could be anything behind the sheet – mines, a ditch, a tank. While the idea appeared in Tom Winteringham's *New Ways of War*, published by Penguin Books in 1940, the General Officer Commanding Home Forces was described as being interested in this tactic as early as 28 July 1940.[22] Correspondence in September

Figure 8.11.
Home Guard putting the rails into a roadblock in Wester Ross (Imperial War Museum H7330).

Figure 8.12.
Horizontal-rail block with 'broken column' block, East Lothian (Author).

1941 shows that 200,000 square yards of canvas had already been supplied for this purpose, and an estimated 250,000 square yards was still required.[23]

Roadblocks were built in considerable numbers in 1940, at first as part of linear defence systems, as elements in the defence of focal points and as elements in increasingly complex local defence plans. In July 1940 Scottish Command noted that 'The numbers of tank "stops" [the context making clear this means roadblocks] which are being erected are inadequate. Considerably more energy is to be devoted to their erection.'[24] Decision-making about their siting was to be devolved even to LDV (Home Guard) company commanders to turn every town and village into a tank-proof locality. Yet by December 1940 the situation had changed completely: *Scottish Command Operation Instruction No. 2* ordered that no more roadblocks were to be built, as they were more likely to hold up British counter-attacks.

FLAME AT ROADBLOCKS

Flame weapons, deployed either as part of a roadblock or in the form of an ambush, were proposed and developed early in the invasion crisis of 1940. The ideal site and form of the 'anti-tank flame trap' were described in July 1940: an oil tank under cover was to supply oil to pipes controlled by taps that spread oil across the road, to be ignited once a tank was in the trap.[25] The flame fougasse, which projected a jet of burning fuel from an oil drum buried in a roadside bank to a maximum range of 25 yards (22.8m) but intended for a target up to 10 yards (9.1m) away), was also approved as a useful form of petroleum warfare in mid-

Figure 8.13.
Barrel flame barrage
demonstration at Mid Calder,
West Lothian on 28 November
1940 (Imperial War Museum
H5772).

August 1940, after a successful demonstration.[26] Revised instructions were issued
for the deployment of flame fougasses in September 1940, which included a
description of a third form of flame weapon, a 'barrel flame trap', which threw
barrels of inflammable liquid from cover (say from behind a hedge) up to 6–10
yards; they were best deployed at bends in the road or at roadblocks. Both fougasses
and barrel flame traps could be deployed in 'batteries' although it was not envisaged
that more than five would be installed in one place. Figure 8.13 shows the effect
of the firing of a group of barrel traps. Hundreds of these traps were installed,
but no definitive list survives.

McNAUGHTON TUBES

McNaughton tubes, or Canadian pipe mines, took advantage of new Canadian
technology which allowed long shallow angled holes to be bored quickly into the
ground, into which steel pipes could be driven by hydraulic rams. The steel pipes

Figure 8.14.
Tank failing to cross an obstacle made by a Canadian pipe mine at a test/demonstration in Scotland in February 1941 (The National Archives, WO 199/52).

were about 55 feet (16.7m) long and were 3 inches (7cm) in diameter, and were placed at 25-foot (7.6m) intervals. They could be arranged in a single line, or, for an instant roadblock, one above the other, or crossing, driven from both sides of the road. These pipes were either filled with explosives straight away (which led to problems with guarding the loaded pipes and the deterioration of the explosive), or when an invasion threat was imminent. When detonated, each pipe created an obstacle from 25 feet (7.6m) to about 50 feet (15.2m) wide and up to a maximum of about 11 feet (3.35m) deep (see below), the sides of which were loose and afforded a good obstacle to tanks (Fig. 8.14). They were also bored under aerodrome runways to 'immobilise' them quickly. A great advantage of this type of obstacle over other kinds of anti-tank obstacle was that it was undetectable to the enemy until detonated, and also did not interfere with existing land uses.

BEACH MINES

The War Office files are full of references to the provision and laying of anti-tank mines behind beaches, in large numbers, either to reinforce beach defences or, with barbed wire, to provide the only barrier. The minefields were both large (hundreds of metres long) and small (blocking narrow beach exits). Minefields had to be both fenced and signposted, but it was permissible to delineate and mark dummy minefields, to 'mystify' the enemy. Regrettably, several deaths were recorded in unit War Diaries, both of infantrymen and engineers killed during the laying of mines, and of civilians who foolishly beat down the fences that surrounded the minefields to get to the beach.

Extraordinarily, tests of the effectiveness of anti-tank mines on beaches do not seem to have taken place until March 1942, after concerns were raised when a Churchill tank strayed into a beach minefield and suffered hardly any damage.[27]

'BEACH' FLAME BARRIERS

The idea of flame barrages on beaches was developed in the Petroleum Warfare Department in the first quarter of 1941 (was no better use to be found for the fuel being taken across the Atlantic at such a high price in lives and ships than burning it on beaches?). It was noted that the 'Commander-in-Chief considers that this obstacle is a valuable addition to beach defences'.[28] The apparatus consisted of a line of jets 600 feet (182m) across, projecting from a buried front pipe from which feeder pipes led back to the pump and reservoir, about 450 feet (137m) behind. Scottish Command originally bid for a total coverage of 3055 yards (2.79km) in 11 separate barrages on beaches and also on anti-tank stop-lines, particularly in Shetland.[29] A reconsideration of the practicalities through 1941 and into 1942 (including the realisation of the difficulties of transporting the equipment to and across Shetland) led, in the end, to Scotland's sole barrage being installed at the mouth of the Burn of Lyth in Sinclair's Bay in Caithness.[30] It was completed in the winter of 1942–43, after all risk of invasion had passed.[31] Perhaps a rather ill-directed effort.

FLOATING BARRIERS

Three floating barriers – intended to foul the propellers of slow-moving craft – seem to have been in place offshore from three Moray Firth beaches by the end of February 1941: Sandend Bay (1 mile long), Cullen Bay (1½ miles) and Spey Bay (7 miles – Portgordon to Boars Head). These locally-manufactured floating obstructions, consisting of old herring nets, installed on the initiative of the Flag Officer-in-Charge at Invergordon, survived the winter of 1940–41 well. Proposals for a further 10, or even 40, miles do not seem to have been carried through. The Flag Officer, whose scheme it was, rather eccentrically rounded off his note on the nets by stating that 'I wish it to be understood that I am, personally, very dubious about the efficiency of this "defence" and consider it very doubtful whether it is worth the effort and cost.' He preferred 'active offence' – 'guns and more guns' instead. 'This is the only proper "defence" that I know, i.e. something to *sink* ships or *kill* Huns with' (his emphasis).[32]

9. PILLBOXES

The most complete study of hardened defences in the UK is that by Dr Mike Osborne, who describes the main standard types, as well as considering a wide range of variants and local styles.[1] There are many other summaries and accounts, both in published and Internet resources, but Henry Wills's pioneering work of 1985 was the first to put the study of pillboxes on an ordered footing.[2]

The main subdivision was between those designed to be bulletproof, with walls 30 to 60cm thick, and shellproof, with walls up to 137cm thick.[3] Bulletproof pillboxes in Scotland were supposed to be 15 inches thick (and tend to be about 35 to 40cm), and shellproof 3ft 6in thick (and tend to be about 90–115cm), with some Polish pillboxes clearly built to metric measurements with 75cm thick walls. In reality, there was a further subdivision – 'not even bulletproof' – as was recognised for some prefabricated types, such as the Norcon, which were incapable of withstanding a burst of fire hitting one part of what was little more than an upended sewer pipe (Fig. 10.8).

A series of standard designs was promulgated by the Department of Fortifications and Works in May 1940, and these are described below. Osborne has set out clearly and sensibly the problems in identifying these on the ground: not all standard type drawings survive; some design drawing numbers seem to have been duplicated (such as Type 27, which may refer both to rectangular machine gun pillboxes and to hexagonal and octagonal pillboxes with central anti-aircraft mountings); some designed types were never actually built; and some design numbers, especially those applied by individual Army Commands, may have referred to minor design changes to a standard type, or to a completely unique design. Osborne has also noted that some designs were derived directly from experience of building pillboxes in France by the British Expeditionary Force. Indeed, there is an exchange on file in late July and early August 1940 between the Commander Royal Engineers of Scottish Command and the Commander Royal Engineers of the team building the Command Line, from whom advice was sought as 'you were responsible for putting up a large number over there [in France]'.[4] The detailed engineering drawing that came back 'as far as can be recollected of the latest design of Hexagonal Bren Pillbox as used with the BEF in

France' was of a shellproof design, with heavy steel reinforcement of the concrete, resembling the pillboxes built on the Cowie Line, in Kincardineshire (see below).

Although there have been attempts (not by Osborne) to impose retrospectively greater consistency on the typology of the surviving pillboxes than was evident in 1940, the 'types' remain a useful shorthand. Through the identification of local characteristics, pillbox styles can occasionally indicate where particular units or forces may have been active. It was, however, the location, purpose and intention of the pillbox in its tactical and strategic scheme, and its likely effectiveness, that mattered.

Pillboxes now often survive in splendid isolation; some indeed were 'one-offs', placed by individual units for a specific purpose, now not recorded, but many were designed to be part of larger complexes. Pillboxes on or near a beach had a clear relation to each other, but the purpose of those in the countryside may be more difficult to comprehend. Many pillboxes are also now very visible, for example standing right on the edge of a road or clearly outlined against the sky. In 1940–41 most would have been camouflaged using paint, netting or vegetation; and often their surroundings have changed – a pillbox once hidden on the edge of a wood might now stand on a bare hill or a straightened road line might now lie much closer to a pillbox than it did in 1940. On the other hand, wartime aerial photographs show that in some cases no effort whatsoever seemed to have been made to camouflage some pillboxes. In contrast, there is a series of photographs in the Imperial War Museum, taken at the behest of the Commander Royal Engineers of 51st Division in 1940 (and therefore possibly in Scotland) showing the extent to which pillboxes were disguised – in the one reproduced here, it is painted very effectively as a pile of wood beside a railway line (Fig. 9.1).

GHQ *Operation Instruction No. 1* (5 June 1940)[5] stated that all defences were to have a barbed wire fence around at least 40 yards (36.5m) from the position, and if possible another at 60 yards (54.8m) to prevent the approach of flamethrowers. In many cases on the defended beaches of Scotland it is clear from contemporary aerial photographs that pillboxes (and other firing positions around them) stood within enclosures of barbed wire; sometimes only the wire enclosure reveals the presence of a structure.

In October 1940 the construction programme of pillboxes in Scotland was to number 949 to bulletproof specification (of which 150 were still to be built), and 43 shellproof (12 still to be built). Another (undated) document showed even higher numbers of planned pillboxes: 1,141 bulletproof and 325 shellproof.[6]

In December 1940 defence works policy was revised.[7] Beach pillboxes were to be confined to beaches where there were anti-tank obstacles, and were to be considered as a skeleton for the defence rather than as a complete defensive system. They were to be allowed at a frequency of two per 1,000 yards (914m) and beach

Figure 9.1.
A pillbox cleverly painted to look like a pile of wood beside a railway. A War Office photograph taken on 15 October 1940 at the request of the Commander Royal Engineers, 51st Division, and therefore probably somewhere in North-east Scotland (Imperial War Museum H4775).

pillboxes were to have bulletproof walls only. Pillboxes already built were to be checked to ensure that their loopholes and the internal spaces could accommodate machine guns, light automatics or anti-tank rifles. No further anti-tank gun pillboxes were to be built on beaches, as these weapons were to be held in the mobile reserves. On 20 February 1941 the order was given that no further pillboxes were to be constructed. This order was subsequently clarified to exclude aerodrome defence pillboxes, construction of which was to continue.[8]

The pattern that survives of pillboxes on beaches was very much as set out in December 1940, with a box set in or behind the concrete barrier every few hundred metres. The boxes were intended to house either medium or light machine guns to support infantry placed in firing positions around. Only in a handful of places were pillboxes arranged in such a way as to provide mutually supporting fire, for example in Fife, at Tentsmuir and Largo Bay, where the Polish Army built pairs or groups of three pillboxes, at Balmedie in Aberdeenshire, where three pillboxes were placed in a group, at the Bonar Bridge Defended Locality, and in a handful of places on the Command Line and the Cowie Line.

In the summer of 1941 a draft policy was under discussion about when troops should build either concrete pillboxes and other structures, or field positions (built of timber, soil and sandbags). The discussion recorded on file charted the last battle between static and mobile philosophies of warfare.[9] A comment on the second draft of the document, in July 1941, suggested that it had an 'undesirable Maginot complex'. In the absence of progress or agreement there was a meeting on 19 September 1941 at which it was eventually decided not to issue the directive at all, and the minutes effectively sounded the death knell for concrete defences: '... the vast majority of pillboxes were superfluous and ... any directive issued on the subject should stress their limited value.' Arising out of this it was admitted that 'we had gone for pillboxes to excess last year [1940].' By February 1942 GHQ Home Forces could write,[10] 'All experience of modern warfare since [May 1940] points most strongly to the fact that the pillbox is not a suitable type of fortification for either coast or nodal point defence.'

The attitude to pillboxes later in the war is indicated in a letter (from an unknown writer) in June 1944, recommending the removal of a badly sited pillbox in Eskbank, Midlothian, where much better defence positions could be obtained in the houses and gardens in the vicinity. The pillbox was 'a death trap' which 'merely obstruct[ed] the field of fire'. The writer noted that in 1943, when removal had first been suggested, the most important consideration preventing this had been 'the effect on the civil population of pulling it down'.[11]

CONSTRUCTION

Pillboxes were built using a variety of materials, depending in part on availability, although some designs depended upon the use of particular types of shuttering. In Scotland the most prevalent construction was of concrete, either poured into timber shuttering, or into brick shuttering, that was left in place. The concrete was normally heavily reinforced with steel bars, which are often revealed on damaged examples, but many pillboxes seem to have been built without reinforcement, if none could be had. On the Cowie Line west of Stonehaven in Kincardineshire the external shuttering was provided by quarried granite blocks of the kind used throughout the north-east for building houses and farms. The addition of granite to reinforced concrete created a formidably strong 90cm-thick wall. Pillbox roofs were also built of reinforced concrete, poured on wooden or corrugated iron shuttering (where the latter was used, it was left in place). Roof thicknesses varied considerably and a pillbox with shellproof walls would have a relatively thin (e.g. 20–30cm) roof. Some pillboxes were built of individual concrete blocks or even, in a handful of examples, of bags filled with cement, wetted, built into a wall and left to set. Many pillboxes were partly buried, to the bottom of the embrasures, or even higher, and soil or sand might also be placed over the roof.

In many cases the firing loops in the walls were prefabricated or built of prefabricated elements. Most often provision was made for a particular kind of weapon: most frequently, light or medium machine guns, anti-tank rifles or anti-tank guns. Each weapon had particular requirements, such as width and height of embrasure or support for a tripod or other mounting. Many pillboxes show clear signs of larger embrasures (for Vickers machine guns) being reduced in size, probably for a Bren gun, and at least one Scottish Command design was intended to be modified in this way, if the heavier guns were not available. Pillboxes for particular types of weapon could also have embrasures or small loops for lighter weapons for all-round protection. Some early pillboxes had smooth-faced embrasures that might have had the effect of channelling bullet fragments into the pillbox; instructions were issued in September 1940 to cut the embrasures into a stepped profile, which was the pattern built into most pillboxes, made of brick, concrete or even with steel plating.[12] Photographs of pillboxes in use with large, simple embrasures show that sandbags could also be placed to reduce the size of the embrasure and give more cover to the gunners (Fig. 14.7).

Some types of pillbox had as standard the protection of personnel from blast, ricochet or firing in through one embrasure hitting someone standing at another, by the construction of brick or concrete walls running down the axis of the pillbox, or T-shaped or Y-shaped walls that also provided cover from the door. In some cases, protective walls or even enclosed porches were erected outside the door, or simple walls provided cover for the door from a vulnerable flank. Such porches could be provided with their own loopholes for close protection.

In November 1940 the design of the Turnbull mount was accepted by the War Office for manufacture; it comprised a frame to fit the embrasure and a support for a gun – different bars could be supplied to fit different types of machine gun, although Bren and Vickers were the most usual type. Most of the surviving anti-tank gun pillboxes at Bonar Bridge have had the large gun embrasures bricked up to accommodate a Turnbull mount. The presence of these mounts created a bit of a headache in the already complex efforts to find a way of making pillbox embrasures flamethrower-proof.[13]

On 19 December 1940 it was determined by Scottish Command (in response to proposals by the Polish Forces to reinforce the defences on their coast) that any new pillboxes should be tank-gun-proof, and existing pillbox walls should be thickened by sandbags or soil, rather than by adding concrete, owing to supply limitations.[14] Drawings exist in Polish files for the thickening of two types of pillbox:[15] a Type 22 hexagonal pillbox, and one of the Y-shaped Angus variants described below. Scottish Command seems to have sought designs for thickening pillbox walls from GHQ, in July 1941, but were told to devise them themselves.[16]

TYPES

Pillbox policy in Scottish Command was promulgated by the Commander Royal Engineers of Scottish Command, on the basis of UK policy and the views of Scottish Command and its constituent formations. On 20 June 1940 a Scottish Command policy document stated that the General Officer Commanding in Scotland 'prefers the octagonal type' of pillbox and 'the octagonal type will therefore be used in future' (except for hexagonal Bofors gun anti-aircraft pillboxes).[17] Looking at what was actually built, this expression of the GOC's preference seems to have had little effect, as octagonal pillboxes are very rare on the beach and stop-line defences. On 20 August 1940 it was recorded that 'There seems to be considerable doubt as to the approved designs for Pillboxes' and instructions were issued in Scotland.[18] There were to be two main protection classifications. 'Tank gun proof' had 3ft 6in (1.06m) reinforced concrete walls and a 12-inch (30cm) reinforced concrete roof; this was said to be proof also against shells up to 5.9-inch with a low trajectory. Shell- or bomb-proof roofs were, however, ruled out at this time except in the most exceptional circumstances. 'Bulletproof' pillboxes were to have 15-inch (38cm) walls and 12-inch thick roofs, both in concrete. Any brick shuttering was to be added to these thicknesses.

At this point, on 28 August 1940,[19] the only types approved for construction in Scotland were:

- FW3 Drawing No. 28 [Type 28] for anti-tank gun, with or without the Bren gun compartment, which would always have 3ft 6in walls.
- FW3 Drawing No. 24 [Type 24] for Bren guns, with bulletproof walls.
- Commander Engineers Scottish Command (CEScC) Drawing No. 2865 for Bren guns where tank gun-proof protection was required.[20]
- FW3 Drawing No. 27 [Type 27] for one Vickers medium machine gun giving tank-proof protection.
- A design for two Vickers guns, being prepared; four of these were built on the Command Line.

Further clarification was provided on 22 September,[21] when designs for Vickers, Bren gun, Lewis gun or anti-tank rifle were issued in Scotland (unfortunately the drawings have not been located). The implication is that the two designs (CEScC 2894 – firing in two opposite directions and CEScC 2893 – firing in a number of directions) could be used for any of these, but where Vickers guns were not available the loopholes were to be bricked up to the dimensions of the Bren loophole in Type 24 pillboxes, or sandbags would be positioned to allow a Bren gun, Lewis gun or anti-tank rifle to be fired out of the standard loophole. Scottish

Command design 2894 is probably the rectangular pillbox design found on the beaches of Burghead and Lossiemouth East (below) while design 2893 is probably the bulletproof Type 24 with large embrasure and firing table found on the same beaches, and on the beaches north of Aberdeen and in Caithness.

REGULAR AND IRREGULAR HEXAGONS (FIG. 9.2)

Types 22 and 24

These two types and their variants are the most common types built in the UK in 1940–41. Both have six sides: the classic Type 22 is a regular hexagon; the Type 24 has five sides usually of near-equal length, with a longer side, with the entrance, to the rear. There are many variants of both kinds, and it can be unclear whether a variant pillbox was inspired more by one type than the other.

As Osborne has noted,[22] the Type 22 is often seen as the archetypal pillbox. Built to both bullet- and shellproof specifications, these were most usually designed for rifles or Bren guns: very often the embrasure (usually prefabricated) had a small rectangular socket below it to accommodate the folded-up bipod of the Bren. In well-preserved examples on the Scottish Command Line, the timber shelving that covered the concrete within the embrasure had a small hatch to cover the bipod socket, either hinged or to be lifted out. A common, but not invariable, feature of these pillboxes is one, or more often a pair of, small loops flanking the entrance for a pistol or rifle. Most also had a T- or Y-shaped internal ricochet/blast wall. Type 24 was the most common type, and appeared in a number of variants, both bullet- and shellproof. There was usually an angle greater than 90° between the longer rear and side walls. They usually had pistol loops flanking the door.

Type 22/24 Variants

Both Type 22 and Type 24 have many local variants. They are considered together because some could be interpreted as variants of either Type; in particular, there are six-sided types which Osborne interprets as truncated regular hexagons (i.e. a Type 22 variant) but are almost identical to some Type 24s, the only difference being that the two shorter walls adjacent to the entrance wall are set at 90° to the rear wall, rather than at an oblique angle. One documented variant to Type 24 in Scotland was defined for the Command Line, where the entrance was moved from the longest (normally rear) wall which could then accommodate two embrasures side by side, which were intended to house a Bren gun and a Boys anti-tank rifle.[23]

Figure 9.2.
Plans of some British octagonal, hexagonal and circular pillbox types.

CEScC 2865
[Type 22 variant]
Cowie Line

Type 24
Command Line

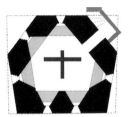

Type 24
Command Line
Bren/ATk rifle variant

Type 27 octagonal
Douglas Wood

Type 27 hexagonal
Aberdeen
(after RCAHMS)

Balmedie/Newburgh Type
Balmedie
(after RCAHMS)

0   5m

Armco
Montrose

CEScC 2893
[Type 24 variant]
Balmedie
(after RCAHMS)

CEScC 2893
[Type 24 variant]
Lossiemouth East

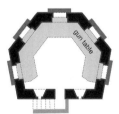

CEScC 2893
[Type 24 variant]
Keiss
(after A Guttridge)

Orkney Type 22/24 variants

The hexagonal pillboxes on Orkney are miniature versions of Type 22s found on the mainland (Fig. 10.7). They have low crawl doorways and smooth-faced (and therefore dangerous) embrasures on all faces. The pillboxes are cast, built of concrete blocks or, in one case, of cement-filled sandbags, wetted and left to harden. They are in general very poorly designed and built.

Polish Variants to Type 22

The Polish Army built several different types of pillbox, some of which did not conform to British designs, possibly reflecting the preferences of different engineer units. At Tentsmuir in Fife most of the pillboxes built were of Type 22, with walls 75cm thick, and large, simple embrasures and no internal features such as gun tables or ricochet walls. Within the same plan the Polish engineers built variants with two and three embrasures, and with embrasures frequently occupying the corners. These are illustrated in Figure 9.5.

ANTI-AIRCRAFT PILLBOXES

Often known as Type 27, these pillboxes are generally regular octagons or hexagons usually with an open well in the centre where an anti-aircraft gun (commonly a Bren gun) would be mounted. Figure 9.2 illustrates a typical example, from Douglas Wood radar station in Angus. It had bulletproof walls and embrasures on every wall; the anti-aircraft well had a platform (raised about 1m above the pillbox floor), below which was a small chamber with three low entrances, presumably for storage or shelter. They are particularly associated with aerodromes, radar stations and other locations where both ground and anti-aircraft fire was likely to be needed, such as Aberdeen Esplanade. A handful had the octagonal ground plan of such pillboxes, but the roof was cast right over the 'well'. For example, the three octagonal pillboxes at Lunan Bay (one of which survives) incorporated the brick wall of the central anti-aircraft well, as usual, but without a matching opening in the roof above. Mike Craib has recorded at Nigg Bay, Aberdeen, what seems to be a Bofors gun mounting on a regular-hexagon Type 22 pillbox base. Throughout the text I have used 'Type 27' to refer to these pillboxes, rather than to Vickers pillboxes (p. 119).

CIRCULAR PILLBOXES (FIG. 9.2)

Type 25

The 'Armco' type of pillbox was a design from the private sector, rather more successful than the Norcon (below), produced by a London-based company in its corrugated iron factory at Letchworth. The pillbox was circular, measuring 8 feet (2.4m) in diameter with walls 12 inches (30cm) thick, and therefore designed to be bulletproof. According to Osborne,[24] the manufacturers intended that the corrugated iron shuttering would remain in place, but this was often removed to be reused. There were between one and three loopholes. The example illustrated, at Montrose (Fig. 9.2; Fig. 13.5), is one of a pair apparently designed to mount a belt-fed Vickers medium machine gun and its ammunition box, firing through a single embrasure. Evidence of an inscription over the door of one points to these specialist pillboxes having been built by men from a machine gun battalion, 8th Gordon Highlanders, one company of which was posted to Montrose in the summer of 1940.[25]

Norcon

Norcon pillboxes (named after the company that sold them to the government) were nothing more than an upended concrete sewer pipe, open-topped or with a concrete top, either flush with the top of the pipe, or overhanging the edge. The 'classic' Norcon, as illustrated in Norcon Ltd's drawings CP/6/40/II and CP/6/40/III,[26] was 4 feet (1.2m) high and 6 feet (1.8m) in diameter over 4-inch (10cm) thick walls. There were four to six 'gun apertures' arranged round the circumference; in the 'III' version, six were clustered on the side away from the low round-topped entrance. With no shelf or table to support a light or medium machine gun, they were more suited to troops armed with rifles (Fig. 9.3).

Osborne has noted that the pipes were not reliably bulletproof,[27] and might not, for example, stand up to a burst of fire from a machine gun hitting the same place. To provide more protection and to aid camouflage, they were designed to be set into the ground to half or more of their depth. Bullet impacts show that someone tested one of the Norcon pillboxes on the Inganess anti-tank line in Orkney, where about half of the height of the Norcon was left above ground (Fig. 10.8). The Orkney Norcons were entered and (most importantly) exited through a hatch in the roof – vulnerable to fire from the advancing enemy – rather than the more protected access to the rear. These Norcons were thus doubly dangerous. The uselessness of the Norcons was recognised by the Army in Orkney at a defence

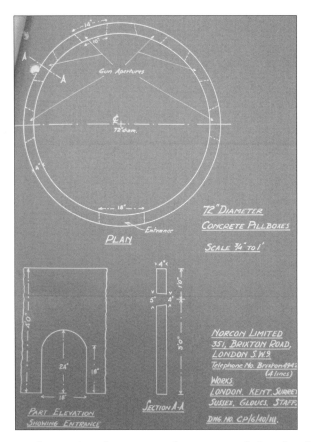

Figure 9.3.
A company blueprint of the Norcon Type III 'pillbox' (The National Archives, WO 199/2657).

conference in February 1941: 'It was agreed that the circular pillbox was not effective and was not bulletproof'.[28] Fifty of these deathtraps, modified for use with a Vickers machine gun, were ordered by Scottish Command on 16 July 1940, for the north and south sectors of the Command Line but fortunately the failure of the contractor to deliver allowed the contract to be cancelled when defence policy changed.[29]

Pickett-Hamilton/Tett Turret/Alan Williams Turret

These three small one- or two-man firing positions were particularly associated with aerodromes. Indeed, the Pickett-Hamilton Disappearing Fort was designed specifically for use close to runways, where, retracted, it offered no obstruction to aircraft. In action a hand-operated pump could partially raise it to expose something that looked very like a Norcon: a simple roofed cylinder with firing apertures and a roof access hatch. Tett Turrets and Alan Williams Turrets were, respectively, small revolving steel or concrete and steel turrets set above a pit. Only a handful of examples is known in Scotland.

RECTANGULAR MACHINE GUN PILLBOXES

'Type 27' for Vickers machine gun

There is a range in Scotland, as in the rest of the UK, of small rectangular pillboxes for Bren light machine guns or for Vickers medium machine guns, which seem to have been designed locally for particular places or purposes. Roughly square or rectangular shellproof pillboxes for Vickers MMGs, to a design sometimes known as Type 27 (confusingly the same type number as the hexagonal and octagonal anti-aircraft pillboxes described above), seem to have been rare in Scotland, although one based on the design, with embrasures on three sides, survives on the north side of Wick harbour (Fig. 9.4). [30]

Scottish Command Un-Numbered Variant:
Command Line Double Vickers (Fig. 9.4)

There are only four of these known in Scotland, all on the Scottish Command Line in Fife and Perthshire (all survive). These rectangular shellproof pillboxes had two large stepped embrasures facing in the same direction. The embrasures had heavy timber gun tables supported on brick pedestals and were designed for Vickers medium machine guns (and War Diaries show that sections from 7th Cheshire Regiment, a machine gun battalion, were to occupy these). [31] Osborne has noted that these boxes resembled a type otherwise found only with the BEF in France and included them under variants of the Type 27 single machine gun pillbox. [32] They had additional, smaller, loopholes for flanking defence, distributed as the siting and topography of the pillbox required and were located in such a way as to provide flanking fire from a two-gun section of Vickers medium machine guns on troops approaching the Command Line's anti-tank barrier.

Scottish Command Drawing No. 2894 Small Rectangular Machine Gun Pillboxes

There were a few small rectangular structures built on Scottish beaches, which can be interpreted either as pillboxes or as observation posts. Indeed, a couple of them are marked clearly as observation posts on Polish Army maps at Tentsmuir in Fife. Those on the Moray Firth coast have heavy concrete gun tables for Vickers machine guns, below large embrasures enfilading the line of anti-tank cubes into which they are set (Fig. 9.4, Fig. 12.12). The handful of rectangular structures evident in East Lothian included both low and cramped machine gun positions, with a single embrasure facing the sea, and observation posts. They are discussed and illustrated in the Edinburgh Area description below.

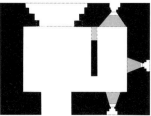

Type 28
Command Line
2-punder ATk Gun with Bren gun chamber

CEScC 2894 for Vickers MMG
Lossiemouth East

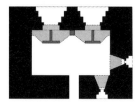

Double Vickers MMG
Command Line

Single Vickers MMG
East Lothian

East Lothian
Observation post:
plan and section

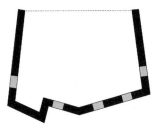

Gun-house for 18 pdr
Ferryden, Montrose

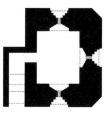

Pillbox, Wick Harbour
(after A Guttridge)

Gun-house for 4-inch naval gun
at Carnoustie (after Scottish Water)

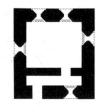

Aerodrome defence pillbox, Wick
(after A Guttridge)

0   5m

Polish Largo Bay/Fife Ness Variants (Fig. 9.5)

In the eastern and central sectors of the long, defended beach at Largo Bay in Fife there survive two pairs of unusual pillboxes. In the eastern sector of the defences (described below) there are two flattened-V-shaped pillboxes, measuring about 7m across their front by about 6m deep; the two parts, which 'hinge' on the front, are of different sizes and are separated by a brick wall. Each chamber has one firing embrasure, pointing along the beach to east and west, but none to seaward. The walls are concrete with brick facing, covered by a thin cement render. The roof is about 1m thick, of poured concrete over corrugated iron shuttering, edged by a single skin of brick. The walls are about 1.15m thick at the entrance but thinner in an area round the embrasures, which are set into a sort of 'alcove', which provides a firing platform, in which there is a *c*.25cm square socket, probably for Bren guns. Both pillboxes have low 'wings' of brick-shuttered concrete at both ends of the front face, apparently intended to protect the embrasures from fire from the sea (Fig. 14.16).

Just west of Lower Largo there are two further rectangular pillboxes, measuring about 4m by 5m, with offset entrances at their eastern ends. The outer side of the wall is faced with brick, which is in turn covered by a thin cement render. The eastern example has two compartments, the rear (eastern) of which has no embrasure. Both pillboxes have only one visible embrasure, in the western face, aligned along the beach. The pillboxes were provided with a dwarf wall protecting the embrasure from fire from the sea. As in the pair already described, the firing embrasure is set in a broad shallow alcove, where the wall is thinner. The walls and roof are around 1m thick.

Further east on the Fife coast, three pillboxes also have embrasures enfilading the beach protected by walls from fire from the sea. One of them, at Fife Ness, bears an inscription, to the west of a seaward-facing observation embrasure, ascribing the construction to Polish engineers in May 1941.

Angus Y-Shaped (Fig.9.5)

Aerial photographs taken during and just after the war suggest that at least 13 Y-shaped pillboxes were built between Barry Ness and Arbroath in Angus, but none survives. Fortunately there is a ground plan preserved in the Polish archives, showing that, as originally built, they measured 18 feet (5.5m) across the 'base' of the Y (where the entrance lay), with the other walls between 8 feet (2.43m) and 12 feet (3.65m) long. There were six Bren gun embrasures, two on the 'stem' of the Y, and four on the tips and inner sides of the 'arms'. There was a ricochet wall on the axis of the Y. As originally built, the walls were 2 feet (60cm) thick. The

Figure 9.4.
Plans of British rectangular pillbox and gun-house types.

Tentsmuir A

Tentsmuir B

Tentsmuir D

Tentsmuir C
for anti-tank gun

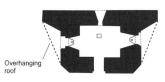

Overhanging
roof

Fife Ness

Tentsmuir E

0   5m

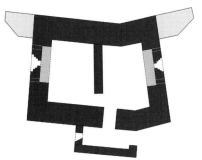

Largo Bay East, with low
wings to shield embrasures

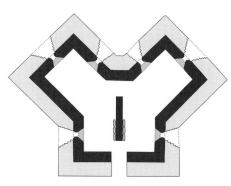

Angus Y-shaped type
lighter outer fill is later/proposed
thickening

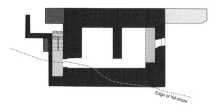

Largo Bay Centre, with single
shielded embrasure

purpose of the Polish engineer drawing was to show proposals to increase the thickness of the walls to 4ft 9in (1.44m) by means of adding a brick wall 1 ft 2in (35cm) thick some 1ft 7in (47cm) from the original wall, the intervening space to be filled with gravel or stones. The embrasures were continued out in concrete with a stepped profile. A weakness of the original design was that there was no porch or covering over the door, and no close-defence firing loops on the entrance wall. The Polish drawn-section of the pillbox also shows proposals, presumably when action was imminent, to block the door with sandbags, with a wood-framed firing loop about midway up its height to allow a kneeling man to fire from cover.

There is no definite proof of who built these pillboxes; they first appeared on a Polish map of the Barry peninsula dated December 1940 with a caption suggesting that what was illustrated might be proposals. Yet all the Polish maps of Barry and Arbroath showed clearly the 'Y' shape of the 13 pillboxes and clearly marked another pillbox (shown as a circle or hexagon on the maps) near Barry Ness as (in Polish) the 'English pillbox'. It seems likely therefore that these pillboxes were Polish-built.

RECTANGULAR ARTILLERY PILLBOXES AND GUN-HOUSES

Type 28 (Fig. 9.4)

The Type 28 was the most common type of pillbox designed to protect artillery, usually a 2-pounder anti-tank gun. They were usually built with shellproof walls. There were two main subtypes: that with a smaller separate chamber for a Bren gun, firing in the same direction as the anti-tank gun, either to right or left of the anti-tank gun; and that where only the anti-tank gun chamber was provided. They were characterised by a large stepped embrasure to the front, with a large entrance at the rear to allow the gun to be wheeled into the pillbox. The gun chamber often had cut-outs below the embrasure to accommodate parts of the 2-pounder carriage. The Bren gun chamber commonly had one or two subsidiary close-defence loops to the flank and the rear, and the gun chamber might also be provided with a flanking loop. They were not particularly common in Scotland; the largest concentration was (and many still survive) at the defended locality at Bonar Bridge (see below) where there were originally around 11. Most of the Bonar Bridge anti-tank gun embrasures have been bricked up and fitted with a Turnbull mount for a machine gun.

Figure 9.5.
Plans of pillbox types certainly or probably constructed by the Polish Army, Angus and Fife, 1940–41.

Polish Variant

A unique anti-tank gun pillbox survives at Tentsmuir (C on Fig. 9.5), built in the same style as the Type 22 variants there, with 75cm thick walls. It has two broad embrasures enfilading the line of cubes within which the pillbox lies, and has a large access for the gun at the rear right. The Polish military maps clearly mark this as an anti-tank gun pillbox.

GUN-HOUSES

Artillery that was likely to remain in a fixed position for any length of time could be sited in a gun-house, which provided variable levels of protection for the gun and its crew. At Montrose, two gun-houses (still surviving) were built on the southern flank of the beach and harbour to accommodate 18-pounder guns (Fig. 9.4). These had thin brick walls. Small embrasures at roof level seem unlikely to have been pistol/rifle loops to provide protective fire to the flanks and rear, but are more likely for ventilation to disperse cordite fumes from firing. Both gun-houses had ready-use ammunition lockers at the rear. The guns of 942nd Defence Battery (Mobile) at Carnoustie were in brick gun-houses with a rectangular fore-part, and a fan-shaped rear, to allow the relatively large naval 4-inch guns to traverse (Fig. 9.4).

CONCLUSION TO PART II

In Chapter 1, the occasional tendency of writers to deal with the defensive structures as a homogeneous mass was mentioned, giving the impression that they were the product of a single coherent plan. In the first two sections of the book it has been demonstrated how convoluted the process of building defences could be.

The impetus for construction had been given in May–June 1940, conforming to Ironside's policy, after he took over, that in the absence of sufficient, adequately equipped mobile troops, defences had to be built to slow down German armoured attacks. Despite his successor's expressed distaste for static defences, work continued during Brooke's tenure on building beach and stop-line defences through the second part of 1940 and well into 1941, and a considerable investment was made in upgrading already-built beach defences after December 1940. The costly beach scaffolding programme was conceived of and implemented during Brooke's tenure, as were flame projectors on beach and other defence lines, and at harbours (although these were a Royal Navy initiative and responsibility).

Table CII. The approximate periods of currency for different types of structure in Scotland

Structure	Period of currency
Anti-tank stop-line (not mere check-lines)	May 1940 to early 1943 (Inganess Line)
Line of cubes (maybe double or even triple)	May 1940 to December 1940
Double or triple line of dragon's teeth	May 1940 to December 1940
Five lines of dragon's teeth, or two lines added to reinforce single line of cubes (to new standard set in *Military Training Pamphlet 30, Pt III*)	January 1941 to May 1942
Pillboxes on beaches and stop-lines	May through summer 1940; ordered to cease February 1941, but one Polish pillbox was dated May 1941

Structure	Period of currency
Aerodrome defences	May 1940 to at least May 1942
Beach scaffolding	October 1940 to February 1942
Scaffolding on anti-tank stop-lines in northern isles	December 1940 to mid/late 1942
Construction of emergency 6-inch coast batteries	June 1940 to autumn 1941

PART III:
WHAT WAS BUILT

This part of the book describes the defences that were built on the beaches, on the anti-tank stop-lines and, to a lesser extent, on aerodromes and in ports and towns. In the text the past tense is used to describe something that was done or built in the 1940s and which does not appear to survive; the present tense is used for the description of, for example, the characteristics of the coast, which have not changed much, and for structures built in the 1940s that can still be seen, and were in the main visited during the fieldwork for this book. The descriptions include what seemed to be interesting or significant information about the units that built and manned the defences, although much detail has been omitted for the sake of readability.

10. ORKNEY AND SHETLAND

*'Under present conditions any landing
in strength is bound to succeed.'*

(Brigadier Kemp, Commander of Orkney & Shetland Defences, 27 June 1940)[1]

I t was perceptively and succinctly stated in April 1942 by the Commander of the Orkney and Shetland Defences that, 'The primary role of all [troops] in ORKNEYS, SHETLANDS and CAITHNESS is the defence of the naval base and installations in SCAPA FLOW. This can only be achieved by denying the enemy the territory surrounding this base and the use of the aerodromes in SHETLANDS and CAITHNESS'.[2]

The internal defensive arrangements for Orkney, Shetland and Caithness are set out separately below, but reference must be made to developments across that whole area. The perceived importance and vulnerability of different parts of Scotland changed rapidly during the first 18 months of the war. The naval base at Invergordon, for example, came to seem less important, and the northern isles and Caithness came to seem both more important for the British war effort, and more vulnerable to attack. But no-one ever seemed to feel that the command structure of the defences of Orkney and Shetland (and Caithness, when it was added) was quite right.

As early as 28 October 1939 the military commander of the defences in Orkney and Shetland Area (the Commander of 58th Anti-aircraft Brigade, RA) was considering the possibility of German landings on Orkney. On 25 November the Weekly Report of the C-in-C Home Forces noted that 'A complete Battalion is now stationed in the ORKNEYS' (5/7th Gordon Highlanders, which had been mobilised in Banchory only on 1 September) and that 'Steps are being taken by the Scottish Command to dispatch two companies with eight AA LMGs to form a garrison for the SHETLANDS'.[3] The island had few facilities for the troops, and when the commander of 9th Division visited his men in January 1940 he was appalled at their living conditions.[4]

General Sir John T. Burnett-Stuart, on a mission from the Chief of the Imperial General Staff, made a flying visit to Shetland on 1 December 1939 and met Brigadier

Opposite.
Anti-tank cubes at Tentsmuir, Fife, with the Tay in the background (Author).

129

Kemp. The general wrote a perceptive report on what he found, noting that he did not think that Shetland could be regarded as an attractive objective for a seaborne raid or an airborne parachute attack, because of the uncertainty of the weather, the difficult terrain and the absence of any site of military importance, apart from Sumburgh.[5] He considered the three fighter aircraft then at Sumburgh to be 'a great addition to the strength of the defence', which at this stage consisted of two officers and 90 men of the 'D' (Shetland) Company of the 10th (Home Defence) Battalion Gordon Highlanders.[6] Burnett-Stuart recommended that the Home Defence battalion should comprise five companies, of which the HQ company (with a mortar platoon but no carriers) would be locally recruited, with the other four provided on rotation by Home Defence battalions elsewhere on mainland Scotland.[7] This report became the basis for the defence of the islands for the months to come.

The threat to Shetland from German troops in southern Norway began to be discussed by CSC in early May 1940, even before Norway had fallen. A possible *coup de main* in Shetland was one of the possibilities considered in the Joint Planning Subcommittee's report on *Seaborne and Airborne Attack on the United Kingdom*, presented to CSC on 5 May 1940: 'In the absence of a sufficient garrison [in Shetland], a raid might succeed in gaining control of the main islands since, as only a small force would be needed to effect this, it might land with sufficient supplies to last it for some time ...' Through the summer, the threat of a German assault on Shetland was much more prominent in CSC discussions than a direct attack on Orkney and the Home Fleet base, although the main aim of such an attack would of course be to threaten Scapa. Shetland was less than 90 minutes flying time (at 160 m.p.h.) from Norway; Orkney only two hours away.

On 27 June 1940, Kemp, by now a major general, made a direct request to HQ Home Forces, over the head of Scottish Command (who had already turned him down), for more men for the Orkney and Shetland Area. He did 'not think that Orkney [was] an unlikely objective for attack' because of the effect on the Home Fleet if Scapa was lost, the neutralisation of Coastal Command and other bases in northern Scotland, the loss of control of northern seas, and the great prestige Germany would gain.[8]

Kemp noted the number of unprotected landing areas in Orkney (both for parachute troops and sandy beaches for seaborne assaults), and his inability to provide anti-tank obstacles because of the priority then being given to aerodrome construction. He stressed that, despite his having large numbers of troops on the island, most were manning anti-aircraft or coast defence guns, and that he had in fact only one half-trained battalion of infantry, plus any other troops (not trained for infantry work) he could raise from searchlight units, Pioneers and RASC, and no anti-tank weapons. His battalion was disposed round Kirkwall and Hatston aerodrome (a 9,000-yard perimeter) while Stromness was guarded by Pioneers and RASC: 'Under existing conditions any landing in strength is bound to succeed.'[9] He considered a larger garrison necessary: two battalions of trained infantry; one Home Defence company for Vulnerable Points; a machine gun company; and a field artillery battery of four guns. Kemp cannot have been entirely happy with the way the admiral in charge of Orkney expressed himself in support: 'However fantastic such an idea may appear at first sight I am of the opinion that in the absence of the Fleet an invasion by sea and air is within the bounds of possibility' and the loss of Scapa Flow would be '. . . a national disaster of the first magnitude'.[10]

In late July 1940 Kemp again wrote noting the unsatisfactory state of the command structure: he was responsible to the admiral for 'local operations', to Scottish Command for operational policy and training of troops other than anti-aircraft units, and to Anti-aircraft Command in relation to operational policy and training for men in anti-aircraft units. By July the garrison comprised 7th Battalion Gordon Highlanders in Orkney (900 men out of the total Army complement of 10,500: anti-aircraft, coast defence, Royal Army Service Corps, Royal Engineers and so on) and in Shetland 7th Battalion Black Watch, a machine gun company of 8th Gordons, two Royal Marine howitzers and the composite Home Defence battalion. He suggested that the garrison should move from the control of Home Forces to direct War Office control, so that the Admiralty could be allotted forces direct; and he asked for the individual battalions and companies to be replaced by a fully found brigade, with commander and staff. By this stage, however, both Orkney and Shetland had been provided with field artillery (a troop each of 75-mm guns – of First World War vintage but first-class weapons) one 3-inch mortar, and Orkney also had five Bren gun carriers. Looking back, and even taking into account the post-Dunkirk equipment crisis, it seems rather cavalier that the defence of the vital fleet base at Scapa could only justify the allocation of eight field guns and two 3-inch mortars.[11]

In late July 1940 CSC was considering the paper by Admiral Sir Reginald Plunket Ernle-Erle Drax, Commander-in-Chief at the Nore, mentioned in the Prologue, which postulated a powerful diversion against the north of Scotland, to strike at the Home Fleet and draw part of the RAF northwards.[12] While initially dismissive, the JIC had, by 7 August, changed its tune, admitting that 20,500 airborne troops with mortars and mountain artillery could be landed in Scotland to capture aerodromes north of the Tay.[13]

Kemp (now only Commander in Orkney, as Orkney and Shetland had been split into two naval commands in July)[14] wrote on 11 August 1940,[15] this time to Scottish Command, 'I desire once more to represent my misgivings over the land defence of ORKNEY . . . Norway is 350 miles from Orkney [the direct flight from

Stavanger Sola aerodrome to Scapa is actually only 310 miles]', there was no chance of reinforcement, and he believed the garrison to be inadequate. Parachute landings of 500 men at Lyness or the northern aerodromes, or 1,000 men on Kirkwall would have, in his view, a 50 per cent chance of success. He concluded, 'In my opinion SCAPA BASE should be impregnable. I shall spare no effort to repel invasion by improvisation, by defence works, and by using my limited forces to attack the enemy if he lands. But without being defeatist I cannot report that I feel confident in my power to succeed in my task with the forces at my disposal. I request that this statement be put on record and it be brought to the attention of the Commander-in-Chief Home Forces.' Clearly, when an officer feels the need to write this sort of thing to a superior, things are very bad indeed and if Scapa fell Kemp clearly had no intention of being the scapegoat.[16] General Carrington, GOC Scotland, forwarded this to HQ Home Forces, suggesting that the numbers of parachutists was 'probably . . . excessive' but offering to delay the departure of one battalion from Orkney, while sending its relief north immediately, thus providing an additional battalion until October 1940.[17] One must sympathise with Carrington: as noted already (p. 14), he had written a rather tetchy minute to Home Forces in late May complaining that he had only nine battalions of trained infantry in Scotland, of which two were already allocated to Orkney and Shetland, and six protecting the areas round Invergordon and Rosyth.[18]

In late June or early July 1940 maps were prepared of both Orkney and Shetland on which the coast was assessed as 'possible for tanks; good [beach] exits; easy sea approach; sheltered from swell', or as being 'tank-proof', or as providing less likely landing spots because of swell or a difficult sea approach. The maps also showed proposed internal defence lines, and the approximate location of naval booms, nets and minefields. Separate maps of defence proposals for Orkney, and in more detail for Kirkwall, were produced during July 1940, and the provisions on this map, where they were implemented, are also shown on Figures 10.4 and 10.6.[19]

Captain Sallis, RE presented a very clear picture of the state of play in defence in the middle of July 1940, in his 'Questionnaire on Orkneys and Shetlands Defences',[20] which provided a detailed snapshot. For example, the Home Guard (numbering 529 in Orkney and 820 in Shetland) were 'Regarded as of considerable value'; 30 pillboxes were planned or being built in Orkney 'to a local hexagonal design for LMGs' (see p. 116); and 50 Norcons had been ordered for Orkney. The 1,400 Pioneers in Orkney and 282 in Shetland were 100 per cent equipped with rifles, as were the RE units, but at the expense of anti-aircraft units, which had only 48–60 rifles per battery.

On 3 July 1940, concerns about an attack from Norway had reached one of their peaks: *Orkney & Shetland Defences Operation Order No. 3* stated bluntly that, 'There are many indications that the enemy are preparing a combined air and sea invasion of the British isles. The enemy have a force of 20,000 including parachutists concentrated at STAVANGER and TRONDHEIM, and they are believed to be collecting a fleet of launches and small boats'.[21]

The newly-appointed admiral in charge of Shetland (in post from July to November 1940, when Orkney and Shetland became one command again) was Lord Cork and Orrery, an energetic seaman in his mid-60s. Shortly after taking command he was agitating for an increase in the garrison of the islands by one battalion and for the provision of light tanks, increased anti-aircraft cover, searchlights, mountain artillery, three 3-inch mortars and 5 miles of triple Dannert fence. Anthony Eden, Secretary of State for War, considered that the current garrison (which met the recommendations of Sir John Burnett-Stuart in 1939) was adequate and resources must not be 'frittered away'.[22] Given the extraordinary and unexpected developments there had been on the other side of the North Sea since 1939 in the loss of Denmark, Norway, the low countries and France, this seems a rather complacent response.

The garrison of Shetland, reported to CSC on 11 August 1940,[23] comprised:

- one infantry battalion: 900 men; 50 Bren guns; 22 anti-tank rifles; six Bren carriers; and two 3-inch mortars;
- one Home Defence Battalion: 550 men; 62 Lewis guns;
- one machine gun company: 12 Vickers medium machine guns;
- four 75-mm guns (in transit);
- two 3.7-inch howitzers (Royal Marines);
- anti-aircraft artillery: 450 men; 12 3-inch guns; six 40-mm Bofors guns;
- General Construction Coys, RE 400 (with rifles);
- Pioneers 280 (with rifles);
- Home Guard 820 (523 with rifles);
- RAF – two squadrons of Sunderland flying boats; one squadron Blenheims; one flight of three eight-gun fighters [presumably Hurricanes].

The Committee agreed to recommend reinforcement (apart from tanks) and also decided that Orkney and Shetland Defences were to come under direct War Office control (that is, removed from the control of Scottish Command and GHQ Home Forces).[24] This took effect on 20 August 1940.[25] The prime minister also approved the despatch of a further battalion, further anti-aircraft guns and the minor pieces of equipment, such as mortars.[26]

The fact that the Orkney and Shetland Defences were now outwith Home Forces (and thus Scottish Command) control clearly caused significant irritation, especially as Scottish Command believed that it would to have to find any reinforcements if the War Office wanted to send more troops north. On 26 December 1940 Carrington complained to GHQ Home Forces that the situation was rather as if 'the Isle of Wight was run by the War Office'.[27] At least Orkney and Shetland had been reunited as a single command under the Admiral commanding Orkney and Shetland late in November 1940.

1941 began with discussion of the transfer of operational control of Orkney and Shetland back to C-in-C Home Forces, the arrangements since August 1940 having been found 'unsatisfactory'.[28] Brooke seemed very anxious to take OSDEF back, but also suggested that Caithness should be added, which was not welcomed at this stage by the admiral commanding Orkney and Shetland.[29]

General Brooke, in a paper to CSC on 2 March 1941, agreed to the addition of a battalion each to Orkney and Shetland and proposed a command structure to allow the admiral to continue to have local operational command of all troops, once control of the islands had reverted from the War Office to GHQ Home Forces, which happened in June 1941. General Thorne, by then GOC Scotland, shared the Army view that the defence of Scapa Flow depended on the security of the land both north and south of the Pentland Firth and he ensured that Caithness was added to the Orkney and Shetland Defences.[30]

In early 1942 the local commanders of the Navy, Army and RAF still believed that a force of 7,000–12,000 airborne troops might descend on the islands and, 'have results comparable to a successful invasion in the South and that with [the enemy's] limited resources it might well be that an effort to capture these islands may be the enemy's main objective in the West during 1942. . . . It seems to me that we are taking a tremendous risk of possible disaster for the sake of . . . comparatively few additional troops . . .'[31] By April 1942 the garrison of Orkney had increased to a brigade. The 207th Infantry Brigade comprised four infantry battalions; an independent field battery, RA; two anti-aircraft brigades; three coast artillery regiments, RA (20 batteries); and a Home Defence battalion. Shetland's garrison had risen to an infantry brigade (three battalions); one independent light battery, a heavy anti-aircraft regiment and four coast batteries, RA; and a Home Defence company. Caithness was garrisoned by 227th Independent Infantry Brigade (three battalions); a field regiment, RA, a coast defence battery, RA and a Home Defence battalion. In effect, the north was garrisoned by the equivalent of an infantry division with a very formidable anti-aircraft and coast defence capability. This was a major change from the state of play in 1939, and even in 1940, and probably better reflected the strategic importance of the area.[32]

THE DEFENCES OF SHETLAND

Mainland is around 90km long north–south and a maximum of about 30km across, with an area of 967 sq km, but nowhere in Shetland is more than 5km from the sea. A great part of Mainland is only 4–6km across, separated into segments by even narrower necks which constrain the road network; these usually coincide with valleys across the island, within which the few east–west roads run. In May 1940 a number of defensive lines were chosen to take advantage of the topography. There is no evidence that any of these positions were fortified at this stage, and indeed the nature of the island is such that little or nothing would be needed to allow a small force (probably hurrying from Lerwick) to block progress. It was calculated, however, that an Army convoy averaging 10 m.p.h. would take 3 hours from Lerwick to Sumburgh, and 2 hours and 40 minutes to Scatsta. The description below is based on three key documents setting out the means of defending Shetland, dated May 1940, March 1941 and June 1941, and these documents are referred to as, for example, 'the May document', below.[33]

In 1942 the Commanding Officer of the Argyll & Sutherland Highlanders set out his experiences of soldiering in Shetland at this time. The country was 'unsuitable for normal operations' and most infantry training was in guerrilla tactics. Because of the generally boggy conditions, Bren carriers had few chances to leave the road, and mortars were similarly road-bound, not because they could not be carried, but because the recoil of a 3-inch mortar buried the weapon in the peat.[34]

At least 19 major defensive positions were planned and most seem to have been built. In addition there were many defensive strongpoints (not described here) in hamlets and at junctions. The mainland defences are described in three parts: defences north of Lerwick; the defences of Lerwick and Scalloway; and the defences south of Lerwick. Throughout, it can be assumed that beaches adjacent to the ends of defence lines were obstructed by barbed wire, as listed in the 1941 document.[35] Roadblocks were also placed in association with defence lines, strong-points or in other useful locations; most are shown on the maps here, but are not generally referred to in the description.

North Shetland

Eight defensive systems were proposed or constructed in northern Shetland (Fig. 10.1).

The Garths Voe/Scatsta area was the location (2 on Fig. 10.1) of, first, a key seaplane base and second, the Scatsta aerodrome, which was under construction in 1940–41. Instead of an abandoned Garths Voe defence line (1 on Fig. 10.1), the airbases were to be defended by a wired perimeter, part of which, at the north-east, was formed by an anti-tank ditch, one mile long.[36]

A defence line was identified in May 1940 as 'North Brae' (3 on Fig. 10.1) with a forward position at Mavis Grind, intended to cut off access from the large penin-sula called North Mavine. Mavis Grind is an isthmus about 90m across at the

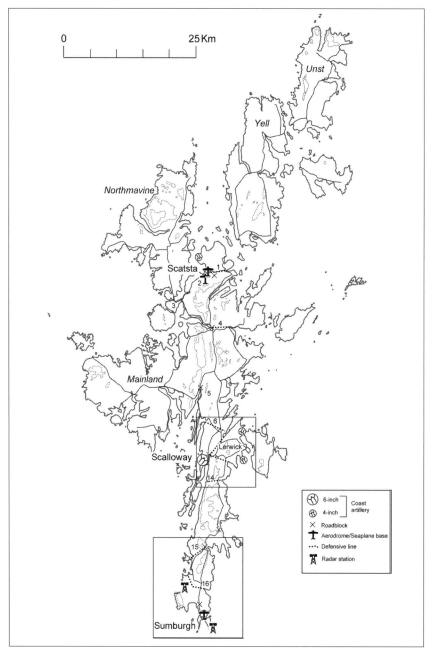

Figure 10.1.
Shetland, showing defences and other sites operational or under construction in 1940 and the earlier part of 1941. The rectangles show the extent of Figs 10.2 and 10.3.

southern end of North Maven where dragon's teeth were arranged in a complex pattern up to five deep to block it; the number of rows suggests that they were built after December 1940, to conform to the standards set in *Military Training Pamphlet 30*.

A line about 3.9km long between the east and west coasts, from Laxa to Voe, was identified in May 1940 (4 on Fig. 10.1). Not specifically listed as a 'defence line', the roadblock at Weisdale (on the west coast) and the 'inland strong point' at Girlsta on the east straddle the only two roads from the north (5 on Fig. 10.1).

The list of defence lines dated June 1941 noted that a 'striking force' – a reserve of almost a battalion strength – was based at Point of Scotland, north of Lerwick.[37] It was responsible for two 'Stop Lines' (one north and one south of Lerwick). The northern ran from Wormadale (at the head of Whiteness Voe, whose beach was blocked by wire) south-east to Hill of Herrislee (above Dale). The line comprised only light firing positions and no wire (6 on Fig. 10.1 and Fig. 10.2).

In the May 1940 document two defence lines hinged on Scalloway – to the north-east a line ran to Dale; to the south-east (actually south of Lerwick but noted here) the second runs to Trebister, at the head of Gulber Wick (7a and 7b on Fig. 10.2). Although referred to in the May 1940 document in such a way as to suggest they were the main defence lines for Lerwick, they were not, however,

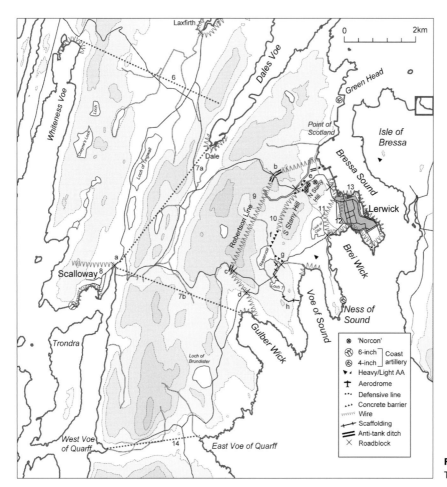

Figure 10.2.
The defences around Lerwick.

137

mentioned again and were most likely ephemeral, their function being replaced by other defence systems.

Scalloway and Lerwick

In the March 1941 document Scalloway was described as having a wire perimeter along its waterfront (8 on Fig. 10.2), and along the high ground north of the town, from the Hill of Barry to a roadblock (a on Fig. 10.2) where the main road crosses the head of East Voe of Scalloway. The northern perimeter was described as a 'defence line' in the June 1941 document. A coast battery of two 4-inch guns was established at the western edge of the town, on Ness of Westshore.

The defences of Lerwick were more complex. To the three key documents (of May 1940 and March and June 1941) can be added a series of papers from the War Diaries of units that had a role in the defence of Shetland, in which we find the expected confusion caused by the same defence line being described using different way-points. At certain times some of the lines were intended to operate in both directions: to defend Lerwick from outside and to contain an enemy force that had taken Lerwick.

Lerwick: The Robertson Line

The outermost line was usually known as the *Robertson Line* (9 on Fig. 10.2), presumably named after the commanding officer of the 7th Black Watch, in whose War Diary 'good progress' on the line was recorded on 24 June 1940, with Pioneers giving 'tremendous help' digging. The line was 'well sited', and about 5 miles long from Gremista, via Hill of Shurton to Gulberwick, and was wired throughout with dug, but unrevetted, firing trenches.

The detailed list of defence sites dated March 1941 also mentioned two short sections of hand-dug, but only 'partially effective', anti-tank ditch at the points (b and c on Fig. 10.2) where the Robertson Line crossed the roads north and west out of Lerwick.[38] It also listed four defensive lines around Lerwick: the 'Outer (Outpost Line)' (give or take some slightly erratic grid-referencing, typical of this document), is the Robertson Line. In June 1941 the Officer Commanding Shetland Defences described it as 'well sited . . . but far too long, very wet and inaccessible'.[39]

Lerwick: The Stany Hill Line

Something resembling this line was first mentioned in May 1940, as 'An additional emergency line [which] has been reconnoitred in the immediate vicinity of LERWICK to be occupied only if [other] lines [7a and 7b] cannot be reached'.[40]

In March 1941, a document in the 7th Seaforth Highlanders' War Diary notes that 'The STANY HILL LINE when sufficiently completed will become the main defence line for LERWICK facing west.'[41] Until the line was prepared, the 'Outpost (Robertson) Line' would be manned (10 on Fig. 10.2). The Stany Hill Line was still being built in June 1941 but it had already been made accessible by the provision of a rough road, and could be held by five companies (albeit with a gap 700 yards (640m) wide in the centre covered by patrols).[42] The line comprised an anti-tank obstacle, part natural, part artificial. Pimples, and then a short anti-tank ditch, ran from the coast to the South Burn of Gremista. The burn itself was improved as an obstacle, by 'tar barrels' (an alternative term for a flame trap), stone walling, dragon's teeth and deepening of the burn. Positions were also to be dug facing east, to allow Lerwick, if captured, to be isolated. Additionally, survey and aerial photographs have revealed three pillboxes (probably Norcon type) and a loopholed wall overlooking the South Burn of Gremista (e on Fig. 10.2); dragon's teeth blocking a track over the hill just north-east of the reservoir (f); and cubes between the reservoir and the roadblock (g) and on the burn to the south-east. A line of beach scaffolding is visible on aerial photographs running from the edge of the reservoir, to and then south-west along the road, cutting across to the Loch of Trebister and from the loch to Voe of Sound (h on Fig. 10.2).

Lerwick: The Inner Defensive Line (The Bridgewater Line)

The War Diary of 7th Black Watch mentioned an 'Inner Defensive Line' (11 on Fig. 10.2) with north and south roadblocks which ran from Shearer's Wharf to North Loch to Clickimin Loch, and ended at the road bounding the south edge of the loch.[43] In June 1941 it had apparently been neither reconnoitred nor begun.

Lerwick: The New Inner Defence Line (The Carpenter Line)

It was noted in March 1941 that a 'new INNER DEFENCES Line facing EAST', which was within the town facing towards the seafront, was to be built from Braewick Manse, through Gilbertson Park to Shearer's Wharf (12 on Fig. 10.2), to be manned by ancillary troops (that is, Pioneers, RASC, etc.).[44] It was mentioned again in June 1941 when it was partly constructed.[45] The space between the Bridgewater and Carpenter Lines contained the two 3.7-inch howitzers, Brigade HQ, the force reserve and the prisoner of war cage.[46] The line was to be lightly wired.

Lerwick's Waterfront Defences

Lerwick's waterfront defences (13 on Fig. 10.2) were mentioned frequently in the documents, manned at different times by Home Guard, Pioneers, anti-aircraft troops, Shetland Defence Battalion, a company of 7th Black Watch and a motor transport section.[47] The defences ran from Holmsgarth in the north, at the east end of the Robertson and Stany Hill lines, round the coast to the end of the Inner Line, at the south end of Clickimin Loch at Breiwick.[48] It was described as a string of posts each with an open trench and beside it splinter-proof living quarters; the waterfront was 'wired wherever possible'.[49]

There was a mobile column (a company of Black Watch, carrier and mortar platoons, the two Royal Marine 3.7-inch howitzers and four medium machine guns from 8th Gordons) based in Lerwick, but ready to tackle a landing anywhere on Mainland.[50] There were other defended areas around Lerwick, at Point of Scotland and Green Head coast battery, both north of Lerwick, the coast battery on Ness of Sound, and the heavy anti-aircraft battery across Bressay Sound at Hill of Cruster on the island of Bressay.

The May 1940 document included a line (14 on Fig. 10.2), about 2.6km long, across Mainland between West Voe of Quarff and East Voe of Quarff. The line comprised only light firing positions and no wire.

South Shetland

The southernmost defences were erected in considerable depth to protect Sumburgh aerodrome from an advance from the north. In May 1940 the aerodrome's garrison comprised two companies of the Home Defence battalion with elements of two anti-aircraft batteries. By September, 'Sumforce' had grown to comprise the heavy anti-aircraft battery and the section of light anti-aircraft guns, a troop of four 75-mm guns, most of three companies of 7th Seaforth Highlanders, most of a company of medium machine guns from 8th Gordon Highlanders, two platoons of the Shetland Defence Battalion, various Royal Engineer and Pioneer detachments working in the area, and a large number of RAF personnel.[51]

The May 1940 document identified a line (15 on Fig. 10.1) running north-east to south-west from Channer Wick to Bigton. The main north–south road, which here runs along the east coast, had a roadblock where it crossed the Burn of Claver.

About 6km north of Sumburgh, at a point where Mainland is about 3.8km across, the Loch of Spiggie and the Loch of Brow constrain the road system, on the north-west, to an isthmus only a few metres across, and on the east, to a strip of land about 1km broad. This point was chosen for a defensive line (16 on Fig. 10.3). Although not mentioned specifically in the files, a roadblock and dragon's teeth were built to bar the road on the isthmus at the north-west end (j on Fig. 10.3) and a zigzag line of beach scaffolding (clearly visible on 1940s aerial photo-

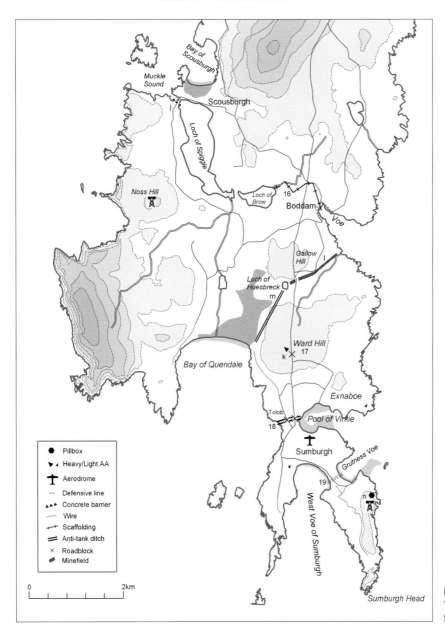

Figure 10.3.
The defences around Sumburgh.

graphs) was built to close the gap between the eastern end of Loch of Brow and the sea at Boddam.

A 'Sumforce' Operation Order of September 1940 noted that positions at Ward Hill and Exnaboe were to be held by parts of B Company 7th Seaforths (17 on Fig. 10.3). In March 1941 three sections of medium machine guns from 8th Gordons were positioned in this area covering the approaches from the north.[52] This position can probably located exactly by the location of a roadblock mentioned in a March 1941 list (k on Fig. 10.3). A tank obstacle was to be prepared along the front of the main position comprising mines from the east coast to Loch of Huns-breck (l), and a dug ditch from there to a point east of the Bay of Quendale (m).[53] This barrier lay about 1.5km in advance of the defended positions. These defences were noted in June 1941 as to be reviewed in the light of events in Crete, and the ditch was not to be 'started meanwhile'.[54] It is not known if this was ever dug.

The May 1940 list included a line blocking the narrow isthmus (about 400m across) south of Tolob, on the northern boundary of Sumburgh aerodrome (18 on Fig. 10.3).[55] The March and May 1941 documents mentioned two roadblocks and an anti-tank ditch running from sea to sea. The March 1941 document places platoons of 7th Seaforths and a section of medium machine guns of 8th Gordons in and around Tolob (in advance of the anti-tank ditch) as what are described as the 'Inner Defences'.[56] Guns of 152nd Field Regiment, RA were located south of Tolob to fire onto the aerodrome. The March 1941 list of defensive positions gives grid references for a 'Reserve Line' in the vicinity of Exnaboe and Tolob.

The southernmost defence line on Mainland was listed in May 1940 and closed a neck of land at the south-east edge of the aerodrome (19 on Fig. 10.3), cutting off any advance of paratroopers from the flat ground between the Jarlshof ancient monument and the hamlet of Sumburgh. The Sumburgh Chain Home Low radar station, guarded by a pillbox, was built on this peninsula (n) at some point in 1940–41.[57]

THE DEFENCES OF ORKNEY

The main purpose of the anti-invasion defences of Orkney was to protect the fleet anchorage and its infrastructure in Scapa Flow (Fig. 10.4), and the RAF and Fleet Air Arm aerodromes around it. A detailed description of the Scapa defences is beyond the scope of this book and mainly those anti-invasion defences that were in place or were built from September 1939 until mid-1941 are described here. The mapped remains are generally what was in place in July 1940 (with some additions up to December 1940). The Inganess Line is an exception; it was the most substantial 'conventional' anti-invasion defensive structure in Orkney, but construction continued into 1943.

Anti-invasion planning was already taking place in Orkney in 1939, when preparations were made to meet various eventualities arising from a seaborne landing in Inganess Bay or parachute landings in north or east Mainland, or in Hoy close to Lyness.[58] There was also a need to prevent an invader approaching Kirkwall and Hatston (Fig. 10.5) from any direction, and to protect Netherbutton radar station. Defensive positions were to be reconnoitred by nightfall on 27

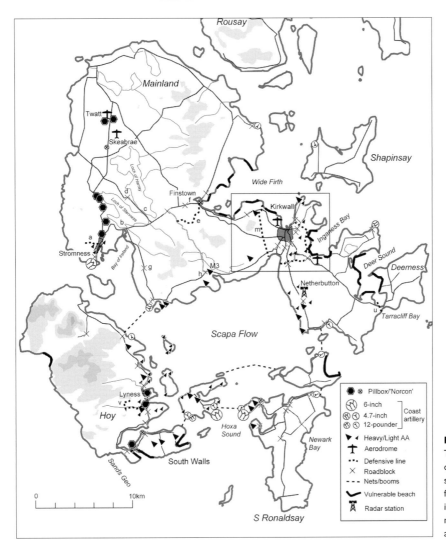

Figure 10.4.
The central and southern part of Orkney. The coast batteries shown on the map are those fully in place and operational in June 1940 (although others may have been partly built and armed).

October 1939 and digging would begin on Sunday 28th.[59] Positions to deal with these eventualities were built near Finstown and Bridge of Waith; near Wideford Hill; near Inganess; around Netherbutton; and around Lyness. Wired perimeters were to be erected round Stromness, Kirkwall and the aerodromes.[60]

As the anti-aircraft defences were focused on Scapa Flow, large parts of Mainland and the other islands were ill-defended against landings (Fig. 10.4),[61] and the coast guns at that time covered only the entrances to Scapa Flow and the northern approach to Kirkwall.[62] At the same time the only operational aerodrome (Hatston) lay close to Kirkwall, while three further aerodromes (Grimsetter, Skeabrae and Twatt) were in the early stages of construction.[63]

The majority of vulnerable beaches lay in the bays off Wide Firth, north of

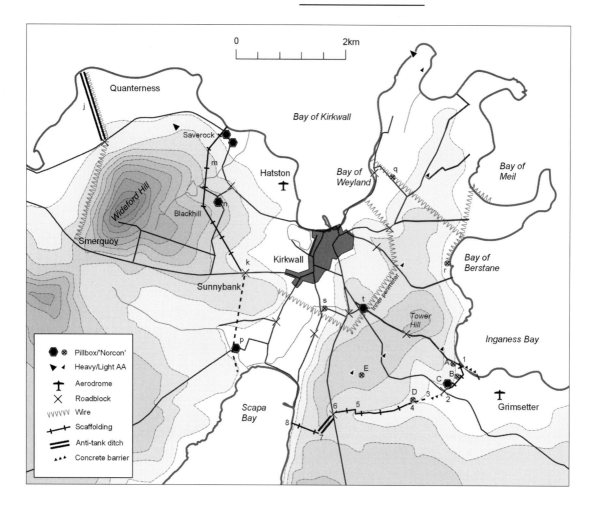

Figure 10.5.
The defences in the central part of Mainland, around Kirkwall.

Kirkwall, in Inganess Bay and in Deer Sound.[64] Lines of concrete cubes or dragon's teeth were not as a rule built on the beaches of Orkney but some were obstructed by wire or mines. In many cases, defence was undertaken by blocking an access from the beach to the strategic areas, some distance from the beach itself.

Kirkwall is the focus of the road system of Mainland and is also the point where the island is at its narrowest, between the open sea in Wide Firth and Scapa Flow. As the site of key elements of the command structure (including Hatston aerodrome and the Gun Operation Room, which controlled the anti-aircraft barrage) it was seen as the key to the capture of the island. While Stromness was defended because of its intrinsic value as a port, it was also one route of approach to Kirkwall, and all the defences described below, to west, east and north of Kirkwall, were intended to stop an enemy force from reaching the capital. The road network is constrained by water and high ground, the result being a limited number of exits from the mass of Mainland to the north-west, where landings

144

could take place untroubled by coast or anti-aircraft artillery. All of these exits were defended.

Stromness (Fig. 10.4) was defended by positions around the town, which covered a continuous wire obstacle that ran, by March 1941, from Bay of Navershaw (east of the town), to the junction of the Kirkwall road with the road north to Twatt. There were roadblocks on both roads, covered by a pillbox on a small hill to the west of the junction,[65] and the wire continued to the coast.[66]

The approach from the north towards Stromness was protected in depth by four further pillboxes (Fig. 10.6), sited to cover the road with fire from its flanks. None of the files seems to mention this arrangement but a map on file has an annotation suggesting that the sites for 34 pillboxes (probably Norcon type) had been chosen in the Stromness area.[67] A sketch map of defensive lines in Orkney in March 1940 shows what may be a defensive line closer in to Stromness over Brinkies Hill (a on Fig. 10.4) about which no other information has yet come to light.[68]

About 3km north-east of Stromness, the route from the town towards Kirkwall was to be blocked by a defensive position[69] and then a planned demolition at Bridge of Waith (b on Fig. 10.4), whence the Loch of Stenness flows into the sea.[70] About 3km further to the east, the next route from north-west to south-east was to be blocked at the narrow causeway under which the waters of the Lochs of

Figure 10.6.
A small Orkney Type 22 variant pillbox north of Stromness at Pallast (Author).

Stenness and Harray mingle (c); 440 yards (402m) of beach scaffolding was needed to block the area.[71] There was a roadblock at Bookan, to the north (d).

Finstown, where high ground and the watercourse known as the Ouse constrain traffic to a single road, was the site of proposed defences from 1939 onwards. At first, positions were to be built on Hill of Heddle, south of the village and possibly further to the south-west.[72] A demolition (f on Fig. 10.4) was proposed for the main road over the Bridge of Ouse, cutting off access from the beaches on the west side of Wide Firth. The bridge was overlooked by a surviving Norcon type pillbox on its south side.

In July 1940 an 'Outpost line' was noted in a file running from Finstown right across the island to the heavy anti-aircraft battery (number M3) at Kirbister.[73] The less direct of the routes from Bridge of Waith to Kirkwall, by the north shore of Scapa Flow, was defended by roadblocks at Clestrane (g on Fig. 10.4) and Kirbister (h).[74]

From Finstown two roads run east and east-south-east to Kirkwall, to the north and the south of Wideford Hill, which is a major barrier to movement (Fig. 10.5). A third road runs along the north shore of Scapa Flow towards Kirkwall. The island is about 6km across here and positions and lines of defence were planned, and to some extent implemented between 1939 and 1941, to block the approach along these roads. But what was actually built, and by whom, is difficult to untangle. The map shows the outpost line of wire and an anti-tank ditch (j on Fig. 10.5) planned, in February 1941, on the west side of the hill, from Quanterness to Smerquoy.[75]

The line marked 'm' on Figure 10.5 is the best estimate of the final line across the island, with a roadblock at the point marked (k) and scaffolding from the coast to Wideford Hill, which was to be constructed as 'a second priority as soon as beach hurdles [scaffolding] were available'.[76] Two pillboxes have been recorded at the northern end of the line, near the main road. A third survives at Blackhill (n on Fig. 10.5) standing a little behind the scaffolding line; it is a rather eccentric Type 22 variant built of cement-filled sandbags (Fig. 10.7). A further pillbox may be visible on an aerial photograph near the Scapa distillery (p on Fig. 10.5), where a roadblock was proposed in February 1941.[77] It is not clear what was built of the southern sector of the barrier.

The documented line of the Kirkwall inner perimeter is marked on Fig. 10.5 and there was also continuous wiring from Berstane Bay to Bay of Weyland cutting off the peninsula to the north-east of the town.[78] This line was tied into wire defences running from the north side of Bay of Meil, southwards to, and along, the Bay of Berstane and along Inganess Bay, accompanied by beach mines in the Bays of Meil and Berstane, all documented at various times from September 1940 to March 1941.[79] Three Norcon pillboxes have been identified, behind Bay

Figure 10.7.
A small Orkney Type 22 variant pillbox made of wetted bags of cement on the flank of Wideford Hill at Blackhill. A candidate for the least effective pillbox of 1940–41 (Author).

of Weyland (q on Fig. 10.5) and Bay of Berstane (r), and on the eastern road from Scapa Bay to Kirkwall (s), just inside the wire perimeter. A further pillbox – an Orkney Type 22 variant – has been recorded on the south-east side of the perimeter (t).

The Inganess Line

The most substantial anti-tank line in Orkney was the Inganess Line, south of Kirkwall, running from Inganess Bay (where the beach was blocked by concrete obstacles) to Scapa Bay (Fig. 10.5). An original line (October 1939 defence plan)[80] on Tower Hill gave way during 1940 to the final line along the valley of the Burn of Wideford and over the watershed towards Scapa. The geology created considerable difficulties for the construction of an anti-tank ditch and possible solutions were debated in the files over a long period. By March 1941 it was stated that the barrier was complete apart from a length of about 880 yards, for which that quantity of beach scaffolding was required.[81] It seems, however, that the work was later not considered satisfactory.[82]

The line can be considered in a number of sections (marked on Fig. 10.5), conforming to divisions marked on maps of October 1941 and March 1942:

(1–2) From Inganess Bay to the road that now runs from Kirkwall to Orkney Airport (Grimsetter) the barrier was originally intended to be provided by steepening the hillside, with part of the front covered by the marshy valley bottom. But by December 1941 this was to be replaced by beach scaffolding.[83] This sector has two Norcon pillboxes (Pillboxes A and B on Fig. 10.5) and a hexagonal pillbox (C) all of which are barely bulletproof (Fig. 10.8) and, because of their design, would have been deathtraps. There was a roadblock at point 2 on Fig. 10.5.

(2–3) To the west of the roadblock was a dog-legged stretch of about 300m of dragon's teeth, laid five deep (and visible on wartime aerial photographs), which were under construction in October 1941 (even though a 'beach flame barrage' for this area was still under consideration; see p. 107 above).[84]

(3–4) This section was blocked by the stream valley being given a vertical face. The final pillbox on the Inganess Line (Pillbox D on Fig. 10.5 – a third Norcon) was set on the high northern side of the stream gorge.

(4–5–6) The sector between 5 and 6 had been completed with beach scaffolding, by October 1941. An attempt to dig an anti-tank ditch between points 4 and 5 was not a success and, in the end, beach scaffolding was also used to make the barrier.[85] There was a roadblock at point 6 on Figure 10.5.

(6–7) This sector was blocked by the only satisfactory length of anti-tank ditch on the line.

Figure 10.8.
Norcon pillbox B on the Inganess Line, showing three impacts from bullets (1, 2 and 3), the last of which has penetrated the wall (Author).

(7–8) This sector was the most problematic; rock close to the surface meant that the ditch was only 3ft deep. Beach scaffolding was proposed but in the end (apparently early in 1943), about 100 McNaughton tubes were bored into the ground on its south side to allow a ditch to be 'blown' when needed.[86]

The defensive position, first mooted in October 1939, and partially completed by March 1941, was thus finally completed in early 1943.

Other Defences

The final anti-tank defence on Mainland was erected at the narrow isthmus separating the Deerness Peninsula from the rest of Mainland (u on Fig. 10.4) to block it and to defend the potentially vulnerable beaches to the north (Sandi Sand) and south (Tarracliff Bay). It comprised three lines of dragon's teeth (the eastern being a crude local variant made with concrete-filled steel drums set onto a concrete base) running westwards along the beach for over 500m and then running some 200m north out onto Sandi Sand. The scaffolding probably ran from the eastern end of the dragon's teeth and then across the isthmus to the western part of Tarracliff Bay, known as Dingyshowe Bay.[87]

The naval base at Lyness, on the south-east corner of Hoy, was the key land installation for the Fleet at Scapa. It occupied a peninsula about 900m square and its defence from landward attack was considered as early as October 1939, when defensive positions were planned at Rysa, to the north, Ore to the south and the hill of Wee Fea to the west.[88] They included, in 1940, a range of roadblocks and at least one pillbox (v on Fig. 10.4).[89]

The main sea entrance to Scapa Flow lay through Hoxa Sound, and during the war the armament of its flanking headlands was developed, with the establishment of coast defence guns. Measures were also taken to protect the landward approaches to South Walls, Herston Head and Hoxa Head, including a small hexagonal pillbox covering the causeway to South Walls (The Ayre).[90] The area seems to have been scaffolded too. A Norcon type pillbox was positioned at South Ness (possibly covering a roadblock there) and at Hoxa Head.

11. SUTHERLAND SUB-AREA

North Highland Area was created on 21 July 1940 and in October was divided into Sutherland and Aberdeen Sub-areas.[1] On 18 June 1941 Caithness became part of the Orkney and Shetland defence area and North Highland Area had no further role in its command.[2]

Sutherland Sub-area at first covered the counties of Caithness, Sutherland, Ross & Cromarty, Inverness-shire and Nairn (Figs. 2.2, 11.1, 11.9). In 1940–41 the most important areas strategically were Caithness, close to Scapa Flow, with vulnerable beaches, aerodromes and the port of Wick; the naval oiling base at Invergordon; and the area near Nairn with its aerodromes. The areas between were of limited strategic significance. With only two roads south, Caithness is isolated from the rest of Scotland and, once captured, would have been comparatively easy to hold against a British counter-attack. If the enemy succeeded in seizing Caithness, the naval anchorage at Scapa Flow would have become very difficult to hold, and the passage of convoys by the north coast would have been seriously interfered with. The road distances between Inverness and Wick (coast route) and Thurso (inland route via Forsinard) were then 140 and 156 miles (225km and 251km) respectively, the driving times for military convoys (at an average speed of 10 mph) being 14 and 15.5 hours.

South of the vulnerable beaches of Caithness, stop-lines were planned to bar the route of an enemy force that had established a foothold. The topography of Caithness, Sutherland and Ross & Cromarty constrains road communication to only a few roads. The two main routes south were linked east to west between Lairg and Loch Fleet (on the east coast), and were, in 1940, forced to converge at Bonar Bridge by a major natural barrier formed by the Dornoch Firth and the Kyle of Sutherland (Fig. 11.10). The railway lines from Thurso and Wick meet at Georgemass Junction, by Halkirk, and then head south-west across trackless moorland for about 35km, to Forsinard and then to the coast at Helmsdale. From this point south the railway and road run together to the crossing of Loch Fleet, where the main line runs inland to Lairg, crossing the Kyle of Sutherland a little north-west of Bonar Bridge, at Invershin. The road bridge at Bonar Bridge and the Invershin railway bridge were therefore in a very strategically important position (Fig. 11.9).

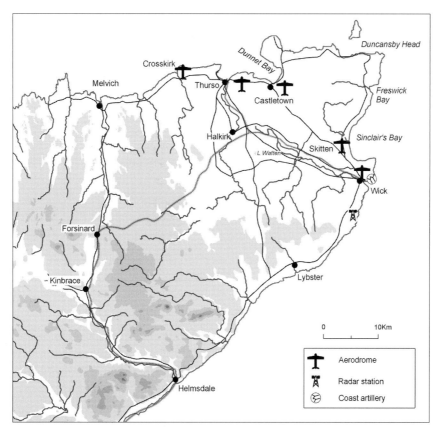

Figure 11.1.
Caithness, the northern portion of Sutherland Sub-area, showing aerodromes and radar stations operational or under construction in 1940 and the earlier part of 1941.

At Evanton the single main route was once again constrained to the coast, through Dingwall and Beauly. From Dingwall, road and rail routes ran west towards Kyle of Lochalsh and, most importantly, the subsidiary fleet anchorage at Loch Ewe, which also served, from 1941, as a major mustering point for Arctic convoys.

PORTS AND AERODROMES

There was only one 'major defended port' in Sutherland Sub-area, the naval base at Invergordon (Fig. 11.9), with three coast batteries each of two 6-inch guns. The only 'minor defended port' was Wick, which had a two-gun 6-inch 'emergency' battery put in place in June 1940.[3] In the *North Highland Area Defence Scheme* for December 1940 the list of ports to be prepared for immobilisation included, in Sutherland Sub-area, Scrabster, Wick, Lybster, Helmsdale, Balintore and Inverness.[4] The installation of flame projectors at harbours in Scotland in 1942–43 has already been mentioned: Wick was to have two such devices fitted, while Helmsdale was to have one.[5]

Wick is the only town and port in the area for which detailed maps of the defence in 1940–41 have so far been found.[6] The defence comprised a wire boundary some 300–600m out from the edge of the town, with 10–12 pillboxes and numerous other firing positions, abutting the even larger defended area of the aerodrome on the north side of the town, and the 6-inch coast battery to the north-east.

In 1940–41 there were four aerodromes either in active service or under construction in Caithness: Wick, Castletown, Skitten and Crosskirk (Fig. 11.1). The December 1940 list also includes an aerodrome or landing ground at St Fergus ('Not in use') and a civil aerodrome at Thurso ('blocked').[7]

SUTHERLAND SUB-AREA: MANNING AND DEFENCE

In the period before North Highland Area was established, 26th Infantry Brigade of 9th Division, based in Inverness, was responsible for the defence of northern Scotland (defined in April 1940 as extending from the Pentland Firth to Banff). A key responsibility was the defence of the naval installations at Invergordon. In spring 1940, what was known as 'Sub-area A' extended from Caithness south, through Sutherland, Ross & Cromarty and Inverness-shire. This sector, with HQ at Alness, was manned by the 'Cromarty Mobile Garrison', which comprised 5th Seaforth Highlanders (Strathpeffer), 5th Cameron Highlanders (Tain and Edderton), 275th Field Company, RE (Alness), with two companies of 7th Seaforth Highlanders as reserve at Dingwall. The reserve for 26th Brigade was the Infantry Training Centre of the Cameron Highlanders at Inverness.[8] Should the brigade require support, 9th Division's reserve was provided by 28th Infantry Brigade, based far to the south at Callander, near Stirling.

When, in September/October 1940, Sutherland and Aberdeen Sub-areas came into being, *North Highland Operation Instruction No. 5* set out the roles of the two battalions of Field Force infantry that were now in the Area: the 7th Battalion Cameron Highlanders in Wick was to cover Sinclair's Bay, Dunnet Bay, Wick itself, and Wick, Castletown and Skitten aerodromes; 9th Seaforth Highlanders were to cover the area between Tain, Edderton and Nigg, guarding Invergordon naval base and Evanton aerodrome and, under certain circumstances, to hold the Bonar Bridge defended locality.[9]

In November 1940, the Field Force units in Sutherland Sub-area had been reinforced by 152nd Field Regiment, RA whose role was to protect Wick and Skitten aerodromes and Sinclair's Bay with one troop of 18-pounder guns, by indirect fire from a point about 4.5km west of Wick, and to protect Castletown aerodrome and Dunnet Bay, with fire from Hill of Olrig.[10]

Static defence roles were allocated to two Royal Engineer companies and seven Pioneer companies in the area, the latter having roles in defending the small towns where they were based, such as Tain, Dingwall and Bonar Bridge. The two Home Defence battalions were responsible for guarding Vulnerable Points and for sectors of the Inverness and Wick town defences. The two Infantry Training Centres were responsible for defending Inverness (Queen's Own Cameron Highlanders) and Fort George (Seaforth Highlanders) with the latter also providing the counter-attack force for Dalcross and Brackla aerodromes.[11] The local Home Guard battalions had clearly-defined roles in supporting the static defence troops throughout the area,[12] including manning the defences of Inverness and smaller towns, the defences at Loch Garve and Bonar Bridge, and petrol depots in Tain, Lairg and Dingwall.

In December 1940 Scottish Command issued instructions both to review requirements for new defence works within the Command and to prepare to bring existing defences up to the new standards set out in *Military Training Pamphlet 30*, which had been published in October 1940.[13] Defensive works on two beaches in Caithness – Dunnet Bay and Sinclair's Bay – were to be strengthened and many of the barriers on Caithness beaches seem to show the addition of a double line of dragon's teeth to an original single row of cubes (a standard reinforcement strategy). It is possible that Murkle and Freswick were both reinforced with dragon's teeth at the same time, even though they were not on the priority list.

Throughout 1941 the possibility of 'diversionary or subsidiary attacks' in parts of Scotland remained, and in February 1941 Scottish Command recognised both the importance and the vulnerability of Caithness by forming an independent brigade (227th Independent Infantry Brigade) there. It was composed of three 'beach battalions' (at a lower level of equipment than Field Force units): 12th Cameronians (moved from Lossiemouth), 10th Black Watch and 7th Cameron Highlanders (who were already in the area).[14] 'Caithness', as defined for the purposes of the Army, was the area north-east of the main road between Helmsdale and Melvich, thus including part of the county of Sutherland. Brigadier Rose-Miller MC, DSO, the commander, comes across in the files as a real 'live wire', getting to grips with his responsibilities and wanting to build a thoroughly efficient integrated team, including the local naval and RAF forces. Interestingly, he had only been given substantive promotion to lieutenant colonel on 4 November 1940. He had been, as a major, an acting lieutenant colonel commanding the 1st Battalion Cameron Highlanders during the fighting in France, with great distinction.

In the first months of 1941 Rose-Miller based his planning on the expectation that Scotland would face attack from two infantry divisions, two light tank battalions and an airborne brigade, and that, under the worst circumstances, the greater proportion of the airborne brigade, one infantry brigade and the bulk of the tanks available to the invaders would be directed against Caithness.[15]

On the creation of the brigade, on 11 February 1941, the troops under Rose-Miller's command comprised:

(a) his independent brigade of three infantry battalions, HQ at the Pulteney Distillery in Wick;

(b) two troops of 152nd Field Regiment, RA (four 18-pounders; four 4.5-inch howitzers) – the third troop had no guns but was used in an infantry role;

(c) one troop of 942nd Defence Battery (Mobile), RA (four 4-inch guns, based at Sinclair's Bay);

(d) 303rd Coast Defence Battery (the two 6-inch guns covering the approach to Wick Harbour);

(e) one general construction company Royal Engineers (increased to two companies, 665th and 668th, by March 1941);

(f) one company 8th (Home Defence) Battalion Seaforth Highlanders (two companies by March);

(g) one company 70th (Young Soldier) Battalion Argyll & Sutherland Highlanders;

(h) one Animal Pack Transport Company, RASC;

(i) two companies of Pioneers (141st and 146th);

(j) one battalion Home Guard.

By March there were also two anti-aircraft batteries. He considered, however, that the war establishment of an independent brigade was hopelessly inadequate for the job, judging that more field and anti-tank guns and a machine gun company should be added.[16]

Of the two vulnerable beaches – Dunnet Bay and Sinclair's Bay – Rose-Miller felt that if the latter fell into enemy hands it would create 'a very serious situation' because of its proximity to Skitten and Wick aerodromes and the port of Wick.[17] The small fishing harbours (of which Helmsdale was the largest) were not seen as a significant risk; but he felt that the demolition of the major bridge at Helmsdale could seriously disrupt communications.

The brigadier considered the three aerodromes in operation at this time (Wick – bomber; Skitten and Castletown – fighter) as vital not only for the defence of Caithness but also for the conduct of the whole war. All convoys passing round the north of Scotland were escorted by aircraft from these bases. His position was that 'This Brigade will defend CAITHNESS and drive any enemy who may land from air or sea back into the sea. The word "withdrawal" will not be used in this Brigade, and Battalions will defend their posts to the last man and last cartridge.'[18]

In setting out his policy for defence and training in March 1941, Rose-Miller did not mince his words: bold leadership was needed from junior commanders; the whole brigade must train as a team; everyone must know their job and be kept in the picture; counter-attack would be practised night and day; men were to be inspired with viciousness and the will to kill; and the catch-words in the brigade were to be 'ATTACK, SPEED, INQUISITIVENESS, VICIOUSNESS and last but not least TEAMWORK'. He wanted the men to be kept active as he believed that 'The war may be won by the Army which is least bored'.

The brigadier spoke to the assembled Home Guard of the area in July 1941, explaining the risks of invasion; why Caithness might be a target; and the role the Home Guard would have in getting information to the regular forces, hindering the concentration of airborne enemy troops and guiding regular forces: 'You – the Home Guard, are my eyes. I rely on you to hold and delay the enemy sufficiently long for me to attack and destroy him.' It was also reiterated that officers and NCOs in both regular and Home Guard units should make sure they knew their opposite numbers in other units.[19]

The War Diary of 12th Cameron Highlanders showed the cunning and capacity of the local Home Guard in the area. In the brigade exercise 'Windup' at the end of August 1941 a Home Guard disguised as a mechanic managed to get into the compound round the 6-inch guns at the port 'to repair the fog signal' and managed to place a dummy time bomb on the battery range-finder. Similarly, a group of Home Guards disguised as an ambulance crew and casualties penetrated the Battalion HQ of 12th Camerons and captured it.[20]

THE CAITHNESS BEACHES

Thurso Bay

Thurso Bay, with the town at the south-east end and Scrabster harbour at the north-west, was consistently thought of as a lower risk invasion beach than Wick, as the approach from the sea was more difficult and the geomorphology of much of the shore provided a natural barrier. At the north side of the harbour a roadblock (still in place) was erected to bar access along the shore from the east and north-east. In 1970 an Aberdeen University beach survey noted scattered anti-tank cubes around the harbour, now swept away by redevelopment,[21] and along the bottom of the cliffs towards the town. The harbour was backed by a steep cliff, up which the access road still rises from north to south. It appears to have been blocked where it crossed a small gorge ('The Gill') at a point where a pillbox (visible on contemporary aerial photographs) was built into a wall at a road junction. The mouth of a burn was blocked by a line of cubes about 200m long, covered by a pillbox (still surviving) on the cliff, among the ruins of Scrabster Castle; cubes near here are marked '710–40' and '14/10/40'. Thurso beach itself seems to have been adequately blocked by the wall of the esplanade, but some anti-tank cubes were placed from the east end of the esplanade to the west bank of the River Thurso, at Thurso's small quay.

The 656th General Construction Company, RE began work on the defences of Thurso in August 1940, while 146th Pioneer Company was erecting anti-tank defences at Thurso and on adjacent beaches, and wiring the port at Scrabster, a task that took all of September, while also preparing to take their share of the defence of the area.[22]

Murkle Bay

Murkle Bay is a small bay lying within the larger unit of Dunnet Bay (Figs 11.2, 11.3), facing north-east and containing a shell and sand beach.[23] The beach is split in two by the Murkle Burn, which also separates a steeper dune face to the beach (to the north) from a lower dune face (to the south-east), which affected the strength and extent of the defences required. The bay is about 1.2km around from headland to headland, and the sandy beach is about 550m long. Pre-war mapping shows a broader beach than today.

The built defences were in three sections. The westernmost comprised dragon's teeth, five deep, out onto a wide rocky platform called The Spur and three deep

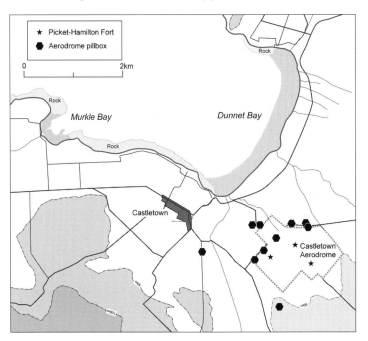

Figure 11.2.
The area of Dunnet Bay, Murkle Bay and Castletown aerodrome.

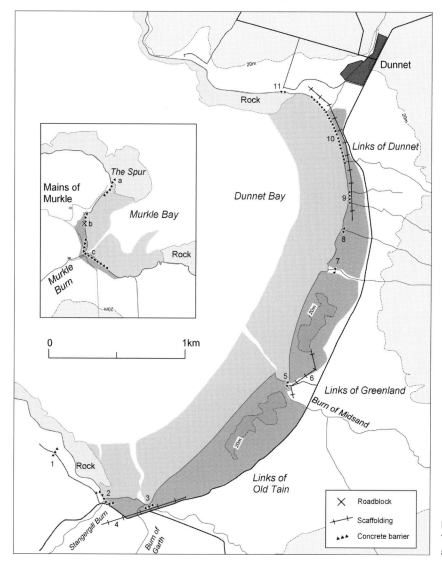

Figure 11.3.
The defences of Murkle Bay and Dunnet Bay.

along the low cliff (a on Fig. 11.3; Fig. 11.4). The second section comprised cubes fronted by dragon's teeth, within which there was a horizontal-rail roadblock (b on Fig. 11.3). The visible surviving cubes have sharp-edged pieces of Caithness flagstone set along one diagonal axis of their tops and steel rings to aid wiring. They have been poured into a mixture of wood and corrugated iron shuttering, over shallow, irregular holes dug into the shingle. One cube has, crudely scratched into its top, what appears to be '6 WAR'; the Defence of Britain database also records the graffiti '4×3' and 'W M 1941'. The burn was blocked by a double line of dragon's teeth (c) which continued for about 300m along the beach to the east (possibly backed by cubes in places).

Figure 11.4.
Dragon's teeth at the northern end of Murkle Bay (Author).

Dunnet Bay

The defence of the beach was crucial to the security of Castletown aerodrome, which lay close behind the dunes. The dune system is more than 350m across in places, but narrows to the north. The long beach is broad and compact, providing a good landing surface. In the southern two-thirds of the bay, the dunes are 12–20m high and were a substantial barrier to an invading force, except where the mouths of burns and erosion hollows allowed an exit. Nine burn mouths were blocked and the narrow road running north-west was also blocked with cubes and dragon's teeth (1 on Fig. 11.3). At the south-west end of the beach two burns were blocked by a line of cubes and a line of dragon's teeth (2) and by dragon's teeth (3). Virtually nothing survives at this end of the beach. In the autumn of 1941 this barrier was reinforced by beach scaffolding running behind the dunes (4).[24]

The beach exit along the Burn of Midsand was blocked by a double line of dragon's teeth, of which 11 survive (5 on Fig. 11.3). A zigzag line of beach scaffolding was added behind the dunes during 1941, obstructing a greater length (6). Four further burns north-north-east of the Burn of Midsand were also blocked by cubes, a short way inland (7); and by cubes and dragon's teeth (at 8 and 9). Fragments of both of these last survive. In the northernmost part of the beach, where the dune belt is narrow and low, a continuous triple line of pimples ran for about 550m (10); a length of the barrier survives north of the Burn of Dunnet. Some pimples have what seem to be the characters '27' or '2F' inscribed in the wet concrete. During 1941 a 1km-long line of beach scaffolding was erected behind the dunes from south of point 9 to north of the dragon's teeth (10). The final barrier in the bay was a short line of cubes and dragon's teeth blocking a track down through the cliff to a fishing station (11).

Castletown Aerodrome

Castletown lay immediately behind the southern end of Dunnet Bay (Fig. 11.2). It was a fighter aerodrome and was heavily defended: at least nine pillboxes have been recorded, mainly on the seaward side, along with a rock-cut battle HQ (from which the defence of the aerodrome would be commanded) and at least three Pickett-Hamilton forts beside the runways. There is little in the file about who built the defences, or when, but 692nd (Costain) General Construction Company, RE a specialist aerodrome-construction unit, was involved in construction at Castletown until October 1940, when the bulk of the unit went to London leaving a detachment to complete the battle HQ.

Freswick Bay

Freswick Bay lies on the east coast of Caithness between Duncansby Head and Sinclair's Bay (Fig. 11.5). To north and south the shore is rocky, with high cliffs to the north, and lower to the south. There are exits to the beach at the north and at the south and what was probably a low section of dunes was blocked for about 40m (nothing now surviving) at point 2 on Figure 11.5.

The northern part of the beach was the most heavily defended (Fig. 11.6). A line of anti-tank cubes runs for about 120m from the end of the cliff southwards to a horizontal-rail roadblock on the track to the beach. These cubes have been reinforced with a double line of dragon's teeth in front, almost certainly after December 1940. The cubes and dragon's teeth continue south of the roadblock, the cubes to the landward side for about 80m, the dragon's teeth to seaward, for about 50m. The defences are well preserved at this end of the beach.

At the southern end of the bay, on the northern side of the mouth of the Freswick Burn, a single line of anti-tank cubes was fronted by two rows of dragon's teeth; some still survive. The dragon's teeth here, perhaps to take account of the instability of the sand, have huge concrete bases. In one tumbled case, the foundation has a volume of 5–10 times that of the 'tooth' (Fig. 8.6). On the southern side of the burn mouth, the land rises to a height of over 10m where Freswick House, a seventeenth-century domestic castle, sits. The seaward boundary wall of the house is fronted, for no apparent reason, by two lines of dragon's teeth, some of which have tumbled down the slope onto the beach. There is, perhaps unexpectedly, no sign of the castle wall having been loopholed.

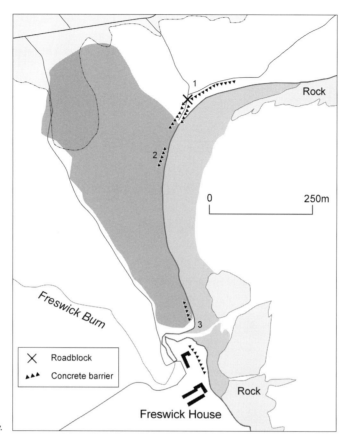

Rock

0   250m

Freswick Burn

3

✕   Roadblock

▲▲▲   Concrete barrier

Rock

Freswick House

Figure 11.5.
The defences of Freswick Bay.

Figure 11.6.
Cubes fronted by two lines of
dragon's teeth, at the north
end of Freswick Bay (Author).

160

Sinclair's Bay and Wick

Brigadier Rose-Miller saw Sinclair's Bay (Fig. 11.7) as his most vulnerable and important beach because of its proximity to two aerodromes, at Skitten (1.2km behind the beach) and at Wick (1km south of Ackergill in the southernmost part of the bay), and to the port of Wick. Because the dunes were lower or non-existent at the two ends of the bay, and because these areas also had easier access to the

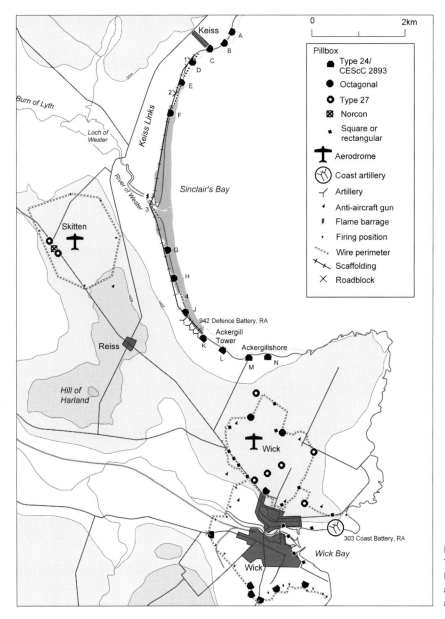

Figure 11.7.
The defences of Sinclair's Bay, Wick town and the aerodromes at Wick and Skitten.

main road behind the beach, the defences were stronger at the northern and southern ends.

The bay is split in two by the mouth of the River of Wester (the name for the short watercourse draining the Loch of Wester to the sea; it is referred to in Army files as the Burn of Lyth – the watercourse feeding the loch). The mouth of the river itself provided an exit from the beach, only 1,200m from the edge of Skitten aerodrome.

The northernmost structures of the defences are two identical pillboxes 270m and 540m north-east of Keiss harbour (A and B on Fig. 11.7), now lying close to or on the very edge of the land, at the top of the shingle beach (Fig. 11.8). They are brick-built pillboxes probably conforming to CEScC 2893 (the Scottish Command Type 24 variant), with 9-inch thick (barely bulletproof) walls, but set into the ground to the height of the bottom of the embrasure. The seaward wall of the southern pillbox is now exposed by erosion and it can be seen that a brick apron was built below each embrasure, to thicken and strengthen the wall. The bricks were of local manufacture: 'Hunter of Brora'. This style of pillbox was also built on other parts of the bay. There is no evidence of any concrete barrier along the steeply sloping shingle beach here.

The cliff above Keiss harbour provided an adequate barrier for a short distance, and a pillbox was erected on top of the cliff. This has been reduced to its base and a small part of the rear walls; it was probably a further Type 24 variant (C on Fig. 11.7).

About 250m to the south-west of the village the cliff ceased to be an adequate anti-tank barrier and an artificial barrier was therefore constructed from here

Figure 11.8.
Pillbox north of Keiss, showing the brick aprons below the large embrasures for medium machine guns (Author).

for about 1.3km, covering a section where there are no dunes and the beach backs straight onto flat agricultural land. Within this section the barrier is formed by a single line of concrete cubes (peculiarly badly made and with very shallow foundations) reinforced by two lines of dragon's teeth. Near the southern end of this sector, one of the cubes was marked 'A Hendry 7–1940' in the wet concrete; the Defence of Britain database records 'Wm Miller Sept 1940' written on another. Within the line are two roadblocks (at 1 and 2 on Fig. 11.7) on tracks running parallel to and onto the beach. There are also the shattered remnants of three CEScC 2893 pillboxes (D, E and F) which seem to have been placed among the dragon's teeth, or, in the case of F, south of the end of the concrete barrier.

No concrete barrier seems to have been required for the next 2km southwards to the mouth of the River of Wester, as the dunes were high enough. The mouth of the river was blocked about 100m inland from the beach by two double lines of cubes across the river and a second line ran along the shore a little to the south (3 on Fig. 11.7). Many pieces of the barrier survive here, although some have been moved.

There is no trace of any concrete barrier in the southern part of the bay, apart from three large concrete blocks lying at the head of the beach about 1.8km south of the river, where there is now no obvious need for an obstruction (4 on Fig. 11.7). However, three pillboxes have also been recorded at various times in the last 30 years along this stretch of beach at the points marked on the map, although none is now visible (G, H and J).

In the early autumn of 1941 it was decided that the defences described above were inadequate, and beach scaffolding was erected along the whole length of Sinclair's Bay, between pillboxes D and K on Figure 11.7. Unusually, the scaffolding was erected behind the dunes to conceal it from the sea, while being close enough to the beach to prevent a tank having a clear run at it.[25] Also, in the autumn of 1941 it was recorded that 'a flame-thrower is in the course of construction at the entrance of the Burn of Lyth for a distance of 300 yds'.[26] This flame projector was eventually completed over the winter of 1942–43 but was put on a care and maintenance basis in spring 1943.[27] I have mentioned the unedifying story of the flame barrage (p. 109).

At the south end of the sandy beach, and along the low shoreline cliffs immediately to the north of Wick aerodrome, were four further CEScC 2893 Type 24 variant pillboxes, 400–600m apart. The first (K on Fig. 11.7) does not survive. That at Ackergill Tower (L) survives only as a hexagonal concrete base and some brickwork immediately below the wall of the castle, on the edge of the rocky top of the beach. The surviving elements of the structure show that it was the same style as pillboxes A and B at Keiss. In two places the curtain wall of Ackergill Tower was breached at a high level to provide wide machine gun embrasures, which are still visible. At Ackergillshore the pillbox sits at the shoreward end of the pier, covering the small harbour (M). The final pillbox, built of concrete blocks, but otherwise of similar pattern to the extant pillboxes north of Keiss, sits on top of the low cliff with a good field of fire over the bay and foreshore (N).

In October 1940 Scottish Command allocated beach searchlights to Sinclair's Bay, but their location is not known. The four 4-inch naval guns of the beach battery (942nd Defence Battery (Mobile), RA) were placed in 1940 at the south end of the beach near pillboxes J and K (Fig. 11.7).

Wick

Wick aerodrome (Fig. 11.7) was a key fighter base from the beginning of the war, and its proximity to Norway, sandwiched between a vulnerable landing beach and the largest civil port north of Peterhead, inevitably meant that it was, in time, heavily defended. The aerodrome perimeter was joined to the defensive perimeter of the town and the harbour, which incorporated the 6-inch coast battery covering Wick Bay. There were at least six Type 27 pillboxes, 12 further pillboxes on and around the aerodrome, and a further 12 in the town perimeter and around the harbour, along with other firing positions. Andrew Guttridge has made plans of one of the rectangular pillboxes on the aerodrome perimeter, and a classic Vickers pillbox at the harbour (Fig. 9.4).

Work is recorded on the defences in Caithness in the War Diary of 656th General Construction Company, RE from the beginning of July to October 1940.[28] Wick aerodrome was wired in July but pillboxes 'already erected' by mid-June were not considered satisfactory and were being rebuilt.[29] Indeed, the only battle at ground level in Wick in the summer of 1940 was the bitter feud apparently running between 656th Field Company, RE, (under local command) and 692nd (Costain) General Construction Company, RE (working for the Air Ministry building aerodromes). On 1 August, 692nd Company noted that pillboxes they had built were 'being demolished and rebuilt at a lower level by [656th] Company'.[30] 692nd Company countered by complaining about trenches dug by 656th Company just outside the aerodrome where the heaps of spoil would make 'excellent cover for an attacking force' and checking to see whether the field of fire of the rebuilt, lower pillboxes would be impaired. Pillbox no. 4 (built by contract for 656th Company) was in fact found to have poor visibility and 692nd Company gleefully reported this to the Air Ministry. 692nd Company also seemed pleased to be able to report that the farmer on whose land the trenches had been dug had written to complain to his MP about 656th Company. The pillbox feud continued with 692nd Company deciding that the reinforcing of some pillboxes on the aerodrome (by 656th Company) had been badly planned and central piers would have to be built to support the roofs. On 21 August 1940, Major Berridge, the CO of 692nd Company, sent a report critical of the defences in the Wick area to the Commander Royal Engineers in charge of aerodrome works stating that, 'The whole defensive attitude in this area seems to be sit tight and wait for the enemy to attack rather than to attack the enemy before he can organise.'[30] Major Berridge – driven either by frustration or perhaps by an innate tactlessness – felt he had to point out forcibly to Major General Chalmers – the Commander of North Highland Area – when he called in at the unit's offices for a chat, that 'we did not come under his command'.

That 'independent' Royal Engineer units were a cause of friction is further hinted at by the experiences in early September 1940 of a detachment of the same 692nd Company working at Sumburgh aerodrome in Shetland. The Shetland Garrison Engineer, Captain Augier, RE had seized some of 692nd Company's stores and was refusing to return them or to give them any help at Sumburgh until they came under his command.[32] It is not clear how many of poor Major Berridge's problems were the result of what may have been an abrasive personality, but Augier's bloody-minded obstructiveness in Shetland at the height of the invasion scare and a couple of weeks into the Battle of Britain is scarcely believable.

Sinclair's Bay, by February 1941, was wired throughout its length and anti-tank mines were being laid wherever the enemy might move inland. The Burn of Lyth/River of Wester were themselves believed to be enough of a barrier to localise any attack to the north or south of it. The infantry garrison of the entire length of the beach comprised about 150 men, split between the southern sector (a platoon around Ackergill Tower; a platoon area 600 yards (548m) south of river; with a reserve platoon at the crossroads north-north-east of Reiss) and the northern (platoons in the area between the river and Keiss and one platoon to the west in reserve). A Bren gun carrier section was to provide a mobile reserve for counter-attack from the southern sector.[33]

Rose-Miller did not relish the idea of his field troops being dispersed in pillboxes – a not uncommon feeling in 1941 – preferring positions on the flanks of the beach. At Sinclair's Bay, in particular, he arranged for a dozen medium machine guns (additional to the equipment of the battalion) to be left in position to be manned as necessary by 7th Cameron Highlanders. He wanted the brigade to have supplies of food and ammunition, well-distributed around the area, adequate for two weeks of fighting without resupply.[34]

In the Defence Orders for Thurso and Scrabster, issued on 6 February 1941, the limited scale of defence available away from the beaches was only too clear. Scrabster was to be defended by only 14 staff from the 'Officers Movement Control' office, 25 Home Guard and three sections from 146th Pioneer Company (about

25–30 men) with the support of two Naval Maxim guns. Thurso was defended by just six sections of 146th Pioneer Corps (about 50–60 men). Incidentally, the same document notes 11 pillboxes in Thurso,[35] the location of which are not known.

DEFENCES SOUTH OF CAITHNESS

The tasks of the Sub-area included manning a series of defended localities and stop-lines to prevent an enemy force that had occupied Caithness from moving south. A list of stop-lines, intended to take advantage in most cases of natural barriers, was produced in July 1940, when 9th Division listed five stop-lines in Sutherland Sub-area (Table 11.1) and the troops to hold them.

A second list, in June 1941, included only one of these – the Bonar Bridge defended locality, albeit described using different place names.[36] The Caledonian Canal had been added by spring 1943.[37] Of the five listed in June 1940, the first (Helmsdale to Melvich) has the appearance of a line drawn on a map by someone who did not know the country, or as a line very poorly described: crossing the stop-line would have merely taken an enemy from one area of trackless, inhospitable, boggy hills to another. The four lines south of Caithness (nos. 2, 3, 4 and 5) take advantage of four major bights – three of them striking 30km and more into the eastern coast: the mouth of the Fleet, the Dornoch Firth, the Cromarty Firth and the Beauly Firth (Fig. 11.9).

The effect of the Loch Fleet to Lairg stop-line could have been achieved by blocking only the road crossing Loch Fleet, on the causeway known as the 'The Mound', and the road at Lairg. Between the two, the River Fleet, the boggy ground

Table 11.1. Stop-lines listed by 9th Infantry Division in July 1940

Line	Object
1. Helmsdale – Kinbrace – Forsinard – Melvich	To confine enemy to north-east Caithness
2. Loch Fleet – Rogart – Lairg	To prevent enemy moving south
3. Bonar Bridge – Inveran	To prevent enemy moving south
4. Dingwall	To prevent enemy moving south and to deny the road and railways to Kyle of Lochalsh
5. Kessock – Beauly – River at military grid J.07 – Kilmorack.	To cover Inverness and routes for reinforcements from south and south-west

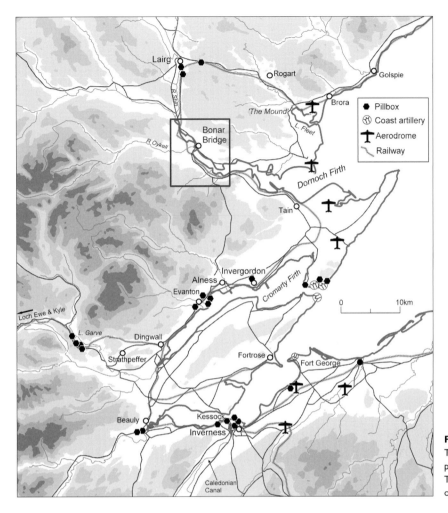

Figure 11.9.
The defences in the southern part of Sutherland Sub-area. The box indicates the extent of Fig. 11.10.

near its mouth and the high ground to the south, provide an effective barrier. There is no evidence that The Mound was blocked, but three pillboxes were built at Lairg.

The third 'line', at Bonar Bridge, more accurately referred to in files as a 'defended locality', was developed as a major block, as befits such a strategic point, the structures extending over an area 7km north-west to south-east and 2.5km north-east to south-west. The Kyle of Sutherland is a tidal inlet above the Dornoch Firth, fed by two major river systems: the River Oykell, draining the land to the west, and the River Shin, draining the hills to the north and north-west. The normal tidal limit is 35km inland from the inner edge of the Dornoch Firth, at Inveroykel, west of the area shown in Figure 11.10. The water barrier was bridged in 1940–41 at three points: at Inveroykel; by the railway viaduct at Invershin (adapted in 1941 to carry both road and rail traffic);[38] and finally, at Bonar Bridge.

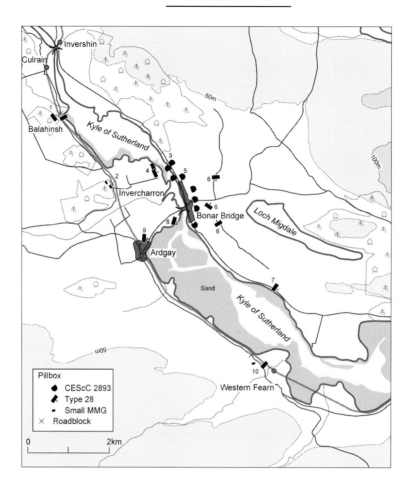

Figure 11.10.
The Bonar Bridge
defended locality.

There seem to have been some 21 pillboxes near Bonar Bridge, on both sides of the Kyle of Sutherland (including the largest concentration of Type 28 anti-tank gun pillboxes in Scotland), and two known roadblocks. Some of the anti-tank pillboxes have the integral Bren gun chamber often seen in this type; some do not. Most of the survivors have had their large embrasures reduced in size with brickwork and fitted with steel Turnbull mounts (probably for Vickers medium machine guns) – the Home Guard who took over the manning of these pillboxes were not armed with 2-pounder anti-tank guns at this stage of the war (Fig. 11.11).

Two anti-tank gun pillboxes covered the northern approach on the west side at a roadblock at Balahinsh (1 on Fig. 11.10). Some 2km south-east, at the entrance to Invercharron House a second roadblock (still in situ) (2) closed the road and was covered by two rectangular medium machine gun pillboxes, one on the uphill, western, flank, the other tucked into the roadside firing north at the roadblock. All elements of this complex survive.

Figure 11.11.
Bonar Bridge Type 28 pillbox (no. 8 on Fig. 11.10) converted for use with a machine gun by the large embrasure being bricked up to take a Turnbull mount (Author).

The approach to Bonar Bridge from Invershin, to the north on the eastern bank, was covered by three pillboxes sited close to the road (3 on Fig. 11.10) and a double anti-tank gun pillbox on the other side of the Kyle (4), firing north-east into the flank of any column on the road. A CEScC 2893 (Type 24 variant) medium machine gun pillbox set to the east of and above the road (5), seems to have been tasked mainly with covering the north-east approaches to the village.

An enemy approaching along the minor road from the east would face fire from three anti-tank gun pillboxes (all marked 6 on Fig. 11.10), the northern set on high ground to the north, firing south (surviving in excellent condition). The south-east approach, along the coast road from Dingwall, was blocked by a roadside Type 28 pillbox about 2.5km south-east of the village (7). Closer in to the village on the eastern and southern side were four pillboxes (not numbered on the map and only one surviving, half-buried) probably a CEScC 2893 (Type 24 variants) facing east and south-east. As the enemy approached the village the road was also covered by two further anti-tank pillboxes, on the western side of the Kyle, firing eastwards, one just SSW of the bridge, the other on the outskirts of the village of Ardgay (8 and 9).

If an enemy penetrated all these defences, the final block lay at Western Fearn on the road to Tain, to the south-east (10 on Fig. 11.10), where a roadblock was covered by two pillboxes, one an anti-tank gun pillbox firing from among the farm buildings and the other a smaller rectangular medium machine gun box.

The beach between Dornoch and Tarbat Ness was identified on the list of vulnerable beaches of May 1940[39] and October 1941,[40] and the small beach at Shandwick Bay appeared on the vulnerable beach list in October 1941. There were references in a number of files to the obstruction of these beaches with anti-glider poles and wire, but there is no evidence that anything more substantial was built there.

The Cromarty Firth was the site of the important naval oiling depot at Invergordon and its associated defences. Invergordon had been a major naval base in the First World War but Scapa was considered more secure from bombing, and Invergordon served mainly as a refuelling depot in the 1939–45 war. The narrow entrance into the Firth was defended in 1940–41 by three batteries, each of two 6-inch naval guns. The North Sutor battery had at least two pillboxes. A third pillbox was built at the northern end of the Cromarty ferry. The northern approach to Invergordon village was guarded by a Type 24 pillbox and, although no other concrete defence posts are recorded, there are hints on contemporary aerial photographs of pillboxes or other firing positions in woods round the site's perimeter. Four pillboxes were recorded as being provided for the defence of Evanton aerodrome (originally built as a land base for carrier-borne aircraft).

The Norwegian Brigade had been formed on 3 March 1941 in south-west Scotland. After its legal status was clarified by the military agreement signed on 28 May by Trygve Lie (Foreign Minister in the Norwegian government-in-exile) and Anthony Eden, it was given operational responsibilities in the Sub-area, moving on 10–11 June 1941 to the area around Invergordon, to defend the naval base, the aerodromes and the beaches.[41]

The topography around Dingwall, Strathpeffer and Conon Bridge, where there is only a narrow gap between the Cromarty Firth and high ground, offered a good choke point. The line at Dingwall listed in June 1940 (No. 4 on Table 11.1) had two purposes: 'To prevent enemy moving south and to deny the road and railways to Kyle of Lochalsh'. Both would have been achieved by blocking the main road just north of Dingwall, where the main road and railway cross the River Peffery, at Kinnairdie. However, no defence structures have been recorded on the main road here. The route to Kyle of Lochalsh is also the only road from the east to Loch Ewe, the temporary Fleet anchorage established in September 1939.[42]

There is, however, a 'defended locality' at Loch Garve, 13km as the crow flies (and over 17km as the road wanders) west of Dingwall. Here, the road and the railway to Kyle of Lochalsh run along a narrow strip of land between high, steep ground on the south and Loch Garve on the north-east. This narrow gap was closed by a roadblock and four pillboxes: one is a Type 28 anti-tank gun pillbox and two were for Bren guns; the fourth has not been examined. Unexpectedly, the pillboxes here actually face north-west and are designed to stop an enemy coming from that direction. The three inspected had no capacity to fire in the other direction.

The fifth line listed in 1940, around Kessock to Kilmorack, is formed by the Beauly Firth, the final major natural barrier to movement southwards. Two pillboxes have been recorded, which are likely to have been part of the stop-line. A possible Type 24 was built to the east of the road from Kessock into Inverness, perhaps covering the approach from what was then the ferry across the Firth. A brick-built pillbox of unknown type, with embrasures facing west and north, lay just west of the mouth of the Caledonian Canal. Above Beauly the river meanders across the floodplain and the lowest bridge across it is that for the railway line. About 1km upriver is the Lovat Bridge, which carries the main road. A junction between it and a minor road was covered by a pillbox, reported as being rectangular with five embrasures, and a roofless Norcon type pillbox has been recorded on the east side of the bridge. A minor airfield (Inverness Longman) lay just to the east of the town and three Type 27 pillboxes (the kind with the integral anti-aircraft mounting, particularly associated with aerodromes) have been recorded on it.

References to the use of the Caledonian Canal as a stop-line (Fig. 11.9) do not always make clear what part of the 90km or more of the canal, and the lochs it links, was being referred to. In July 1940 the 5th Division was, in the event of an enemy landing in the north-west of Scotland, to hold 'strong bridge-heads on the Caledonian canal from Fort Augustus (at the south-west end of Loch Ness) to Colvoullin' (to the south-west, near Corran).[43] In December 1940 52nd Division had the same role.[44] The canal and lochs would have made a formidable barrier, requiring only roadblocks, field positions and possibly demolitions (although none were formally approved by Scottish Command) to block the handful of crossings. In early 1941 an additional temporary bridge was built at Ferry Lochend, at the north-east end of Loch Ness, to replace the ferry there, as one of four or five extra crossings needed to relieve bottlenecks in the Scottish road network.[45]

The coastal strip between Inverness and the Sub-area boundary, just east of Nairn, contained three aerodromes that were active in 1940–41: Dalcross, Brackla and Leanach. None had any known defence-related structures, and Leanach, in use from 1933, does not appear in any of the aerodrome defence lists consulted. The sea approaches to Inverness were guarded by the narrows between Fortrose and Fort George, where an emergency coast battery (304th Coast Battery, RA) was established in the summer of 1940. Indeed the flag officer in charge of Inver-gordon had, on 6 July 1940, stressed the extreme urgency of a battery being estab-lished there.[46]

The beach west of Nairn appeared on the Scottish Command lists of vulnerable beaches of April and October 1941, described as defended by wire and minefields only. The beach to the east of Nairn was not close to any strategic assets, such as a port or aerodrome, and does not appear on any lists of vulnerable beaches. It was, however, immobilised by the erection of hundreds of anti-glider poles, many of which survive. The pattern of posts continued some distance to the east and the whole pattern is described in the next section: Aberdeen Sub-area.

12. ABERDEEN SUB-AREA

Aberdeen Sub-area took in the historical counties of Moray, Banffshire, Aberdeenshire and Kincardineshire. The total length of beach in north-east Scotland (including the length of coast west of the Sub-area boundary between Nairn and Inverness) is about 275km, of which 44 per cent is sandy beach. The western part of the Sub-area comprises difficult hill and mountain, but much of the north-east is rolling lightly wooded agricultural land, good tank country, with few natural barriers within it.

The Sub-area is described in two parts: the north-facing coast and its hinterland; and the east-facing coast and its hinterland. The northern coastline falls into two parts: the western sector between Nairn and Buckie is dominated by long beaches vulnerable to enemy landings while the sector from Buckie to Fraserburgh is predominantly cliff, with a small number of sandy inlets. The east-facing coast breaks down in the same way: between Fraserburgh and Aberdeen much of the coast is sandy beach vulnerable to landing, while south of Aberdeen the coast is rocky, with a small number of sandy inlets.

THE MORAY FIRTH COAST

Behind the beaches in the western part of the Moray Firth coast is the narrow coastal plain, rising quickly to the foothills of the mountains to the south. Along the coastal plain are the main road and rail links to the east and south-east. The western part of this zone had, in 1940–41, a very high density of airfields either in use or with construction far enough advanced to make them possible targets for enemy landings. Between Nairn and the River Spey (a distance of less than 50km) there were seven RAF or Fleet Air Arm aerodromes and airfields: three (Kinloss, Rosevalley and Lossiemouth) lay right beside vulnerable beaches – the first two behind Burghead Bay, the last behind Lossiemouth east beach; Elgin Milltown, less than 2km from the sandy beach of Spey Bay was not operational at this stage of the war (Fig. 12.9).[1]

There were no 'major defended ports' in Aberdeen Sub-area, apart from

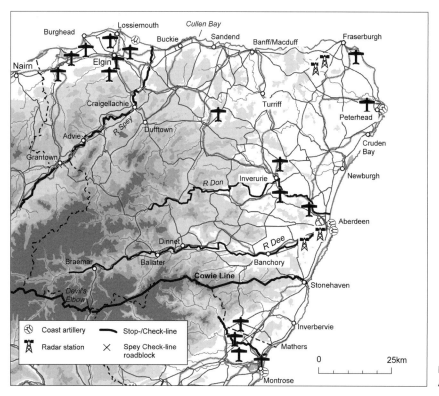

Figure 12.1.
Aberdeen Sub-area.

Aberdeen itself, and the only 'minor defended port' between Inverness and Fraserburgh was Buckie, which was provided with no gun armament. On 11 September 1940 there were 11 harbours that apparently needed 'immobilisation' on this stretch of coast, ranging from three block-ships for Lossiemouth, to one at Findochty.[2] It was reported that, although 'Portsoy, Whitehills, Banff and Macduff, obstructions [were] the most efficient yet seen . . . None of the obstructions would stop a trawler'. What then, one must wonder, was the point at these tiny ports, let alone the more robust 'Floating Defence Type H. A/B Mk III' that was to be installed in them in 1941?[3]

The armoured train based at Aberdeen included in its patrol pattern the branch line to Lossiemouth and the line along the coast from Lossiemouth to Macduff.[4] The officer in charge noted that the line ran close to the coast for about 1½ miles west of Banff, and also between Cullen and Garmouth, and that on the Burghead to Hopeman line (west of Lossiemouth), the train 'could cover any approach from the sea'.[5]

In May 1940 there was in existence a small 'Moray Striking Force', equivalent to the longer-lived 'Cromarty Force' for Invergordon. Its purpose was to protect the aerodromes and airfields at Kinloss, Lossiemouth, Waterside and Rosevalley.[6] It comprised three companies of 7th Seaforths; a troop of howitzers from 126th

Field Regiment, RA; a troop of 61st Anti-tank Regiment, RA; two medium machine gun platoons of 8th Gordons; as well as Royal Engineers.

The 150th Pioneer Company arrived in the Findhorn area on 4 July 1940 to begin work on immobilising beaches and fields within 5 miles of Kinloss aerodrome.[7] The erection of anti-glider poles continued to the end of September, as the poles were often washed away, despite several different methods of securing them in the sand. The company also provided masons and stone-dressers to assist in the erection of pillboxes, some of the work being done by civilian contractors. Two companies of Polish Engineers were based in the area, building coastal defences and erecting anti-glider poles in fields, from 16 August 1940 until they moved to Dundee at the beginning of 1941 (Fig. 8.1). They described their life there in the 'Kronika' (Chronicle) of the 1st Engineer Company, living in a camp in the forest, where they were much troubled by midges, but could indulge in the Polish love of mushroom-hunting. The building of the cubes was very 'zmudne' – tedious – and unpleasant, because of the continuous wind that covered the men with sand and cement, and their cement mixers constantly broke down.[8]

In December 1940 the 216th Independent Infantry Brigade, based in Aberdeen but under the direct command of North Highland Area, was responsible for defending the coast from 'Blowupnose' (a point on the coast south of Aberdeen) all the way to Spey Bay – a length of coastline of over 150km.[9] The brigade, which had been formed that month, comprised 12th Battalion Royal Scots, 13th Highland Light Infantry and 15th Argyll & Sutherland Highlanders. It was reported by their commander that, unfortunately, 'The troops under command, while numerous, have never constituted a very formidable fighting force'. Not all the men had rifles, and the Royal Engineer and Pioneer companies only had rifles for half and a quarter of their men respectively.[10]

In February 1941 the probable scale of attack on Scotland was expected to comprise two infantry divisions, two light tank battalions (stated as comprising about 400 tanks) and an airborne brigade. Up to half of this available force was expected to be directed against the vulnerable beaches between Aberdeen and Findhorn. The 154th Infantry Brigade of 51st Division was to hold itself ready to reinforce the coastline anywhere between Buchan Ness and Findhorn.[11] On 'Stand To'[12] an infantry battalion and a machine gun company from 8th Gordons were to occupy the Lossiemouth to Burghead coast. At the same time two platoons of 8th Gordons were to occupy previously selected positions on the Kingston to Lossiemouth beach and the Burghead to Findhorn beach in support of Area-commanded static troops and Home Guard on these beaches. Presumably their Vickers guns were to be positioned in the medium machine gun beach pillboxes. Even this long after Dunkirk the 126th Field Regiment, RA was still armed with a ragbag of guns, in three batteries, the first comprising eight 4.5-inch howitzers;

the second, four 75-mm guns and two 25-pounders; and the third, four 18-pounders. The two 25-pounder guns were 'the first guns of this type to come to the unit'. The 25-pounder, 75-mm and 60-pounder gun positions marked on the Findhorn to Burghead map (2 and 3 on Fig. 12.3) are probably the guns of 126th Field Regiment, RA and 71st Medium Regiment, RA.

From late March 1941 6th Training Battalion, Royal Engineers, in Elgin was to be responsible for the defence of the town and the coast from Kingston to the mouth of the River Lossie – basically the single stretch of beach at Innes Links, east of Lossiemouth. The battalion had artillery support from the 60-pounders of the 71st Medium Regiment, RA, (1 on Fig. 12.9) covering the whole Lossiemouth East beach as far as Spey Bay, and two troops of 297th Field Battery, RA (4.5in howitzers, part of 126th Field Regiment) positioned further east (2 and 3 on Fig. 12.9), to cover the west and east portions of the beach. 68th Pioneer Company was to defend the beach from Lossiemouth westwards to Burghead, with support from 490th Battery, RA.[13]

By July 1941 153rd Infantry Brigade had taken on responsibility for counter-attacking Lossiemouth and Kinloss aerodromes, and the defence of the Findhorn to Portgordon beaches. Two 60-pounder guns were allocated for artillery support at Lossiemouth (with a secondary firing role on Spey Bay beach) and two 60-pounders for Kinloss were shown on the Burghead Bay map on the War Diary of 1st Battalion Black Watch.[14]

Scaffolding

In 1941, and the first two months of 1942, when beach scaffolding was being erected, huge quantities were earmarked for this section of coast, as follows, from west to east (listed 21 November 1941): Findhorn to Burghead (7 miles); Lossiemouth to Kingston (8 miles); Cullen Bay (1.5 miles); Sandend Bay (1 mile); and Banff Bay (1 mile). By February 1942, the situation was that of the 15 projected miles between Kingston and Findhorn none had been erected, although 85 per cent of the material needed had been dumped on site. Major General Grant, Commander of North Highland District, considered that erecting scaffolding was a distraction from the men's proper defensive role.[15] The order to stop erecting scaffolding in the UK was given in March 1942 and hundreds of tons of steel were just abandoned on the beaches.[16]

Nairn to Burghead

In the May 1940 list of vulnerable beaches, 'Nairn to Burghead' appears as a beach 16 miles long, which fairly closely matches the distance between the two towns.

On the beach lists for April 1941 and October 1941 'Nairn' appears as a separate entry, apparently referring to the beach west of the town. In both lists it appears as protected by mines and wire only. In 1940 the section of beach from Nairn to the mouth of Findhorn Bay was backed, as now, by forestry plantation, albeit not so dense during the war. Despite the barrier provided by the trees, this section of beach was clearly considered at risk from glider or seaplane landings, as the sand bars, salt marsh and lagoons, extending for over 10km, were obstructed in 1940 by the erection of hundreds of anti-glider poles, of which a large proportion survive (Fig. 12.2). Admiral Dreyer, in his beach survey in August 1940, noted that anti-tank cubes were being built on the western side of Findhorn Bay to block tanks passing the east end of the dunes, and these are marked 1 on Fig. 12.3.[17]

Burghead Bay

In the beach lists for October 1940, April 1941 and October 1941 Burghead Bay appeared as a separate entry. The beach is the easternmost of a complex of long beaches and broad open bays.[18]

Admiral Dreyer surveyed the beach in August 1940, as follows:[19]

BURGHEAD westward to FINDHORN: 7 miles of beach judged suitable for tank landings. Anti-aircraft stakes placed the whole of its length . . . Triple Dannert wire rolls placed just below High Water Mark and reinforced concrete blocks along the edge of the sand dunes, just above High Water. Pillboxes for machine guns and anti-tank guns – 24 of former and 34 of latter to be placed every 1/4 mile along beach. Taken 2 months to complete

Figure 12.2.
Anti-glider poles on the salt-marsh and lagoons between Nairn and Findhorn (Author).

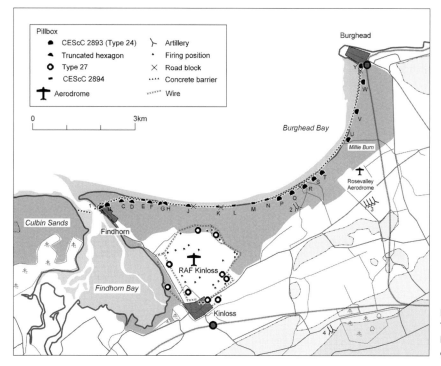

Figure 12.3.
The beach defences from Findhorn to Burghead and of RAF Kinloss.

blocking of this beach. Blocks at first made 4ft high – in process of being heightened by another foot. Blocks extend to below Low Water on eastern side of Findhorn Bay to seaward of Findhorn village.

There were substantial anti-invasion defences but this beach was also used for training for the D-Day landings; one or two of the structures recorded on the beach seem to be for this purpose, and some of the 1940–41 structures may also have been blown up for practice. Almost all the remains described below now lie well within the intertidal zone or at least on the beach: although mid-twentieth-century maps suggest that in 1940 they were well above the high-tide mark.

The anti-invasion barrier comprised a line of cubes (double at the west, but mainly single) starting below low water in Findhorn Bay (1 on Fig. 12.3), on the west, running for about 1km across the links north of the village of Findhorn until it met the beach, where it turned along the beach for about 3km. There was one original break in the line (near pillboxes L and M) but otherwise the cubes ran for about 5.5km in an unbroken line to Burghead. There were three types of pillbox (Fig. 12.4; 12.5; 12.6): at the western end were seven truncated hexagons (some of which survive) set behind the cubes or in the line, probably a variant of Type 22, with three embrasures facing the sea and often with a rear porch (pillboxes A, C, D, F, G and H on Fig. 12.3). The central sector was dominated by four rectan-

Figure 12.4. (left) Pillboxes G and H, truncated hexagons, on Burghead beach. They were originally within a salient in the line of cubes, which has long since disappeared into the sand (Author).

Figure 12.5. (right) A small machine gun pillbox of type CEScC 2894 on Burghead beach (Author).

gular medium machine gun pillboxes of type CEScC 2894 which would have sat within the cube line (K, L, M and N), but a fifth lay to the west (E). The western half of the beach contained nine CEScC 2893 (Type 24 variant) pillboxes originally behind and above the cubes, most of which are still visible. They had the characteristic heavy gun table and large apertures, and also external cast concrete walls covering the door. The remains of three roadblocks through the cubes onto the beach survive, near pillboxes J, K and R.

In October 1940 (and until June 1941) the beach from Findhorn to Burghead was the responsibility of 200th Pioneer Company (with only around 100 men) as part of a defence scheme led at first by 12th Cameronians and later by 154th Infantry Brigade.[20] Pillbox E was marked on a 1st Battalion Black Watch map of the bay (October 1941) as the location of a medium machine gun position, firing east, and the centre of the positions of D Company[21] as well as the position of a 3-inch mortar. Pillboxes Q, R, S and T (Fig. 12.3) were marked on the same map[22] as the centre of the positions of B Company, with a 3-inch mortar. A pair of 25-pounder guns was sited just behind (2 on Fig. 12.3). Just west of pillbox Q a length of about 95m of concrete with a corrugated surface is visible, now lying almost flat. While on the line of the cubes, it seems more likely that this was a length of anti-tank wall erected for D-Day training, as it closely resembles training structures (including replica sections of the German 'Atlantic Wall') erected at Sheriffmuir in Stirlingshire.[23] On the map of October 1941 Burghead is shown as being held by A Company of 1st Battalion Black Watch, with a 3-inch mortar.[24] The same map shows the positions of four 75-mm gun (3) and two 60-pounders, well behind the beach (4), to provide supporting fire.

The major bomber aerodrome at Kinloss was immediately behind the western part of the beach, and its satellite airfield at Rosevalley near the middle portion.

Analysis of wartime and post-war aerial photographs by RCAHMS has revealed the location of at least nine Type 27 pillboxes at Kinloss. While this seems a large enough number, the Black Watch map dated October 1941 showed 20 or more other firing positions, indicating a considerable density of defence.

Between Burghead and Lossiemouth, the minor beaches at Hopeman and Covesea, in an area otherwise characterised by rocky shores and cliffs, did not seem to have been defended. The next major beach was that to the west of Lossiemouth, which was split into two parts – Covesea Links and Stotfield Links – by a rocky headland on which stands Covesea Lighthouse (Fig. 12.7). Immediately behind the links was the important RAF Bomber Command base at Lossiemouth. While few concrete defences were built, wartime aerial photographs reveal a large barbed wire enclosure around what may have been a wide-embrasured gun-house (1 on Fig. 12.7). Three clearly marked minefields were visible on a 1941 aerial photograph: one south of the gun position (2); the largest running for about 1km, from the foot of the steeper slope at the west end (3), with a short length of anti-tank cubes; and the third on the shore below the lighthouse (4).

To the east of the lighthouse the defences of Stotfield Links were more substantial. Four CEScC 2893 pillboxes (Type 24 variants) have been recorded, but only pillbox A, on a crag in front of the lighthouse, survives, dominating the beaches to east and west (Fig. 12.8). It has been provided with a cladding of stones to help disguise it. From the outcrop to the east there was originally a single line of anti-tank cubes along the back of the beach, much of which is still visible. By May 1942, however, about half of the cubes were already unstable or overturned by the sea.[25] The cubes terminate close to Lossiemouth in a line running about 100m into the sea. At the point where they turn out to sea there are the remains of a roadblock, presumably controlling access onto the beach. Behind the beach on

Figure 12.6.
CEScC 2893 (Type 24 variant) pillbox P on Burghead Beach. The cubes show signs of having been raised in height by a foot, the point at which some of those visible in this photograph have failed. Admiral Dreyer noted the raising of the height of the cubes when he visited in August 1940 (Author).

179

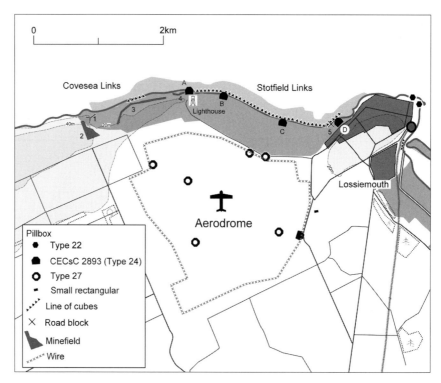

Figure 12.7.
The beaches west of Lossiemouth and the aerodrome.

the aerodrome were at least six Type 27 pillboxes (identified on aerial photographs). Two further pillboxes at the east may have been a Type 22 or 24 and a rectangular one. The boundary shown on Figure 12.7 is of the rather limited extent of the aerodrome prior to expansion later in the war.

Lossiemouth East

This beach appeared on the lists of vulnerable beaches of May and October 1940 and April and October 1941. There were two airfields behind the beach: Elgin/Milltown, in 1940 a satellite to Lossiemouth, less than 2km behind the beach; and a civilian airfield, about which little is known, at Lunan Wood, 3.5km up the Spey from its mouth, which was noted as immobilised on lists of 1940, but was not mentioned in later lists.

On pre-war mapping, the dunes between Lossiemouth and Kingston, at the mouth of the Spey, now densely forested, were relatively clear of trees, and the central part of the beach has since seen the formation of a high shingle bank, changing its appearance considerably.

Two Type 22 pillboxes, visible on wartime aerial photographs, covered the mouth of Lossiemouth harbour (Fig. 12.7) and a single line of anti-tank cubes, about 150m long, blocked access from the mouth of the river into the town. These

Figure 12.8.
CEScC 2893 (Type 24 variant) pillbox, with stone cladding to aid camouflage, on the headland below Covesea lighthouse (Author).

cubes have been removed or buried under subsequent remodelling of the quayside.

The coast to the east of the town required no engineered anti-invasion defences for the first 3km, as an effective barrier was provided by the River Lossie and the Innes and Spynie Canals. Anti-invasion defences were only built from the point where a subsidiary channel of the Innes Canal originally branched off to the north-east. A small causeway between the main and subsidiary channels was blocked by a line of eight anti-tank cubes and a roadblock, covered by a CEScC 2893 pillbox (A in Figs 12.9, 12.10). The subsidiary channel still holds water and would have made a formidable anti-tank barrier for its entire length of 750m, which was covered by a further three pillboxes: a rectangular CEScC 2894 medium machine gun pillbox (B in Fig. 12.9) and two CEScC 2893s (C and D). The rectan-

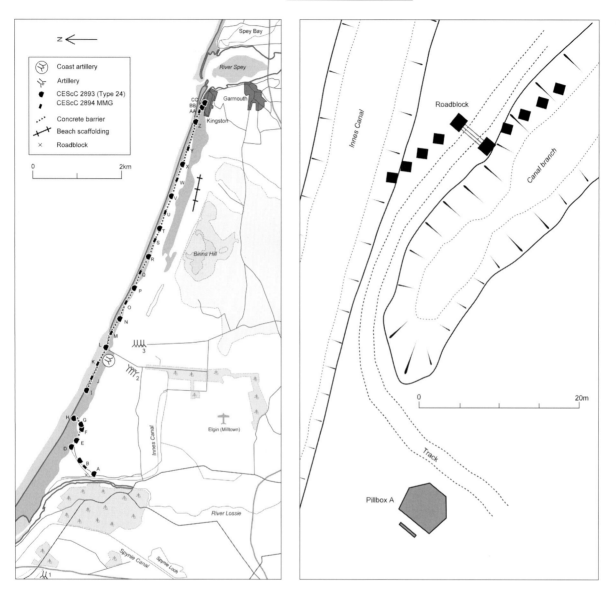

gular pillbox is very well preserved, to the extent that it still has lengths of wire netting tented out from the roof to a short distance from the wall foot, to hold vegetation for camouflage (visible on Fig. 12.11).

From the north-east end of the canal branch for 8km to the village of Kingston at the mouth of the River Spey runs the longest and best-preserved length of anti-invasion cubes and pillboxes in Scotland. It is also, because of its simplicity and regularity, one of the easiest to describe. A line of anti-tank cubes, single apart from the easternmost section, stretched from the canal to the beach. Within this sector of cubes sit three CEScC 2893 pillboxes (E, F and G on Fig. 12.9) which

Figure 12.9. (opposite left) The beach between Lossiemouth (beyond the edge of the map, to the west) and Kingston on Spey. This is the most completely surviving section of beach defence in Scotland. Elgin (Milltown) aerodrome may have been operating as a decoy site for Lossiemouth aerodrome in 1940-41 and seems only to have become operational in 1943. The pillbox and roadblock at the western end of the complex are shown in more detail on Fig. 12.10.

Figure 12.10. (opposite right) Road block and pillbox A closing the track between the Innes Canal and its north-easterly branch, at the west end of the defences between Lossiemouth and Kingston. (Author, for Forestry Commission Scotland)

Figure 12.11. (left) Rectangular pillbox B of type CEScC 2894 with surviving wire netting to hold camouflage (Author).

occupy the points where the line of cubes changes direction. A fifth CEScC 2893 (pillbox H), now tumbled on the beach, originally sat on top of the beach dune in advance of the line of cubes.

There is a break of about 500m in which the sand dunes appear to have provided an adequate barrier before the single line of cubes recommences. It then runs unbroken for about 6.8km to Kingston, with, along the whole length apart from the western end, a CEScC 2893 Type 24 variant alternating with a rectangular CEScC 2893 medium machine gun pillbox (Figs 12.12, 12.13). The final surviving pillbox is a rectangular CEScC 2894 (Y). From this point to Kingston the cubes (a double line for the last few hundred metres) and the pillboxes have now either been buried in the shingle or removed. The pillboxes are of a remarkably consistent plan; all have bulletproof walls with simple, fairly large embrasures for medium machine guns. All have low rear doors covered by a low external wall, and in the CEScC 2893s, usually flanked by two small rifle loops.

A unique feature of this complex of defences is a very well-preserved 6-inch gun battery at Innes Links, just behind the line of cubes (Fig. 12.14). It was one of the emergency batteries erected in 1940–41 but was the only one in Scotland built to defend a beach. The battery has two gun-houses (with crew shelters and ready-use ammunition stores), two searchlight housings on both flanks, a battery observation post, forward and main magazines, and three engine houses, all largely roofed and intact (Figs 12.15, 12.16). In addition there are about 18 concrete bases for accommodation buildings. The contract for the battery's construction was signed on 28 April 1941.[26] Behind the beach, two troops (eight guns) of 4.5-inch

Figure 12.12. (left) Rectangular pillbox K of type CEScC 2894 for a medium machine gun, at a change of angle in the line of cubes (Author).

Figure 12.13. (right) Pillbox 'I' on the beach between Lossiemouth and Kingston (Author).

howitzers of 297 Battery, RA (of 126 Field Regiment) were placed to cover the beach to east and west (marked 2 and 3 on Fig. 12.9), with heavy artillery cover provided from a point south-east of Lossiemouth (1 on Fig. 12.9).[27]

The defence of the beach from Covesea Lighthouse to Kingston was, in October 1940, the responsibility of three companies of the 12th Cameronians.[28] While the battalion continued to have a role in defending the beach, static units assumed a greater role in the defence of the coast from Findhorn to Kingston: Findhorn to Burghead – 200th Pioneer Company (with about only 100 men); Burghead to Lossiemouth – 150th Pioneer Company; Lossiemouth to Kingston – 6th Training Battalion, RE while the villages of Lossiemouth, Kingston and Garmouth had a Home Guard garrison.[29] This arrangement lasted until early 1941, when 12th Cameronians moved to Caithness.[30]

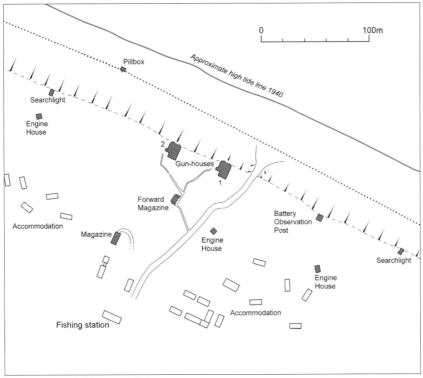

Figure 12.14. (above) The two gun-houses of the 6-inch gun battery at Innes Links, east of Lossiemouth, behind the line of cubes (Author).

Figure 12.15. (left) Plan of the 6-inch battery complex at Innes Links, redrawn from a plan by AOC Archaeology, but with an approximate tide line for 1940–41 (Author, for Forestry Commission Scotland).

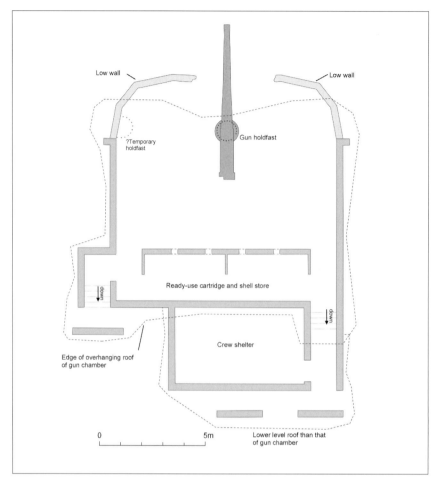

Figure 12.16.
Gun-house 2 of the Innes Links 6-inch gun battery, redrawn from a plan by AOC Archaeology Ltd, with the addition of the plan view of the gun. The irregular roof shape seems to have been designed to break up the line of the building as seen from the air (Author, for Forestry Commission Scotland).

Speymouth to Fraserburgh

The last of the long beaches in this part of the coast runs for about 4.2km from the mouth of the Spey eastwards to Portgordon, where the coast becomes less suitable for landings. This beach seems never to have been heavily defended, as it was probably too distant from any strategic target, such as a port or airfield. However, two Norcon pillboxes have been noted about 3km east of the river's mouth.[31] It is not until Portnockie–Cullen that the next vulnerable beach is encountered. However, North Highland Area was preparing a number of small harbours on this coast for immobilisation: Portgordon, Buckpool, Buckie, Findochty, Portnockie, Cullen, Portsoy, Whitehills, Banff, Macduff, Rosehearty and Sandhaven.[32] Of these, only Buckie and Macduff were identified at Scottish Command level.[33]

Cullen Sands appeared as a vulnerable beach on the Scottish Command October 1940 and April and October 1941 lists; it also appeared on a North

Figure 12.17.
The pillboxes (Bren gun to left, anti-tank gun Type 28 to right), at the eastern end of the double line of cubes blocking Sandend beach (Author).

Highland Area list of beaches in its defence plan of December 1940.[34] Part of the bay was blocked by a double line of anti-tank cubes on the east side of the Burn of Cullen, barring access into the village, and a double line (with a hexagonal pillbox, now destroyed), about 400m long, covered the eastern third of the main beach.

Five kilometres to the west of Cullen, the sandy beach at Sandend appeared on Scottish Command lists of vulnerable beaches of October 1940, April 1941 and October 1941, as well as in the *North Highland Area Defence Scheme* of December 1940.[35] It was defended by an almost classic arrangement: three pillboxes, well-positioned to enfilade the beach while themselves being protected from fire from the sea, covered a double line of cubes running along the beach and blocking the mouths of two burns. Most of the defences survive. One pillbox is that rarity on a beach, a Type 28 for an anti-tank gun (Fig. 12.17). This one has no Bren chamber, as covering fire was provided by an adjacent Bren gun pillbox, of indeterminate type, set into the hill-slope. A very similar pillbox sits at the western end of the bay, among buildings which protect it from seaward fire.

Boyndie Bay, just west of Banff, did not appear on any Scottish Command lists of vulnerable beaches. However, it does seem to have been obstructed by anti-glider poles and was included on a list of beaches in the *North Highland Area Defence Scheme* of December 1940 and again in 1941, when it was described as 'prepared for defence'.[36] Macduff harbour, unlike that at Banff, had water in it at all states of the tide, but the only recorded defence structure for the two harbours was a pillbox at the head of the east breakwater of Banff harbour.

The area between Spey Bay and Fraserburgh was not heavily manned for defence. In October 1940, 13th Battalion Highland Light Infantry was responsible for defending the coast between Spey Bay and Troup Head, with 12th Cameron Highlanders to the west and 12th Royal Scots at Fraserburgh. The four companies of the HLI were spread thinly, each responsible for a section of coast 12–15km long. The Banff Company of the Home Guard (240 men) reinforced the coast defences from Whitehills (west of Banff) to Troup Head.[37]

Spey Stop-Line

Only one anti-tank stop-line was identified in the western part of Aberdeen Sub-area – the line of the River Spey (Fig. 12.1), which appeared in an amendment of the Aberdeen Sub-area Defence Scheme, dated 27 April 1941,[38] and on a Scottish Command list of stop-lines in July 1941.[39] The River Spey provided a substantial barrier to movement from north-west to south-east. Apart from the coastal strip, the high ground to the north-west of the river effectively channelled movement to a very limited number of routes approaching the river from that side. Eight roadblocks have been documented, at the bridges across the river between Fochabers, near the mouth of the river, and Grantown. There were no defensive constructions directly associated with the River Spey line, but a scatter of pillboxes has been recorded across the counties of the north-east, and a group of these lay not far south-east of the Spey at Craigellachie and Dufftown, probably as part of a focal point defence.

THE EAST COAST OF ABERDEEN SUB-AREA

The east-facing coast of the Sub-area has two types of beach formation: bays such as Fraserburgh Bay and Cruden Bay, and extensive continuous beaches, which may be partly subdivided by river outlets, such as the long beach between Sands of Forvie and Aberdeen harbour. The coast between Fraserburgh and Aberdeen measures about 75km, of which some 47km is sandy beach of the kind considered most vulnerable to a landing. The longest continuous section, between the Rivers Ythan and Don, measures over 15km. In 1940–41 this area was considered particularly vulnerable because of the proximity of its beaches to Peterhead and Aberdeen, and to aerodromes close to the coast. The landscape for many miles behind the eastern beaches was open, rolling lightly wooded countryside, good tank country, with few natural barriers to movement, with an extensive and complex road network and, in 1940, an extensive rail network.

Ports and Aerodromes

In June 1940 General Carrington noted that 'Aberdeen, if captured, would be capable of maintaining a large force.'[40] Peterhead was included in all lists of 'minor defended ports' and ports that had to be prepared for immobilisation, while Aberdeen was the only civilian 'major defended port' listed north of Dundee. In April 1940 the position of the 6-inch guns to rearm the Victorian battery at Torry Point, covering the approaches to Aberdeen harbour, was approved; the city was one of four places in the UK where accelerated installation was required, the holdfasts for the guns being despatched on 14 May 1940 (Fig. 6.3). The Peterhead battery comprised two 6-inch guns on Salthouse Head, at the south-west end of the South Breakwater of the harbour. The final configuration of the Aberdeen batteries was two pairs of 6-inch guns, facing north and south-east from the Girdle Ness headland. In December 1940 five harbours were to be prepared for immobilisation on the east coast of the Sub-area: to the 'usual suspects' (Fraserburgh, Peterhead and Aberdeen) were added Boddam and Port Errol, both of which were very small.[41]

In 1940–41 there were two aerodromes very close to the coast near Fraserburgh and Peterhead. The more northerly, Fraserburgh (Inverallochy), between the beaches of Fraserburgh Bay and St Combs, was under construction in 1941 and was included as a Category A aerodrome from March. The major airbase at Peterhead was under construction in 1940–41 and appeared on a list of aerodromes to be defended as early as August 1940, and as a Category A aerodrome by December. It was the only one in the area to require a battle HQ and a suite of pillboxes. On 24 June 1941 ten pillboxes were listed to be built there, nine of which were for 'internal' defence, that is, against airborne troops landing on the aerodrome rather than an assault on its perimeter.[42] The surviving pillboxes are of an aerodrome defence design known as 'Mushrooms', because of their low domed roof.[43]

The aerodrome at Dyce also had a suite of defensive pillboxes and appeared in lists of aerodromes to be defended in August and October 1940; it had been reduced to a Category C aerodrome by December 1940 after the relocation of the fighter sector control. On the night of 15–16 June 1941 the defences of Dyce were tested by a troop of No. 6 Commando at 01.15 hours, attempting to penetrate the defences in teams of three to eight men. While some were captured by the RAF guard, the perimeter wire was cut in two or three places and much damage could have been done to aeroplanes.[44] There were two aerodromes in use inland, carrying non-military traffic diverted from Dyce; first, Kintore, which was replaced in time by East Fingask.

Manning

By July 1940, 682nd General Construction Company, RE was erecting wire and building pillboxes at various aerodromes up the east coast, including Dyce.[45] From 14 August 1940, 1st Battalion Gordon Highlanders formed a mobile defence column between Buchan Ness and Aberdeen 'dashing in commandeered buses and lorries to Rattray Head and other points where their presence appeared to be urgently required'.[46]

Aberdeen Sub-area was created on 5 October 1940, and 216th Independent Infantry Brigade (of four 'beach' battalions and a Field Regiment, RA) was established in Aberdeen by the beginning of December.[47] As already noted, while formidable on paper, it was recorded that, 'The troops under command, while numerous, have never constituted a very formidable fighting force'.[48] The brigade's role in the eastern part of the Sub-area was to defend the coastline and to counter-attack against any enemy attack on Dyce aerodrome. Home Defence troops (10th Gordons) defended Vulnerable Points and provided the garrison of Dyce, supported by Royal Engineers.[49] 98th Pioneer Company patrolled roads and railways in the Stonehaven area and manned the Cowie Line (see below).[50]

In addition to the heavy 6-inch coast batteries at Peterhead and Aberdeen, 942nd Defence Battery (Mobile), RA provided further cover for the beaches in the area (and at Wick), originally with ten static 4-inch naval guns, which were replaced in April 1941 by eight 18-pounders. By the end of May 1940 the 18-pounders were themselves replaced by 75-mm field guns which, in June 1941, were moved from beach defence to provide artillery cover for the aerodromes in the area.[51]

In February 1941 it was reported for the area that 'In general the concrete work, including pillboxes and anti-tank obstacles, is nearing . . . completion. Minefields are some 50% finished . . . On the vulnerable beaches the static defences at present consist of one line of pillboxes, roughly a quarter of a mile apart. So far no works have been sited to give depth to the beach defences.'[52] Given the near completion of these defences, the instructions, recorded on the same file in the same month, for the siting and construction of further beach defences seems difficult to explain.

Throughout this period the three brigades of 51st Division (152nd, 153rd and 154th) had roles to play in the event of an invasion in support of the more 'static' troops who would bear the first brunt (which included 216th Brigade in the north-east). In February 1941, 152nd Brigade was to be prepared to occupy the Rattray Head beach.[53] The tasks of 153rd Brigade included (one or more of) occupying any part of the Sub-area's coastline from Milton Ness (at the Sub-area's southern boundary) to Banff; placing a battalion with a machine gun company on the beach from north of Aberdeen to Newburgh; occupying Aberdeen beach with the whole brigade group;[54] and counter-attacking Dyce airport. The 154th Brigade was located at this time in the north-west part of the Sub-area; it and the other two brigades had roles in the Moray Firth coast sector of the Sub-area, and were intended to act in mutual support.[55]

The 216th Independent Infantry Brigade (without 15th Argyll & Sutherland Highlanders, which transferred to Orkney) moved away from the north-east of Scotland to Northumberland in March 1941.[56] To reinforce the weakened defences, 70th (Young Soldier) Battalion Argyll & Sutherland Highlanders, apart from two companies, was moved from Glasgow to Peterhead and Kincardineshire.[57] 11th Lancashire Fusiliers also moved to the area, as 'the only normal infantry [battalion] under command [of Aberdeen Sub-area] and as they were comparatively well trained and equipped they provided a considerable strengthening'.[58] In March 1941 this battalion was responsible for the defence of Cruden Bay, Peterhead (with the Home Guard), Fraserburgh (with the Home Guard and 128th Pioneer Company) and for any counter-attack needed on Peterhead and Fraserburgh aerodromes.[59] 70th (YS) Argyll & Sutherland Highlanders was to provide the garrison of the two aerodromes, as well as guarding seven Vulnerable Points (including the four radar stations) and contributing a company to the defence of Aberdeen.

In March 1941 Aberdeen city was defended not only by a company of 10th (Home Defence) Gordon Highlanders but also by three Home Guard battalions, the Infantry Training Centre of the Gordon Highlanders (although during 1941 the Infantry Training Centre was so weak that it had to be relieved of its role in the defence of the city),[60] 50th Pioneer Company (which had a vital role in defending the 6-inch coast guns),[61] and the men of the two 6-inch coast batteries and two anti-aircraft batteries.[62] In the same month the Canadian Forestry Corps was tasked with defending the crossings of the Dee at Banchory, Kincardine O'Neil and Aboyne, along with the Home Guard.[63]

In June 1941 51st Division had a brigade group in each of Inverurie, Turriff and Elgin. In the same month the C-in-C Scotland noted the importance of forces being placed south of the Forth, but 'could not agree to the emptying of BUCHAN and MORAY' because the beaches would be left undefended.[64] At the same time, the change of emphasis of defence away from the beaches to the aerodromes (after the loss of Crete) led to the reorganisation of beach artillery. In addition to the 75-mm guns of 942nd Defence Battery (Mobile), RA already mentioned, four 60-pounder guns near Rattray Head were to be split between Fraserburgh, to cover the port and the landing ground at Inverallochy, and Peterhead to cover the new aerodrome (although still capable of firing on Peterhead beaches). With the growing emphasis on mobility for the Field Force, the defence of the beaches and towns was increasingly devolving on static support troops and the Home Guard; by June 1941 responsibility for the defence of Peterhead had, for example, devolved entirely onto the Home Guard.[65]

Aberdeen was the base for Armoured Train No. 11 from the end of July 1940, and it made a series of reconnaissance sorties for 51st Division and the Aberdeen Garrison in August, as far north-west as Fort George (see pp. 79–81) and as far south as Broughty Ferry, near Dundee. The report of the train's commander was that the train would have little effect in the undulating and wooded country of the interior of the county, but Dyce and Inverurie aerodromes could be covered by its fire. Neither the beach at Cruden Bay nor the harbour at Peterhead were in sight of the railway and the train could not therefore provide supporting fire.[66]

Fraserburgh

In April 1941, Fraserburgh had a scheme of defence based on a perimeter split into three sectors: the north end of Fraserburgh Bay round the shore of the town, and two sectors covering the outskirts of the town. The coast sector was the most heavily defended (a company of 11th Lancashire Fusiliers with three Bren guns); the two shoreward sectors were manned by 128th Pioneer Company and the Home Guard. 67th Pioneer Company was erecting Dannert and barbed wire obstacles round the town in August 1940 and three pillboxes at the harbour.[67]

Fraserburgh Bay lies between Kinnaird Head to the west (occupied by the burgh of Fraserburgh) and Cairnbulg Head to the east (Fig. 12.18). For most of its length the bay is backed by a single high dune ridge, up to 15m high, which seems to have provided a barrier adequate to stop tanks, except at particular points, where concrete obstacles were erected. The harbour, which lies at the western end of the bay, was protected by at least three pillboxes, a Type 27 on the breakwater, a Type 24 on the central pier and one of unknown type, and whose precise location is not known, on the north breakwater.

Short rows of anti-tank cubes were built in three places in the westernmost part of the bay; the first closed an easy exit from the north-west extremity (1 on Fig. 12.18), the second and third obstructed a culvert and a blow-out in the dunes, just east of the esplanade (2 and 3 on Fig. 12.18). The wall of the esplanade itself would have provided an adequate anti-tank barrier. A barbed wire enclosure (visible on aerial photographs) from the east end of the esplanade to behind the line of cubes suggested the presence of a minefield. Three pillboxes were built in a north-north-east to south-south-west line over about 500m: nearest the sea was a Type 22 (A on Fig. 12.18), which survives; then a Type 24, probably one of the CEScC 2893 medium machine gun variants (B); and finally a Type 27 (C), the last possibly associated with a wartime radio installation. A fourth pillbox – another Type 24/CEScC 2893 (D) – was visible on a 1943 aerial photograph where a blow-out in the dunes left an access open to the south; there was a complex firing trench to the east of it. All the surviving pillboxes from here to the Loch of Strathbeg are the medium machine gun CEScC 2893 type, with bulletproof walls and heavy gun table for a Vickers. Many of the embrasures have, however, subsequently been reduced to a Bren gun sized loop, with concrete blocks and steel

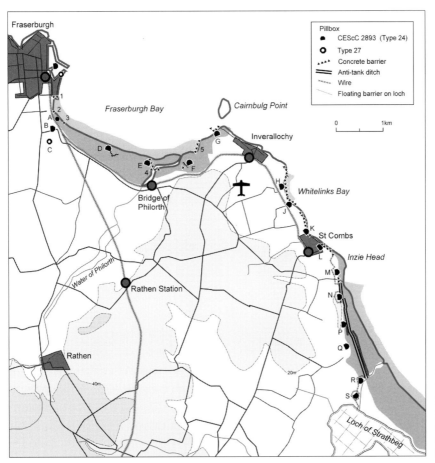

Figure 12.18.
The coast from Fraserburgh to the Loch of Strathbeg. The pattern of lines on the Loch shows the locations of floating anti-seaplane obstacles in spring 1941.

plate. Some of the survivors have a cruciform ricochet wall.

Four places in the eastern half of the bay required a concrete obstruction and three of these had a covering pillbox. First, the mouth of the Water of Philorth was blocked a little inland by a double line of cubes and the western bank was also obstructed (4 on Fig. 12.18) while pillbox E stood to the west. Second, a short line of about eight or ten cubes in the dunes blocked an access through the dunes called 'Maggie's Trink', covered by pillbox F. Third, a short stretch of beach to the east was obstructed by a double line of cubes about 170m long (5). Finally, a short line of cubes lay along and at right angles to the shore of the harbour at West Haven. Its accompanying pillbox (G) survives, and on a 1941 aerial photograph seemed to have been disguised as a fisherman's hut.

Inverallochy to St Combs

The RAF aerodrome of Fraserburgh, behind the village of Inverallochy, was under construction in 1941; it first appeared on a list of important aerodromes in the list of March of that year. The rocky shore of Inverallochy village did not seem to have required a concrete barrier, but the cubes resumed south-east of the village, just north of Whitelinks Bay, which was backed by the branch railway to St Combs. The barrier continued south-east to beyond St Combs, broken only where a rocky shore made it unnecessary. Many cubes have since been removed to shelter a simple harbour at Corse Craig, but many of the cubes north of St Combs survive. 67th Pioneer Company was building 'tank traps' at St Combs in late August 1940 and continued work there into November.[68] Four pillboxes were erected on this short stretch of coast: three on Whitelinks Bay (H, J and K on Fig. 12.18) and one just east of St Combs (L). The survivor (K) is of the CEScC 2893 pattern, with embrasures reduced in size.

St Combs to Loch of Strathbeg

South-east of St Combs, from where the line of anti-tank cubes ended at a steeper slope, a heavy barbed wire fence (clearly visible on low-level oblique aerial photographs taken in 1941) zigzagged along the plateau above the raised beach, behind another pillbox set on the edge of the plateau (M on Fig. 12.18). This pillbox, with a good field of fire over the dunes, marked the beginning of an unusual sector of the coast defences, running for over 13km from Inzie Head to St Fergus Links (Figs 12.18, 12.20); here the main anti-invasion barrier was provided by an anti-tank ditch rather than cubes or dragon's teeth. It may be in part because this section of coast was so exposed it was realised that anti-tank cubes on the beach would not have lasted long, and because most of the obstacle could be adapted from a deep pre-existing drainage ditch dug long before the war.

The anti-tank ditch started with a newly dug 350m-long section, south of pillbox M, which was sited to fire along it (Fig. 12.19). Two further pillboxes (N and P on Fig. 12.18) were placed about 100m behind the ditch. South of P there were minefields (very obvious on wartime aerial photographs); one 250m long on the landward side of the ditch and another about 1km long on the seaward side. The minefields seem to have been intended to strengthen a sector behind which there was no raised beach to impede exit from the links.

The anti-tank ditch/drain ends where it ran into the canalised channel that drains the Loch of Strathbeg; the junction was reinforced by anti-tank cubes, and a pillbox (R on Fig. 12.18, still surviving) covered it. A final pillbox (S, facing south) lay between R and the Loch.

The Loch of Strathbeg is over 3km long, running north-west to south-east about 1km behind the beach, and formed an adequate anti-tank barrier. The anti-invasion defences resumed at the eastern end of the loch, where the main barrier

Figure 12.19.
Pillbox M (on Fig. 12.18) viewed from the south along the anti-tank ditch (Author).

was again provided by an anti-tank ditch (looking recently dug in July 1941 aerial photographs). The loch itself was considered vulnerable to seaplane landings and was, by May 1941, one of three in Aberdeen Sub-area that had been immobilised by floating log obstacles.[69]

In March 1941 the entire beach from St Combs to the south-east was covered by a pair of 60-pounder guns of 71st Medium Regiment, RA located south-east of the Loch of Strathbeg (1 on Fig. 12.20).[70]

Loch of Strathbeg to Peterhead

The anti-tank ditch resumed at the south-east corner of the Loch of Strathbeg and ran, apparently continuously, in a shallow zigzag line, for almost 7km to the mouth of the Blackwater, which now forms the southern boundary of the St Fergus gas terminal (Fig. 12.20). The dune system is higher than to the north (up to 15m) but was very active and unstable in 1940, and the defence line was built inland of extensive areas of shifting sand-dune. The 73rd Pioneer Company was working on the anti-tank ditch south of the Loch from 25 July 1940 onwards; some men were diverted from erecting anti-glider poles to digging the ditch in late August.[71] The anti-tank ditch ran east and then south, along the back of the unstable dunes, skirting the high ground on which the first of six pillboxes on this 'corner' (A to F on Fig. 12.20, all surviving) were sited (Fig. 12.21). Two (C and

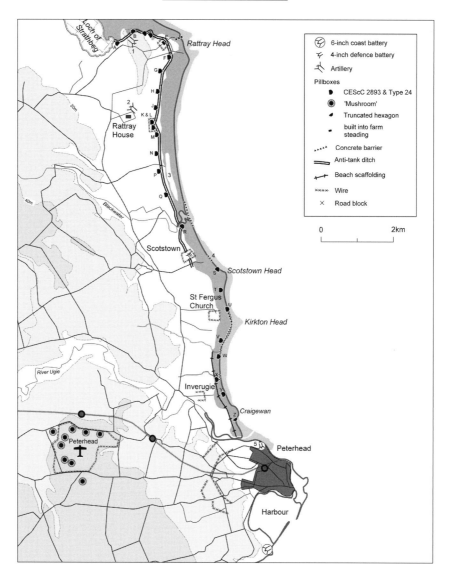

Figure 12.20.
The defences from the Loch
of Strathbeg to Peterhead.

D) covered a salient in the ditch and a third (E) was built into the corner of Seaton
Farm steading (Fig. 12.22). Pillboxes A and B occupied high ground and had
extensive fields of fire over the dunes and links to the north. The ditch continued
to the east of the shore station of Rattray Head lighthouse. Where the low-level
oblique aerial photographs are clear enough, there was a strong fence visible on
the enemy (eastern) edge of the anti-tank ditch. 67th Pioneer Company was
erecting wire in the Rattray Head area from late November 1940.[72]

The pattern of the ditch, with a pillbox every 400–600m, usually in a salient
where the ditch changed angle, continued for some distance. Near Rattray House
there was a group of three pillboxes (K, L and M on Fig. 12.20) concentrated over

Figure 12.21. (top)
The view from pillbox B (Fig. 12.20) over the Loch of Strathbeg and the dunes. The gorse in the foreground covers a complex of firing trenches (Author).

Figure 12.22. (left)
The adapted outbuilding at Seaton Farm; the two loopholes in the middle are within pillbox E; those to the right are outside it (Author).

a length of 350m, two of them within a single barbed wire enclosure. A small fragment of the anti-tank ditch survives here as a water-filled trench. A troop (equiped with two 60-pounders) of 71st Medium Regiment, RA was recorded in April 1941 as being positioned near Rattray House (2 on Fig. 12.20),[73] covering the beach from that point to Scotstown.

In the dunes in front of pillboxes N, P and Q (Fig. 12.20) a winter-flooding loch was 'immobilised' by having anti-glider ditches dug across it from east to west (3 on Fig. 12.20). Post-war aerial photographs show the characteristic wired outlines of minefields in this area (the position of mines in this case appear as regular patterns of post-clearance craters).

The pattern of ditch, with spaced pillboxes, continued to the Blackwater, the mouth of which was blocked at the head of the beach by a 790m-long triple line of dragon's teeth. A pillbox still stands close to the southern bank (R on Fig. 12.20), with firing positions to its south. All the surviving pillboxes on this stretch (and most do survive) are CEScC 2893 variants of Type 24, with the gun table and larger embrasures; the embrasures, however, tend to be the same width as those in the Moray Firth examples, although their height is lower. Many have subsequently been reduced in size for Bren guns.

South of the Blackwater it seems likely that another pre-existing water channel running south for about 1km may have provided an adequate anti-tank barrier to just beyond Scotstown Farm, which had around it a very large barbed wire enclosure. In the part of the enclosure nearer the sea, a 1941 aerial photograph shows the presence of a complex of trenches and weapon pits, and also what appear to be three open-topped concrete gun-houses facing south-south-east. The road to the beach south of Scotstown was blocked by anti-tank cubes at its beach terminal (4 on Fig. 12.20).

From this point south the emphasis of the defence shifted from an inland anti-tank ditch back to a more normal barrier on the beach. Two pillboxes have been recorded about 620m apart, to the north and south of Scotstown Head (S and T on Fig. 12.20).

Kirkton Head was obstructed by a line of cubes about 750m long, with two pillboxes (U and V on Fig. 12.20) with a wired strongpoint behind, around the St Fergus Church graveyard. There were three further lengths of cubes, just south of pillbox V and near pillboxes W and X, both blocking watercourses. The only surviving pillbox on this sector (W), unlike the others described to the north, had embrasures that were built from scratch for Bren guns, rather than reduced in size from medium machine gun embrasures. It also had an internal ricochet wall. It seems likely that the pillboxes in this sector (S to Y) were more typical Type 24 pillboxes than those on the beaches to the north and north-west. On the top surface of a cube blocking an unnamed burn north-west of Mains of Inverugie is inscribed 'James Alexander 17/10/40', which neatly dates this bit of work.

A final pillbox (Z on Fig. 12.20) – a truncated hexagon reminiscent of those at Findhorn – still sits at the northern end of the short beach between Craigewan and the mouth of the River Ugie. The fields behind the beach were criss-crossed by anti-glider ditches, and the steading of Mains of Inverugie was surrounded by a barbed wire fence, implying the presence of a strongpoint.

As noted above, until June 1941 the beaches north of Peterhead were covered by two 4-inch naval guns of 942nd Defence Battery (Mobile), RA in Buckhaven (5 on Fig. 12.20).[74]

The defences of the shore north of the River Ugie were reinforced by beach scaffolding.[75] Apparently 143rd Pioneer Company was erecting scaffolding on beaches in the area as early as October 1941.[76] In March 1942 a trace map was drawn, showing continuous scaffolding running from just north of the Ugie to the unnamed burn beside pillbox W. This was part of a request for permission to extend the scaffolding further north to the 'dragon's teeth' (actually cubes) protecting Kirkton Head, and south to the River Ugie. Permission was denied. In February 1942, 50,000 scaffolding tubes, as well as over 100,000 couplers, were lying in dumps on beaches between Peterhead and Fraserburgh.

Peterhead

By April 1941 Peterhead was defended by two perimeters, described in the Defence Scheme devised by 11th Lancashire Fusiliers.[77] The inner perimeter was held by the Peterhead Home Guard (with 71 men, 36 rifles, nine Lewis guns and one Vickers medium machine gun), the outer by a company of the Fusiliers (with eight Bren guns). It is not clear if the separate posts forming the perimeters were linked by wire but approximate lines are marked on the map.

Cruden Bay

Cruden Bay lies about 10km south-south-west of Peterhead. It was included in both the April and October 1941 lists of vulnerable beaches (Fig. 12.23). The height of the dunes and the cliffs behind meant that in the central and northern parts of the beach an anti-tank barrier was required only at possible exits from the beach, while the southern section needed a near-continuous barrier. There were seven pillboxes in this relatively small beach, from Port Errol harbour at its north, to its southern end. The three surviving pillboxes at Cruden Bay are simple bullet-proof Type 24 pillboxes, with no gun table (indeed no firing shelf of any kind) and with small embrasures for Bren or Lewis guns.

The port facilities at Port Errol were blocked, first by a massive concrete road-block to prevent access round the east end of the harbour (1 on Fig. 12.23) and, second, by a concrete wall to prevent vehicle access up a ramp from the outer harbour to the quay (Fig. 12.24). A pillbox lay south-east of the harbour but it is not known whether this was on the cliff-top or, more probably, on a rocky shelf at the level of the harbour.[78] A second pillbox (B on Fig. 12.23) still overlooks the entrance to the mouth of the Water of Cruden and the northernmost part of the beach (Fig. 12.25). The only vulnerable section of the frontage of Port Errol was obstructed by a single line of anti-tank cubes, which joined the end of a double line of concrete-filled sewer pipes blocking the mouth of the river (2 on Fig. 12.23).

The northern part of the beach was obstructed in two places: by a single line

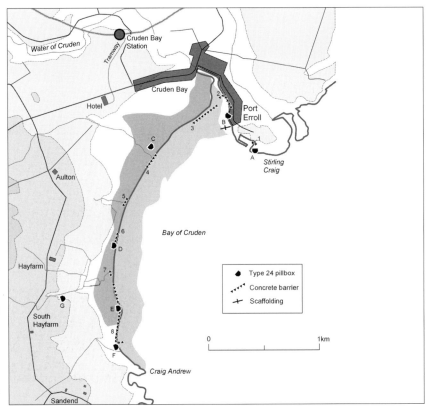

Figure 12.23. (right)
The defences of Cruden Bay.

Figure 12.24. (opposite top)
Complex block at the head
of the ramp out of the outer
harbour at Port Errol, Cruden
Bay, with the remains of a
massive concrete roadblock
behind (Author).

Figure 12.25. (opposite
below) Pillbox B at Port Errol,
Cruden Bay (Author).

of cubes about 270m long (3 on Fig. 12.23); and a line about 150m long that blocked a gap in the dunes formed by an unnamed burn (4). A pillbox (C on Fig. 12.23) was mentioned in this locality in the War Diary of 11th Battalion Lancashire Fusiliers in April 1941 but is not visible.[79] In the middle of the bay two short lines of cubes blocked a watercourse (5) and a low section of dunes (6); pillbox D, now almost overwhelmed by the dunes behind it, lay at the south end of the line. The southernmost part of the bay was blocked by a short line of cubes covering the mouth of a burn (7), and then, to the south, a continuous line of cubes (8), almost 1km long, ending in a short seaward turn onto a rock platform. A pillbox midway along the line (E) is not currently visible, but that covering the southern end of the line (F) survives in good condition. A final pillbox (G) was located on the only practicable exit from the southern part of the bay, as mentioned in the 1941 Lancashire Fusiliers Defence Scheme.[80]

The 50th Pioneer Company was wiring up Cruden Bay beach into January 1941. By the autumn of that year the area was garrisoned by the Norwegian Brigade, and the HQ of the Rifle Battalion and the HQ Company were based in the village.[81] The list of scaffolding for removal at the end of the war recorded only a very short length at Port Errol.[82]

The most detailed account of the defence of Cruden Bay was provided by 11th Lancashire Fusiliers in April 1941. The troops available were 'D' Company (with four Bren guns) and two platoons of HQ Company (No. 6 Platoon with two Brens and No. 5 (Pioneer) Company). The bay was split into four areas:

Area 1 Pillboxes G to D: No. 6 Platoon of HQ Company, with their two Brens.
Area 2 Pillbox C: a platoon of 'D' Company with two Brens.
Area 3 Estuary: No. 5 Platoon of HQ Company. Pillbox B was not mentioned.
Area 4 Pillbox A: a platoon of 'D' Company with two Brens.

The basis of the fire plan for the whole beach was to be two Bren guns each in pillboxes A, C and D. By June 1941, the burden of defence was to fall more heavily on the Home Guard – 'A' Company (less a platoon) of 1st Buchan Home Guard was responsible for Cruden Bay.[83]

Sands of Forvie to Aberdeen

For about 10km south-south-west of Cruden Bay the coast was not suitable for landing but, thereafter, for almost 25km from the Sands of Forvie southwards to Aberdeen harbour, it was. The beach is broken in only two places, by the estuaries of the Ythan and the Don. Behind the beach runs the main trunk road to Aberdeen, with its major harbour and the key aerodrome at Dyce. At first, the War Office files did not differentiate between the beaches north of Aberdeen, up to Hackley Head (that is, north of Forvie, north of the Ythan); in 1941 the beaches north and south of the mouth of the River Ythan were listed separately.[84]

The Sands of Forvie is a major dune system, the fifth largest and least man-disturbed of the large sand-dune systems in Britain, and important for both nature and archaeological conservation.[85] The northern portion lies over a rock platform which forms a cliff face at the coast; the southern part had a beach suitable for landing and appeared in the April and October 1941 lists of vulnerable beaches but was marked as blocked by minefields only.[86] Clearly this decision was changed at some point, as the whole of the beach, a length of about 2km, was blocked by a single line of cubes visible on 1940s aerial photographs, and a CEScC 2893 type pillbox survives on the northern bank of the Ythan (A on Fig. 12.26). The 143rd Pioneer Company was working on defence works north of Newburgh in October 1941, in bad weather.[87] The 4-inch naval guns of 942nd Defence Battery (Mobile), RA were positioned at Newburgh Bar, apparently on the northern bank.[88]

The southern 'shoulder' of the mouth of the Ythan is dominated by a high sand-hill, from which point south there is a continuous line of anti-tank cubes

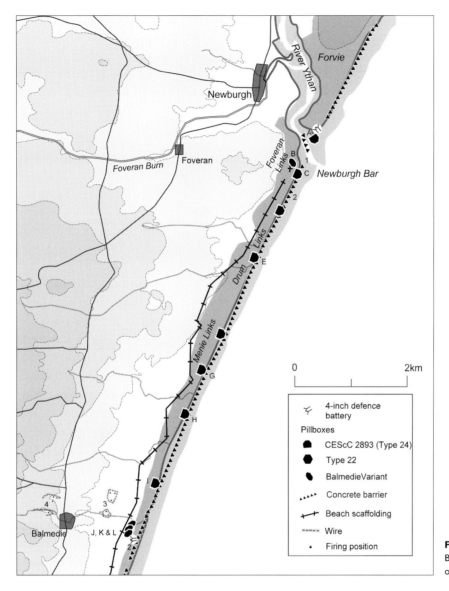

Figure 12.26.
Beach defences from Sands of Forvie to Balmedie.

for approximately 9.5km. The shoulder itself was obstructed by a short run of cubes, which dog-legged out into the river. The line of cubes southwards was covered by fire from a series of medium machine gun pillboxes of the CEScC 2893 pattern, many of which survive.

The defences just south of the Ythan, on Foveran Links, were quite complex. The high sand-hill immediately behind the beach seems to have provided a fairly substantial natural barrier, but immediately to the south and west of it there was, and still is, a low, shallow 'valley' providing an easy exit northwards from the beach. The line of anti-tank cubes ran across its seaward entrance, but for some

Figure 12.27.
Pillbox variant and scaffolding at Foveran Links, Newburgh; the unusual concrete structures illustrated in Figs 12.28 and 12.29 lie just to the top left of the photograph (Author).

reason a length of beach scaffolding (still surviving) was built running north–south along the bottom of the 'valley'. It may be that minor changes in topography have made the original purpose of the scaffolding unclear. The northern end of the scaffolding was dominated by an unusual pillbox (B on Fig. 12.26) – a rectangle in shape with its corners knocked off (Fig. 12.27). The pillbox has two embrasures on the long, west-facing side and one each in the corners and sides. Its entrance is located in a porch to the south-east. The pillbox is constructed in a hard, bright red brick and resembles a group of pillboxes at Balmedie, to the south (p. 207) (pillboxes J, K and L on Fig. 12.26). What appear to be the blown-up fragments of a further reinforced concrete pillbox with bulletproof walls (C) are visible at the southern end of the 'valley'.

South-east of the pillbox a narrow 'pass' through the crest of the sand ridge has been fortified. Its eastern end is blocked by two thick concrete walls running across the 'pass'. The western end is likewise blocked by two walls, but the western of this pair (which faces and probably originally looked down upon the rear of pillbox B) has firing loops angled steeply downwards into the valley. In the centre of the wall is an opening, leading into a lower flat-roofed western extension, now buried in sand, which has a single further firing loop (Figs 12.28, 12.29). The landward wall with the seagull-wing profile is bulletproof, while the straight wall 4m behind it is shellproof. In the tops of both walls there are four sockets arranged in such a way as to suggest that beams between them supported a roof of some sort. About 30m seaward, at the other end of the 'pass', the pattern is replicated: a seagull-wing plan wall facing outward (but in this case shellproof and without firing embrasures) and a bulletproof straight wall behind it, towards the 'pass'. This wall has eight firing embrasures, sloping downwards, mirroring those on the wall inland. These have no sockets for roof beams. The two pairs of walls

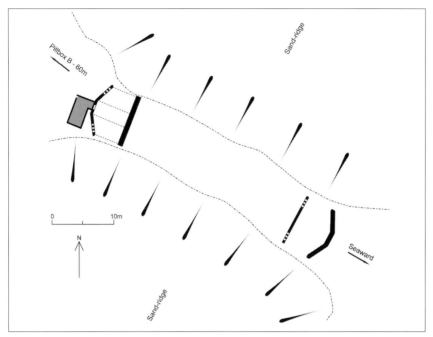

Figure 12.28.
The fortified 'pass' in the sand-hill at Foveran Links. The north-west pair of walls seems to form a firing position overlooking the beach exit to the west; the pair of walls to the south-east seems designed to protect the rear of the firing position. Sand movement continues to reveal features here and this plan will no doubt have to be amended in the future.

Figure 12.29.
The walls of the north-western point of its fortified position (Author).

seem to form a defended position within the upper part of the sand-hill, with fire being concentrated inland towards the beach exit.

The line of anti-tank cubes to the south is remarkable for one of the most elaborately decorated cubes recorded (Fig. 12.30; 2 on Fig. 12.26), featuring a caricature of a recumbent Hitler about to receive a bomb on his forehead with another, anonymous figure on the other side, also being bombed. The centrepiece is an elaborate heart pierced with an arrow and bearing the words 'Louis Lawson BORN

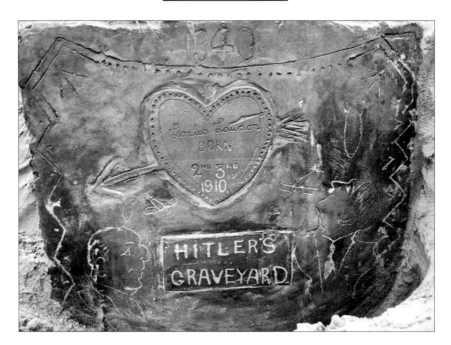

Figure 12.30.
Louis Lawson's 'work of art' on a cube at Newburgh (Author).

2nd 3rd 1910', above the title 'HITLER'S GRAVEYARD'. One face of another cube just to the south has an incised face of Hitler and, on the rear, an illegible name and a date of birth. Further decorated cubes have been reported between here and Aberdeen, including one inscribed 'A Humphrey 1940' and one with scribbled initials and swastikas (not located).

The cubes in this area have large pieces of granite and other rock set into their tops. There is, among the cubes, the occasional concrete-filled sewer pipe (or a group of up to a dozen or so) (Fig. 8.3) on flat concrete bases. The movement of the coast since the war has, in some places, buried the line of cubes, with the odd one visible in the face of the dunes, or where the line crossed the mouth of a burn. In many places cubes are now within the range of the tide and are much tumbled or have been obliterated. Damage caused by the sea was in some places reported within months of the cubes being put in place (see p. 209).

For the whole distance between Newburgh and the mouth of the Don (Fig.12.31) the line of cubes was covered by simple CEScC Type 2893 pillboxes set just behind the line, every 300–500m. Although, at first sight, there seem to be larger gaps in the pattern, careful examination of contemporary aerial photographs reveals the barbed wire enclosures that typically covered the rear and flanks of a pillbox and it has been presumed that a pillbox was present. The line of cubes was generally built along what was then the top of the beach, with the pillboxes on the dunes behind. Many of the pillboxes survive, although most are now canted over because of coast erosion, and some have vanished under the dunes and occasionally

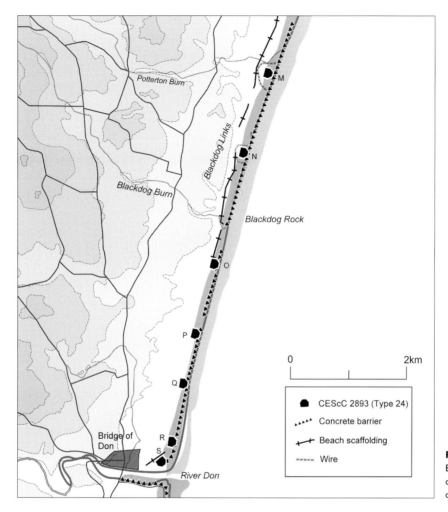

Figure 12.31.
Beach defences from south of Balmedie to the mouth of the River Don.

reappear. Erosion has also revealed the massive scale of foundations provided to try to make the pillboxes secure (Fig. 12.32).

The CEScC 2893 pillboxes on this coast are almost identical to those built in great numbers in Burghead Bay and to the east of Lossiemouth, but do not generally have rearward-facing pistol loops or external walls covering the doors.

Balmedie

At Balmedie Links there is an unusual concentration of pillboxes well behind the line of cubes on the beach (J, K & L on Fig. 12.26). As in the case of the pillbox at Newburgh (B), these have been built of, or shuttered with, brick and are of an unusual shape. Two are small, almost circular, boxes with four embrasures and distinctly thicker walls facing the sea. The third is in the same building style but,

207

Figure 12.32.
One of the pillboxes on the Ythan-Don coast, with its massive foundations exposed by erosion (Author).

like pillbox B at Newburgh – a rectangle with the corners knocked off, with two embrasures on each long face and one on the corner walls – has a total of ten embrasures (Fig. 9.2). These pillboxes seem designed to command the flat links behind the high coast dunes.

A pair of 4-inch naval guns of 942nd Defence Battery (Mobile), RA was sited at Balmedie in March 1941.[89] Their precise location is not known, but 4-inch guns were usually sited for direct fire on the beaches and a position seaward of the group of pillboxes seems plausible (2 on Fig. 12.26).[90]

A Department of Agriculture for Scotland plan of its smallholdings at Balmedie at the end of the war showed the defence works on its land, including four wired perimeters surrounding many firing positions (3 & 4 on Fig. 12.26).[91]

The defences south of Balmedie (Fig. 12.31) continued the general pattern of a simple line (or lines) of cubes with occasional pillboxes behind, the final pillbox lying at the mouth of the Don.[92] The 50th Pioneer Company was reported as wiring the beaches from the Don to Newburgh from October 1940, with work still continuing into January and February 1941.[93] Pillbox O was the subject of a high-level exchange in March 1941 between General Ritchie, the commander of 51st Division, and Scottish Command. The general had been informed that 'the detachment of 8th Gordons [a medium machine gun battalion] which is . . . earmarked to occupy No 5 pillbox on the ABERDEEN beach, has been told that this pillbox is to be used as a dummy searchlight position in conjunction with two dummy guns that have been erected in the neighbourhood'.[94] He considered it was essential that the pillbox should continue to be available for a medium machine gun. The outcome of the exchange was not recorded on file.

This was not an easy coast to protect. In April 1941 it was estimated that for 2 miles north of Aberdeen about 1,320 cubes required replacement.[95] In July 1941 between Blackdog Rock and the mouth of the Ythan over half the cubes (about 2,300 of them) no longer provided an obstacle.[96] A March 1941 report by 50th Pioneer Company noted that most of the pillboxes in the area were 'very badly sited and will be taken by the sea eventually'.[97]

This part of the east coast is one of the few where scaffolding was actually erected in 1941–42, for over 6 miles from south of Newburgh to south of Blackdog. There was a further short section across the beach on the north side of the mouth of the Don, beside pillbox S.[98]

Aberdeen

Aberdeen esplanade, between the mouths of the Dee and the Don, was heavily defended during the war (Fig. 12.33). Almost the entire beach was backed by a high sloping sea wall, but during the war the northern part of the beach had a more natural and unstructured slope up to the coast road, and a double line of cubes obstructed this from the Bridge of Don to where the sea wall then began

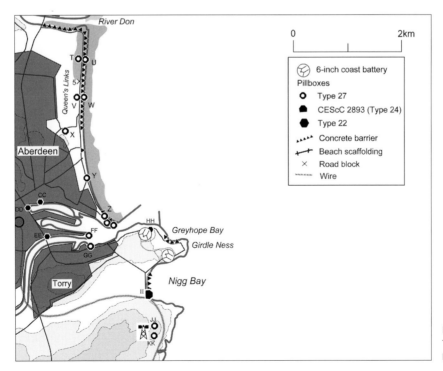

Figure 12.33.
The defences of Aberdeen beach and harbour.

Figure 12.34.
Anti-tank cubes being destroyed on Aberdeen seafront, 1946. Pillbox T is visible in the background (Aberdeen Journals).

(Fig. 12.34). There were four pillboxes in this sector, all Type 27 anti-aircraft pillboxes with a central well, in pairs (T and U; V and W on Fig. 12.33), one pair west of the coast road and the other to the east, seaward of the cubes; T survives. Between the two pairs of pillboxes an underpass under the road, from the Queens Links to the beach, was blocked by a roadblock (5 on Fig. 12.33). A Type 27 pillbox was built about 250m west of the beach, on the flank of Broad Hill, with a good field of fire over the links (X).

There was a short double line of cubes at the back of the beach at the foot of the Beach Boulevard – the main road from the city to the beach – but from that point south cubes were deployed only where flights of steps led up the sea wall from the beach. Only one Type 27 pillbox was positioned in this sector (Y on Fig. 12.33). A short L-shaped double line of cubes, with a Type 27 pillbox at its corner (Z), closed off the southernmost section of beach.

The final section of defence was a double line of cubes running east of the village of Footdee to the west end of the North Pier, fronted for part of its length by what seem on aerial photographs to be dragon's teeth. Two Type 27 pillboxes were built, one behind the cubes, one behind the dragon's teeth (AA & BB; they lay south-east of pillbox Z, although there is insufficient space on Fig. 12.33 to label them).

The harbour itself was protected by a continuous high barbed wire fence. Five pillboxes have been identified on the perimeter, three of Type 22 guarding the northern approaches to the docks and the approach from the lowest bridge over the Dee (CC, DD and EE on Fig. 12.33; DD is illustrated in Fig.6.4), and two of Type 27 (FF and GG) flanking the entrance to the Dee, at the southern side of the entrance to the port.

The port was defended from the sea by two 6-inch gun batteries. One, at the Victorian Torry Battery, replaced a First World War 6-inch battery, disarmed in the 1930s (Fig. 6.3). The other was erected on the other side of the same headland, Girdle Ness, to cover the southern approaches to the harbour. Aerial photographs show that much of the headland was enclosed within extensive barbed wire fences and that a Type 22 pillbox protected the Torry Point battery. Nigg Bay, to the south of the headland, was obstructed by a double line of cubes with, at its southern end, what was probably a Type 24 pillbox (II on Fig. 12.35). The direct approach to the harbour from the sea to the east was defended by a controlled minefield, and there were three fixed torpedo tubes covering the mouth of the harbour.[99]

There was a handful of other pillboxes in other parts of the city but not described here. On the southern edges of the city a lone Type 27 guarded the BBC station at Nigg, and two pillboxes (probably Type 27s) have been recorded protecting the radar station at Doonies Hill, just south of Nigg Bay (Fig. 12.33, JJ and KK).

Figure 12.35.
Nigg Bay's defences looking towards Girdleness, with a pillbox visible in the right foreground, 1945 (Aberdeen Journals).

SMALL BEACHES AND HARBOURS SOUTH OF ABERDEEN

For most of the 45km south of Aberdeen the coast comprises steep, rugged, meta-morphic cliffs entirely unsuitable for large-scale enemy landings. Even where there is a sandy beach, it is most often backed by an inland cliff or a raised beach that restricts exit. Indeed, Stonehaven is the only substantial beach with an easy exit in this sector. Anti-tank cubes and roadblocks were built, however, to obstruct some rather unlikely landing places, such as Altens Haven, Cove, Broad Haven, Portlethen, Newtonhill and Skatie Shore, north of Stonehaven.

Stonehaven

Stonehaven Bay, extending for about 2km from the eighteenth-century battery (1 on Fig. 12.36) at Cowie to Downie Point, contains cliffs, rock platforms and reefs which considerably restrict the length of beach suitable for landing. The northern part of the bay, in front of the hamlet of Cowie, was blocked by a double line of cubes, ending where the concrete sea wall of the esplanade began. South of the mouth of the Cowie Water the shore was obstructed by a double line of cubes 125m long (in the early years of the war the Cowie flowed behind the back of the beach to a mouth nearer the harbour). A double line of cubes ran along the north bank of the Cowie between the beach and the road bridge over it, to prevent the outflanking of the barrier formed by the sea wall and the Cowie cubes to the north. Cubes west of the bridge are more properly dealt with as part of the Cowie Line (below).

At least one pillbox (a Type 22) was erected on the front (A on Fig. 12.36); its post-war demolition was reported in the local paper, at a cost of £507 2s 6d (£17,200 in modern value). Stonehaven, as the point where the two main roads from the south meet, was a key focal point. The Home Guard defence plan for the town, issued in October 1941, listed a series of outposts (2–9) well outside the town, as well as an inner perimeter of six 'defended localities' based on roadblocks (10–16).[100] Flame fougasses or static flame traps were at that stage being installed at all of these sites.[101]

Catterline, about 8km south of Stonehaven, is one of the small bays/harbours separated from their associated settlement by a steep cliff, charcteristic of this coast. A large number of cubes, dragon's teeth and concrete-filled pipes have since the war been piled up to form a sea wall. The 217th Pioneer Company was recorded as erecting defences at Catterline from September to November 1940.[102]

Braidon Bay lies only 800m or so south of Catterline. The beach is about 300m long, backed by steep cliffs, with a central shingle section between rocky platforms. The sole access was along a track up the narrow valley of the Braidon

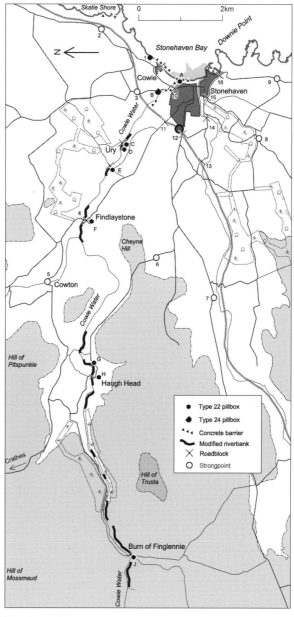

Figure 12.36.
Stonehaven and the Cowie Line.

Burn, which was blocked by a line of 12 anti-tank cubes (Fig. 12.37) with a possible machine gun post on the higher ground. The 217th Pioneer Company was recorded as erecting defences in Braidon Bay from September to November 1940.[103]

The shingle beach at Inverbervie is about 500m long, between a cliff and rock platform to the north and a rock platform to the south; the Bervie Water enters the bay at its northern end. A dozen cubes bar the foreshore on the north side of the river's mouth, with a pillbox tucked into the bottom of the cliff (Fig. 12.38).

213

Figure 12.37.
Anti-tank cubes block the
only exit from Braidon Bay
(Author).

Figure 12.38.
The pillbox and cubes at the
north end of the bay at
Inverbervie (Author).

From within the mouth of the river the entire length of the beach to the south was blocked by a double line of anti-tank cubes, of which few remain, with a Type 22 pillbox near the southern end. The 217th Pioneer Company was erecting defences at Inverbervie from September to November 1940.[104]

For almost 9km south of Inverbervie the coast is fronted by rock shelving and the raised beach behind forms an almost continuous barrier. At Mathers, near the southern boundary of Aberdeen Sub-area, a sand and shingle beach about 1,100m long and 150m across, split into two parts by a rock shelf, backed by a high cliff. The bay was covered by three pillboxes, one each in the north-east and south-west parts with a third near the only (narrow) road exit, which was blocked by a short line of cubes.

EASTERN ABERDEEN SUB-AREA STOP-LINES

There were three formal stop-lines in the eastern part of Aberdeen Sub-area: the lines of the Rivers Dee and Don, and the Cowie Line (9, 10 and 11, respectively, on Fig. 7.2). The Cowie Line was the most southerly, and after the Scottish Command Line, it was the most substantial in Scotland. The Dee and Don lines are of uncertain status.

The March 1941 version of *Aberdeen Sub-area Defence Scheme* identified the Canadian Forestry Corps, in conjunction with the Home Guard, as being responsible for the defence of the Dee crossings at Banchory, Kincardine O'Neil and Aboyne.[105] Amendment No. 4 to the scheme, in April 1941, listed check-lines on the bridges over the Spey (see above), Don and Dee, and over the Cowie Water at Stonehaven. The revised list of check-lines of June 1941 was the first Scottish Command document in which the Rivers Don and Dee appeared.[106] The Aberdeen garrison issued a note about check-lines in September 1941: the defence lines on the Rivers Dee and Don (only within the area of the city) were referred to in the future tense, and were to allow 'The inspection of all vehicles and check identity of occupants'.[107]

While there are no records of constructed defences on these two lines, there was a handful of pillboxes near both rivers. One of which was where one would expect it, on the south side of the river looking north across the bridge to Dinnet, but now buried, while the reasoning behind the positioning of others, for example on the north bank of the Dee, is not now so obvious.

The Cowie Line was first mentioned on 9 June 1940, in General Carrington's report to GHQ Home Forces, in which he identified six possible 'demolition belts' in Scotland.[108] The Cowie Line exploited the topography of eastern Scotland to block off the north-east where the foothills of the Grampians most closely approach the coast, the geographical feature known as The Mounth. Carrington noted the need for subsidiary posts on the road south of Braemar (at the Devil's Elbow) and on the Perth–Inverness road in the area from Kingussie to Dalwhinnie 'to prevent any enemy turning movement' and these blocks were an integral part of the line as built (Fig. 7.2). At this latitude the mountains constrain communications to a handful of routes, the mountain passes being easy to block. Only near the coast was there a choice of routes, and the Cowie Water was exploited to block these (Fig. 12.36). Wherever a road crossed the line, defended positions were established: pillboxes, cubes and roadblocks. Between them, the bank of the Cowie Water was raised or made steeper where the bank was not already high enough to form a barrier.

Work was in hand by 21 June 1940,[109] and the line was already part of 9th Division's operational plans by 7 July, in which the role of the line was described as 'To prevent Southward movements from MORAY or ABERDEEN and turning movement from N.W'.[110] In December 1940, 98th Pioneer Company was responsible for providing patrols on the line, while the Home Guard was to man roadblocks and pillboxes in the area.[111] At the same time, elements of the Field Force were to be prepared to occupy the Cowie Line if it became 'operationally necessary'.[112]

No structures have been identified near Drumochter, at the western end of the line, but anyone who has driven the A9 will know just how narrow the pass of Drumochter is, even after improvements in the 1970s; and in 1940 the road and railway would have been easy to block or blow up.

The next pass to the east is the main road running south from Braemar to Blairgowrie. The pass is narrow and traffic cannot move off the road. The pass was blocked south of its summit, at the notorious hairpin bend known as the Devil's Elbow by a roadblock formed of vertical rails that could be slotted into sockets, and by a line of cubes that obstructed the whole width of the valley bottom. One pillbox covered the roadblock from the south, and a second, tucked into the hillside 450m to the north-west, and still visible, covered the top of the pass and the approach to the roadblock (Fig. 12.39).

The next motorable road, 51km to the east, is the narrow road from Strachan on the River Feugh to Fettercairn, striking out over hills up to 400m above sea level. It was blocked about 7km south of Strachan, at Bridge of Dye, where a high narrow seventeenth-century bridge crossed the gorge of the Water of Dye. Unusually, the two pillboxes which covered the road were placed north of the

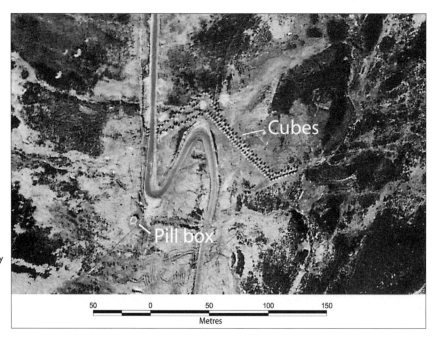

Figure 12.39.
The Devil's Elbow defences on the Cowie Line. The enemy would be expected from the north, at the top of the photograph (RAF/National Collection of Aerial Photography).

bridge (that is, on the expected enemy side). Both pillboxes survive, built into a granite wall. The loopholes of one face to both south and north, the other only south, towards the bridge.

About 10km further east the Cowie Line proper began, in the sense of a continuous anti-tank obstacle (Fig. 12.36). About 750m west of the highest crossing of the Cowie, the alteration of the south bank of the Cowie Water is first visible; the bank was cut back to a vertical face about 2m high and the face was revetted with timber held in place by loops of galvanised wire pegged back into the ground. It is only in this first section that the timber survives, although the wire loops turn up in many places on the line (Fig. 12.40). Without revetting the vertical face might have collapsed, especially in wet weather.

The highest crossing, probably a ford at that time, at Finglennie, was covered by a Type 22 pillbox of the kind characteristic of the Cowie Line (shellproof granite and concrete, designed for Bren guns), which is still so well camouflaged that it is invisible from a few metres away. East of the track the anti-tank barrier was formed by a very substantial constructed embankment.

The next defended crossing of the Cowie was 4.5km east, at Haugh Head. Between Finglennie and here, about a third of the riverbank needed modification to make it an adequate anti-tank barrier. The bridge at Haugh Head was heavily defended: the bank was made vertical for some distance on both sides of the bridge, while a double line of cubes was built beside the road on the south side of the bridge, to stop tanks driving off the road to the west. Two Type 22 pillboxes

Figure 12.40.
Timber revetment of the south bank of the Cowie Line (Author).

(H and G on Fig. 12.36) covered the bridge: one with a line of fire along the bridge, the other about 200m to the west covering the approach to the bridge.

For much of the 4.5km between Haugh Head and the next crossing at Findlaystone the valley of the Cowie was steep and narrow, and only about a fifth of the riverbank needed modification. The bridge at Cowton (5 on Fig. 12.36) regularly appeared in lists of demolitions. At Findlaystone, as at Haugh Head, the bank was raised or made vertical for some distance on both sides of the bridge, and a ford a few metres to the west of Findlaystone Bridge was blocked with cubes. A Type 22 pillbox (F on Fig. 12.36, Fig. 1.1) covered the bridge and, unusually, two weapons pits survive – both providing lines of fire along the bridge. One still has the remains of the wire mesh used for its camouflage.

Down river, three bridges within the Ury estate carried private roads over the Cowie. The magnificent nineteenth-century viaduct carrying the main drive to Ury House towers above a more modest earlier bridge. The viaduct had a horizontal-rail roadblock built at its southern end, while the older bridge was permanently blocked by cubes. Both were covered by fire from a Type 22 pillbox (E on Fig. 12.36) to the west.

About 500m to the east-south-east, in front of Ury House, was one of the most vulnerable crossing points. Here, as elsewhere, the bank was raised in height above and below the crossing, strengthened by cubes. The vulnerable area and the bridge were also covered by two Type 22 pillboxes (D and C on Fig. 12.36). To the east, the river once again enters a narrow gorge, where a constructed anti-tank barrier was not needed. It emerges from the gorge into a wide flood plain as it passes under the Glenury railway viaduct (on which there was a railway block). From here to the Cowie Bridge, within Stonehaven, most of the south-west bank of the river was obstructed by anti-tank cubes. These are visible on post-war aerial photographs but now, apart from a handful at the Cowie Bridge, have been removed or buried beneath flood defences. A final pillbox (B) was located, unusually, on the 'enemy' side of the river, where the river's course turns south, about halfway between the railway and the Cowie Bridge. It appears to be a modified Type 24 set back into the hillside, with lines of fire along the river to the west and the south.

13. ANGUS SUB-AREA

A s early as November 1939, the risk of an air and sea attack on the beaches north of Montrose and at Lunan Bay was being considered; a large force might be landed there to threaten Dundee (Fig. 13.1).[1] While these two beaches were the chief risk, the beaches of Arbroath and Barry to the south-west were also considered vulnerable. The area behind the beaches is one of the largest tracts of high-quality agricultural land in Scotland, with low hills and broad, lightly-wooded valleys. Two main roads ran across the area from the north-east to the south-west, one along the coast through Montrose, Arbroath and Carnoustie to Dundee, and an inland route through Brechin and Forfar towards Perth. A third north-east to south-west route, along the foot of the hills through Cortachy, was, and still is, narrow and twisting, and could be discounted.

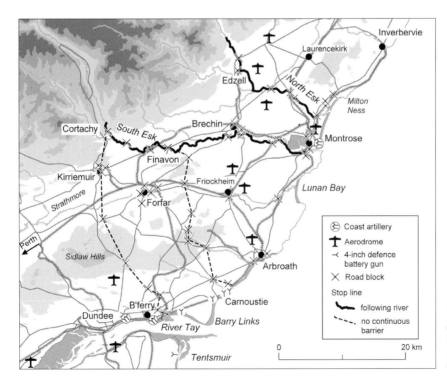

Figure 13.1.
Angus Sub-area, showing the locations of aerodromes active in 1940–41, coast artillery, stop-lines and roadblocks.

Only two aerodromes lay close to beaches in the Sub-area (Arbroath and Montrose), with four others within 15km of the coast. Of the three ports in Angus only Dundee was a 'major defended port' and was the likeliest enemy target in the Sub-area. At the outbreak of war it had no defences against attack from the sea, but by June 1940 the programme of Emergency Coast Batteries and the establishment of 943rd Defence Battery (Mobile), RA at Carnoustie had remedied this. In the 15km transit from the mouth of the Tay to Dundee, an attacker (constrained by the river's narrow channels) would have come under fire from three 4-inch guns of 943rd Battery, RA at Carnoustie and a further two guns of the battery at Monifieth and, more distant, at Tentsmuir in Fife. At Broughty Ferry and Stannergate in Dundee were the two batteries of 6-inch naval guns of 503rd Coast Regiment and 308rd Coast Battery, RA covering the distant and final approaches to the harbour.[2] There was also a controlled minefield near the mouth of the river, with its control point at Buddon.[3]

Montrose harbour is formed by the broad outlet of the River South Esk, with quays on both sides of the river. The vulnerability of the harbour was reflected in the construction of an emergency battery of two 6-inch guns just north of the river mouth; the harbour entrance was also covered at various times by two 18-pounder guns and two 75-mm guns firing from the southern side of the river mouth, and by machine gun pillboxes and other firing positions, described below. An old sand-hopper at Dundee, named *Edie*, was identified as the block-ship for the harbour.[4]

Arbroath was listed as a vulnerable port, albeit not among the most significant (as it is largely dry at low tide), as early as May 1940, when the port authorities were instructed to prepare immobilisation schemes. There was also a plan for it to be 'immobilised' by a boom and a block-ship.[5]

BEACHES

Montrose Beach

Montrose Bay was the first large, vulnerable beach south of Aberdeen. Measured along the top of the beach it is about 8.8km long. To the north are high cliffs; to the south the mouth of the South Esk, which also forms the southern boundary of the town of Montrose and its harbour. The strategic risk posed here was significantly increased by the presence of a military aerodrome on the northern outskirts of the town, just behind the beach.

The bay is in two parts (Fig. 13.2), divided about 2km from the northern end by the mouth of the North Esk. In the northernmost part of the bay, below the village of St Cyrus, the high lava cliffs that form the coastline north of the bay come closest to the shore.[6] To the south, the cliffs reduce in height and retreat from the shore but they still dominate the dunes. The dunes are cut off by a tidal inlet, and the flat area between cliff and beach could only be exited to the south-west through an area of salt marsh via a narrow 2km-long track leading to North-water Bridge. Polish maps from 1941 show that this beach had no more than a fence of Dannert wire along its top and that there was a handful of firing positions on and behind the beach. Wartime aerial photographs show a pedestrian bridge over the tidal inlet, probably to allow troops to man the positions in dunes quickly. The Chain Home Low radar station at Kirkside, 200m inland from the top of the

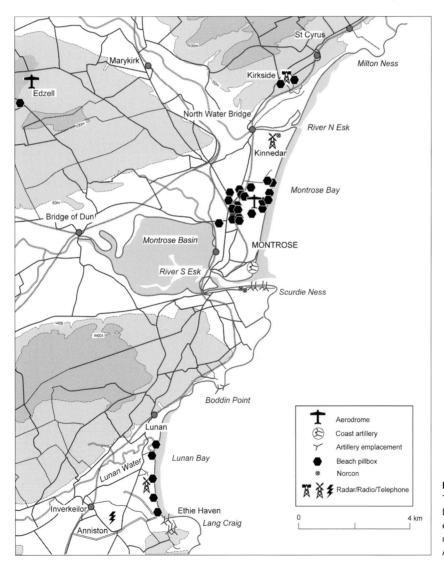

Figure 13.2.
The Montrose Bay and Lunan Bay area. The artillery emplacements are those marked on 1941 Polish Army maps.

cliffs, was, however, the sort of important Vulnerable Point that might be raided by the enemy, and was consequently defended by at least two pillboxes within a barbed wire boundary.

Immediately south of the North Esk are the links of Charleton and Kinnedar, the northern half of the 6km-long beach. An anti-tank barrier was generally only needed where the dunes – between 4m and 12m high – were pierced by a track. However, the low southern bank of the North Esk and the northernmost part of the beach were vulnerable. Cubes and a roadblock were built at Fisherhills (1 on

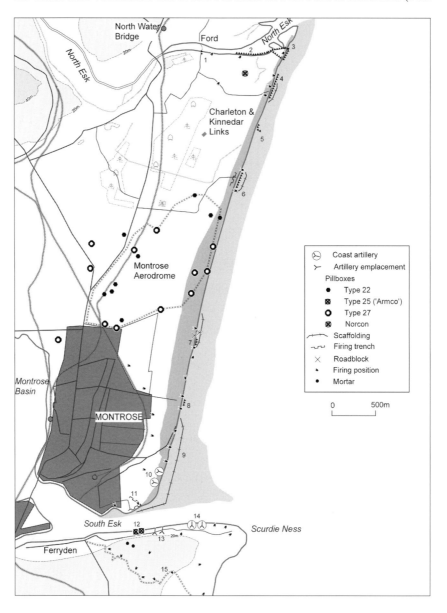

Figure 13.3.
Montrose Bay south
of the River North Esk.

Figure 13.4.
Concrete defences at the mouth of the North Esk, showing the tumbled cubes on the beach and their replacement by five lines of dragon's teeth. (RAF/ National Collection of Aerial Photography).

Fig. 13.3), about 1km in from the beach, to obstruct a ford across the river. A substantial barrier was built of cubes and some dragon's teeth for about 750m along the riverbank to the sea, and then turned south along the beach (2). By the time an aerial photograph was taken in 1942, the cubes at the mouth of the river (3) had been damaged by the sea and replaced by a line of five rows of dragon's teeth cutting across the links (Fig. 13.4); this repair work was probably the work of the Polish Army.

Two vulnerable exits from the beach were blocked in this sector (4 and 6 on Fig. 13.3) by a mixture of barbed wire and concrete cubes (reinforced by beach scaffolding in 1941) and covered by machine gun positions shown on Polish Army maps.[7] A short length of cubes, with a dog-leg out onto the beach (at 5), survives between sections 4 and 6.

The southernmost 3km portion of the bay was backed by the aerodrome and the town. The dunes fall in height from 10m to about 8m in the south and the beach narrows from about 200m at low tide to about 10m near the southern end. There seem to have been at least 20 pillboxes within the aerodrome, with four more to the west of the main road and on the western approach to the town. The majority of these were Type 27 pillboxes: large octagonal pillboxes with an anti-aircraft position in a central well. Others were more standard Type 22 pillboxes. There were also at least two Pickett-Hamilton forts close to the runways. Six of the pillboxes were sited on, or close to, the dunes on the vulnerable eastern side of the aerodrome.

A single short line of cubes (7 on Fig. 13.3) and a roadblock barred a blow-out in the dunes. These were reinforced in 1941 by beach scaffolding, which itself had a roadblock within it, controlling access to the beach. The final section of anti-tank cubes on the beach (8) lay just north of the beach pavilion; there has been so much change here since the war that it is now not clear why a barrier was needed.

A long section of beach scaffolding was erected in 1941 from just south of point 8 round into the mouth of the South Esk (9 on Fig. 13.3).[8] Behind this was the coast battery of two 6-inch guns, in separate gun-houses (10). The southernmost feature on the beach was a complex firing position, comprising a zigzag firing trench covering the entrance to the harbour (at 11).

Major parts of the beach defence were built to the south of the South Esk, on the high ground between Ferryden and Scurdie Ness. When the Poles were responsible for Angus the whole headland was enclosed by barbed wire (15 on Fig. 13.3), and contained many firing positions. Two Type 25 circular Armco pillboxes (12 on Fig. 13.3; Fig. 13.5; Fig. 9.2) survive beside the road to Scurdie Ness, each with a single embrasure overlooking the entrance to the harbour and the links beyond. Both had short lengths of wall added to protect the entrances from flanking fire. The inscription '8th Gordons', and the shelf for the ammunition box, confirms that they were built by or for that battalion's Vickers medium machine guns.

Figure 13.5.
One of the two Armco pillboxes at Scurdie Ness, overlooking the mouth of the South Esk and Montrose Harbour. They were built by or for 8th Battalion Gordon Highlanders for two of their Vickers medium machine guns (Author).

Two gun-houses with thin brick walls and thin concrete roofs (13 on Fig. 13.3; plan on Fig. 9.6), both provided with loopholes for close defence to side and rear, looked northwards over the beach and the links behind it. The files (and local memory) suggest that these gun-houses contained 18-pounder guns, later manned by the Home Guard.[9] To the east, two large artillery emplacements were quarried out of the face of the cliff by Polish engineers during 1941, not far above the height of the sea (14 on Fig. 13.3; Fig. 13.6). References in British files suggest that these were likely to have held 75-mm guns, four of which were in fixed defences in Angus, under Polish command.[10] The emplacements were complex structures of reinforced concrete with imposing facades, entered by a tunnel from the road above.

In late 1939, 'B' Company of 9th (Home Defence) Battalion Black Watch was stationed in Montrose, while the rest of the battalion was distributed widely on guard duties across eastern Scotland.[11] The commander of 128th Field Regiment, RA (part of the 9th Division's artillery), was in charge of the defences of Montrose, and in June 1940 he wrote to the HQ of what was then Dundee Sub-area expressing, in the strongest terms, his concerns about the weakness of the defence.[12] He wrote that the garrison of Montrose consisted of his own unit (very much under strength); one platoon of machine guns of 8th Gordons; the men of the 6-inch guns, of which more later; and a Royal Engineer detachment which would be fully occupied during an invasion in immobilising petrol and electrical installations and demolishing bridges. These forces had to cover, in all, 8,000 yards of front. He noted that even when all hands, including cooks, turned out it was impossible

Figure 13.6.
One of the two Polish artillery positions quarried into the cliff near Scurdie Ness, to fire north just above sea level. Inset is the inscription, in Polish: 'Position "Bandit Leader"'. Constructed by sappers of Second Platoon. To POLAND and VICTORY. Polish Sappers 1941.' (Author).

to man all the available rifles or the defended localities up to minimum strength. Furthermore, he had no troops in reserve. To make matters worse, the 6-inch coast artillery guns were, in his view, located badly with a view to their defence and badly commanded. He clearly despised the commander of the 307th Heavy Battery, RA – a Captain Veitch – and wanted him replaced: 'In my view he has proved to be an extremely inexperienced officer with very little Military Knowledge, and no sense of discipline, and I consider that his presence here under the existing conditions constitutes a menace to the defence of Montrose.' 128th Field Regiment, RA was posted away to Tain on 8 August, and Veitch and his coast battery were no longer the commander's problem.[13] Unfortunately we do not have the captain's side of the story.

The 282nd Battery of 71st Field Regiment, RA arrived in Montrose on 8 July 1940[14] but by August the War Diary suggests that only one section of A Troop of this regiment (two 18-pounder guns, presumably in the gun-houses on Scordie Ness) remained.[15] At the end of the month, three officers and 149 other ranks of the 9th (Pioneer) Battalion York & Lancaster Regiment arrived to reinforce the Montrose defences.[16] It was during this period that Montrose experienced one of the worst known outbreaks of military 'Fifth Column' hysteria (see p. 32).

On 10 and 15 August, the commander of the armoured train based in Aberdeen undertook reconnaissance journeys along the main line, which then, as now, passed the western edge of the town, and also along the branch line to Inverbervie. The main line would allow the train to fire onto Montrose Basin (Fig. 13.2), which was seen as vulnerable to landings by seaplanes. The Inverbervie line usefully ran through the middle of the aerodrome and the commander noted that the train could provide fire at any point of the aerodrome.

By November 1940, the troops and heavy weapons available to defend Montrose were 10th Black Watch; 98th and 195th Pioneer Companies; the two 6-inch guns of 307th Coast Battery, RA; and the two 18-pounders of 151st Field Regiment, RA (on the south side of the South Esk). A platoon of the Black Watch (with two Home Guard machine guns in support, presumably in the two Armco pillboxes) was stationed at Ferryden, on the south side of the South Esk, to guard the switches of the controlled minefield at the Lifeboat Station and to protect the 18-pounder guns. Another platoon was posted at Kirkside House to support the garrison of the radar station (half a platoon of B Company, 9th Black Watch),[17] as it was feared that there might be 'combined air and sea raids . . . near R.D.F [radar] stations, at ST CYRUS and MONTROSE Aerodrome, for the purpose of obtaining secrets that are not known to the enemy'.[18] In general, indeed, there was a concern about 'hit and run raids . . . which may take as little as an hour in which to complete'.[19]

In March 1941, in a review of the defence of Scotland, it was mooted that the boundary of the Polish forces should be extended north to Milton Ness to take in Lunan Bay and the Montrose–St Cyrus beaches. One advantage was that Milton Ness provided a better northern flank, as there was no large vulnerable beach to the north until Stonehaven and Aberdeen. At first, the Polish unit responsible for the area was 5th Brygada Kadre (a unit made up largely of surplus officers designed as a cadre to absorb further Polish soldiers as they became available). A Polish map delineates a large defended area wired off on the hill between Ferryden at Scurdie Ness, around the 18-pounder artillery position, with many machine gun positions (15 on Fig. 13.3).[20]

The internal defence of Montrose aerodrome was the responsibility of the RAF, with the assistance of the anti-aircraft gunners on the station and one company of 9th (Home Defence) Battalion Black Watch; 10th Black Watch also had as one of its primary roles the assistance of the defence of the aerodrome.[21] The reality of the 'guard' was, however, described as follows by Ed Preston, an armourer: 'The airfield was guarded day and night by two Erks each armed with a pick and whistle ... If an enemy patrol had infiltrated by sea and over the bents [dunes] a vigorous counter attack was expected from the two guards, smiting the invaders hip and thigh with their pick handles and blowing their whistles with all their might to sound over half a mile away ... What good would two pick handle carrying Erks [have] been against a well armed Wehrmacht patrol?'[22]

The defences of Montrose airfield were tested twice in June 1941. On 2 June an exercise revealed that 'the defences of this aerodrome are weak both in troops and in effective weapons, many of the weapons available not being complete.'[23] In the middle of the month a troop of No. 6 Commando arrived in the area, mainly to train the Home Guard, but they also tested airfield security at Montrose and Arbroath: 'The defences of this aerodrome were known to be very weak owing to shortage of men and weapons and extreme difficulty of defence through the lay-out of the Aerodrome', and found 'to be quite incapable of keeping the attackers out'.[24]

Nevertheless, by August 1941 there were better-developed plans for the co-ordination of Polish troops, Pioneers, Royal Artillery and Home Guard to defend the town, deny the harbour to the enemy and assist the 120 or so RAF and anti-aircraft gunners defending the aerodrome. These plans were timely as, even into the spring of 1942, Montrose still counted as one of the five most 'dangerous', that is vulnerable, beaches in Scotland.[25]

Lunan Bay

Lunan Bay, about 4km long with deep water close inshore, was included in the first list of vulnerable beaches prepared in May 1940, although it was not one of the highest priority. The 250–300m wide stretch of beach between upper and lower tides is smooth and shelves at only one to two degrees, making it an easy beach on which to land small vessels (Fig. 13.7). Work began on the defences there in late June.[26]

The bay is split into two parts by the Lunan Water. North of the river mouth the dunes were high enough to act as a barrier, and concrete obstacles were erected only to block two accesses from the beach: near Buckie Den (two lines of dragon's teeth and a roadblock (1 on Fig. 13.7)) and on another beach exit (2; a triple line of dragon's teeth). In the summer of 1941 it was felt necessary to erect beach scaffolding (3) from the mouth of Buckie Den, along the upper part of the beach, to

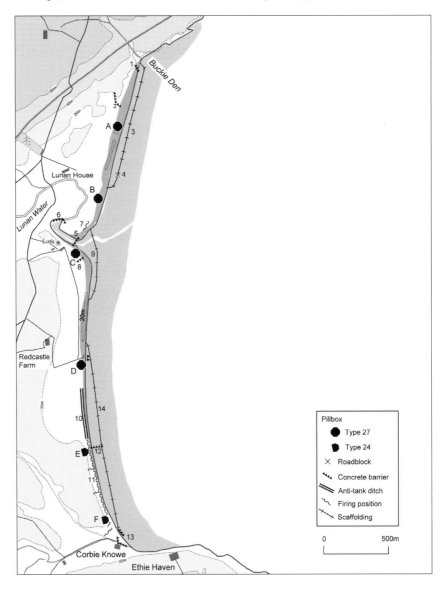

Figure 13.7.
The defences of Lunan Bay.

opposite Lunan Links. There seems to have been a roadblock in it near its southern end (at 4), presumably to allow access to the salmon nets. Polish maps show the presence of what seems to be the northernmost pillbox (A on Fig. 13.7).[27]

The mouth of the Lunan Water was blocked by a single line of cubes at the mouth (5 on Fig. 13.7) and another a little way inland (6), and it was covered by two pillboxes (C and D on Fig. 13.8); a short line of anti-tank cubes protected the approach to the pillbox from the south-east (at 8 on Fig. 13.7). Pillbox C survives and is a Type 27 variant: a large, octagonal pillbox with a covered porch. All the walls and the porch had a pre-cast concrete embrasure, probably for a Bren gun. There is an internal chamber which, on most Type 27 pillboxes, would be the well with an open top for an anti-aircraft position. The roof of the surviving pillbox, however, has been cast as a single unit. Aerial photographs suggest that pillboxes A, B and D (Fig. 13.7) were of the same type.

In the summer of 1941, it was felt necessary to erect a line of beach scaffolding over 500m long, from just north of the mouth of the river to about 330m south of pillbox C (9 on Fig. 13.7). Some of the beach scaffolding is still occasionally exposed by storms.

The beach south of the mouth of the river is in two distinct parts.[28] For about 1.5km there is, behind the dunes (which are 5–20m high), a broad flat expanse of arable land. About 250 to 300m behind this sits the fossil cliff: the face of the 20m-high raised beach. One pillbox (D on Fig. 13.7) was erected in the middle of this section of beach and is visible in the background of Figure 8.10. There are the remains of a continuous ditch, possibly an anti-tank ditch, just behind the beach (at 10 on Fig. 13.7), where there are no dunes to act as a barrier.

The final portion of the bay starts where the fossil cliff curves back close to the back of the beach. This sector is fronted for over 750m by a continuous firing

Figure 13.8.
Pillbox C on Lunan Bay, a Type 27 variant with the central anti-aircraft well roofed over (Author).

trench, with crenellated plan (11 on Fig. 13.7), accessed by lengths of trench zigzagging down the face of the cliff at two points. There are two pillboxes on this stretch, one at the north (E on Fig. 13.7), the other at the south (F). The latter has been demolished and its shattered remains lie on the beach. The former, set into the hillside, has been converted into a bird-watching hide. From what is now visible it was a fairly standard Type 24 pillbox. Just to the north, a line of anti-tank cubes runs down the beach (12 on Fig. 13.7), presumably to restrict access along it at high tide.

At the southern end of the beach is the hamlet of Corbie Knowe, a collection of beach huts and caravans through which flows the Keilor Burn. This exit from the beach was obstructed by three short sets of anti-tank cubes, along the top of the beach just north of the burn's mouth (13 on Fig. 13.7), a line across the burn at a slight angle; and a line along the beach south of the watercourse. Further anti-tank cubes have been recorded at the tiny hamlet of Ethie Haven, 600m east of Corbie Knowe.

In addition to the two lengths of beach scaffolding erected on the northern part of the beach and over the mouth of the Lunan Water, scaffolding was recorded from just north of pillbox D to the north end of the anti-tank cubes at Corbie Knowe (14 on Fig. 13.7; Fig. 8.10).[29]

While the Polish Army was stationed in this area, artillery cover was provided by five guns sited on the high ground above Ethie Haven. These lay in a large barbed wire compound with nine machine gun positions protecting its landward side (not illustrated). A map on a Polish file[30] showed a regular arrangement of lines of anti-glider posts, 120–150m apart, running down the beach with cross-lines erected between them.

Manning and Use

As early as February 1940, 'selected riflemen' of 126th Field Regiment, RA were, in the event of enemy action, to 'defend the sands of LUNAN BAY and the Railway Bridge at INVERKEILOR.' under the command of Captain MacDonald and 2nd Lieutenant Cowie.[31] The use of artillerymen as infantrymen in this period often reflected the shortage of artillery pieces after Dunkirk; 120 unarmed gunners were also to be offered to the police in Dundee and Arbroath to aid the civil power.

The 71st Field Regiment, RA also had a responsibility for the defence of Lunan Bay. On the night of 8 September 1940 (the night of the 'Cromwell' signal) a patrol under Captain Barber responded to reports of parachute and small boat landings in the bay by enemy agents. He returned at 07.00 on the 9th 'with nothing to report.'[32]

In October 1940, one platoon of 10th Black Watch was based at Redcastle

Farm, above the centre of the beach, to report on activity in Lunan Bay and to protect the GPO telephone repeater station behind the beach at Annieston.[33] Meanwhile, the local Home Guard was to man two machine guns, positioned on either side of the mouth of the Lunan Water, as well as the three pillboxes in the middle of the bay (B, C and D on Fig. 13.7).

At the beginning of December 1940, the 143rd Pioneer Company moved to Montrose and began to work on the defences in the area, including barbed wire and firing posts at Lunan Bay.[34] Work continued there, and at St Cyrus and Montrose, during January 1941: sandbagging and revetting firing positions; constructing machine gun posts; wiring; making concrete pimples; and camouflaging pillboxes. This sort of work continued into March, but in April and May 1941 all available personnel were put to erecting tubular steel scaffolding defences in Lunan Bay. This caused problems. On 17 June, British officers from Angus Sub-area visited with officers of the Polish 10th Mechanised Cavalry Brigade to discuss the problem of the new scaffolding masking the Polish guns.[35]

On Boddin Point, to the north-east of the bay (Fig. 13.2), a Polish map of 1941 showed the presence of two artillery pieces, marked by the Polish symbol for 'coast artillery', positioned to fire back onto the northern half of the bay. It was probably sited on the massive platform provided by the monumental limekiln.[36] Only a circular emplacement about 4m across, which may be a gun-site, and a scatter of anti-tank cubes now show that this area was ever defended.

Arbroath

From Ethie Haven, at the southern end of Lunan Bay, the coast is formed for over 10km by high cliffs fronted by rock shelves occasionally accessible by steep, narrow gullies, which did not seem to have needed defence. Arbroath itself was seen as vulnerable because of a combination of factors: a long sandy beach to the south-west of the town; the presence of a military aerodrome a short distance outside the town to the north; and good road and rail access to the south-west to Dundee, and northwards, to Lunan Bay and Montrose.

During the period of the Polish presence in the area, field guns were positioned within three heavily defended enclosures to cover the beaches and the aerodrome (marked 1, 2 and 3 on Fig. 13.9); the barbed wire perimeter of the West Seaton Farm site (at 1) was attached to the wire perimeter drawn around Arbroath.[37]

The seafront of the town had been transformed in the 1930s by public works schemes for the unemployed, which, among other projects, saw the construction of esplanades at the east and west ends. A consequence not foreseen by the burghers of Arbroath was that these would act as anti-tank walls in 1940.[38]

Arbroath's eastern beach is fronted by intertidal rock shelves and these made

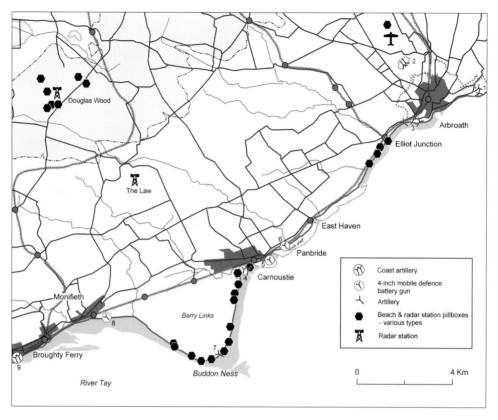

Figure 13.9. (above) Angus Sub-area from Arbroath to Broughty Ferry.

Figure 13.10. (opposite top) The beach defences from Arbroath to the Dowrie Burn.

Figure 13.11. (opposite below) The Arbroath Summer Pavilion, decorated for war, in a Polish Army photograph (Polish Institute & Sikorski Museum, London).

this side of the town a poor prospect for an enemy landing. To the west, the sea wall formed by the promenade originally ended at the Summer Pavilion, now demolished (3 on Fig. 13.10). At two points small slipways and ramps through the promenade were blocked by a handful of anti-tank cubes (2 on Fig. 13.10).

Beyond the end of the promenade, to the south-west of the Summer Pavilion, there was no pre-existing wall and the dunes at the back of the beach were not high enough to block access. From here, therefore, a new anti-tank barrier had to be built for about 3.5km. A Polish photograph from the summer of 1941 (Fig. 13.11) showed the Pavilion painted in camouflage colours and its access to the beach blocked by anti-tank cubes and barbed wire.

From the Summer Pavilion, the anti-tank cubes ran south-west for about 1,900m to the Penston Burn (5 on Fig. 13.10). In part this was a double line, but it was mainly single further from the town. At the mouth of the Elliot Water (at 4) the defences were at their deepest: between one and three lines of dragon's teeth were added to the riverbank (Fig. 13.12). There were also two Y-shaped pillboxes (A and B on Fig. 13.10) between the Summer Pavilion and the mouth of the Elliot Water, 400m apart: one near the Junction (A) and one on the narrow spit between the Elliot Water and the beach (B). Neither survives. A third example of this type

232

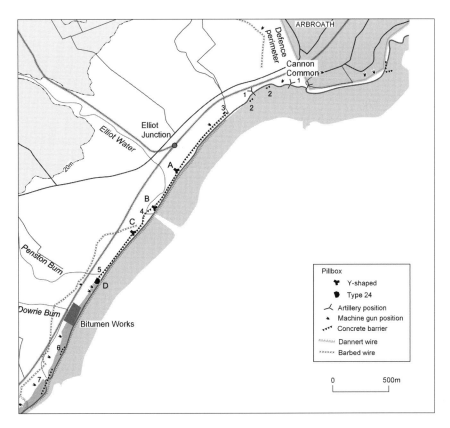

Figure 13.12.
Anti-tank cubes, with dragon's teeth added, and a Y-shaped pillbox (B) at the mouth of the Elliot Water, SW of Arbroath (RAF/National Collection of Aerial Photography).

of pillbox lay a little to the south-west (C). The line of cubes terminated at a Type 24 pillbox (D) on the western side of the mouth of the Penston Burn (5 on Fig. 13.10), where the height of the dunes rose, to provide an adequate barrier. Until the 1970s the next section of dunes to the south was occupied by the densely-packed buildings of a bitumen factory.

About 700m south-west of pillbox D a small arrow-shaped setting of ten anti-tank cubes (which still survives) blocked a low point on the dunes (6 on Fig. 13.10). After a further 150m the dunes fell away again to a height of less than 2m, and required a 160m-long line of anti-tank cubes (at 7), capped with cement with steel uprights, which run to the south-west end of the sandy beach.

The beach south of Arbroath was described in February 1940[39] as 'very exposed and impossible to craft drawing more than four feet'. It was thus not noted on the Scottish Command's lists of vulnerable beaches of May 1940[40] or October 1940.[41] It only appeared on the lists of April[42] and October 1941.[43] Despite this, 27th Pioneer Company was constructing anti-tank obstacles on Arbroath and Elliot beaches in August 1940, under the supervision of 665th General Construction Company, RE.[44]

In February 1941 the defences of the Fleet Air Arm aerodrome outside Arbroath were tested. Although a locally-mounted test and an attack by No. 6 Commando both revealed weaknesses, the results were better than they had been at Montrose.[45]

Barry

For 5.5km from the western end of the Arbroath/Elliot beach defences to Carnoustie, a rocky shelf provided a satisfactory barrier to enemy landings. From Carnoustie there is a continuous sandy beach for the 14km around the Barry peninsula (jutting out into the mouth of the River Tay), past Monifieth, to Broughty Castle. The Barry peninsula (with Tentsmuir on the other side of the estuary) was mapped even more intensively by the Polish Army than the beaches of eastern Angus and is therefore one of the few places in Scotland where there is really good documentary evidence for the complexity of defence preparations, in addition to the concrete remains.[46]

The first 800m or so of this section of coast, fronting the town of Carnoustie, was blocked by lines of anti-tank cubes and dragon's teeth. Carnoustie beach is about 600m long and up to 400m across at low tide, stretching from the intertidal rock platform at the east to the mouth of the Barry Burn at the west. The barrier started at the east with a line of cubes running out from the beach onto the rocky platform (1 on Fig. 13.13). The line of cubes was fronted by a double or triple line of dragon's teeth, probably a later addition by the Poles (Fig. 8.5). A combined barrier of cubes and dragon's teeth ran along the head of the beach to the mouth of the Barry Burn. Set in breaks in the lines of cubes were two Y-shaped pillboxes. A photograph taken by the Poles shows five lines of dragon's teeth at this point, looking north-east towards the town (Fig. 13.14).

Three shelters for artillery pieces were erected in or near Carnoustie: one at Panbride, 1.5km to the east; one at the eastern end of Carnoustie beside the Coast-guard Station (still surviving, Fig. 9.4) and the third in the middle of the blocked beach (2 on Fig. 13.13). These were, respectively, 4-inch guns numbers 6, 5 and 4 of 943rd Defence Battery (Mobile), RA (marked on Fig. 13.9). The rear part of the gun-houses was fan-shaped, to allow the 4-inch guns to traverse (Fig. 9.4). As elsewhere, by June 1941 the 4-inch naval guns had been replaced by 75-mm guns of French pattern.[47] The Poles pointed out to Scottish Command that changing from 4-inch naval guns would reduce the battery's capacity to engage with ships, but the reply reminded them that the battery's role was to fire at barges or other small craft being run ashore, and that field guns were just as capable of this task. Like the other Mobile Defence Batteries, the guns were repositioned in mid-1941, once regunned, to prioritise the defence of ports and aerodromes.[48] The defences of Carnoustie and Barry, including the 4-inch guns, were visited by General Alan Brooke in December 1940, and later by the King and Queen, accompanied by General Sikorski (Fig. 13.15).

The defences of Barry Links can be considered in five parts (Fig. 13.13), starting at the Barry Burn: (a) north-east – the northern half of the east face of Barry

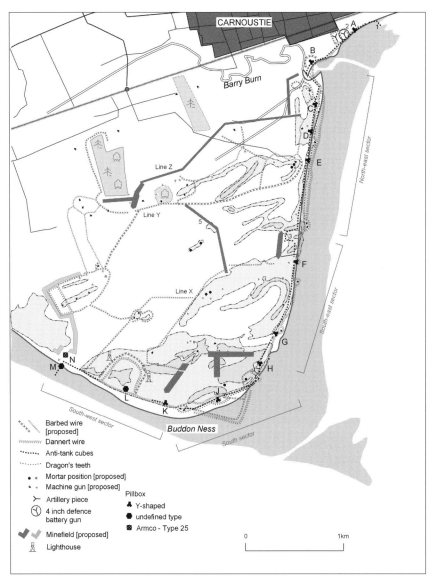

Figure 13.13.
Barry Links, showing the
defences mapped by the
Polish Army, and proposals
for strengthening, 1940–41.

Links; (b) south-east – the southern half of the east face; (c) south – Buddon
Ness; and (d) the south-west sector. Finally, sector (e) comprises the three north-
west defence lines running across the links from north-east to south-west. The
most heavily defended are the first and third. The entire beach in front of Carnoustie
and round the Barry peninsula was shown on Polish military maps as covered by
anti-glider poles. They are not marked on the maps here.

(a) North-east sector
South of the Barry Burn, the barrier of cubes, fronted by two lines of dragon's

Figure 13.14.
Dragon's teeth at the west end of Carnoustie Beach, built by the Polish Army and recorded by one of their photographers (Polish Institute & Sikorski Museum, London).

Figure 13.15.
The King and Queen at the defences of Barry with General Sikorski (on the Queen's left) (Polish Institute & Sikorski Museum, London).

teeth, ran across what was then apparently unconsolidated sand, but what is now stabilised links, turned a sharp corner and then headed southwards for about 1.5km. There were three Y-shaped pillboxes, 250–350m apart, set into the line of cubes in the northern part of this sector (pillboxes C, D and E on Fig. 13.13). There were also a dozen or so firing positions for machine guns (both light machine guns (Brens) and medium machine guns (Vickers)) and mortars on or close behind the beach, which lay within a maze of barbed wire entanglements. Three of the machine gun positions were set forward on the beach to allow them to enfilade the beach to north and south.

(b) South-east sector

At the boundary between the north-east and south-east sectors (3 on Fig. 13.13), the line of cubes (with no fronting dragon's teeth) jinked inland (west) for about 150m to form a re-entrant about 150m across (north–south). Contemporary aerial photographs suggest that the cubes followed what was then the edge of the line of dunes, stabilised by vegetation, around an area of unstable sand. This sector, where the anti-tank barrier was provided by a single line of cubes fronted by Dannert wire, had two Y-shaped pillboxes (F and G on Fig. 13.13) and two machine gun emplacements enfilading the beach. The Polish sketch maps suggest that the relative weakness of the defences here may have reflected the presence of a more effective natural barrier provided by high sand-hills at this point.

(c) South sector – Buddon Ness

The southern tip of Barry Links, starting a little east of Buddon Ness, was the most heavily defended point of all, even though parts of the beach were backed by relatively high dunes. There were three Y-shaped pillboxes (H, J and K on Fig. 13.13) over a front of about 1,300m. Tucked into the south of the easternmost pillbox, the Polish maps showed a well-placed artillery position (just south of pillbox H) that could fire over a wide arc from the approaches to Carnoustie in the north, across the mouth of the Tay to Tentsmuir Sands in the south. Most of the frontage of this sector was blocked by a line of cubes fronted by a double line of dragon's teeth and a line of Dannert wire. The shattered remains of pillbox J, as well as a short stretch of cubes and dragon's teeth, survive in a tidal pool on the sands, as the coast has retreated here. There were two substantial minefields behind the beach.

(d) South-west sector

Within the last sector of the beach defences there were three pillboxes (L, M and N on Fig. 13.13), none of them the Y-shaped type. The pillbox close to the lighthouses (L) was described on the Polish maps (in Polish) as the 'English pillbox'. The north-west end of the beach defences was formed by a 500m-long line of cubes along the top of the beach, which turned out to sea for 100m or so, closing off the beach to the north. Some of the surviving cubes are unusual in still having their wooden shuttering in place, albeit now rather rotten (Fig. 13.16). Pillbox M, still visible, albeit partly buried, is an unusual shape, providing machine gun embrasures firing along the line of the beach to the south-east and north-west. Its style is reminiscent of Polish-built pillboxes in Fife (Fig. 9.5). Pillbox N, the last, appears to be an 'Armco' Type 25. One of the Polish maps annotates a feature in its approximate position as 'Schr[on] dla ludzi' – 'bunker/shelter for people'. To the north-west there were no further defences on the beach, and at first the height of the

Figure 13.16.
Anti-tank cubes on the
western coast of Barry, with
timber shuttering still in place.

older inland dunes, behind the coast dunes, may have been considered an adequate anti-tank barrier. A Polish map of April 1942 illustrated a proposal to complete the defence of the north-west coast of Barry and the coast to Monifieth using beach scaffolding and mines. There was no record of scaffolding in this area and it seems likely that this was never built.[49] There was a 500m-long line of anti-tank cubes covering the front of Monifieth, west of the position of gun No. 3 of 943rd Defence Battery (Mobile), RA until Spring 1941.[50] None of these survives and they are not separately mapped here.

(e) North-west sector (not labelled on the map)
The Polish maps revealed the complexity of the defence behind the beach. There were three north-east to south-west defence lines within Barry Links (labelled lines X, Y and Z on Fig. 13.13), made up of Dannert wire, barbed wire and minefields, within and around which there were many machine gun and mortar positions.

The written record for the building and occupation of Barry is patchy, and troops mentioned as being stationed there may only have been living in Barry Camp, rather than building or manning defences. Although Barry fell within the boundaries of 137th Brigade of 46th Division in the summer of 1940, it seemed that none of their men were positioned east of Dundee, and that the Dundee garrison was responsible for Barry.[51] Units came and went rapidly over the summer. Two batteries of 61st Anti-tank Regiment, RA, were there from May to July, when a detachment of 10th Black Watch took over.[52] On 18 August, elements of 71st Field Regiment, RA became responsible for Barry, and by the 22nd eight of its newly acquired 75-mm guns were positioned there. The mixed equipment of this regiment on that date is perhaps indicative of the problems of the supply of artillery pieces after Dunkirk: it had four 18-pounders, sixteen 75-mm and four 25-pounders.

The 10th Battalion South Staffordshire Regiment (a Pioneer battalion) became responsible for the defence of Barry at the end of August or beginning of September 1940,[53] with support from Royal Engineers (272nd Field Company), 168th Pioneer Company) and a detachment of 9th (Home Defence) Battalion Black Watch. Wire obstacles were to be provided along the whole front; forward defence locations were also to be wired; anti-tank obstacles were to be covered by pillboxes; and field positions were to be constructed.

The Polish Army took over the defence of Angus in mid-October 1940. Its customary energy is visible in its files. A map dating from November–December 1940 showed the ten Y-shaped pillboxes, the Polish gun position beside the coast artillery in Carnoustie, and Dannert wire east of Barry pillbox A (Fig. 13.13), between pillboxes D and F, and behind pillbox H.[54] The Barry area was garrisoned in 1941 by the Polish 14th Lancers and the 10th Polish Engineer Company.[55]

ANGUS INLAND

It was considered important to block the north-east to south-west routes across Angus, and consequently two anti-tank stop-lines were planned as early as 7 July 1940 (Fig. 13.1).[56] The 'Kirriemuir Line' ran from the coast in the eastern suburbs of Broughty Ferry to Kirriemuir, in the shadow of the hills. The other, without a name, ran from Montrose to Brechin (that is, along the South Esk), then to Edzell and then along the line of the North Esk, presumably northwards towards Cortachy. The purpose of both lines was 'To check enemy advancing on DUNDEE-PERTH' and the primary manning was to be undertaken by the Home Guard, with support from troops stationed in Angus.[57] Nothing more was heard of the first line; like one or two other lines planned at that time it seemingly ignored the grain of the country or natural barriers.

By November 1940 four lines were listed in the Sub-area. The first two seem to have been created out of parts of the second of the July lines, using the rivers North Esk and South Esk as separate barriers – a much more sensible idea. In addition, taking them in order as one moves south, there was a line from Carnoustie to Finavon and one from Monifieth to Cortachy. This last line was identical to the 'Kirriemuir Line' listed in July.

By April 1941, only the North and South Esk lines were still listed, but the two other lines were there in the wider pattern of roadblocks in the area, which reflected the move away from linear defence systems to the fortification of 'nodes'. By 1943 none of the stop-lines appeared in Scottish Command's list.[58]

The North Esk Line

The North Esk Line was intimately associated with the defence of the beach north of Montrose (Fig. 13.1). The river emerges from the hills above Edzell in a gorge called The Rocks of Solitude, about 17km from the river's mouth as the crow flies. The river formed a very effective barrier across the coast plain, where there were only four road bridges and two rail bridges. Of the three fords, only that close to the mouth had any evidence of blocking.

The South Esk Line

The coastal plain is only about 20km wide north-west of Montrose, but the South Esk takes a more meandering course, so that the South Esk anti-tank line was some 40km long. The river flows into the western side of Montrose Basin, which in turn drains into the sea to the south of Montrose. From the basin, the river runs north-north-west for around 8km, where it skirts the town of Brechin on its southern side. The river then runs west across rolling agricultural land, and then north into the hills, for about 23km. There were only three road crossings between the basin and the fringes of Brechin and in 1940 the next crossing upstream was over 9km west, at Finavon. On 22 June 1941, Exercise 'Finavon' was mounted by a troop of Commandos (probably the same outfit who had been testing aerodrome defences to destruction round Angus). They were pretending to be German parachute troops ordered to take and hold two crossings over the South Esk in advance of a larger force that had managed to cross the North Esk Line. The Commando troop attempted to penetrate the defences of the roadblocks on the bridges at Finavon and Justinhaugh. At the former, the defences were penetrated by 'magnificent stalking' which taught the Home Guard troops about all-round observation and alertness. At Justinhaugh, the Commandos made a more direct approach and managed to take the bridge.

The Carnoustie–Finavon Line

This line (Fig. 13.1) appeared as an entity only in the list of November 1940. It did not follow or use any particular watercourse or other natural barrier. Instead, it utilised well-positioned roadblocks placed on roads and junctions that would have slowed down a German advance. It is possible that the line was also known as the Maclagan Line.[59] From Finavon the line would have been completed to the hills by using the river and the north-westernmost roadblocks on the South Esk Line. The listing makes it clear that the six roadblocks in and around Forfar, behind the line, were an integral part of it. Like an optical illusion, the Carnoustie–Finavon 'Line' disappears as an entity after November 1940, but remained as a line of points, manned by the same people. In the changed philosophy of the time, however, it represented a series of defended nodes, rather than a linear defence.

The Kirriemuir Line

The Kirriemuir Line appeared in the list of stop-lines for Highland Area in July 1940[60] and in the Angus Sub-area list for November 1940.[61] The line ran from near the western end of the Monifieth beach defences and comprised roadblocks closing all the north-east to south-west roads south of the Sidlaw Hills, and, north of the hills, the main road at Glamis. As with the Carnoustie–Finavon Line, it had disappeared as a 'line' by April 1941, but its component roadblocks remained active, among a wider series of blocks within Angus.

Inland from Barry and Monifieth, between the Carnoustie–Finavon and Kirriemuir Lines, at Douglas Wood, was one of the most heavily-defended radar stations in Scotland, with at least seven Type 27 pillboxes (Fig. 13.1). One of them is illustrated on Figure 9.2.

Dundee

Dundee's harbour was by far the most significant potential enemy target in the Angus Sub-area. It was much larger than Arbroath and Montrose and, with its open front to the Tay estuary, it was at risk of a major landing by a mechanised force. Indeed, the J.C. Plan of November 1939 included Dundee as one of the six ports in eastern Britain that might be a conceivable landing place.[62]

In 1940, Dundee was rather smaller than it is now (Fig. 13.17), but the combined Home Guard force available in the city, and in Monifieth and Broughty Ferry, was large: 2,635 men, with 1,310 rifles and 67 light machine guns. On 17 July 1940 the Army garrison of Dundee comprised 50th (Holding Battalion) Black Watch,

9th Black Watch, two Pioneer companies of 9th York & Lancaster Regiment and the 242nd and 243rd Batteries of 61st Anti-tank Regiment, RA.[63]

Between 15 October 1940 and 1 March 1941, 5th Brygada Kadrowa of the Polish Army (one of the surplus-officer battalions) was responsible for the defence of the area from Monifieth to the west of Dundee.[64] By June 1941 a Polish Engineer battalion, about 100 strong, had assumed responsibility for the defence of Dundee. The Polish forces liaised with the Dundee Home Guard and set out detailed plans for its defence.[65] There were at least 23 pillboxes, many of them at or near road junctions on the defence perimeter along the Kingsway (Fig. 13.17).

Figure 13.17.
Dundee's defences, largely as represented on a Polish map of 1941.

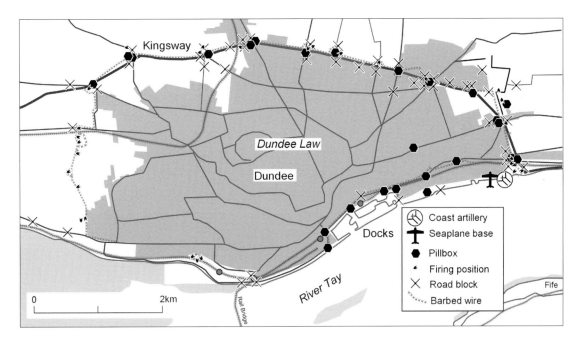

14. FIFE SUB-AREA

Fife Sub-area was very much larger than the historical county. It took in Kinross and a large part of eastern Perthshire, including Perth itself, the valley of the Earn as far west as Dunning and Forteviot, and the Tay as far north as a line from Luncarty to Burrelton (Fig. 14.1). The Sub-area was believed to be vulnerable to direct assault on the beaches of north-east or south Fife, and to penetration towards Perth by an attacking force from the north-east, from Dundee or the Angus beaches.

The Forth was one of Scotland's six 'major defended ports' and within it on the Fife side were significant port facilities, both military and civil: the naval base at Rosyth, Methil (and the convoy assembly area in Largo Bay), as well as Kirkcaldy. All of these lay within the outer fixed defences of the Forth, while all but Methil and Kirkcaldy lay within the middle line (from Burntisland to Edinburgh), with the key batteries on the island of Inchkeith.

In 1940, there were four major RAF and Fleet Air Arm aerodromes in the eastern part of Fife Sub-area – Leuchars, Dunino, Crail and Stravithie – two of which lay on the coast. A fifth, civil airfield north-west of St Andrews, at Craigie Barn, appeared in an August 1940 list of aerodromes to be defended, but not thereafter. The key aerodrome near Rosyth at Donibristle lay well within the Forth defences and was less vulnerable. Three minor aerodromes lay to the north-east of Perth, at Perth Racecourse, Scone (the most important of the three) and at Whitefield.

There is little information about the period of defence construction before the Poles took over the area on 15 October 1940. Two weeks later, on 3 November, their British liaison officer informed Scottish Command that the Poles had already given instructions for the safeguarding of beach defences to protect them from damage by the sea, and were preparing to insert mines to replace concrete defences destroyed by the sea.[1]

On 10 December, Major General Kossakowski, C-in-C of Polish Engineers, raised concerns about the defences that the Polish Army had inherited in Angus and Fife. He reported that they had been built in haste in the summer and had 'neither a homogeneous nor an accomplished character'.[2] Some 57 new emplace-

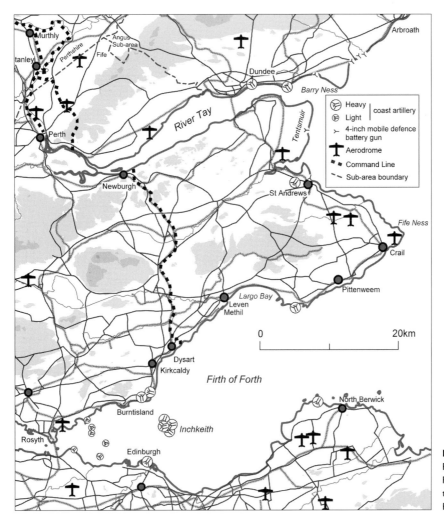

Figure 14.1.
Plan of Fife and part of
Perthshire Sub-areas, including
the coast batteries of the
Forth Fixed Defences.

ments and observation posts were needed and 15 extant emplacements required reinforcement; 700 anti-tank cubes were to be moved; and 150,000 yards of wire obstacle was to be created; 18,600 mines were to be laid; and almost 5,000 anti-glider posts were to be erected. Scottish Command responded a few days later, generally positively, but requested an input into the design and location of these additional defences.

It is clear that work to build and repair the concrete coast defences continued into 1942, but in May of that year it was decided that no more concrete obstacles were to be constructed at Tentsmuir. Cement and aggregate contracts were to be cancelled and tubular scaffolding, already supplied to South Highland Area to replace concrete obstacles 'which have become ineffective owing to the drifting sands', was to be used instead.[3]

BEACHES

Tentsmuir, Edenmouth and St Andrews

Tentsmuir is one of the largest areas of dunes in Scotland (Fig. 14.2). It is also one of the rare cases where the coast is, in general, growing rather than eroding;[4] there are, however, parts of the east-facing coast where there is active erosion. Comparison between wartime and more recent maps shows considerable change and the anti-tank cubes – originally sited along the top of the beach – provide a useful fixed line against which coastal change can be marked. Now, many of the cubes are well inland, while some are over 50m out onto the intertidal sands.

Tentsmuir was seen as particularly vulnerable to an enemy invasion, since a good beach for a landing was close to an aerodrome (Leuchars) and to ports on the south Fife coast. If an invader penetrated the beach and the woodland behind

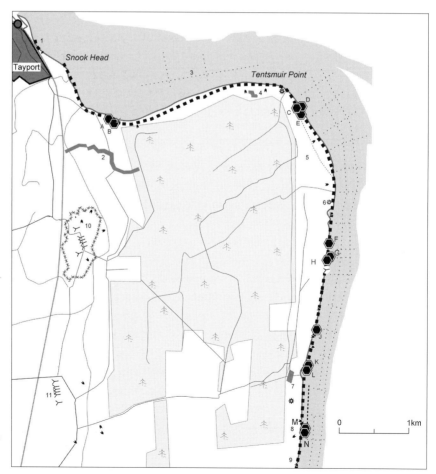

Figure 14.2.
The defences of the northern part of Tentsmuir. The key for the drawing is on Fig. 14.9.

it, he would find a series of good roads running south-west through favourable tank country across Fife towards the major port at Methil and the naval base at Rosyth. Beyond, via the road bridges at Kincardine and Stirling and the Forth and Alloa rail bridges, was the administrative and industrial heartland of Scotland. As a consequence of this vulnerability, a 'backstop' was created in the form of the southern part of the Scottish Command Line, crossing Fife from the Forth at Dysart to Newburgh on the Tay. This is described below.

In 1940–41, most of the area behind the Tentsmuir beach had been densely afforested for almost 20 years,[5] although routes from the beach were more open then than they are now. As with Angus Sub-area, understanding of the defence of the beaches has been enhanced by the thoroughness of the map record created by the Polish Army between December 1940 and September 1941.[6]

There was a continuous line of anti-tank cubes from Snook Head at the north-west, round the coast for about 12.5km into the mouth of the Eden, with separate lengths of barrier to the north-west at Tayport (1 on Fig. 14.9) and at Shelley Point on the edge of Leuchars aerodrome (16 on Fig. 14.11). In places, the Polish engineers recorded large-scale replacement of cubes tumbled about by the sea, and in one sector (at 5 on Fig. 14.2) replaced a long section of fallen cubes 150m *further out* to sea; the rationale for this is no longer obvious. The pattern of anti-glider poles on the beach, shown on the Polish maps, is marked '3' on Figures 14.2 and 14.9. The line of cubes was fronted throughout its length by a line of Dannert wire; in some places there was also a parallel line of barbed wire. Behind the cubes, machine gun and observation posts were marked on the Polish maps as surrounded by a profusion of barbed and Dannert wire enclosures, which are not shown on the maps here. The locations of beach searchlights were identified at various times by the Poles and the four most persistent locations along the frontage are marked on the maps here.

Thirteen pillboxes have been recorded on the beach. All but one of the survivors are based on the hexagonal Type 22. They are of a markedly different style from 'normal' examples, and built to metric dimensions (75cm thick walls); they are also grouped to provide mutually supporting fire in a way not often observed in British defence systems, in which pillboxes were usually strung out along a line. The Poles had far more experience of building linear defence systems incorporating pillboxes with interlocking fields of fire, on their pre-war eastern and western frontiers. In all but the two pillboxes at the north-west end (A and B on Fig. 14.2), the surviving boxes' walls were cast in timber shuttering; in contrast, A and B had had corrugated iron shuttering (Fig. 14.3). The embrasures were very large – effectively occupying the whole of a facet of the hexagon, or placed in a corner. They were simple and had no support for a gun other than the thick wall of the box. Some had two embrasures, others had three. The pillboxes look

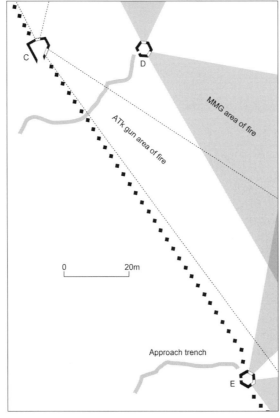

tall, partly because they have reinforced concrete roofs far thicker than the 30cm that was specified at the time for British pillboxes.

The single anti-tank gun pillbox (C on Fig. 14.4; Fig. 9.5) had two broad embrasures, to allow the gun to enfilade the line of cubes, and a broad entrance behind the cube line. It was clearly marked as an anti-tank gun pillbox on the Polish maps.

The north-westernmost pillboxes (A and B on Fig. 14.2; 14.3) are set on higher ground with good fields of fire to north-west and north-east, the forward one covering a complex roadblock (with sliding steel beams on rollers) giving access through the line of cubes. A machine gun position was mapped to the east and there was a long narrow minefield to the rear (at 2 on Fig. 14.2).

Tentsmuir Point was heavily defended, with a small minefield (4 on Fig. 14.2), firing positions, and three pillboxes – two Type 22s (D and E) and the anti-tank gun pillbox (C) – which were positioned to provide mutual support, while protecting each pillbox from accidental shots from the others (Fig. 14.4). Both Type 22s have surviving sunken access trenches.

To the south was another major defence complex, a wired enclosure measuring about 680m by 120m, containing three pillboxes on the line of cubes (F, G and H on Fig. 14.2), accommodation huts and a 4-inch naval gun, No. 2 of 943rd Defence Battery (Mobile), RA (raised in Carnoustie in August 1940) (Fig. 14.5).[7] As noted

Figure 14.3. (opposite top) Tentsmuir pillbox B, with its simple, large embrasures and clear signs of its corrugated iron shuttering (Author).

Figure 14.4. (opposite below) Tentsmuir pillboxes C, D and E, set within and in front of the line of cubes, showing their interlocking fields of fire. All are of Polish design. Pillbox C was built for an anti-tank gun while D and E were for medium machine guns. D and E have covered approaches in trenches, which are still visible (Author, for Forestry Commission Scotland).

Figure 14.5. (left) Tentsmuir: 4-inch naval gun, No. 2 of 943rd Defence Battery (Mobile), RA, with pillbox H in the background (Fife Council Museum Service).

above, 4-inch guns were returned to the Navy in April 1941, being replaced first by 18-pounder, and then, in June, by 75-mm field guns. The two surviving pillboxes (F and G) are Type 22 boxes of the familiar pattern; F is unusual in having the shapes of two anti-tank cubes cast onto its roof, presumably to make it look like an unbroken line of cubes from the air (Fig. 14.6) About 300m further south was another barbed wire enclosure, within which were section firing posts, an anti-aircraft medium machine gun and a pillbox (J on Fig. 14.2). This area is now in the intertidal zone and there is no trace of any of those structures.

The two pillboxes, K and L (Fig. 14.2), are those illustrated in a well-known series of contemporary photographs (Fig. 14.7) showing Polish soldiers working on revetting the coast, presumably because of erosion. The boxes also appear in detailed engineering diagrams showing how the revetting was to be built (Fig. 14.8).[8]

Pillbox K has previously been identified as for a beach searchlight,[9] but it was mapped by the Poles as a medium machine gun pillbox, and contemporary photographs of the pillboxes ready for use show that the large embrasures were reduced in size using sandbags. A photograph in the Imperial War Museum shows Polish troops using a light railway to move materials around the site, as appears on one of their photographs at Carnoustie; the base of one of these rail-hoppers has been conserved and displayed on site. There is a minefield just behind these pillboxes (7 on Fig. 14.2), apparently blocking the road to what is now the Forestry Commission car park, which partly occupies the site of the minefield. At point 8 on Figure 14.2 a Dannert wire enclosure surrounded firing positions and two light machine gun pillboxes (M and N on Fig. 14.2; 14.9) marked on the Polish

Figure 14.6. (right) Tentsmuir pillbox F with the shapes of two concrete cubes cast onto its top, probably to assist camouflaging the pillbox (Matthew Ritchie).

Figure 14.7. (opposite top) Tentsmuir pillbox H being revetted, showing how sandbags were used to reinforce the walls and reduce the size of embrasures (Fife Council Museums Service).

Figure 14.8. (opposite below) Polish engineers' drawing of the revetting work to be done at Tentsmuir pillbox H (Polish Institute & Sikorski Museum, London).

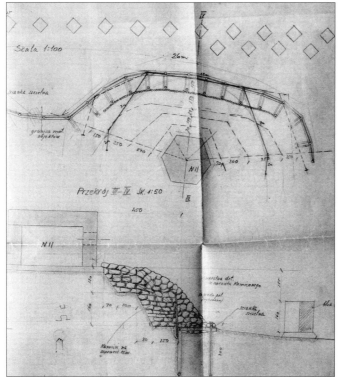

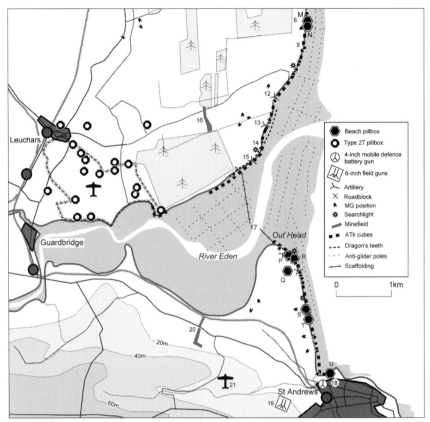

Figure 14.9.
The defences of the southern part of Tentsmuir Sands, the mouth of the River Eden, and the west beach of St Andrews. The boundary of Leuchars aerodrome is that in 1940–41, before major wartime expansion and the extension of the runway eastwards.

map and visible on an undated wartime RAF vertical aerial photograph.

The southernmost elements of the defence visible on the map were a series of firing positions and a rectangular concrete structure set on a low hill (9 on Fig. 14.2). While this has six small embrasures to the sea and to both flanks, and there are the remains of a table of some kind that might have been used for supporting a gun – the embrasures are more the size for Bren guns than Vickers – the structure was marked as an observation post on Polish maps, rather than a pillbox. There is a small square hole in the roof that may have accommodated a periscope. To the west of the forestry plantation, Polish maps showed the location of artillery and medium machine gun firing positions, particularly around Morton (10) in the north and Rhynd in the middle sector (11).

South of pillboxes M and N the line of defence began to curve westwards into the river mouth. The positions there comprised scattered light machine gun emplacements behind the cubes, two defended barbed wire enclosures behind the beach, a searchlight site and a pair of anti-tank guns (12 and 13 on Fig. 14.9). In what must have been seen as a vulnerable section of beach, the anti-tank cubes were reinforced by dragon's teeth, in front or behind (14 on Fig. 14.9; Fig. 14.10).

These probably reflected a strengthening of the original line after the Scottish Command directive of December 1940. An anti-tank gun emplacement, mapped at point 15 (Fig. 14.9), may be identified with a timber and steel emplacement surviving in the sand cliff just behind the cubes. A minefield lay behind the line of defence to block a gap between two areas of forestry plantation (16). Interpretation of many aerial photographs of Leuchars aerodrome by David Easton has revealed at least 18 Type 27 pillboxes around the boundary of what was then a much smaller aerodrome, and to its north and west. A line of beach scaffolding ran inland of the anti-tank cubes on the north side of the Eden to the edge of the main channel and the line resumed on the south side, running to Out Head (17).[10]

The defences shown on the Polish maps resumed on the south side of the River Eden (Fig. 14.9), where a line of cubes curved round the northern tip of Out Head and ran along its eastern side towards St Andrews, becoming a double line about halfway to the town. The line was covered by a number of machine gun emplacements protected to the front and rear by barbed wire, and the beach in front of the cubes was planted with anti-glider poles. Post-war changes mean that little is now visible, other than a few lengths of half-buried cubes. Three machine gun pillboxes were mapped near the northern end in a characteristic Polish group (P, R and Q); two lay on the line of cubes, the third to the rear. These were flanked by two anti-tank guns and a searchlight, and were protected from the rear by a barbed wire entanglement. At one time the Poles had an artillery

Figure 14.10.
A single line of anti-tank cubes reinforced by two lines of dragon's teeth. Beyond the seated figure the teeth have been added to the landward (right) side of the cubes (Author).

piece on Out Head. A pair of pillboxes was mapped (S and T), accompanied once again by an anti-tank gun.

A simple pillbox has been recorded at the south end of the beach (U on Fig. 14.9), but this was not shown on Polish maps. Behind it was No. 2 gun of 943rd Defence Battery (Mobile), RA (18 on Fig. 14.9). The 4-inch naval gun, complete with shield, looking as if had just been plucked from the deck of a destroyer, sat in an incongruous position in what is now the beer garden of Rusack's Hotel (Fig. 14.11). Two further guns located west of the town (19 on Fig. 14.9) were clearly labelled on one Polish map as 6-inch coast guns (which Scottish Command record as being in Polish hands). A Polish archive photograph shows one of these formidable guns on its First World War field mounting (Fig. 14.12).

The town of St Andrews itself was the subject of detailed defence planning by the Polish Army, whose files contained dozens of plans of buildings and their surroundings, with intended firing positions and fields of fire.

A further Polish map, indicating dispositions between 15 October 1940 and 1 March 1941, showed that the area between the Tay and the Eden was the responsibility of 6th Infantry Battalion of Polish 1st Brigade.[11]

Figure 14.11.
4-inch naval gun, No. 1 of 943rd Defence Battery (Mobile), RA, sited at Rusack's Hotel in St Andrews. (Fife Museum Service).

St Andrews to Elie

From St Andrews south-east to Fife Ness, and then south-west along the coast to Elie (Fig. 14.13), a few Vulnerable Points were blocked, and firing positions for machine guns and artillery were established at key points. The triangle of land defined by St Andrews, Fife Ness and St Monans contained three aerodromes: Crail Naval Air Station, Dunino (a satellite to Leuchars) and Stravithie (an Emergency Landing Ground for Leuchars). Of these, Crail and Dunino had pillboxes built (11 and 5 of them are recorded, respectively). The overambitious Polish proposals for the defence of Dunino in August 1941, and the sceptical Scottish Command response, have already been mentioned (pp. 71–2).

Away from the airfields, small-scale defences were built on the coast at Kinkell Ness, where two machine gun positions lay behind barbed wire. The next defences were located on Buddo Ness, where a pair of what are clearly Polish-built pillboxes facing east and west is linked by a tunnel; at Boat Haven, where a pair of pillboxes faced the sea – the fragments of one survive, along with fortified firing positions in a stone wall; and at Babbett Ness, where two field guns were positioned to fire west-north-west and south-east along the coast.

Cambo Sands was included on the lists of defended beaches created in October 1940 and April and October 1941. The two later lists described the beach as protected by mines only. The beach is about 800m long and the Polish map showed a

Figure 14.12.
One of the two 6-inch naval guns on a First World War field carriage operated by the Polish Army near St Andrews (Polish Institute & Sikorski Museum, London).

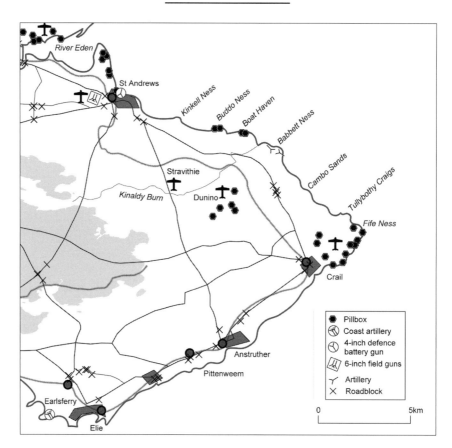

Figure 14.13.
The defences of the East Neuk of Fife. Artillery positions are those marked on Polish Army maps.

minefield about 1,100m long and about 60m across, closing off the whole beach and the area to its north. At Tullybothy Craigs, included in the October 1941 beach list, the Poles mapped four separate minefields covering much of the vulnerable area from just east of Randerston Castle to the east end of Balcomie Links. Between the minefields was a pair of machine gun posts and an anti-aircraft machine gun.

At least 11 pillboxes have been recorded in and around Crail Naval Air Station, mostly a mixture of Types 24 and 27. Many of the former have had their walls doubled in thickness (Fig. 14.14). Short lines of anti-tank cubes blocked a section of beach at the very easternmost tip of the aerodrome, near Kilwinning Castle, and a further line of anti-tank cubes ran out from the coast in the middle of Crail village. A pillbox sharing some characteristics of the unusual examples at Largo Bay was built on the very tip of Fife Ness; an inscription inside states that it was built by Polish engineers in May 1941 (Fig. 9.5).

Between 15 October 1940 and 1 March 1941 the 3rd Infantry Battalion of Polish 1st Brigade was responsible for the area from the mouth of the River Eden southwards to about Kinkell Ness.[12] What seems to be an independent Company ('7 Kompania') manned the coast from Buddo Ness and Fife Ness.

Figure 14.14.
Aerodrome defence pillbox
at Crail, showing the thickening
of the wall (Author).

Elie and Largo Bay

There are four separate, relatively small beaches over a distance of about 7km from Ardross to Shell Bay. The first constructed defences are found at the head of the narrow bay, known as Wood Haven, on the western side of Elie Ness. Although the sandy beach is backed by a slope 9m high, a single line of anti-tank cubes was built along its top (1 on Fig. 14.15). Only a short run of the cubes now survives. To the east and north-west all the flat areas were immobilised by a pattern of neatly-dug anti-glider trenches.

Elie was itself a barrier to invading forces, and only the road from the harbour and four lanes through the houses to the beach were blocked. Beside the westernmost lane is a machine gun embrasure set into the sea wall below a garden (Pillbox A on Fig. 14.15) providing flanking fire over the western half of the beach. Behind the village, and to the east, all the flat fields and the golf course were immobilised by a pattern of anti-glider trenches (2 on Fig. 14.15). On the western side of Chapel Ness is Earlsferry Links, fronted by a sandy beach broken up by rocky shelves. No new defences were built here, but Kincraig Point was the site of a coast battery comprising (in 1940–41) two 6-inch guns – part of the fixed defences of the Forth.

Shell Bay is a narrow but deep sandy beach about 500m across between the heights of Kincraig Point and the lower Ruddon's Point to the west (Fig. 14.15). A burn at the east end was blocked by a triple row of dragon's teeth, which survive, and a longer triple line closed off the western part of the beach and the headland separating Shell Bay from Largo Bay. A triple line of dragon's teeth ceased to be a standard part of the defensive repertoire after the *Military Training Pamphlet* 30 specifications were issued in Scottish Command in December 1940, when five lines became the norm.

Largo Bay appeared on the Scottish Command lists of vulnerable beaches

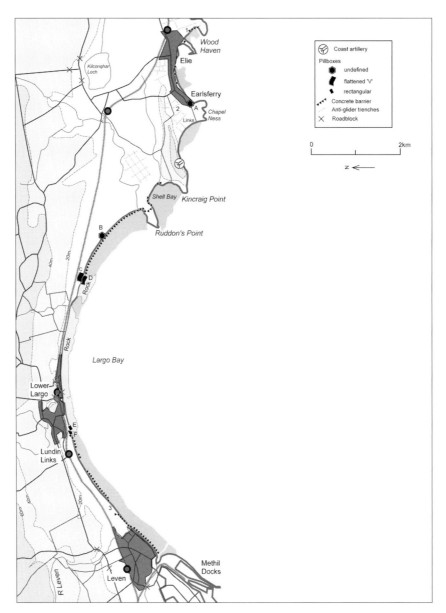

Figure 14.15.
The defences of Elie, Shell Bay and Largo Bay.

dated October 1940 and May and October 1941 (but oddly, not that for April 1940). It incorporated by far the most attractive beach for a landing between Tentsmuir and the beaches of East Lothian. It is split into two roughly equal parts by the conjoined villages of Lundin Links and Lower Largo.

For about 1.3km east of Ruddon's Point the beach is sandy and the dunes behind it are low, and as a consequence it was blocked by a mixture of concrete cubes and dragon's teeth to a point where the beach gives way to a rocky platform. Three pillboxes were built, one about midway along (B on Fig. 14.15 – not surviving) and two, described below, at the western end of the cubes. Near the western end of the line one cube bears the marks '15 AUG J.C. 1940' inscribed in the concrete.

The two surviving pillboxes (C and D on Fig. 14.15; Fig. 14.16; Fig. 9.5) stand one behind the other, providing interlocking fire. Although they bear a passing resemblance to the Y-shaped pillboxes noted in the Arbroath–Barry sector of the Angus coast, they are of a unique flattened V-shaped design. Both have only two embrasures, facing east and west along the beach, and in both cases the embrasures are protected from fire from the sea by dwarf walls, jutting out from the seaward corners (see p. 121). They are certain to be of Polish design.

The sector of beach from the pillboxes to Lower Largo/Lundin Links is backed by high dunes and the steep embankment of the former railway, and also is mainly rocky; consequently, it seems to have required no concrete barrier. The village itself, with its high stone walls to the sea, and the cliffs in the western part, formed a barrier to landing, until the golf course, immediately west of the village.

The first defence features south of Lundin Links were two rectangular Polish-built pillboxes, which still survive; they were set at an angle into the steep dune face below the golf clubhouse (E and F on Fig. 14.15), to direct fire from a single embrasure westwards along the beach. Because of the curve of the beach, the eastern pillbox fired past the western pillbox. In both cases the embrasure was protected from fire from seaward by a dwarf wall (Fig. 9.5). This sector of the beach has high dunes behind it, and short lengths of anti-tank cubes were built only where an additional barrier was required. About 600m to the west the height of the dunes dropped, and from there a near-continuous barrier of cubes ran to

Figure 14.16.
One of the two Polish pillboxes (C) in the northern half of Largo Bay (Author).

the mouth of the River Leven (3 on Fig. 14.15). To the west of the river lies the port of Methil, which was a major entry port for Atlantic convoys for much of the war, and was included on various lists of Vulnerable Ports.[13]

Between 15 October 1940 and 1 March 1941,[14] 4th Brygada Kadrowa (a surplus-officer battalion) was responsible for the defence of the area from Anstruther to Dysart.

Anti-invasion defences were erected in a few vulnerable places on the coastline between Largo and the Forth Rail Bridge and Rosyth. Where there were sandy beaches they were in the main backed by steep natural slopes. The list of beach obstacles to be cleared at the end of the war, however, included anti-tank cubes at Blair Point, just north-east of Dysart. These formed the southernmost terminal of the Scottish Command Line (Chapter 15).

Kirkcaldy and Dysart were included in lists of beaches to be blocked dated April and October 1941.[15] At Kirkcaldy, the construction in 1922–23 of the 1,400m-long sea wall and esplanade provided an effective anti-tank barrier for most of the town. As a consequence, anti-tank cubes were needed only on Pathhead Sands to the north-east of the harbour; to the south of the esplanade, closing the mouth of the Tiel Burn and an area to its south; and at the southern end of the beach. A carefully-drawn Polish map, dated November 1941, showed the location and extent of about 35 defended localities (existing and proposed) protected by Dannert wire, covering approaches by road and cross-country to Kirkcaldy and Dysart, and noting the location of existing and proposed roadblocks and demolitions.[16]

Burntisland was included in the April and October 1941 lists of beaches to be blocked. Only three exits through the esplanade wall and a small unwalled section at the west end of the esplanade wall actually required a barrier. In the eastern part of the bay, a combination of high ground and the steep railway embankment along the coast provided an adequate barrier to landing. A pillbox was built covering the south pier of Burntisland dock.

The very extensive Burntisland Sands were covered by a square pattern of anti-glider poles, many of which survive, albeit cut down to just above ground level. At Pettycur, the headland between Kinghorn and Burntisland – far less built-up in 1940–41 than it is today – there were two coast defence batteries, both comprising two 6-inch naval guns,[17] part of the fixed defences of the Forth. There were at least two pillboxes at the east and west ends of the barbed wire compound around the batteries.

No anti-invasion defence was specified for the stretch of coast from Aberdour to Dalgety Bay, but the headland between Barnhill Bay and Dalgety Bay was the site of a 6-pounder coast defence battery at Charles Hill.[18] This point also acted as the northern anchoring point for the anti-submarine boom which blocked Mortimer's Deep out to Inchcolm island. There was a pillbox at Braefoot Point, overlooking a naval pier and Dalgety Bay. Donibristle aerodrome lay just behind Dalgety Bay and one pillbox of its defences has been recorded.

The naval base at Rosyth was one of the key strategic locations in central Scotland. At Pitreavie Castle, north of the town, was located the combined RAF and Naval command HQ, which was surrounded by at least six pillboxes (five of them apparently Type 27). Details of the defence of the dockyard were provided in the files of the Polish Army. These showed a boundary of triple Dannert coils, roadblocks, machine gun and anti-tank rifle positions. No pillboxes were mapped, and the pillboxes recorded to the west of the dockyard area and to the east of Inverkeithing do not seem to have been incorporated in the Polish defence plans.

The files also show a high level of preparation for the defence of the towns of Rosyth and Dunfermline. Sketch plans of the surroundings of individual buildings, or parts of streets, showed the planned location of gun positions and fields of fire. One from Dunfermline is reproduced here (Fig. 14.17).

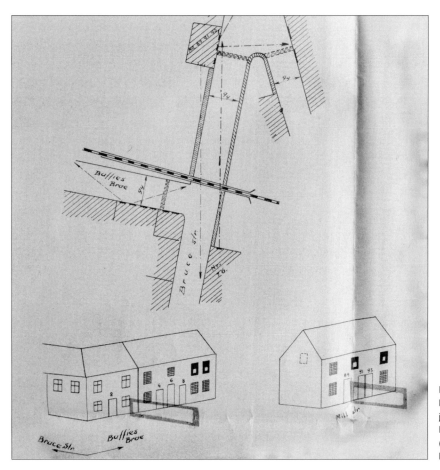

Figure 14.17.
Polish defence plan for the junction of Buffies Brae and Bruce Street in Dunfermline (Polish Institute and Sikorski Museum, London).

15. THE SCOTTISH COMMAND LINE

The Scottish Command Line was described in Scottish Command's October 1940 Defence Scheme as, 'A defensive line, to cover the approaches in favourable country to the FORTH–CLYDE isthmus ... constructed from DYSART ... on the FIRTH OF FORTH along the railway line to NEWBURGH ... From KINFAUNS ... to a mile south of STANLEY ... the line forms a bridgehead covering Perth to the East and North-East. From STANLEY ... the line follows the railway and river to DUNKELD ... with extensions to TUMMEL BRIDGE. A continuous anti-tank obstacle is included.'[1] Its depth and complexity reflected the perceived levels of risk, and therefore the deepest defences blocked the easiest routes towards Perth from Forfar and across Fife towards the naval base at Rosyth (Fig. 15.1; 15.7).

On 9 June 1940, in his appreciation of Scotland's strategic position, General Carrington proposed the Perth–Dunkeld–Rannoch line (which was to become the northern sector of the Command Line) as the most effective one to defend the industrial capacity of central Scotland.[2] GHQ Home Forces gave permission on 14 June for the line to be constructed, but suggested that it be extended across Fife to the Firth of Forth. This line – Dysart to Newburgh – would become the southern sector of the Command Line.

The Command Line comprised the following elements: the anti-tank barrier; over 100 road, rail and river-blocks; over 400 firing positions, including 21 pillboxes; demolitions; and minefields.

THE ANTI-TANK BARRIER

On 2 April 1940, the Commander Royal Engineers (CRE), Scottish Command drew up instructions about anti-tank ditches:[3] 'Anti-tank ditches must be sited on the same principles as other obstacles, i.e. they should be sited tactically to canalize the attack into positions from which they can best be dealt with by weapons. They should be enfiladed by anti-tank weapons and defended by machine gun and small arms fire, in order to prevent destruction of the obstacle'. Thus,

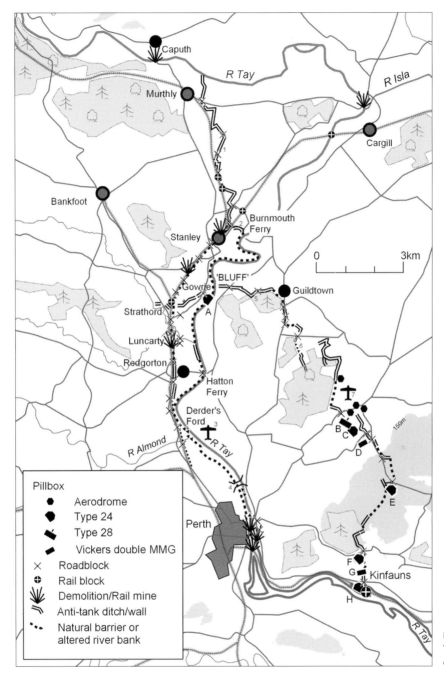

Figure 15.1.
The northern sector
of the Command Line.

the V-shaped salients visible on the Command Line (as in Fig. 15.2) were designed
to allow anti-tank guns to enfilade the ditch, without the danger of hitting each
other.[4] That the line was marked out on the ground with considerable care was
shown by a reference to a partly completed ditch in a War Diary in August 1940.

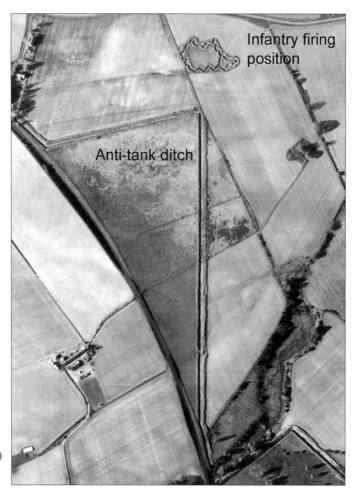

Figure 15.2.
Aerial photograph of the anti-tank ditch zigzagging north towards Murthly. A complex infantry firing position lies to the east of the ditch here, one of three on the Line (the others being at Kinfauns and near Dunkeld) (RAF/National Collection of Aerial Photography).

It was stated that part of it had been dug on the wrong alignment, the consequence being that 'the fire plan would be upset'.[5]

There were up to four parallel lines of anti-tank barrier, most often two anti-tank ditches, revetted with timber and brushwood held in place with galvanised wire. In a couple of places some of this galvanised wire is still visible; in one location, at Loanfolds (5 on Fig. 15.1), upright timbers survive in the ditch. Existing obstacles were exploited or strengthened wherever possible: watercourses; railway cuttings and embankments; woodland; and bogs. The parallel lines of anti-tank ditch were sometimes linked by roughly perpendicular cross-ditches to form closed cells. In three places, south of Kettlebridge, at Thornton and at Balfarg (Fig. 15.7), an arm of the anti-tank ditch ran westwards, perpendicular to the primary ditch, to block what was then the main north–south road.

There were also many anti-tank cubes, anti-tank walls and occasionally dragon's teeth, all designed to fill in vulnerable parts of the line or associated with a road or rail-block (Fig. 15.10). In two places, major stretches of dragon's teeth were built to form the main anti-tank barrier. As on the beaches, there was a great deal of barbed wire, much of it Dannert concertina coils. It was suggested that, 'Wire obstacles should, where possible, be erected on both sides of the anti-tank obstacle'.[6]

Road-, Rail- and River-Blocks

There were blocks of some kind at every point where the anti-tank barrier met a road, railway or tram track, or on road bridges under or over the railway line where that was close to, or itself formed, the anti-tank barrier. There were also fixed blocks in watercourses. On roads and railways there were three kinds of movable barriers: vertical rail on busy roads; horizontal rail on minor roads or tracks; and wire (although there were only two clearly identified examples of the last). Some minor tracks were blocked permanently to vehicular traffic by concrete walls, while allowing pedestrians to pass, and some of these still survive, on minor roads and tracks.

Firing Positions

The firing positions for infantry and guns took different forms: loopholes in walls; slit trenches and weapon pits (the files suggest there were 385 of these); four more complex firing positions, formed by trenches and weapon pits; and 21 pillboxes (8 in the northern sector and 13 in the southern). A further seven pillboxes were built in positions where they would have reinforced the Command Line, three protecting Ladybank army depot and four recorded at Perth/Scone aerodrome (although there is no evidence that these pillboxes were built at the same time as the Command Line). In turn, three of the Command Line pillboxes (B, C and D on Fig. 15.1) would have materially aided the defence of the aerodrome, which lay immediately to the east of the anti-tank ditch.

Pillboxes

Seventeen of the original 21 Command Line pillboxes survive. Four types are represented and the destroyed boxes probably conformed to two of the types. All had 'shellproof' walls (1.3m thick):

- Hexagonal Type 24 (Osborne 2008) designed for a Bren gun, usually with one loophole per side; there were certainly 9, and probably 12, of these on the line (Fig. 9.2).

- A hexagonal pillbox based on Type 24 and designed by Scottish Command Royal Engineers, 'modified for use as a combined anti-tank Rifle and Bren gun by altering the two rifle loopholes in the long face [which usually flanked the door] accordingly and shifting the doorway to one of the opposite faces'.[7] Four pillboxes on the Command Line seem to have been of this type; three (C, L and V on Figs 15.1 and 15.7) survive, while W (Fig. 15.7) has been destroyed (a plan of V is on Fig. 9.2).
- Four rectangular pillboxes with a pair of large loopholes facing in one direction for two Vickers medium machine guns, with subsidiary flanking rifle loops (all four survive – D, G, T and U on Figs 15.1 and 15.7; a plan of D is on Fig. 9.4).
- A single classic Type 28 pillbox for a 2-pounder anti-tank gun with separate Bren chamber (B on Fig. 15.1, Fig. 9.4).

Demolitions and Mines

The original preparations for defence included a range of planned demolitions in the northern part of the Command Line. There were no watercourses on the Fife section of the Command Line large enough to act as a barrier but, on the Tay, demolitions were planned for all the rail and road bridges from the centre of Perth in the south and as far north-west as Tummel Bridge. In three places there were also plans to mine the railway: at Luncarty; at a point just south of Stanley; and at Stanley Junction. The Poles, however, took a much more radical approach to tactical demolitions, and made at least outline preparations for the demolition of *every* significant road and rail bridge in Angus, Fife and western Perthshire. This was wholly contrary to Scottish Command doctrine, but the Poles were clearly intending to make the Germans fight for every yard of Scottish soil.[8]

COMMAND LINE, NORTHERN SECTOR

The Command Line has already been described in print in some detail and what follows is therefore very much a brief summary, from north to south.[9] From Murthly northwards the anti-tank obstacle of the Command Line was formed by the River Tay, which from that point upstream would provide a substantial barrier, once the road and rail bridges over it were blown. The most northerly constructed anti-tank obstacle began at the top of the steep southern bank of the Tay, just north-east of what was then the Perth District Lunatic Asylum in Murthly. A single line of ditch ran south to the railway line and then zigzagged back and forth to the east of the railway for about 5km (Figs. 15.1, 15.2). There was a roadblock at every point where a road, or even a track, crossed the line of the ditch. The railway itself was used to provide the obstacle only in a couple of short stretches. In Black Wood (1 on Fig. 15.1) one of the best-preserved sections of the anti-tank ditch is still visible, with an intact horizontal-rail roadblock where a minor road crosses it.

To the south of Stanley on the west side of the Tay the barrier was doubled. The bank of the river was modified, where necessary, to form an obstacle, right into the centre of Perth, and cubes were built to block Derder's Ford across the Tay, the mouth of the River Almond and burns at Luncarty and on the North Inch in Perth. To the west of the river, a second barrier was provided by a combination of lengths of anti-tank ditch and railway embankment; every bridge under or over the railway or ditch had a roadblock. In a number of places blocks or demolitions on the railway itself were planned. North of Perth there was a temporary bridge, one of five built or adapted to bypass bottlenecks on the Scottish road network.[10] At Strathord (2 on Fig. 15.1) a line of anti-tank ditch ran roughly east to west; near its eastern end, on the bank of the river, a Type 24 pillbox still stands (A on Fig. 15.1), positioned to fire on the roadblocks to the north-west.

There was a Command Line forward position on the east bank of the Tay, in the form of a mainly single line of anti-tank ditch covering the two most important approaches to Perth, from Forfar and from Dundee. The ditch ran from the point called 'Bluff' in the army files (Fig. 15.1), to Guildtown, past the western boundary of Scone aerodrome (at 7 on Fig. 15.1) and south to the Tay again at Kinfauns. The area enclosed included the emergency landing ground at Perth Racecourse (3). The heaviest defences were concentrated on the two main routes, from Forfar to Perth and from Dundee to Perth. On the northern of these, where it passed Scone aerodrome, three pillboxes covered the road from high ground to the south: the Type 28 anti-tank gun pillbox (B on Fig. 15.1; Fig. 15.3); a Type 24 variant for

Figure 15.3.
The large embrasure in Command Line pillbox B to accommodate a 2-pdr anti-tank gun (Author).

Bren and anti-tank rifle (C); and a double Vickers pillbox (D). This last pillbox is very well preserved, including its heavy timber gun tables (Fig. 15.4). Two pillboxes also covered roadblocks on minor roads over the hills (E – where lengths of anti-tank ditch are visible (Fig. 15.5) – and F on Fig. 15.1). Finally, a double Vickers pillbox (G on Fig. 15.1; Fig. 15.6 – still surviving), as well as a Type 24, covered the Dundee to Perth road and railway at Kinfauns. At point 6 on Figure 15.1 the barrier was formed for 350m by five lines of dragon's teeth.

Figure 15.4. (opposite top) Heavily-built timber and brick gun table for a Vickers medium machine gun in Command Line pillbox D (Author).

Figure 15.5. (opposite below) A surviving portion of the Command Line anti-tank ditch above Muirton Farm, near Pillbox E (Author).

Figure 15.6. (above) Pillbox G – one of the double Vickers machine gun pillboxes on the Command Line – at Kinfauns (Author).

Southern Sector

The southern sector of the Command Line ran across Fife, from Newburgh on the Tay to Dysart on the Forth. As in the northern sector, although the barrier was continuous, the defences were concentrated at the points of greatest threat – where the main roads crossed it from east to west. Thus the narrow coast plain at Newburgh was obstructed by a double ditch, covered by fire from a Type 24 pillbox (J) on high ground. Road- and rail-blocks at Den of Lindores were likewise covered by a second pillbox (K).

South of the hills (where the barrier was relatively weak), it was built with a double line of obstacles: to the east a ditch, and behind it a combination of ditch and railway embankment. North of Collessie (9 on Fig. 15.7, a 300m-long section of dragon's teeth, five deep, took the place of the anti-tank ditch, where bedrock close to the surface prevented it being dug (Fig. 15.8). A further length of dragon's teeth, three deep, lay just west of the village. Collessie itself was intended to be a major obstacle, with two lines of anti-tank ditch to the north and south, and

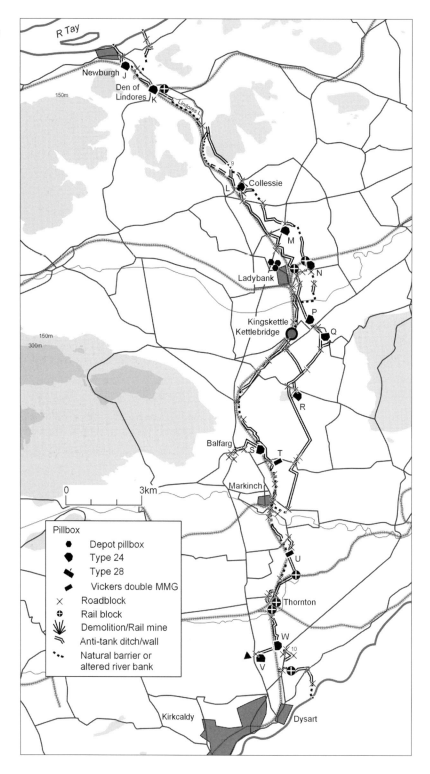

Figure 15.7.
The southern sector of the Command Line.

Figure 15.8.
Dragon's teeth on the Command Line, above the village of Collessie in Fife. The two lines to the right are larger and may reflect a reinforcement of an original three lines of teeth (Author).

Figure 15.9.
Command Line pillbox L on the edge of Collessie in Fife. This is an example of the Type 24 variant found on the Command Line, with two embrasures on the longest wall, to accommodate a Bren gun and a Boys anti-tank rifle side by side. The pillbox has been camouflaged using fieldstone, to merge into the wall in which it is built (Author).

roadblocks within the village and on the approaches to it, all covered by a Bren gun and anti-tank rifle pillbox (L on Fig. 15.7; Fig. 15.9).

The main road from the east, through Ladybank and Kingskettle (Fig. 15.7), was blocked by up to three lines of ditch, with pillboxes that covered road and rail-blocks on the main routes (M, N, P and Q on Fig. 15.7) – all of Type 24. South of Kettlebridge, a cross-ditch between east and west ditches was designed to block the main north-east to south-west road.

Pillbox R (Fig. 15.7) now destroyed, covered a complex roadblock on a minor road on the eastern ditch. The routes through Balfarg were blocked by a Type 24 which covered a bridge over the railway (S) and a double Vickers pillbox (T) which could fire north into the rear of an attacking force. Balfarg was one of the places where a length of anti-tank ditch ran westward, behind the main ditch line, specifically to block the main north–south route. South of Markinch, a fourth double Vickers machine gun pillbox (U) would have provided flanking fire on an enemy approaching the major railway junction at Thornton, where the rail-lines were also blocked.

South of Thornton there was another westward branch of the anti-tank ditch specifically to block the north–south main road. The roadblock there was covered by one of the Command Line Type 24 variant pillboxes (V on Fig. 15.7) with embrasures for both a Bren gun and an anti-tank rifle on the long, north-facing, wall.

In places, there are large sections of concrete anti-tank wall, including a length of 300m at Kettlebridge, and one 43m long adjacent to a roadblock at Cowdenlaws Farm, near the south end (10 on Fig. 15.7; Fig. 15.11); the latter was covered by a pillbox, now destroyed (W on Fig. 15.7).

Construction and Manning of the Command Line

Figure 15.10.
The remains of part of a Command Line railway block on the main line at Ladybank Junction in Fife. The line would have been blocked by lengths of rail set vertically in sockets between the cubes shown on the photograph (Author).

The construction of the Command Line was a major enterprise which involved many Royal Engineers, requisitioned digging machines, civilian contractors, specially hired labourers and volunteers. The first construction units were in place by 19 June 1940. Under the overall command of Lieutenant Colonel Nutt, based in Perth, the construction of the Fife sector (with HQ at Kinross) was recorded

as requiring five Royal Engineer companies; 100 locally sourced labourers; 1,000 men from Westfield Colliery; 2,000 men from labour exchanges; and local volunteers. Twenty mechanical excavators were requisitioned.[11] The construction of the Tay sector (with its HQ at Murthly) was undertaken by four companies of Royal Engineers, one company of Pioneers, 170 locally employed men, 200 additional men from labour exchanges, local volunteers, eight mechanical diggers and four rail-mounted excavators, usually used for track maintenance. Among the volunteers and ancillary troops working on the ditch were, at various times, the Home Guard; 100 LNER railwaymen; 250 men from Nairn's linoleum works in Kirkcaldy; and 240 miners. At one stage 400 men from 4th Stevedore Battalion were being carried by train from Rosyth naval base to Thornton Junction every day for ditch-digging. By mid-July 500 civilian labourers from Edinburgh, Leith and Falkirk were engaged on the work.[12]

Originally, in July, no infantry trenches or concrete works were to be built on the Command Line.[13] In August, however, it was decided that there would be a total of 50 machine gun and anti-tank gun pillboxes, although only the 21 already described were eventually built. It was also decided that a second anti-tank ditch was to be dug in advance (i.e. to the east) of the one already planned.

By 7 July 1940, the line, although scarcely begun, was already appearing in battle plans. The 9th Division, for example, included among its wide-ranging roles across eastern Scotland manning either the north or south sectors.[14] One gun of 205th Anti-tank Battery, RA was to be in pillbox B (Fig. 15.1) overlooking Scone airfield, and four of the Vickers medium machine guns of the 7th Battalion, the Cheshire Regiment, were to be in the specially-designed machine gun pillboxes D and G.[15]

Figure 15.11.
A horizontal-rail roadblock and a length of concrete anti-tank wall at Cowdenlaws, on the Command Line (Author).

If 9th Division had to occupy the northern sector, however, the Commanding Officer of 15th Infantry Brigade (responsible for the section from Stanley to Dunkeld) planned to ignore the Command Line (which he considered an inadequate barrier). Instead he would deploy his men to the east of the river, to protect the approaches to the bridges at Dunkeld, Caputh and Kinclaven, and the approaches to Burnmouth Ferry. This more flexible and 'modern' approach highlighted the growing irrelevance of 'static' defence systems like the Command Line.

By 27 August, 34.5 miles of the anti-tank ditch had been completed, with 9.75 miles of dug ditch still to be revetted; 70 road and railway blocks had been completed; and 18 pillboxes were projected or in hand.[16] In late September 1940 it was planned that all work would be completed by mid-October. By 2 November, apart from salvaging equipment and stores and making good problems reported by farmers, the line was complete, including all the pillboxes and 385 infantry firing trenches. The 157th Pioneer Company remained in the area to maintain the structures of the line until June 1941.[17]

The Polish Army took over responsibility for the defence of Fife and southern Angus in mid-October 1940. Its files for 1941 included detailed plans for the manning of the forward positions of the northern Command Line, east of the River Tay, from Kinfauns to the point known as 'BLUFF'.[18] They also included proposals for a further length of anti-tank ditch to be dug running east–west to the north of Scone. Very much more extensive minefields along the anti-tank ditch were planned.

Over in Fife, the Polish dispositions seemed not to take any account of the Command Line; their forces were positioned well to the east, closer to the east Fife beaches.[19] In February 1941, the War Diary of 110th Army Troops Company, RE reported on progress on the creation of over 120 roadblocks in Fife; these clustered round towns and villages, and blocked routes of communication, in conformity to the doctrine of the defence of 'nodal points', rather than linear defensive systems.[20] The Command Line had become irrelevant.

16. EDINBURGH AREA

Edinburgh Area comprised that part of mainland Scotland between the Forth estuary and the border with England), and contained the country's administrative capital, and major ports and aerodromes. In 1940–41 Edinburgh also formed the hub for the road and rail transport networks for south-east Scotland. To the east of the city were the vulnerable beaches of East Lothian and Berwickshire, largely lying outside the Forth fixed defences. These gave access to the main road and rail-lines to England, and running in the main through gently rolling arable land – good tank country. An invader here could strike west to Edinburgh, and beyond to Scotland's industrial heartland, or south-east into England.

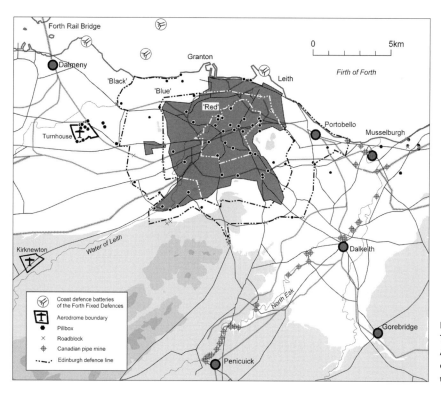

Figure 16.1.
The central part of Edinburgh Area, including the three defence lines of the city and the stop-line of the North Esk.

In 1940–41 there were nine aerodromes or landing fields, either operational or under construction, in Edinburgh Area (not all within the sectors mapped in Figs 16.1 and 16.2). The most important were the Category A fighter stations at Drem and Turnhouse and their (also Category A) satellites at East Fortune (which seems to have replaced Hatty's Plantation by the end of 1940), Tranent and Kirknewton. Two further satellite aerodromes near the border, at Charterhall and Winfield (Horndean), were at a sufficiently advanced stage of construction to require a guard from June 1941. Finally, although the RAF landing ground at Lennoxlove (Haddington) had appeared on none of the Army lists until November 1941 (when it was listed as a satellite Aircraft Storage Unit to Dumfries), it was active from early in 1941. Of these aerodromes, Turnhouse seems to have been the most heavily fortified (with 11 pillboxes recorded), with Tranent having two and Drem having eight and a battle HQ. One of Drem's pillboxes was sacrificed to a demonstration of how to blow one up on 12 May 1941.[1] In Border Sub-area, the Drone Hill radar station, less than 4km inland but about 7km from the vulnerable beaches, was heavily defended by at least ten Type 27 pillboxes.

The Forth was one of Scotland's six 'major defended ports' and within it, on the Edinburgh side, were significant port facilities: the large civil port of Leith, and the naval harbours at Granton and Port Edgar (the latter lying on the opposite bank from Rosyth naval base). All of these lay within the outer and middle defences of the Forth, while Port Edgar lay within the inner defence line. Two 6-inch coast batteries, each comprising two guns, lay within the Area boundary as part of the defences of the Forth; one at Leith Docks (part of the middle line of the Forth fixed defences); the other on the coast just north of Dirleton (although known

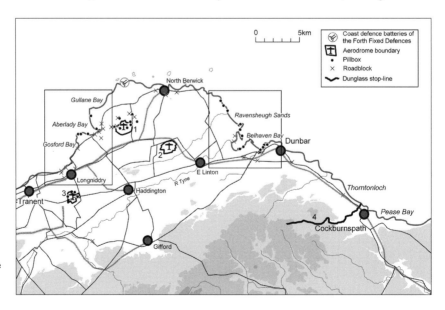

Figure 16.2.
The defences of the East Lothian sector of Edinburgh Area. Aerodrome 1 is East Fortune, 2 Macmerry and 3 Tranent. The boxes indicate the boundaries of Figs 16.3 and 16.4.

by the name of the small island of Fidra, just offshore). The 6-inch battery at Berwick-upon-Tweed was initially in Scottish Command but was handed over to Northern Command in October 1940.[2]

There were no Mobile Defence Batteries on the beaches here, apart from the two 6-inch naval guns on First World War field carriages (at first split between Dunbar and west of North Berwick and then both at Bourhouse, south of Dunbar). Their role was to engage enemy landing craft and cover the beaches north-west of Dunbar (see Fig. 14.12 for one of these near St Andrews). It seems likely that an instruction to the Fife- and Angus-based 943rd Defence Battery (Mobile), RA in April 1941 to take over an existing unit at Dunbar referred to those guns. The guns before and after this seem to have been commanded by whatever RA Regiment was based in the area (e.g. 70th Field Regiment in July 1940, and 71st Medium Regiment, RA and 155th Field Regiment, RA during 1941).[3] In March 1942, the harbour entrances at Dunbar and Eyemouth were reported as having flame projectors either in place, or to be installed; the point of this so late in the war is open to doubt.[4]

The Polish Forces took over responsibility for the defence of East Lothian in the spring of 1942, on giving up Angus; they had been lobbying hard to be moved south for training for active service, especially armoured training. As in Fife and Angus their maps were detailed and informative, although they may record some structures erected after the middle of 1941.[5]

BEACHES

The number of separately-listed vulnerable beaches in the Area rose from two in May 1940 to seven by October 1941. Aberlady and the beaches north-west of Dunbar were two of the three highest priority beaches in June 1940.[6] A year later, the 'most dangerous beaches' in Scotland were recorded as those 'in the vicinity of North Berwick' (along with Montrose, Newburgh–Aberdeen and Lossiemouth); consequently they were defended by a brigade group.[7] As late as September 1941,[8] in a 52nd Division Royal Engineers Operation Instruction, 155th Brigade was still preparing beach defences from Belhaven Bay to Gullane Bay, while those from Gullane Bay to Gosford Bay were to be reconnoitred with a view to short-term defensive preparations being made.[9]

Seton Sands to Gosford Bay/Green Craig

The beach areas at Seton Sands (Fig. 16.3) are fronted by intertidal sand flats up to 400m in width; extensive bedrock platforms are uncovered at low water, especially at Port Seton.[10] About 2.25km of the beach between Port Seton and Longniddry was obstructed by cubes and anti-glider poles, while a pre-existing sea wall covered the front of Port Seton village itself. One horizontal-rail type roadblock survives about midway along the line of cubes, blocking a track from the main road to the beach, and there were two roadblocks on the main road itself. The line of cubes seems to have been double in its eastern and western portions, but triple in the central section. At the east end of the beach the line turned out onto a rock platform (1 on Fig. 16.3). Significant lengths of the cube line survive in the central and western sectors.

The line of cubes resumed after a short break of rocky coast and ran in a continuous line round Ferny Ness, where many cubes still survive in a double row.

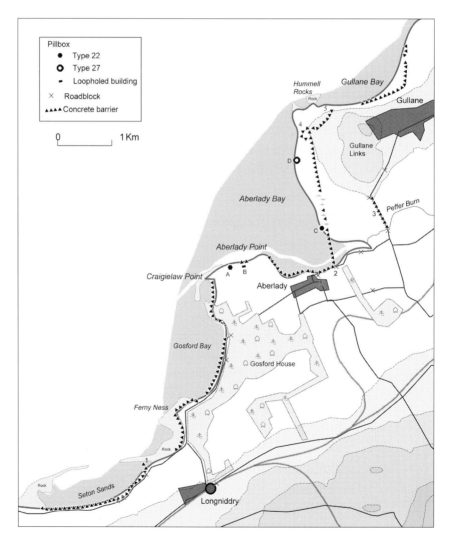

Figure 16.3.
The defended beaches from Seton Sands to Gullane Bay.

After a further short break where an existing sea wall provided a barrier, a near-continuous double line of cubes stretched to the north end of Gosford Bay, where the line turned north-west (as a single line) through woodland. The double line along the beach, through which there was one roadblock, was largely buried, removed or reused as erosion defence after the great storm of 1953.[11] RCAHMS has recorded that some of the tumbled cubes in Gosford Bay still show traces of camouflage paint. The single line of cubes survives in the wood for around 500m, about 75m behind the beach. After the point at which the line returned to the beach, the cubes on the shore have suffered considerable erosion and display signs of wartime brick repairs to their bases; this line originally ran to Craigielaw Point.

Aberlady to Gullane

In June 1940 the Aberlady beach was second in priority (after Sinclair's Bay in Caithness) in the list of 13 vulnerable beaches in Scotland. At low tide, the bay contains a vast area of firm flat sand, which was obstructed by glider poles, and around which anti-tank obstacles were built where necessary.[12] At low tide the course of the Peffer Burn runs through the tidal sands close in to the southern shore, along a rock platform. A short length of tumbled cubes may have been constructed where some barrier was required, and two pillboxes were also built on this shore: a Type 22 (A on Fig. 16.3) is visible in 1940s aerial photographs and was marked on a Polish map of 1942,[13] and a little to the east, a tile-roofed, stone-walled building (B) was adapted as a strongpoint by having two windows reduced to form long, narrow firing embrasures.

A continuous line of anti-tank cubes ran from Aberlady Point for about 1.5km before turning sharply northwards and running for 500m across the Peffer Burn and the tidal sands. Virtually nothing survives here, apart from a short length of anti-tank wall flanking the main road on the southern side of the Burn (2 on Fig. 16.3), probably part of a roadblock.

The line of cubes originally ran northwards almost continuously for about 2.3km from the south side of the Peffer Burn, broken only where boggy ground made the construction of a barrier unnecessary. The southern part the line was double and even triple in places. Two pillboxes have been recorded in this section, in front of the cubes, near the shore: a Type 22 at the south (C on Fig. 16.3) and a Type 27 to the north (D). The line of cubes near the coast was backed up by a second line of cubes and a roadblock along the main road, across the valley of the Peffer Burn (3 on Fig. 16.3).

At the northern end of the long straight line of cubes (4 on Fig. 16.3), there survives an unusual enclosure formed by double and triple lines of cubes, round a high sand-hill, which on the Polish map was the site of an artillery piece (firing north-west) and machine gun positions. The line of cubes ran north-east to a point on a high cliff at Hummel Rocks, where it stopped (5). This last section was photographed from the air, already complete, in July 1940. The anti-tank cubes (reinforced or replaced by short sections of dragon's teeth by the time of the May 1942 Polish map) resumed a little to the east, in Gullane Bay.

Meanwhile, decisions were made in November 1940 that the short stretches of sandy beaches east of Gullane, including the frontage of North Berwick, would not be obstructed by concrete.[14] The Polish map, however, showed heavy wiring.

Ravensheugh to Dunbar

Ravensheugh (Fig. 16.4) had been on the list of beaches to be obstructed in the *Scottish Command Defence Scheme* of October 1940. A map drawn by 17th Battalion Durham Light Infantry[15] showed the defences in the same month, including pill-boxes, annotated for Vickers machine guns and anti-tank guns, and other firing positions. Further pillboxes seem to have been added to the map; these may have been built before the unit left the area in December. The Polish forces and 157th Brigade again drew maps of the defences in the spring of 1942.[16] Although these make the sequence of construction fairly clear, the 1940 and 1942 maps were not entirely consistent. The existence of mapped pillboxes could only be confirmed by field observation in very few cases: post-war clearance seems to have been particularly thorough in this area.

No anti-tank obstacle is marked on the Durham Light Infantry maps from 1940; file documents make it clear that Scottish Command and the local garrison commander were still at the time only discussing what might be needed. The map published here shows the accretion of defences between November 1940 and May 1942; as in so many cases, the features were emphatically not part of a single process nor built over a short period.

The northernmost pillbox (A on Fig. 16.4), just north of Scoughall, was marked on both the Durham Light Infantry and Polish maps. The earlier map also showed a pillbox (B) just north of the mouth of the Peffer Burn (visible on a 1941 aerial photograph), and both maps agreed on the location of an observation post in the area. Between the two was a horizontal-rail roadblock, with a 'broken column' barrier too (Fig. 8.12). The mouth of the burn was blocked by a line of cubes about 270m long, extended northwards by scaffolding in 1942 (1 on Fig. 16.4). The observation post survives and has brick walls about 45cm thick through which there are narrow horizontal embrasures to seaward and to the south-east (the entrance faces towards the roadblock). Another of these structures now lies tumbled onto its face on the beach (2); the strength of the structure was demon-strated by it remaining completely intact despite its current position. The profile

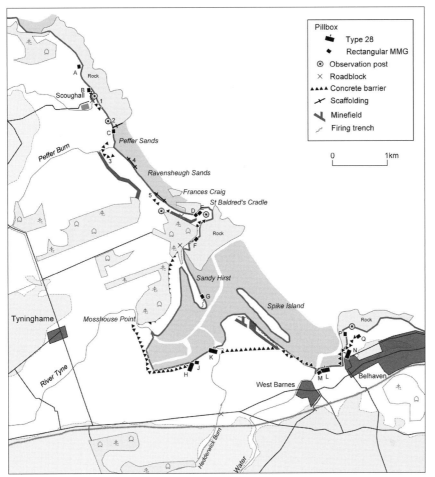

Figure 16.4.
The defended beaches from Scoughall to Dunbar; the defences mapped were built over a period of almost two years, from some point in the summer of 1940 to March–May 1942. The map only shows structures, not individual field positions.

of the embrasure in the observation post strongly suggested that it was not intended for firing a gun (Fig. 16.5). The maps both showed pillbox C (Fig. 16.4) in this area, and, in 1942, a short length of scaffolding ran perpendicular to the beach.

The mouth of the Peffer Burn was blocked above its broad and meandering mouth by about 500m of cubes accompanied in places by dragon's teeth (3 on Fig. 16.4).[17] A 1km-long minefield started behind the cubes, and short lengths of scaffolding (the eastern fronting a line of dragon's teeth) were mapped by the Poles (4 and 5 on Fig. 16.4).[18] The dragon's teeth were proposed in November 1940 and presumably built over the winter of 1940–41; the scaffolding was erected in March 1942. South of point 5 an observation post occupied a high crag; to the south-east, the flank of a further minefield was covered by a double line of cubes running perpendicular to the shore. A track through the minefield was blocked by a horizontal-rail roadblock, strengthened by 'broken column' cylinders. The

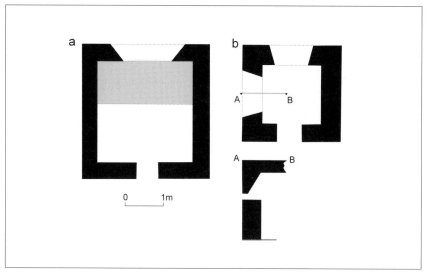

Figure 16.5.
The two types of rectangular structure on the beaches from Scoughall to the mouth of the Tyne. The structure on the left is one of three survivors likely to have been small Vickers medium machine gun posts. On the right is an example of what was probably an observation post: the profile of the embrasure seems unlikely to be for a weapon.

western part of Bathan's Strand was covered by two small rectangular pillboxes (D and E on Fig. 16.4), which are still visible, although one is tumbled onto the beach and the other has lost its front wall and roof. A third of the same kind, in good condition, survives on the other side of St Baldred's Cradle, covering Belhaven Bay and the Tyne Sands (F). Their size and shape is reminiscent of the observation posts to the north-west, near Scoughall, but the plan of the intact one shows considerable differences (Fig. 16.5). They are larger, have a single splayed embrasure facing onto the beaches (in the case of those covering Bathan's Strand, positioned to fire onto the rear of troops landing on the beach (Fig. 16.6)), and have what seems to be a gun table occupying part of the floor area. Although they were only about 1m high, that would have been enough to operate a Vickers medium machine gun, in the sitting firing position. St Baldred's Cradle was the site of the observation post for the guns of 155th Field Regiment, RA.[19]

Belhaven Bay

In June 1940 the beach north-west of Dunbar was third in priority (after Sinclair's Bay and Aberlady) on the list of 13 vulnerable beaches in Scotland.[20] The whole area of the exposed sand and salt marsh here was obstructed by a regular pattern of anti-glider poles. The mouth of the River Tyne is partly obstructed by two substantial sand spits: Sandy Hirst running out from the western side of the bay, and Spike Island from the east, although Spike Island was, in the 1940s, not then such a major feature. Both spits were heavily defended by firing positions and wire; the 1940 map showed a pillbox (G on Fig. 16.4) (annotated 'Vickers') on Sandy Hirst. A low wall of boulders, visible at low water, runs across the mouth

Figure 16.6.
The probable small Vickers post, pillbox E, positioned to fire onto Ravensheugh Sands. Its roof has tumbled onto the beach below (Author).

of the Tyne from the rock shelf seaward of Sandy Hirst, most of the way across the river. Its effect would have been to snag any small craft travelling up the river. It is not clear, however, if this was a defence-related structure.

The concrete anti-tank barrier – mainly a single line of cubes, but occasionally triple – recommenced on the south side of St Baldred's Cradle, with the pillbox already mentioned (F on Fig. 16.4), and ran continuously for about 2.5km to a bluff known as Mosshouse Point, overlooking the River Tyne (Fig. 16.7). There were two horizontal-rail roadblocks through the cubes, reinforced with 'broken column' cylinders. Many of the cubes survive.

The line of cubes resumed on the southern bank of the River Tyne, running southward along the head of the bay behind a pre-existing flood bank. This section

Figure 16.7.
The cubes on the south side of the River Tyne, on Mosshouse Point, west of Dunbar (Author).

(about 850m long) was fronted for a distance of about 475m by a minefield, already in place by the time of the Polish map of 1942 (but not marked on Fig. 16.4). The line of cubes, here double and still in good condition (Fig. 16.8), turned sharply east along the bay's southern edge for about 650m, to the mouth of an unnamed burn, where the line curved inland and then ended where the sand cliff rose sharply to form a natural barrier.

On the high sand cliff to the east there are the blown-up remains of a heavy concrete pillbox (H on Fig. 16.4); surviving features suggest that it was a Type 28 anti-tank gun pillbox, and this is confirmed by marks made on both the 1940 and 1942 maps. The two maps, however, disagree as to which side of this a further pillbox lay (J marked as 'Vickers' on the 1940 map).[21] Both maps showed a further Type 28 pillbox near the mouth of the Hedderwick Burn, and its shattered remains can be seen on the beach. The burn was obstructed by cubes and dragon's teeth, and a triple line of cubes then ran eastwards towards Belhaven Bay. The area isolated to the north of the line of cubes – Hedderwick Hill – was defended by a line of Dannert wire, a number of firing positions and a firing trench along much of its north-east face. Aerial photographs from the 1940s reveal the presence of two large minefields behind the north-east shore. The usefulness of the firing trenches, dug in the summer of 1940, and those on Spike Island, was called into question by the commander of 157th Infantry Brigade in late 1941; he not only suggested that they were too obvious from the air, but was concerned that they might be occupied by an invader. He also believed that it was more important to train his men than have them refurbish these firing positions.[22]

From where the cube line reached the beach, the line of cubes zigzagged along

284

Figure 16.8.
The double line of cubes on the east side of the mouth of the Tyne (Author).

the coast to the mouth of the Biel Water, from which point eastward, for over 400m, an existing high masonry wall provided an adequate anti-tank barrier. The 1940 map showed an anti-tank gun pillbox (L on Fig. 16.4) and a further pillbox marked as 'in cottage' (M), just east of the river. The final barrier, two parallel lines of cubes, ran across the golf course towards the cliffs that protected the frontage of Dunbar town. Within this last section, there was a further anti-tank gun pillbox (N) and a pair of other pillboxes, one of which (Q) was annotated '1 Vickers machine gun (Middx Reg)' – the Middlesex Regiment was a machine gun regiment.

Whitesands to Coldingham

The October 1941 list of vulnerable beaches included an entry for 'Whitesands to Thorntonloch' (Fig. 16.2), a distance of over 6.4km. This section of coast is characterised by limestone pavement running out from the coast, with sectors (and not only the sandy portions) considered, in 1940–41, as being vulnerable to tank landings.

The beach at Thorntonloch was obstructed by about 850m of dragon's teeth, five deep facing the beach and three deep on the west flank (mapped by the Poles in 1942), in a broad line well behind the dunes and behind Thorntonloch farm steading. The line ended at a natural barrier formed by a raised beach at the south. The hundreds of dragon's teeth placed here have now been moved to form a sea wall behind the beach.

Pease Bay is narrow and backed by high cliffs. It appeared in the October

1941 list of vulnerable beaches as to be blocked by wire only. It was, however, described in a document about the Dunglass stop-line (below) as being 'regarded by the naval authorities as a particularly feasible landing place'. Considering its small scale, the height of the cliffs that tower behind it and the ease of blocking the narrow road exits, it is difficult to understand this view. Nevertheless, the Polish maps showed proposals for a minefield across most of the bay, and scaffolding blocking the access up the Tower Burn, at the south-east. The headland to the north-west of the bay (Hawk's Heugh) was occupied by a radar station, defended by at least two Type 27 pillboxes.

Coldingham Bay was the southernmost vulnerable beach listed by Scottish Command in October 1941, but was annotated to be defended by wire only. The narrow beach is backed by a steep slope and no constructed defences have been recorded.

STOP-LINES

In June 1941, two 'check-lines' were listed in Edinburgh Area, based on the River Tweed and the River North Esk, the latter running inland from Musselburgh.[23] In September, the Esk Line was described as running from Musselburgh to Carlops.[24] The purpose of this line was perhaps reflected in 52nd Division's instructions to its 155th Brigade, in September 1941. One of the brigade's tasks was for its reserve battalion 'To occupy a covering position, pending the taking up of a line by 155 Bde gp to cover EDINBURGH from South and S.E. until arrival of remainder of Div.'[25] The records of 10th Battalion Edinburgh Home Guard[26] contain a map showing 33 sites, road and rail bridges and roads and junctions over or near the Esk which were to have Canadian pipe mines installed to create 'surprise' roadblocks by cratering the roads.

A 1943 Scottish Command described two security check-lines: first, along the River Esk from Musselburgh to Penicuick, and thence to the foot of the Pentland Hills on the Penicuik–Biggar road; and second, a line along the River Tweed from the sea to Peebles, and thence via Broughton, Biggar and Symington, to Lanark.[27]

The Dunglass to Elmscleugh anti-tank line (4 on Fig. 16.2) does not appear on any Scottish Command list of stop-lines but had its origins in concerns expressed by 155th Brigade about the protection of its flank. Permission had been given by 8 April 1941 for a demolition belt along this line, and inland, on the roads through the Lammermuir Hills south-east of Gifford.[28] The line made excellent use of the topography to block the main communication routes from Edinburgh towards north-east England. The valley of the Dunglass Burn was both steep-sided and heavily wooded and there were few roads across the hills, inland from the coast. Redfern[29] has described a later, more elaborate scheme, which proposed a large number of road craters (a quick and cheap way of blocking a road) and demolitions on these inland roads. But the initial scheme, which seems to have been built, comprised wire, roadblocks and the modification of the bank of the Dunglass Burn for about 1,300 yards (1,188m) (out of a total length of 7,000 yards (6,400m)) to provide a 'prepared face on those portions not naturally tank proof'.[30] Nothing is now visible of the work done to strengthen the natural barrier.

EDINBURGH

Edinburgh's defences were complex and elaborate. Redfern has collated many sources to list the locations of Home Guard (five battalions) and other units, and their many defended positions, pillboxes and roadblocks.[31] Drawing on his research, the map presented here summarises the locations he identified (Fig. 16.1). There were three main defence lines, from outside in, the Black Line, the Blue Line and the Red Line, with over 80 pillboxes within the city, and around Musselburgh to the east, which was part of the defence system.

Manning

After its return from Norway on 6 May 1940, the 148th Infantry Brigade was posted briefly to Edinburgh Area, with battalions posted across a wide area, including Gullane, Dysart and Newburgh. The brigade was one of the few trained, equipped, experienced and mobile formations in the Command and its loss to Northern Ireland on 6 July 1940, where it was involved in the preparation for the possible pre-emptive invasion of Eire, was a blow to Scottish Command.

The 46th Division, having been evacuated from Dunkirk, was posted to Galashiels, in the Border Training Area, on 1 July 1940, with its 139th Brigade moving, on 6 July, to the Firth of Forth area.[32] The 2nd/5th Battalion Leicestershire Regiment was located in North Berwick and Gullane (and its War Diary mentions work on defences on the 7th);[33] 9th Battalion Sherwood Foresters was at Tyninghame, west of Dunbar; and 2nd/5th Battalion Sherwood Foresters, as the brigade reserve, was in Haddington. While the division had been supposed only to work on rail communications behind the front line in France, and was neither trained nor equipped to fight the battles that it had to on the retreat to Dunkirk, the troops that returned had at least had some battle experience.[34] The brigade group included 70th Field Regiment, RA and an anti-tank battery; a detachment of 71st Medium Regiment, RA operated the two 6-inch naval guns on First World War field carriages near Dunbar.[35]

The War Diary of 9th Sherwood Foresters for July 1940 provided some light relief, after the strain of fighting in France.[36]

1 July. THE RACKETS start: general mutual admiration in high places leads to CB, DSO, OBE to everyone who landed in France on Staff jobs – interesting to see how brave some people [had been whom] we met hurrying down the Dunkirk road ... 46 Div. staff very patriotic collecting scrap metal but keeping it on their chests.

6 July 1940. Given transport, God's blessing and three shovels and sent to this dangerous part of our island fortress, we must win the war.

7 July 1940. Find that anti-tank obstacles have been sited by 5th Columnists or an ignorant Sapper – try to rectify it.

8 July 1940. Hurried visits from Div. Cmdr who withdraws God's blessing, leaving three shovels, one of which has been broken by Pte Alcock.

4 August 1940. Chiefly remarkable that one soldier managed to shoot two others while attending a concert. Apart from this the concert was quite amusing.

18 August. An amusing item [at a swimming gala] was the Sergeants Paddle Boat Race, which made us realise how lucky we were to have the navy to take us from DUNKIRK.

By September 1940, the regular infantry garrison of Edinburgh had been increased from 1st/5th Leicestershire Regiment (with two Home Defence and Young Soldier battalions and signals and training units) to three battalions of the Durham Light Infantry: the 14th, 16th and 17th.[37] The 14th and 17th battalions had been created in July 1940 as so-called 'Dunkirk Battalions', formed from the remnants of units evacuated from France, in this case by officers and men from no fewer than 15 different units.[38] In Edinburgh they received drafts of 800 civilians, to be turned into soldiers. The vetting of men was not as carefully done as in more leisured times, and at least one recruit arrived in a wheel-chair, having been 'lame from birth'. By October, the 14th and 17th Battalions, Durham Light Infantry were manning defences in East Lothian.[39]

In November 1940, the 206th Independent Infantry Brigade (with four infantry battalions) was formed, in part from units already in the area, and was made responsible for the East Lothian coast between Dunglass Viaduct and the western county boundary at Prestonpans. Two of its battalions were spread along the coast from west of Dunbar to Prestonpans, with 165th Officer Cadet Training Unit (in Dunbar) responsible for the coast between West Barns and Cockburnspath.[40] Artillery support was provided by 155th Field Regiment, RA (who also took over the two 6-inch naval guns on First World War field carriages, as C Battery). Other of the regiment's guns were tasked with firing onto enemy landings at Drem and Macmerry. The poor state of the artillery, even six months after Dunkirk, is illustrated by the mixture of equipment (eight 75-mm; eight 4.5-inch howitzers and two 6-inch naval guns – no modern 25-pounders) and the fact that two of the regiment's troops still had no guns (a troop of a field regiment should have had four 25-pounder guns).[41] The 206th Brigade moved out of Scotland in mid-December 1940 and was replaced by 155th Brigade of 52nd Division, which had moved into southern Scotland in November. Most of the division was based in the area between Crieff and Stirling as the Command Reserve, but 155th Brigade was posted to the Gullane–Haddington–Dalkeith area.

The Dunglass railway viaduct marked the east end of the Edinburgh Area's section of vulnerable coast. South-east of that point the Infantry Training Centre of the King's Own Scottish Borderers in Berwick-upon-Tweed was responsible for the limited coastal garrison required.[42]

Substantial numbers of regular infantry, artillery, Royal Engineers and Pioneers were based 40km or more inland, in the Borders Training Area at Galashiels, Selkirk and Greenlaw in June 1940, and again by spring 1941. They were not, however, in Scotland during the late summer and autumn of 1940, when the invasion risk was at its highest, nor were troops in the training area normally given operational roles by Scottish Command.

ARMOURED TRAIN

Edinburgh Area was the base of one of Scotland's armoured trains. From the first allocation in July 1940, train K was based at Longniddry, under Captain B.B. Richards, RE and two NCOs, with a fighting crew from 50 Royal Tank Regiment.[43] Balfour mapped the patrol route of this train: north-west towards Stirling, west towards West Calder, south to Peebles and St Boswells, and east and south-east to Haddington, Gullane, North Berwick, and down the coast to Berwick-upon-Tweed.[44]

17. CONCLUSION

My intention in this book was first, to present a comprehensive overview of what was built in Scotland to prepare for an expected German invasion in 1940–41, and second, using that overview, to demonstrate that the defences were not a homogeneous entity that appeared suddenly in 1940 in conformity to a single coherent plan. Rather, I hoped to show that they were complex reflections of significant shifts in defence policy, of the recognition of changing risks to Scotland and to the UK as a whole, and of, it must be admitted, the shortcomings of British military (and naval and air force) thinking. The relationship between defence policy and what was built was itself not a simple one. The history of defence construction shows that supposedly radical differences in the views of successive Home Forces Commanders actually made rather less difference to the scale of what was done than might have been expected. Although Brooke took over from the supposedly 'static' Ironside in July 1940, and in public at least distanced himself from the building of fixed defences, the construction of those defences went on, apparently unabated, until the middle of 1941. Not only were existing defences strengthened after December 1940, but new and expensive types of fixed defence, such as scaffolding and beach flame barrages, were added to the mix.

The survey of the contemporary documents has made it clear that those who planned the defences were labouring under a series of major misconceptions. Britain believed itself the chief enemy of Germany, as the only combatant left in play in the summer of 1940. It is clear, in retrospect, that Hitler did not intend to invade Britain, but was using the threat of it to try to bring to the table an enemy that he would probably have preferred not to be at war with, before turning on his real enemy, to the east. In the view of the British, their status as chief enemy made it certain that Germany would make a superhuman effort to defeat them, probably by invasion. This assumption was made more powerful because of British misunderstandings and prejudices about Germany and its armed forces. The Germans were supposedly unimaginative, all their military action had to be planned to the last detail, long in advance, and if the plans did not survive contact with the enemy, the Germans could not react quickly. The opposite was the case.

The consequence of this misunderstanding was, however, that the British believed that German victories in 1939–40 were planned in tremendous detail far in advance, and that Germany's next moves, including an invasion of Britain, had 'of course' been planned in the same detail.

British ignorance of the characteristics of foreign armies, and their assumptions, in training, that other armies would organise and react in the same way as themselves, thus led on the one hand to the overestimation of the planning capacity of the German armed forces and, on the other, to the underestimation of their flexibility and adaptability. It also led to certain assumptions about the way in which Germany thought about the projection of military force over long distances. While Britain and the USA had a long history of waging war overseas against distant enemies or in far-flung colonies, Germany, as a continental power until the end of the nineteenth century, had not developed what Dildy has termed 'expeditionary mindedness.' The British armed forces undertook many small-scale military operations during the 1939–45 war, such as the capture of the Lofotens and the Commando raid on the German radar station at Bruneval in France in 1942, spurred on it must be said by a prime minister who valued this sort of warfare. Some German operations might have reinforced a British fear of greater capacity in this area than was actually the case: the assault on Norway (a surprise attack on a lightly armed and ill-prepared neutral); the assault on Crete in May 1941 (a very risky operation that came close to failure); and, later in the war, the daring rescue by German parachutists of Mussolini from captivity. Yet, although there was never any German 'raiding' of the British coastline (and the individual German agents who did land were singularly inept), many of the precautions taken in Britain were against just this sort of raid, or against smaller-scale diversionary operations, for example against Shetland. Fear of this sort of 'hit-and-run' raiding also led to the immobilisation of beaches and landing areas around aerodromes in western Scotland, where the chances of enemy operations of this kind were even less likely. But had no one noticed by mid-1941 that the Germans did not fight like that?

The policy behind the anti-invasion defences was also affected by limitations in British thinking on naval and air power. It has been argued that the Navy had an exaggerated fear of the effect of bombing on the sort of ships (destroyers and cruisers) that would tackle an invasion flotilla. And consequently that there was a good chance of German forces reaching British shores. It was also believed that somehow the Navy might have to resist an invasion flotilla for a prolonged period. A more realistic appreciation of the situation might have meant that anti-invasion defences were not considered necessary: the destroyers would surely have wrought devastation in the lightly-protected flotilla whatever losses they suffered; and once beaten off, it would surely have been both physically and psychologically impossible for the Germans to have had another attempt anytime soon.

In summary, Britain expected a major invasion, large-scale diversions, or major or minor 'raids', that would have been planned well in advance and therefore for which all the equipment (landing craft and so on) would be ready to hand. These attacks would be pushed forward using new forms of mechanised or airborne troops (with perhaps more surprises to come – floating tanks, fleets of seaplanes), with close air support from the Luftwaffe of a kind the RAF would not be willing to supply until later in the war. The assault would be aided and accompanied by numbers of ships, tanks and aeroplanes that faulty British intelligence significantly overestimated, and aided by what was expected to be an active Fifth Column. Meanwhile, Britain would be defended by an Army singularly ill-equipped to fight the sort of mobile war the Germans had introduced, poorly armed and equipped after the evacuation from France, and crucially, largely immobile. The Royal Navy felt, for much of 1940–41, that it could not guarantee to interdict this invasion, at least not for several days.

Although I believe that no invasion was really planned, and that, had it come, it would have been defeated at sea, in the circumstances prevailing in 1940 and into 1941, the anti-invasion defences were a prudent precaution to take against what seemed a real and identifiable risk. The level of risk in 1940–41 was exaggerated by circumstances – beliefs, prejudices, unpreparedness, misinformation – that the modern reader, with perfect hindsight, might find difficult to understand. The continuation of active anti-invasion defence after 1941 seems, in retrospect, incomprehensible. However, people did what they thought was best, on the basis of the information available, and using imperfect systems set up by fallible human beings, under great individual and organisational pressure. I would criticise them only if I thought we would do any better.

NOTES

Prologue

1. The National Archives, Kew (TNA) WO 166/933 War Office, Home Forces, War Diaries: 28th Infantry Brigade: Headquarters. 1939 September – 1940 July.
2. TNA WO 166/4186 War Office, Home Forces, War Diaries: 5th Queen's Own Cameron Highlanders. 1939 September – 1941 December.
3. Jefford, C.G., *RAF Squadrons* (Airlife, Shrewsbury, 2001).
4. Ibid.
5. Taylor, L., *Luftwaffe over Scotland: A History of German Air Attacks on Scotland 1939–1945* (Whittles, Dunbeath, 2010), p. 33.
6. Bungay, S., *Most Dangerous Enemy: A History of the Battle of Britain* (Aurum Press, London, 2000), p. 393.
7. National Records of Scotland, Edinburgh (NRS) CAB 80/15 War Cabinet, Chiefs of Staff Committee, Memoranda. Meetings (40) 551 to (40) 600.
8. NRS CAB 80/16 War Cabinet, Chiefs of Staff Committee, Memoranda. Meetings (40) 601 to (40) 651.

1. Introduction

1. Collier, B., *The Defence of the United Kingdom* (Her Majesty's Stationery Office, London, 1957); Schenk, P., *Invasion of England 1940: The Planning of Operation Sealion* (Conway Maritime Press, London, 1990), p. 355.
2. The National Archives, Kew (TNA) CAB 67/6/31 War Cabinet, Memoranda, papers 101 (40) to 150 (40) 'Invasion of Great Britain: possible co-operation by a "Fifth Column". 17 May 1940.
3. Griffiths, R., *Fellow Travellers of the Right: British Enthusiasts for Nazi Germany 1933–39* (Constable, London, 1980).
4. Lukacs, J., *Five Days in London, May 1940* (Yale University Press, New Haven & London, 2001).
5. Addison, P. and Crang, J.A., eds, *Listening to Britain: Home Intelligence Reports on Britain's Finest Hour May to September 1940* (Bodley Head, London, 2010) p. 134, 20 June 1940.
6. Gilbert, M., 'Pacifist Attitudes to Nazi Germany, 1936–45', *Journal of Contemporary History,* 27 (1992), pp. 493–511.
7. Lukacs, *Five Days in London.*
8. Wills, H., *Pillboxes: A Study of UK Defences 1940* (Leo Cooper, London, 1985).
9. Barclay, G.J., 'The Cowie Line: a Second World War "Stop Line" West of Stonehaven, Aberdeenshire', *Proceedings of the Society of Antiquaries of Scotland,* 135 (2005), pp. 119–61.
10. The Defence of Britain Project database can be accessed at archaeologydataservice.ac.uk/archives/view/dob/.
11. The RCAHMS online database can be accessed at www.rcahms.gov.uk/canmore.html
12. Government policy on the criteria for the selection of monuments and buildings for protection are published in the *Scottish Historic Environment Policy: December 2011* (Historic Scotland, Edinburgh, 2011).
13. Foot, W., *Beaches, Fields, Streets and Hills: The Anti-Invasion Landscapes of England, 1940* (Council for British Archaeology, York, 2006).
14. Calder, A., *The People's War: Britain 1939–1945* (Pimlico, London, 1992).
15. Newbold, D.J., 'British Planning and Preparations to Resist Invasion on Land, September 1939 – September 1940', PhD thesis submitted to King's College, University of London, 1988. British Library thesis no. 241932.
16. Redfern, N., *Twentieth Century Fortifications in the United Kingdom: Vol. I Introduction and Sources* and *Vol. V Site Gazetteer: Scotland* (Council for British Archaeology, York, 1998).
17. Howard, M., *Clausewitz* (Oxford University Press, Oxford, 1983) p. 5.
18. Von Clausewitz, C. *On War* (1832) ed. and tr. Howard, M. and Paret, P. (Princeton University Press, Princeton, NJ, 1989), p. 119.
19. As the final draft of this book was actually being printed in October 2012, David Easton emailed me to report the discovery of a hitherto unknown, but still surviving, section of dragon's teeth, 140m long, on the Command Line in Fife. It is visible on Google Earth . . .

2. Complacency: to May 1940

1. Hart, S.A., 'The forgotten liberator: the 1939–45 career of General Sir Andrew Thorne', *Journal of the Society for Army Historical Research,* 79 (2001), pp. 233–49. Hart notes that Thorne's posting to Scotland was perhaps

intended to reinforce German fears of an Allied invasion of Norway. Hitler knew Thorn and had a high regard for his professional capacity.

2. The National Archives, Kew (TNA) WO 166/434 Home Forces, War Diaries, 9th Division: General Staff. 1939 September – 1940 August

3. TNA WO 166/1211 Home Forces, War Diaries, North Highland Area: HQ. 1940 July – 1941 December.

4. Normal usage in the UK armed forces and government in 1940 was to refer to 'the Orkneys' and 'the Shetlands'. Both are frowned on nowadays by the inhabitants of the islands, but 'the Orkneys' was in wider usage in the first half of the twentieth century than now, even by Orcadians. 'The Shetlands' has always been wrong; the modern form of the name of the archipelago is recorded as 'Hetland' (singular) in 1190. The error is left uncorrected and un-noted in quotations.

5. 'Immobilisation' was the term applied, in a very general sense, to the process of denying the enemy something: it was used to describe the process of obstructing an open space or airfield to prevent landing by parachutists or air-transported troops; the process of ensuring that fuel and food supplies were denied to the enemy; the process of making a port unusable, by blocking lock gates, removing important pieces of crane and lock machinery; and the process of blocking a body of water to prevent seaplanes landing.

6. Crang, J.A., 'The Second World War', in Spiers, E.M., Crang, J.A. and Strickland, M., eds, *A Military History of Scotland* (Edinburgh University Press, Edinburgh, 2012), pp. 559–99.

7. TNA WO 73/146 Distribution of the Army; Monthly returns July–September 1940.

8. TNA WO 73/145 Distribution of the Army; Monthly returns April–June 1940. That the quarterly returns must be read with caution is shown by the return for April–June 1940, which shows 7th Royal Northumberland Fusiliers in Edinburgh Area; the battalion (the machine gun battalion of 51st Division) had been in France for some time, had been captured with the rest of the division at St Valery on 12 June 1940, and according to the regimental history, was not re-formed until September (Barclay, C.N., *The History of the Royal Northumberland Fusiliers in the Second World War* (William Clowes & Sons, London, 1952)).

9. The 9th (Highland) Division was a Territorial unit set up in 1939 as a second-line duplicate twin to 51st Division and was based in Scotland in May 1940. Its brigades were numbered 26, 27 and 28 Brigades. After the surrender of most of 51st Division at St Valery on 12 June 1940, three infantry battalions (two of them from 154 Brigade) and some other troops of the division escaped. In August 1940, 51st Division was reconstituted by 9th Division being renumbered, with the traditional 51st Division brigade numbers (26 = 152, 27 = 153 and 27 = 154). The remnants of the original division evacuated from France were merged into the new division.

10. TNA WO 73/145 Distribution of the Army; Monthly returns April–June 1940.

11. Newbold, D.J., 'British Planning and Preparations to Resist Invasion on Land, September 1939 – September 1940', PhD thesis submitted to King's College, University of London, 1988, p. 36.

12. British troops: location statement 31/5/1941 (TNA WO 166/128 Home Forces, War Diaries, Scottish Command, General Staff, 1941 January–July); Polish troops: Manpower return 1/2/1941 (TNA WO 199/602 Home Forces, Military Headquarters Papers, Polish forces in the UK. July 1940 – July 1943); Norwegian Brigade, Fjaerli, E., *Den norske haer i Storbritannia, 1940–1945* (Tanum-Norli, Oslo, 1982).

13. Evans, R.J., *The Coming of the Third Reich* (Allen Lane, London, 2003), pp. 98–9.

14. Newbold, 'British Planning and Preparations', p. 15.

15. Newbold, 'British Planning and Preparations', p. 15.

16. Newbold, 'British Planning and Preparations', p. 15.

17. Newbold, 'British Planning and Preparations', p. 15.

18. French, D., *Raising Churchill's Army: The British Army and the War against Germany 1919–1945* (OUP, Oxford, 2000), p. 45.

19. French, *Raising Churchill's Army*, p. 46.

20. French, *Raising Churchill's Army*, p. 23.

21. Hutchinson, G.S., *Machine Guns: Their History and Tactical Employment (Being Also a History of the Machine Gun Corps, 1916–1922)* (Macmillan, London, 1938), p. 228.

22. Addison, P. and Crang, J.A., eds, *Listening to Britain: Home Intelligence Reports on Britain's Finest Hour May to September 1940* (Bodley Head, London, 2010), p. 116.

23. Newbold, 'British Planning and Preparations', p. 22.

24. Both Germany and the British War Office referred to 'England' when they meant the United Kingdom of Great Britain and Northern Ireland. I leave this erroneous usage in quotations. For variety, I use 'United Kingdom' and 'Britain' interchangeably.

25. TNA WO 193/697 Directorate of Military Operations and Plans, Intelligence and Statistics (Collation Files), Possible invasion by parachute landing, 1939 September – 1940 September.

26. Newbold, 'British Planning and Preparations', p. 25.

27. Newbold, 'British Planning and Preparations', p. 26.

28. TNA CAB 83/1 War Cabinet: Ministerial Committee on Military Co-ordination: Minutes and Papers (MC Series) 1939.

29. Newbold, 'British Planning and Preparations', pp. 33–4.

30. TNA WO 166/1 Home Forces, War Diaries, General HQ: General (G). 1939 Sept – 1940 December.

31. Newbold, 'British Planning and Preparations', p. 43.

32. TNA WO 166/1 Home Forces, War Diaries, General HQ: General (G). 1939 September – 1940 December.

33. TNA WO 166/1 Home Forces, War Diaries, General HQ: General (G). 1939 September – 1940 December.

34. Newbold, 'British Planning and Preparations', pp. 46–8.

35. Newbold, 'British Planning and Preparations', p. 70.

36. TNA WO 166/1 Home Forces, War Diaries, General HQ: General (G). 1939 September – 1940 December.

37. Newbold, 'British Planning and Preparations', p. 58.
38. Newbold, 'British Planning and Preparations', p. 58.
39. Newbold, 'British Planning and Preparations', p. 69.
40. National Records of Scotland, Edinburgh (NRS) CAB 79/4 Chiefs of Staff Committee, Minutes of Meetings 1940. Meetings (40) 101 to (40) 175.
41. Newbold, 'British Planning and Preparations', p. 75.
42. Dildy, D.C., *Denmark and Norway, 1940: Hitler's Boldest Operation* (Osprey, Oxford, 2007), pp. 42–3.
43. NRS CAB 79/4 Chiefs of Staff Committee: Minutes of Meetings, 1940. Meetings (40) 101 to (40) 175.
44. NRS CAB 80/10 Chiefs of Staff Committee, Memoranda, 1940. Memoranda (40) 301 to (40) 350.
45. Newbold, 'British Planning and Preparations', p. 77–8.
46. NRS CAB 80/10 Chiefs of Staff Committee, Memoranda, 1940. Memoranda (40) 301 to (40) 350.
47. Hastings, M., *Armageddon: The Battle for Germany, 1944–45* (Macmillan, London, 2004), p. 105.
48. NRS CAB 80/10 Chiefs of Staff Committee, Memoranda, 1940. Memoranda (40) 301 to (40) 350.
49. NRS CAB 80/10 Chiefs of Staff Committee, Memoranda, 1940. Memoranda (40) 301 to (40) 350.
50. French, *Raising Churchill's Army*, p. 195.
51. TNA WO 166/1 Home Forces, War Diaries, General HQ: General (G). 1939 September – 1940 December.
52. NRS CAB 79/4 Chiefs of Staff Committee: Minutes of Meetings, 1940. Meetings (40) 101 to (40) 175.
53. NRS CAB 80/10 Chiefs of Staff Committee, Memoranda, 1940. Memoranda (40) 301 to (40) 350.
54. NRS CAB 80/10 Chiefs of Staff Committee, Memoranda, 1940. Memoranda (40) 301 to (40) 350.
55. Newbold, 'British Planning and Preparations', p. 70.

3. The May Panic

1. French, D., *Raising Churchill's Army: The British Army and the War Against Germany 1919–1945* (OUP, Oxford, 2000), pp. 63, 279.
2. Forty, G., *Companion to the British Army, 1939–1945* (History Press, Port Stroud, 2009), p. 5.
3. Newbold, D. J., 'British Planning and Preparations to Resist Invasion on Land, September 1939 – September 1940', PhD thesis presented to King's College, London, 1988, p. 36.
4. French, *Raising Churchill's Army*, pp. 190–1.
5. Barclay, C.N., *The History of the Royal Northumberland Fusiliers in the Second World War* (William Clowes & Sons, London, 1952), p. 10.
6. Hutchinson, G.S., *Machine Guns: Their History and Tactical Employment (Being Also a History of the Machine Gun Corps, 1916–1922)* (Macmillan, London, 1938), p. 2.
7. Forty, *Companion to the British Army*, p. 73.
8. French, *Raising Churchill's Army*, pp. 90–1.
9. The National Archives, Kew (TNA) WO 166/1 Home Forces, War Diaries, General HQ, General (G), 1939 September – 1940 December.
10. Forty, *Companion to the British Army*, p. 74.
11. Rissik, D., *The DLI at War: The History of the Durham Light Infantry 1939–1945* (Durham Light Infantry, Durham, 1953), pp. 324–5.
12. TNA WO 166/1 Home Forces, War Diaries, General HQ, General (G), 1939 September – 1940 December. There are many books about the Home Guard. The most substantial are Brian Osborne's *The People's Army: Home Guard in Scotland 1940–1944* (Birlinn, Edinburgh, 2009) and S.P. MacKenzie's *The Home Guard: A Military and Political History* (OUP, Oxford, 1995).
13. Osborne, *The People's Army*, p. 59.
14. Polish Institute & Sikorski Museum, London (PISM). A.VI.16/2 1941–1942. Fife Museums have a photograph of King Peter II of Yugoslavia being greeted in Fife by General Sikorski at some point in 1941.
15. TNA WO 199/602 Home Forces, Military HQ Papers, Polish forces in the UK, 1940 July – 1943 July.
16. TNA WO 166/1407 Home Forces, War Diaries, 7 Royal Tank Regiment, 1939 September – 1940 April, June – August.
17. Addison, P. and Crang, J.A. eds, *Listening to Britain: Home Intelligence Reports on Britain's Finest Hour May to September* 1940 (Bodley Head, London, 2010), p. xi.
18. Addison and Crang, *Listening to Britain*, p. xiv.
19. Addison and Crang, *Listening to Britain*, p. 84.
20. Roskill, S.W., *The War at Sea, 1939–1945* (H.M.S.O, London, 1976).
21. Hewitt, G., *Hitler's Armada: The German Invasion Plan, and the Defence of Great Britain by the Royal Navy, April–October 1940* (Pen & Sword Maritime, Barnsley, 2008); Cumming, A.J., *The Royal Navy and the Battle of Britain* (Naval Institute, Annapolis, 2010).
22. Cumming, *The Royal Navy and the Battle of Britain*, p. 28–9.
23. Roskill, *The War at Sea*, p. 250.
24. Dildy, D., *Denmark and Norway, 1940: Hitler's Boldest Operation* (Osprey, Oxford, 2007), p. 20.
25. Roskill, *The War at Sea*, p. 341.
26. TNA CAB 67/6/31 War Cabinet, Memoranda, papers 101 (40) to 150 (40) 'Invasion of Great Britain: possible co-operation by a "Fifth Column"'. 17 May 1940.
27. TNA WO 166/1407 Home Forces, War Diaries, 7 Royal Tank Regiment, 1939 September – 1940 April, June–August.
28. Addison and Crang, *Listening to Britain*, p. 24.
29. Addison and Crang, *Listening to Britain*, p. 80.
30. Addison and Crang, *Listening to Britain*, p. 114.

31. Griffiths, R., *Fellow Travellers of the Right: British Enthusiasts for Nazi Germany 1933–39* (Constable, London, 1980). Griffiths, R., *Patriotism Perverted: Captain Ramsay, the Right Club and English Anti-Semitism 1939–40* (Constable, London, 1998).
32. Addison and Crang, *Listening to Britain*, pp. 141–2.
33. Addison and Crang, *Listening to Britain*, p. 25.
34. Griffiths, *Patriotism Perverted*, p. 117.
35. TNA WO 166/1540 Home Forces, War Diaries, Royal Artillery, 128 Field Regiment, 1939 September – 1941 December.
36. TNA WO 166/1540 Home Forces, War Diaries, Royal Artillery, 128 Field Regiment, 1939 September – 1941 December.
37. TNA WO 166/1540 Home Forces, War Diaries, Royal Artillery, 128 Field Regiment, 1939 September – 1941 December.
38. TNA WO 166/1540 Home Forces, War Diaries, Royal Artillery, 128 Field Regiment, 1939 September – 1941 December.
39. Osborne, *The People's Army*, p. 62–3.
40. Newbold, 'British Planning and Preparations', p. 85.
41. NRS CAB 80/10 Chiefs of Staff Committee, Memoranda 1940. Nos. (40) 301 to (40) 350.
42. Newbold, 'British Planning and Preparations', p. 88.
43. Churchill, W.S., *The Second World War, Vol. II: Their Finest Hour* (Cassell, London, 1949), p. 439.
44. TNA WO 199/50 Home Forces, Military Headquarters Papers, GHQ, General defensive demolitions, 1940 May – 1945 January.
45. NRS CAB 80/11 Chiefs of Staff Committee: Memoranda 1940. Nos. (40) 351 to (40) 400; WO 166/1 Home Forces, War Diaries, General HQ, General (G), 1939 September – 1940 December.
46. NRS CAB 79/4 Chiefs of Staff Committee: Minutes of Meetings 1940. Meetings (40) 101 to (40) 175.
47. Newbold, 'British Planning and Preparations', p. 101.
48. NRS CAB 80/11 Chiefs of Staff Committee: Memoranda 1940. Nos. (40) 351 to (40) 400.
49. TNA WO 166/4186 Home Forces, War Diaries, 5 Queen's Own Cameron Highlanders, 1939 September – 1941 December.
50. NRS CAB 80/11 Chiefs of Staff Committee, Memoranda 1940. Nos. (40) 351 to (40) 400.
51. TNA WO 166/1234 Home Forces, War Diaries, Orkney and Shetland Area, HQ, 1939 October – 1940 December.
52. NRS CAB 80/11 Chiefs of Staff Committee, Memoranda 1940. Nos. (40) 351 to (40) 400.
53. TNA CAB 65/7/28 War Cabinet Meeting (40) 133, 22 May 1940.
54. NRS CAB 80/11 Chiefs of Staff Committee, Memoranda 1940. Nos. (40) 351 to (40) 400.
55. Newbold, 'British Planning and Preparations', p. 114.
56. Newbold, 'British Planning and Preparations', p. 116.
57. NRS CAB 80/11 Chiefs of Staff Committee, Memoranda 1940. Nos. (40) 351 to (40) 400.
58. Dildy, *Denmark and Norway, 1940*, p. 90.
59. TNA WO 199/50 GHQ, Defence works, General defensive demolitions, 1940 May – 1945 January. Scottish Command's allocation was the same as Southern and Western Commands, and rather less the Eastern and Northern: £250,000 each (modern value £12.8 million), as those Commands were seen as most vulnerable at this stage.
60. Churchill, *Their Finest Hour*, p. 65.
61. Newbold, 'British Planning and Preparations', p. 129.
62. Newbold, 'British Planning and Preparations', p. 131.
63. Newbold, 'British Planning and Preparations', p. 132.
64. Newbold, 'British Planning and Preparations', p. 135.
65. Addison and Crang, *Listening to Britain*, p. 42.
66. NRS CAB 80/12 Chiefs of Staff Committee, Memoranda, 1940. Nos. (40) 401 to (40) 450.
67. Newbold, 'British Planning and Preparations', p. 95.
68. Churchill, *Their Finest Hour*, p. 143.
69. Addison and Crang, *Listening to Britain*, p. 53.

4. Crisis: June to October 1940

1. The National Archives, Kew (TNA) WO 166/1 Home Forces, War Diaries, General HQ, General (G), 1939 September – 1940 December
2. TNA WO 166/1 Home Forces, War Diaries, General HQ, General (G), 1939 September – 1940 December.
3. Newbold, D.J., 'British Planning and Preparations to Resist Invasion on Land, September 1939 – September 1940', PhD thesis presented to King's College, London, 1988, p. 61.
4. National Records of Scotland, Edinburgh (NRS) CAB 80/12 Chiefs of Staff Committee, Memoranda 1940. Nos. (40) 401 to (40) 450.
5. TNA WO 166/1 Home Forces, War Diaries, General HQ, General (G), 1939 September – 1940 December.
6. TNA WO 166/122 Home Forces, War Diaries, Scottish Command Headquarters, Royal Engineers, 1939 November – 1940 December.
7. TNA WO 166/122 Home Forces, War Diaries, Scottish Command Headquarters, Royal Engineers, 1939 November – 1940 December.
8. TNA WO 166/115 Home Forces, War Diaries, Scottish Command Headquarters, General, 1940 January–July.

9. TNA WO 199/568 Home Forces, Military Headquarters Papers, General HQ: Home defence, Defence against invasion, Scottish Command appreciation, 1940 June – 1942 November.

10. TNA WO 199/568 Home Forces, Military Headquarters Papers, General HQ: Home defence, Defence against invasion, Scottish Command appreciation, 1940 June – 1942 November.

11. Newbold, 'British Planning and Preparations', p. 184.

12. Newbold, 'British Planning and Preparations', p. 189.

13. TNA WO 166/115 Home Forces, War Diaries, Scottish Command Headquarters, General, 1940 January–July.

14. TNA WO 166/115 Home Forces, War Diaries, Scottish Command Headquarters, General, 1940 January–July.

15. TNA WO 166/1013 Home Forces, War Diaries, 148 Infantry Brigade, HQ, 1939 August – 1940 March; June – 1941 December.

16. TNA WO 166/115 Home Forces, War Diaries, Scottish Command Headquarters, General, 1940 January–July.

17. Newbold, 'British Planning and Preparations', p. 169.

18. D. Rose-Miller, personal communication.

19. TNA WO 166/419 Home Forces, War Diaries, 5th Infantry Division, General Staff, 1939 August – 1941 December; WO 166/922 Home Forces, War Diaries, 15th Infantry Brigade, HQ, 1939 September; 1940 May – 1941 December; WO 166/924 Home Forces, War Diaries, 17th Infantry Brigade, HQ, 1939 October; 1940 July – 1941 December.

20. TNA WO 166/1013 Home Forces, War Diaries, 148th Infantry Brigade, HQ, 1939 August – 1940 March, June – 1941 December.

21. NRS CAB 79/5 Chiefs of Staff Committee: Minutes 1940. Meetings (40) 176 to 250.

22. Newbold, 'British Planning and Preparations', p. 248.

23. TNA WO 166/1 Home Forces, War Diaries, General HQ, General (G), 1939 September – 1940 December.

24. Newbold, 'British Planning and Preparations', p. 208.

25. NRS CAB 79/5 Chiefs of Staff Committee, Minutes 1940. Meetings (40) 176 to 250.

26. NRS CAB 80/13 Chiefs of Staff Committee, Memoranda 1940. Nos. (40) 451 to (40) 500.

27. NRS CAB 79/5 Chiefs of Staff Committee, Minutes 1940. Nos. (40) 176 to 250.

28. Addison, P. and Crang, J.A. eds, *Listening to Britain: Home Intelligence Reports on Britain's Finest Hour May to September* 1940 (Bodley Head, London, 2010), p. 165.

29. TNA WO 199/573 GHQ, Home Defence, Memorandum on invasion [Denis Wheatley], 1940 July.

30. TNA WO 199/573 GHQ, Home Defence, Memorandum on invasion (Denis Wheatley), 1940 July.

31. TNA WO 199/568 GHQ, Home Defence, Defence against invasion: Scottish Command appreciation, 1940 June – 1942 November.

32. TNA WO 199/568 GHQ, Home Defence, Defence against invasion: Scottish Command appreciation, 1940 June – 1942 November.

33. TNA WO 199/620 GHQ, Defence of Certain Areas, Orkneys. 1940 March – 1941 September.

34. Addison and Crang, *Listening to Britain*, p. 179.

35. Newbold, 'British Planning and Preparations', p. 237.

36. NRS CAB 80/14 Chiefs of Staff Committee, Memoranda 1940. Nos. (40) 501 to (40) 551.

37. NRS CAB80/14 Chiefs of Staff Committee, Memoranda 1940. Nos. (40) 501 to (40) 551.

38. Newbold, 'British Planning and Preparations', p. 248.

39. Ironside, E., *The Ironside Diaries 1937–1940*, ed. Macleod, R. and Kelly, D. (Constable, London, 1962), p. 5. This contrasts rather oddly with the willingness with which CSC had sent significant reinforcements to Ulster, on the basis of rather less reliable indications about a possible German attack on Eire.

40. NRS CAB 80/14 Chiefs of Staff Committee, Memoranda 1940. Nos. (40) 501 to (40) 551.

41. Roskill, S.W., *The War at Sea 1939–1945* (HMSO, London, 1976), p. 251.

42. Newbold, 'British Planning and Preparations', p. 249. For example, the JIC report on Seaborne and Airborne Attack on the British Isles, discussed at CSC on 16 July 1940.

43. NRS CAB 79/5 Chiefs of Staff Committee, Minutes. Meetings (40) 176 to 250.

44. TNA WO 166/120 Home Forces, War Diaries, Scottish Command HQ, Intelligence, 1940

45. Given the very poor state of training of the British troops at this time, arming battle-experienced, highly motivated Polish troops would, objectively speaking, appear likely to have been rather more useful. As Stephen Bungay has written about the Polish airmen (*Most Dangerous Enemy: a history of the Battle of Britain* (Aurum, London, 2000), p. 174): '. . . they were driven by hatred . . . and were animated by a patriotism of a seriousness and vibrancy unknown in Britain. They felt a passionate desire to avenge their defeat'.

46. TNA WO 199/602 Home Forces, Military Headquarters Papers, Polish forces in the UK, 1940 July – 1943 July.

47. TNA WO 199/602 Home Forces, Military Headquarters Papers, Polish forces in the UK, 1940 July – 1943 July.

48. TNA WO 166/122 Home Forces, War Diaries, Scottish Comamnd HQ, Royal Engineers, 1939 November – 1940 December.

49. Addison and Crang, *Listening to Britain*, p. 239.

50. Addison and Crang, *Listening to Britain*, p. 297.

51. Newbold, 'British Planning and Preparations', pp. 251–4.

52. Newbold, 'British Planning and Preparations', p. 255.

53. Churchill, W.S., *The Second World War, Vol. II: Their Finest Hour* (Cassell, London, 1949), p. 256.

54. Newbold, 'British Planning and Preparations', p. 272.

55. Newbold, 'British Planning and Preparations', p. 273.

56. Addison and Crang, *Listening to Britain*, p. 250.

57. Newbold, 'British Planning and Preparations', p. 279.

58. Addison and Crang, *Listening to Britain*, pp. 258–9.

59. TNA WO 166/1 Home Forces, War Diaries, General HQ, General (G), 1939 September – 1940 December.

60. TNA WO 166/1 Home Forces, War Diaries, General HQ, General (G), 1939 September – 1940 December.
61. Alanbrooke, F.M.L., *War Diaries 1939–1945* (Weidenfeld & Nicolson, London, 2001), p. 95.
62. Knox, B.M., *Brief Historical Notes on the Ayrshire Yeomanry, Earl of Carrick's Own, 152 Field Regiment, R.A. 1939–45* (Stephen & Pollock, Ayr, 1946), p. 20.
63. Knox, *Ayrshire Yeomanry*, p. 20.
64. Newbold, 'British Planning and Preparations', pp. 290–1.
65. Churchill, *Their Finest Hour*, p. 238.
66. Newbold, 'British Planning and Preparations', p. 293.
67. Knox, *Ayrshire Yeomanry*, p. 23; Young, I.A.G. and Gray, R.I., *A Short History of the Ayrshire Yeomanry (Earl of Carrick's Own) 151st Field Regiment, RA, 1939–1946* (Ayr Observer, Ayr, 1947), p. 9.
68. Newbold, 'British Planning and Preparations', p. 295.
69. Addison and Crang, *Listening to Britain*, p. 265.
70. TNA WO 166/122 Home Forces, War Diaries, Scottish Command HQ, Royal Engineers, 1939 November – 1940 December.
71. TNA WO 166/122 Home Forces, War Diaries, Scottish Command HQ, Royal Engineers, 1939 November – 1940 December.
72. TNA WO 166/122 Home Forces, War Diaries, Scottish Command HQ, Royal Engineers, 1939 November – 1940 December.
73. TNA WO 166/1 Home Forces, War Diaries, General HQ, General (G), 1939 September – 1940 December.
74. NRS CAB 79/5 Chiefs of Staff Committee, Minutes 1940. Meetings (40) 176 to 250.
75. Addison and Crang, *Listening to Britain*, p. 333.
76. NRS CAB 79/6 Chiefs of Staff Committee, Minutes 1940. Meetings. (40) 251 to 325.
77. Newbold, 'British Planning and Preparations', p. 308.
78. Newbold, 'British Planning and Preparations', p. 394.
79. Newbold, 'British Planning and Preparations', p. 396.
80. Addison and Crang, *Listening to Britain*, pp. 419, 425, 428, 431.
81. Collier, B., *The Defence of the United Kingdom* (Her Majesty's Stationery Office, London, 1957), pp. 221–3.
82. TNA WO 166/419 Home Forces, War Diaries, 5th Division: General Staff, 1939 August – 1941 December.
83. TNA WO 166/993 Home Forces, War Diaries, 137th Infantry Brigade, HQ, 1939 August – 1940 March; July – 1941 December.
84. TNA WO 166/1022 Home Forces, War Diaries, 153rd Infantry Brigade: HQ, 1939 September – December; 1940 August – 1941 December.
85. TNA WO 166/3443 Home Forces, War Diaries, Royal Engineers, No. 2 General Construction Battalion, 1940 June– December.
86. TNA WO 166/3609 Home Forces, War Diaries, Royal Engineers, 110 Army Troops Company, 1940 July – 1941 December.
87. TNA WO 166/419 Home Forces, War Diaries, 5th Division, General Staff, 1939 August – 1941 December.
88. Addison and Crang, *Listening to Britain*, p. 414.
89. TNA WO 166/552 Home Forces, War Diaries, 46th Division, General Staff, 1939 October – 1940 March, July – 1941 December.
90. TNA WO 166/996 Home Force, War Diaries, 138th Infantry Brigade: HQ, 1939 September – 1940 March; July – 1941 December; WO 166/4754 Home Forces, War Diaries, 6 York & Lancaster Regiment, 1939 August – 1940 April, July – 1941 December.

5. Consolidation and (Over-) Elaboration: October 1940 to July 1941

1. The National Archives, Kew (TNA) WO 166/12 Home Forces, War Diaries, General HQ, Chief Engineer, 1940 June – 1941 December.
2. National Records of Scotland, Edinburgh. (NRS) CAB 80/20 Chiefs of Staff Committee, Memoranda 1940. Nos. (40) 801 – (40) 850.
3. NRS CAB 80/20 Chiefs of Staff Committee, Memoranda 1940. Nos. (40) 801 – (40) 850.
4. TNA WO 166/116 Home Forces, War Diaries, Scottish Command Headquarters, General, 1940 August – December.
5. TNA WO 166/4150 Home Forces, War Diaries, 10 Black Watch (Royal Highland Regiment), 1940 October – 1941 December.
6. TNA WO 199/569 Home Forces, Military Headquarters Papers, GHQ, Home defence situation: winter 1940. 1940 November.
7. Polish Institute & Sikorski Museum, London (PISM). 3.2.XII.Sap Sc.C.C.R. S3/96963/31/G(Ops.) Defence Works 1940–.
8. TNA WO 199/620 Home Forces, Military Headquarters Papers, GHQ, Defence of Certain Areas, Orkneys, 1940 March – 1941 September.
9. TNA WO 199/48 Home Forces, Military Headquarters Papers, GHQ, Defence works, 1940 June – 1942 April.
10. NRS CAB 80/25 Chiefs of Staff Committee, Memoranda 1941. Nos. (41) 1 – (41) 100.
11. NRS CAB 80/26 Chiefs of Staff Committee, Memoranda 1941. Nos. (41) 101 – (41) 200.
12. NRS CAB80/25 War Cabinet: Chiefs of Staff Committee: Memoranda. CoS (41) 1 – (41) 100.
13. TNA WO 166/136 Home Forces, War Diaries, Scottish Command HQ, Royal Engineers, 1941 January.
14. TNA WO 199/602 Home Forces, Military Headquarters Papers, GHQ, Polish forces in the UK, 1940 July – 1943 July; WO 199/620 Home Forces, Military Headquarters Papers, GHQ, Defence of Certain Areas, Orkneys, 1940 March – 1941 September.

15. TNA WO 199/568 General HQ: Home defence: Defence against invasion, Scottish Command appreciation, 1940 June – 1942 November.
16. TNA WO 199/568 General HQ: Home defence: Defence against invasion, Scottish Command appreciation, 1940 June – 1942 November.
17. NRS CAB79/10 War Cabinet: Chiefs of Staff Committee: Minutes of Meetings. COS(41) 41st – 100th meeting 1941
18. NRS CAB 80/26 Chiefs of Staff Committee, Memoranda 1941. Nos. (41) 101 – (41) 200.
19. NRS CAB 80/26 Chiefs of Staff Committee, Memoranda 1941. Nos. (41) 101 – (41) 200.
20. Collier, B., *The Defence of the United Kingdom* (Her Majesty's Stationery Office, London, 1957), Map 20.
21. Collier, *Defence of the United Kingdom*, Map 20.
22. TNA WO 166/128 Home Forces, War Diaries, Scottish Command Headquarters, General Staff, 1941 January–July.
23. TNA WO 166/128 Home Forces, War Diaries, Scottish Command Headquarters, General Staff, 1941 January–July.
24. TNA WO 166/128 Home Forces, War Diaries, Scottish Command Headquarters, General Staff, 1941 January–July.
25. TNA WO 166/4150 Home Forces, War Diaries, 10 Black Watch (Royal Highland Regiment), 1940 October – 1941 December.
26. TNA WO 166/12 Home Forces, War Diaries, General HQ, Chief Engineer, 1940 June – 1941 December.
27. TNA WO 166/4128 Home Forces, War Diaries, 70 Argyll & Sutherland Highlanders (Princess Louise's), 1941 July–December.

6. Trains and Boats and Planes

1. The National Archives, Kew. WO 166/1 Home Forces, War Diaries, General HQ, General (G), 1939 September – 1940 December.
2. Oliver, K.M., *Through Adversity: The History of the Royal Air Force Regiment, 1942–1992* (Forces & Corporate Publishing, Rushden, 1997).
3. TNA WO 166/116 Home Forces, War Diaries, Scottish Command, General, 1940 August–December.
4. Osborne, M., *Defending Britain: Twentieth-Century Military Structures in the Landscape* (Tempus, Stroud, 2004), p. 93.
5. TNA WO 166/116 Home Forces, War Diaries, Scottish Command, General, 1940 August–December.
6. TNA WO 199/27 Home Forces, General HQ: Defence of airfields: Scottish Command, 1940 August – 1942 April.
7. TNA WO 166/122 Home Forces, War Diaries, Scottish Command Headquarters, Royal Engineers, 1939 November – 1940 December.
8. TNA WO 199/27 Home Forces, General HQ: Defence of airfields: Scottish Command, 1940 August – 1942 April.
9. TNA ADM 1/15572 The Navy and the threat of invasion in 1940, history of anti-invasion measures and plans produced by Historical Section of T.S.D. Division. 1940–1943; CAB 44/47 War Histories, Draft Chapters and Narratives, History of the defence of the United Kingdom 1939–1945, by Captain G. C. Wynne, 1948; Maurice-Jones, K.W., *The History of Coast Artillery in the British Army* (Royal Artillery Institution, London, 1959).
10. TNA WO 166/115 Home Forces, War Diaries, Scottish Command Headquarters, General, 1940 January–July.
11. TNA WO 166/1742 Royal Artillery, Coast Regiments, 542 Coast Regiment [No. 2 Group Coastal Artillery]. 1940 October – 1941 December.
12. TNA WO 166/1742 Royal Artillery, Coast Regiments, 542 Coast Regiment [No. 2 Group Coastal Artillery], 1940 October – 1941 December.
13. National Records of Scotland (NRS) CAB 80/11 Chiefs of Staff Committee, Memoranda 1940. Nos. (40) 351 to (40) 400.
14. TNA ADM 1/15572 Navy, The Navy and the threat of invasion in 1940, history of anti-invasion measures and plans produced by Historical Section of T.S.D. Division, 1940–1943.
15. TNA WO 166/1 Home Forces, War Diaries, General HQ, General (G), 1939 September – 1940 December.
16. TNA WO 166/122 Home Forces, War Diaries, Scottish Command Headquarters, Royal Engineers, 1939 November – 1940 December.
17. TNA ADM 1/11943 Navy, Defences, UK, Use of blockships as anti-invasion measures at home ports and harbours, 1940–1942.
18. TNA WO 166/1259 Home Forces, War Diaries, Angus Sub-area, HQ, 1940 October – 1941 December; WO 166/4150 Home Forces, War Diaries, 10 Black Watch (Royal Highland Regiment), 1940 October – 1941 December.
19. TNA WO 166/122 Home Forces, War Diaries, Scottish Command Headquarters, Royal Engineers, 1939 November – 1940 December.
20. TNA WO 166/122 Home Forces, War Diaries, Scottish Command Headquarters, Royal Engineers, 1939 November – 1940 December.
21. TNA WO 199/2883 Home Forces, War Diaries, Aberdeen Sub-area: Anti-invasion measures: Immobilisation of landing grounds, 1941 April – 1943 June.
22. TNA WO 199/435 Home Forces, General HQ, Inter-service co-operation, Naval motor boats under operational control of military, inland water patrols, 1940 June–October.
23. TNA WO 199/610 Home Forces, General HQ, Special defence measures, Inland water patrols, 1940 October – 1941 May.
24. TNA WO 199/2663 Home Forces, Scottish Command HQ, Anti-invasion measures, Obstruction of open water spaces, 1940 June – 1942 April.
25. TNA WO 199/2663 Home Forces, Scottish Command HQ, Anti-invasion measures, Obstruction of open water spaces, 1940 June – 1942 April.
26. TNA WO 199/2663 Home Forces, Scottish Command HQ, Anti-invasion measures, Obstruction of open water spaces, 1940 June – 1942 April.

27. TNA WO 199/2663 Home Forces, Scottish Command HQ, Anti-invasion measures, Obstruction of open water spaces, 1940 June – 1942 April.

28. TNA WO 199/435 Home Forces, General HQ, Inter-service co-operation, Naval motor boats under operational control of military, inland water patrols, 1940 June–October.

29. Balfour, G., *The Armoured Train: Its Development and Usage* (Batsford, London, 1981). Suchcitz, A., 'Polish Armoured Trains in Great Britain 1940–1943', in Maresch, E., ed., *Polish Forces in Defence of the British Isles 1939–1945* (Federation of Poles in Great Britain, London, 2006), pp. 76–91.

30. Balfour, *The Armoured Train*.

31. TNA WO 166/115 Home Forces, War Diaries, Scottish Command Headquarters, General, 1940 January–July.

32. TNA WO 199/605 Home Forces, General HQ, Special Defence Measures, Armoured Trains, Operation and Manning, 1940 November – 1942 January.

33. Balfour, *The Armoured Train*, p. 65.

34. TNA WO 166/116 Home Forces, War Diaries, Scottish Command, General, 1940 August–December.

35. Balfour, *The Armoured Train*, p. 72; TNS WO 166/1448 Home Forces, War Diaries, 4 Armoured Train Group, 10 Train Detachment, 1940 July – 1941 January.

36. TNA WO 166/1449 Home Forces, War Diaries, 4 Armoured Train Group, 11 Train Detachment, 1940 July – 1941 March.

37. TNA WO 166/1449 Home Forces, War Diaries, 4 Armoured Train Group, 11 Train Detachment, 1940 July – 1941 March.

38. TNA WO 199/1029 Home Forces, General HQ; Movements; Armoured Trains, 1940 January–August.

39. Suchcitz, 'Polish Armoured Trains in Great Britain', p. 78.

40. Balfour, *The Armoured Train*, p. 97.

41. TNS WO 166/1448 Home Forces, War Diaries, 4 Armoured Train Group, 10 Train Detachment, 1940 July – 1941 January.

42. Addison, P. and Crang, J.A. eds, *Listening to Britain: Home Intelligence Reports on Britain's Finest Hour May to September 1940* (Bodley Head, London, 2010), p. 73 (3 June 1940).

43. Addison and Crang, *Listening to Britain*, p. 81.

44. Newbold, D.J., 'British Planning and Preparations to Resist Invasion on Land, September 1939 – September 1940', PhD thesis presented to King's College, London, 1988, p. 43; TNA WO 166/1 Home Forces, War Diaries, General HQ, General (G), 1939 September – 1940 December.

45. Newbold, 'British Planning and Preparations', p. 60–2.

46. Newbold, 'British Planning and Preparations', p. 62; TNA WO 166/1 Home Forces, War Diaries, General HQ, General (G), 1939 September – 1940 December.

47. NRS CAB 80/11 Chiefs of Staff Committee, Memoranda 1940. Nos. (40) 351 – (40) 400.

48. TNA WO 199/2882 Home Forces, Scottish Command, Aberdeen Sub-area: Anti-invasion measures: defence of aerodromes, 1941 May–December.

7. Beaches and Stop-Lines

1. The National Archives, Kew (TNA) WO 199/88 Home Forces, Military Headquarters Papers, General HQ, Beach Defence Reconnaissance, Scottish Command, 1940 May – August.

2. TNA WO 166/115 Home Forces, War Diaries, Scottish Command Headquarters, General, 1940 January–July; WO 199/88 Home Forces, Military Headquarters Papers, General HQ, Beach Defence Reconnaissance, Scottish Command, 1940 May–August.

3. TNA WO 166/115 Home Forces, War Diaries, Scottish Command Headquarters, General, 1940 January–July.

4. TNA WO 166/116 Home Forces, War Diaries, Scottish Command, General, 1940 August–December.

5. TNA WO 166/128 Home Forces, War Diaries, Scottish Command Headquarters, General, 1941 January–July.

6. Tully-Jackson, J. and Brown, I., *East Lothian at War* (East Lothian District Library, Haddington, 1996).

7. Collier, B., *The Defence of the United Kingdom* (H.M.S.O., London, 1957), p. 129.

8. Barclay, G.J., 'The Cowie Line: a Second World War "stop line" west of Stonehaven, Aberdeenshire', *Proceedings of the Society of Antiquaries of Scotland*, 135 (2005), pp. 119–61 (p. 134).

9. TNA WO 199/568 Home Forces, General HQ, Home defence, Defence against invasion: Scottish Command appreciation, 1940 June – 1942 November.

10. TNA WO 166/434 Home Forces, War Diaries, 9th Division: General Staff, 1939 September – 1940 August.

11. TNA WO 166/128 Home Forces, War Diaries, Scottish Command Headquarters, General, 1941 January–July.

12. TNA WO 166/10362 Home Forces, War Diaries, Scottish Command, G 1943 January–December.

13. Redfern, N., *Twentieth Century Fortifications in the United Kingdom: Vol. I Introduction and Sources* (Council for British Archaeology, York, 1998), p. 17.

14. TNA WO 199/544 Home Forces, General HQ, Civil Liaison, Keeps and fortified villages, nodal points and anti-tank islands, 1940 September – 1942 October.

8. Barriers

1. The National Archives, Kew (TNA) WO 199/54 Home Forces, General HQ, Defence Works: Scheme of anti-tank obstacles for defence of Great Britain, 1940 June – 1943 March.

2. Osborne, M., personal communication.

3. TNA WO 231/182 Directorate of Military Training, Military Training Pamphlet No. 30. Field engineering (all arms). Part III: obstacles, 1940 October 01 – 1940 October 31.

4. Polish Institute & Sikorski Museum (PISM) 3.2.XII.Sap Sc.C.C.R. S3/96963/31/G(Ops.) Defence Works.
5. TNA WO 166/116 Home Forces, War Diaries, Scottish Command HQ, General, 1940 August–December.
6. I believe this may be seen on the Command Line in Fife, where two slightly taller lines of dragon's teeth lie behind three lower rows (Fig. 15.9).
7. TNA WO 199/1723 Home Forces, Southern Command HQ, Home Defence, Experiments with anti-tank obstacles, 1940 August – 1941 August.
8. TNA WO 199/1723 Home Forces, Southern Command HQ, Home Defence, Experiments with anti-tank obstacles, 1940 August – 1941 August.
9. TNA WO 199/2668 Home Forces, Scottish Command HQ, Anti-invasion measures, Defence of beaches, obstacles including beach flame barrage. 1940 November – 1943 February.
10. Barclay, G.J., 'The Scottish Command Line: the Archaeology and History of a 1940 Anti-Tank "Stop-Line"', *Tayside and Fife Archaeological Journal*, 17 (2011), p. 134.
11. TNA WO 199/1723 Home Forces, Southern Command HQ, Home Defence, Experiments with anti-tank obstacles, 1940 August – 1941 August.
12. Roskill, S.W., *The War at Sea, 1939–1945* (H.M.S.O., London, 1976), p. 253.
13. TNA WO 199/1422 Home Forces, Northern Command HQ, Beach defences, Tubular steel scaffolding, Trial of attack by tanks, 1940 November; WO 199/1425 Home Forces, Northern Command HQ, Beach defences, Tubular steel scaffolding, Drawings and reports, 1941 May, June; WO 199/94 Home Forces, General HQ, Beach Defences, Beach mines, 1940 June – 1944 July.
14. PISM A.VI.31/2 Odcinek [Sector] East Lothian, 1940–42.
15. TNA WO 166/5627 Home Forces, War Diaries, Royal Pioneer Corps, 143 Company, 1940 June – 1941 December. WO 166/1259 Sub-areas: Angus: HQ.
16. TNA WO 166/4188 Home Forces, War Diaries, 7 Queen's Own Cameron Highlanders, 1940 June – 1941 October.
17. TNA WO 199/2739 Home Forces, Scottish Command, North Highland District, Anti-invasion measures, removal and salvage of obsolete defence works, 1942 December – 1944 September; WO 199/95 Home Forces, General HQ, Beach defences, scaffolding, 1941 December – 1944 November.
18. TNA WO 199/2726 Home Forces, Orkney and Shetland Defences, Anti-invasion measures, Defence against seaborne landings, 1940 September – 1944 April.
19. NRS CAB79/14 Chiefs of Staff Committee, Minutes, 1941. Meetings (41) 301 to 350.
20. TNA WO 199/54 Home Forces, General HQ, Defence Works, Scheme of anti-tank obstacles for defence of Great Britain.
21. TNA WO 166/12 Home Forces, War Diaries, General HQ, Chief Engineer; WO 199/54 Home Forces, General HQ, Defence Works, Scheme of anti-tank obstacles for defence of Great Britain, 1940 June – 1943 March; WO 231/182 Directorate of Military Training, Military Training Pamphlet No. 30. Field engineering (all arms). Part III: obstacles, 1940 October 01 – 1940 October 31.
22. TNA WO 166/122 Home Forces, War Diaries, Scottish Command HQ: Royal Engineers, 1939 November – 1940 December.
23. TNA WO 199/54 Home Forces, General HQ, Defence Works, Scheme of anti-tank obstacles for defence of Great Britain, 1940 June – 1943 March.
24. TNA WO 166/116 Home Forces, War Diaries, Scottish Command HQ, General, 1940 August–December.
25. TNA WO 166/12 Home Forces, War Diaries, General HQ, Chief Engineer, 1940 June – 1941 December.
26. TNA WO 166/12 Home Forces, War Diaries, General HQ, Chief Engineer, 1940 June – 1941 December.
27. TNA WO 199/94 Home Forces, General HQ, Beach Defence, Beach mines, 1940 June – 1944 July.
28. TNA WO 199/2668 Home Forces, Scottish Command HQ, Anti-invasion measures, Defence of beaches, obstacles including beach flame barrage, 1940 November – 1943 February.
29. TNA WO 199/2668 Home Forces, Scottish Command HQ, Anti-invasion measures, Defence of beaches, obstacles including beach flame barrage. 1940 November – 1943 February.
30. TNA WO 199/2668 Home Forces, Scottish Command HQ, Anti-invasion measures, Defence of beaches, obstacles including beach flame barrage, 1940 November – 1943 February.
31. TNA WO 199/2668 Home Forces, Scottish Command HQ, Anti-invasion measures, Defence of beaches, obstacles including beach flame barrage, 1940 November – 1943 February.
32. TNA WO 199/2668 Home Forces, Scottish Command HQ, Anti-invasion measures, Defence of beaches, obstacles including beach flame barrage, 1940 November – 1943 February.

9. Pillboxes

1. Osborne, M., *Pillboxes of Britain and Ireland* (Tempus, Stroud, 2008).
2. Wills, H., *Pillboxes: a Study of UK Defences 1940* (Leo Cooper, London, 1985).
3. Osborne, *Pillboxes*, p. 91.
4. The National Archives, Kew (TNA) WO 199/2657 Home Forces, Scottish Command HQ, Anti-invasion measures: provision of pillboxes and blockhouses: correspondence, 1940 June–August.
5. TNA WO 166/1 Home Forces, War Diaries, General HQ: General (G), 1939 September – 1940 December.
6. TNA WO 199/48 Home Forces, General HQ, Defence works, 1940 June – 1942 April.
7. TNA WO 166/116 Home Forces, War Diaries, Scottish Command HQ, General, 1940 August–December.
8. TNA WO 166/136 Home Forces, War Diaries, Scottish Command HQ, Royal Engineers, 1941 January–June, August–December.
9. TNA WO 199/44 Home Forces, General HQ, Defence works: Concrete defences: Policy, 1941 July–September.

10. TNA WO 199/36 Home Forces, General HQ, Defence works, Construction of concrete pillboxes, 1940 August – 1944 July.
11. TNA WO 199/2923 Home Forces, Scottish Command, Midlothian sector, Anti-invasion measures, defence works, 1940 May – 1944 September.
12. TNA WO 166/12 Home Forces, War Diaries, General HQ: Chief Engineer, 1940 June – 1941 December.
13. TNA WO 199/1723 Home Forces, Southern Command HQ, Home defence, Experiments with anti-tank obstacles, 1940 August – 1941 August.
14. Polish Institute and Sikorski Museum, London (PISM) 2/22.XII.Sap.40 Polish Troops: Engineering Matters 1940.
15. PISM A.VI.1/105 Plan obrony odc. [Defence plans for area] Angus i Dundee. 1940–41.
16. TNA WO 166/12 Home Forces, General HQ, Chief Engineer, 1940 June – 1941 December.
17. TNA WO 166/122 Home Forces, Scottish Command HQ, Royal Engineers, 1939 November – 1940 December.
18. TNA WO 166/122 Home Forces, Scottish Command HQ, Royal Engineers, 1939 November – 1940 December.
19. TNA WO 166/122 Home Forces, Scottish Command HQ, Royal Engineers, 1939 November – 1940 December.
20. TNA WO 199/2657 Home Forces, Scottish Command HQ, Anti-invasion measures, provision of pillboxes and blockhouses, correspondence, 1940 June–August; I interpret this as the basis of the shellproof Type 22 of the kind being built on the Cowie Line; these may be directly based on drawings prepared for CRE Scottish Command by CRE Command Line.
21. TNA WO 166/122 Home Forces, War Diaries, Scottish Command HQ, Royal Engineers, 1939 November – 1940 December.
22. Osborne, *Pillboxes*, p. 92.
23. TNA WO 166/3443 Home Forces, War Diaries, CRE Royal Engineers, 2 General Construction Battalion, 1940 June–December.
24. Osborne, *Pillboxes*, p. 232.
25. TNA WO 166/1540 Home Forces, War Diaries, Royal Artillery, 128 Field Regiment, 1939 September – 1941 December.
26. TNA WO 199/2657 Home Forces, Scottish Command HQ, Anti-invasion measures, Provision of pillboxes and blockhouses: correspondence, 1940 June–August.
27. Osborne, *Pillboxes*, p. 233.
28. TNA WO 199/2726 Home Forces, Scottish Command HQ, Orkney and Shetland Defences, Anti-invasion measures, defence against air and seaborne landings, 1940 September – 1944 April.
29. TNA WO 199/2657 Home Forces, Scottish Command HQ, Anti-invasion measures, Provision of pillboxes and blockhouses: correspondence, 1940 June–August.
30. Osborne, *Pillboxes* pp. 149ff. Guttridge, A., *WW2 Military Sites in Caithness* (Dunnett Head Educational Trust, Deerness, 2011), p. 13. I have used 'Type 27' in the text to refer to the anti-aircraft pillboxes.
31. TNA WO 166/919 Home Forces, War Diaries, 13th Infantry Brigade; HQ, 1939 September, 1940 July–December; 1941 January–December.
32. Osborne, *Pillboxes*, p. 155.

10. Orkney and Shetland

1. The National Archives, Kew (TNA) WO 199/620 Home Forces, General HQ, Defence of Certain Areas, Orkneys, 1940 March – 1941 September.
2. TNA WO 166/6035 Home Forces, War Diaries, Scottish Command, General, 1942 January–December.
3. TNA WO 166/1 Home Forces, War Diaries, General HQ: General (G), 1939 September – 1940 December.
4. Miles, W., *The Life of a Regiment, Vol. 5, The Gordon Highlanders 1919–1945* (Warne, London, 1980), p. 115.
5. TNA WO 199/620 Home Forces, General HQ, Defence of Certain Areas, Orkneys, 1940 March – 1941 September.
6. TNA WO 199/620 Home Forces, General HQ, Defence of Certain Areas, Orkneys, 1940 March – 1941 September.
7. TNA WO 199/620 Home Forces, General HQ, Defence of Certain Areas, Orkneys, 1940 March – 1941 September.
8. TNA WO 199/620 Home Forces, General HQ, Defence of Certain Areas, Orkneys, 1940 March – 1941 September.
9. TNA WO 199/620 Home Forces, General HQ, Defence of Certain Areas, Orkneys, 1940 March – 1941 September.
10. TNA WO 199/620 Home Forces, General HQ, Defence of Certain Areas, Orkneys, 1940 March – 1941 September.
11. TNA WO 199/620 Home Forces, General HQ, Defence of Certain Areas, Orkneys, 1940 March – 1941 September.
12. National Records of Scotland (NRS) CAB 80/15 Chiefs of Staff Committee, Memoranda 1940. Nos. (40) 551 – (40) 600.
13. NRS CAB 80/16 Chiefs of Staff Committee, Memoranda 1940. Nos. (40) 601 – (40) 651.
14. NRS CAB 80/16 Chiefs of Staff Committee, Memoranda 1940. Nos. (40) 601 – (40) 651.
15. TNA WO 199/620 Home Forces, General HQ, Defence of Certain Areas, Orkneys, 1940 March – 1941 September.
16. TNA WO 199/620 Home Forces, General HQ, Defence of Certain Areas, Orkneys, 1940 March – 1941 September.
17. TNA WO 199/620 Home Forces, General HQ, Defence of Certain Areas, Orkneys, 1940 March – 1941 September.
18. TNA WO 166/115 Home Forces, War Diaries, Scottish Command, General, 1940 January–July.
19. TNA WO 199/622 Home Forces, General HQ, Defence of Certain Areas, Report on the Orkneys by Capt. W.B. Sallitt, 1940 July.
20. TNA WO 199/622 Home Forces, General HQ, Defence of Certain Areas, Report on the Orkneys by Capt. W.B. Sallitt, 1940 July.
21. TNA WO 199/622 Home Forces, General HQ, Defence of Certain Areas, Report on the Orkneys by Capt. W. B. Sallitt. 1940 July.
22. NRS CAB 80/16 Chiefs of Staff Committee, Memoranda, 1940. Nos. (40) 601 to (40) 651.
23. NRS CAB 80/16 Chiefs of Staff Committee, Memoranda, 1940. Nos. (40) 601 to (40) 651.

24. NRS CAB 79/6 Chiefs of Staff Committee, Minutes, 1940. Meetings (40) 251 to 325.

25. TNA WO 199/620 Home Forces, General HQ, Defence of Certain Areas, Orkneys, 1940 March – 1941 September.

26. NRS CAB 80/16 Chiefs of Staff Committee, Memoranda, 1940. Nos. (40) 601 to (40) 651.

27. TNA WO 199/620 Home Forces, General HQ, Defence of Certain Areas, Orkneys, 1940 March – 1941 September.

28. NRS CAB 80/25 Chiefs of Staff Committee, Memoranda, 1941. Nos. (41) 1 – (41) 100.

29. NRS CAB 80/25 Chiefs of Staff Committee, Memoranda, 1941. Nos. (41) 1 – (41) 100.

30. TNA WO 199/568 Home Forces, General HQ, Home defence, Defence against invasion, Scottish Command appreciation, 1940 June – 1942 November.

31. TNA WO 199/628B Home Forces, General HQ, Defence of certain areas: Orkney and Shetlands, 1941 November – 1942 April.

32. TNA WO 166/6035 Home Forces, War Diaries, Scottish Command, General, 1942 January–December.

33. TNA WO 166/1234 Home Forces, War Diaries, Orkney and Shetland Area, HQ, 1939 October – 1940 December; WO 199/618 Home Forces, General GHQ, Defence of certain areas: Shetlands [includes Orkney material], 1941 May – 1942 January; WO 199/2695 Home Forces, Scottish Command HQ, Operations, Defence of Shetlands, 1941 June – 1944 May.

34. TNA WO 199/619 Home Forces, General HQ, Defence of Certain Areas, Orkneys [includes Shetland material] 1942 August – 1943 February.

35. TNA WO 199/618 Home Forces, General GHQ, Defence of certain areas: Shetlands [includes Orkney material], 1941 May – 1942 January.

36. TNA WO 199/618 Home Forces, General GHQ, Defence of certain areas: Shetlands [includes Orkney material], 1941 May – 1942 January.

37. TNA WO 199/618 Home Forces, General GHQ, Defence of certain areas: Shetlands [includes Orkney material], 1941 May – 1942 January.

38. TNA WO 199/618 Home Forces, General GHQ, Defence of certain areas: Shetlands [includes Orkney material], 1941 May – 1942 January.

39. TNA WO 199/2695 Home Forces, Scottish Command HQ, Operations, Defence of Shetlands, 1941 June – 1944 May.

40. TNA WO 166/1234 Home Forces, War Diaries, Orkney and Shetland Area, HQ, 1939 October – 1940 December.

41. TNA WO 166/4653 War Diaries, 7 Seaforth Highlanders (Ross-shire Buffs, The Duke of Albany's), 1939 August – 1941 December.

42. TNA WO 199/2695 Home Forces, Scottish Command HQ, Operations, Defence of Shetlands, 1941 June – 1944 May.

43. TNA WO 166/4146 Home Forces, War Diaries, 7 Black Watch (Royal Highland Regiment), 1939 August – 1941 December; WO 166/4653 Home Forces, War Diaries, 7 Seaforth Highlanders (Ross-shire Buffs, The Duke of Albany's), 1939 August – 1941 December; WO 199/618 Home Forces, General GHQ, Defence of certain areas: Shetlands [includes Orkney material], 1941 May – 1942 January.

44. TNA WO 166/4653 Home Forces, War Diaries, 7 Seaforth Highlanders (Ross-shire Buffs, The Duke of Albany's), 1939 August – 1941 December.

45. TNA WO 199/2695 Home Forces, Scottish Command HQ, Operations, Defence of Shetlands, 1941 June – 1944 May.

46. TNA WO 199/2695 Home Forces, Scottish Command HQ, Operations, Defence of Shetlands, 1941 June – 1944 May.

47. TNA WO 166/4653 Home Forces, War Diaries, 7 Seaforth Highlanders (Ross-shire Buffs, The Duke of Albany's), 1939 August – 1941 December; WO 199/2695 Home Forces, Scottish Command HQ, Operations, Defence of Shetlands, 1941 June – 1944 May.

48. TNA WO 166/4653 Home Forces, War Diaries, 7 Seaforth Highlanders (Ross-shire Buffs, The Duke of Albany's), 1939 August – 1941 December.

49. TNA WO 199/2695 Home Forces, Scottish Command HQ, Operations, Defence of Shetlands, 1941 June – 1944 May.

50. TNA WO 166/4146 Infantry: 7 Black Watch (Royal Highland Regiment).

51. TNA WO 166/4653 Home Forces, War Diaries, 7 Seaforth Highlanders (Ross-shire Buffs, The Duke of Albany's), 1939 August – 1941 December.

52. TNA WO 166/4653 Home Forces, War Diaries, 7 Seaforth Highlanders (Ross-shire Buffs, The Duke of Albany's), 1939 August – 1941 December.

53. TNA WO 199/2695 Home Forces, Scottish Command HQ, Operations, Defence of Shetlands, 1941 June – 1944 May.

54. TNA WO 199/2695 Home Forces, Scottish Command HQ, Operations, Defence of Shetlands, 1941 June – 1944 May.

55. TNA WO 166/1234 Home Forces, War Diaries, Orkney and Shetland Area, HQ, 1939 October – 1940 December.

56. TNA WO 166/4653 Home Forces, War Diaries, 7 Seaforth Highlanders (Ross-shire Buffs, The Duke of Albany's), 1939 August – 1941 December.

57. TNA WO 199/618 Home Forces, General GHQ, Defence of certain areas: Shetlands [includes Orkney material], 1941 May – 1942 January.

58. TNA WO 166/1234 Home Forces, War Diaries, Orkney and Shetland Area, HQ, 1939 October – 1940 December.

59. TNA WO 166/1234 Home Forces, War Diaries, Orkney and Shetland Area, HQ, 1939 October – 1940 December.

60. TNA WO 199/622 Home Forces, General HQ, Defence of Certain Areas, Report on the Orkneys by Capt. W.B. Sallitt, 1940 July; WO 199/2726 Orkney and Shetland Defences: anti-invasion measures; defence against seaborne landings

61. TNA WO 199/622 Home Forces, General HQ, Defence of Certain Areas, Report on the Orkneys by Capt. W.B. Sallitt, 1940 July.
62. TNA WO 199/622 Home Forces, General HQ, Defence of Certain Areas, Report on the Orkneys by Capt. W.B. Sallitt, 1940 July.
63. Delve, K., *The Military Airfields of Britain: Scotland and Northern Ireland* (Crowood, Marlborough, 2010).
64. TNA WO 199/622 Home Forces, General HQ, Defence of Certain Areas, Report on the Orkneys by Capt. W.B. Sallitt, 1940 July.
65. TNA WO 199/618 Home Forces, General GHQ, Defence of certain areas: Shetlands [includes Orkney material], 1941 May – 1942 January.
66. TNA WO 199/618 Home Forces, General GHQ, Defence of certain areas: Shetlands [includes Orkney material], 1941 May – 1942 January.
67. TNA WO 199/622 Home Forces, General HQ, Defence of Certain Areas, Report on the Orkneys by Capt. W.B. Sallitt, 1940 July.
68. TNA WO 166/1234 Home Forces, War Diaries, Orkney and Shetland Area, HQ, 1939 October – 1940 December.
69. TNA WO 166/1234 Home Forces, War Diaries, Orkney and Shetland Area, HQ, 1939 October – 1940 December.
70. TNA WO 199/622 Home Forces, General HQ, Defence of Certain Areas, Report on the Orkneys by Capt. W.B. Sallitt, 1940 July.
71. TNA WO 199/622 Home Forces, General HQ, Defence of Certain Areas, Report on the Orkneys by Capt. W.B. Sallitt, 1940 July.
72. TNA WO 166/1234 Home Forces, War Diaries, Orkney and Shetland Area, HQ, 1939 October – 1940 December.
73. TNA WO 199/622 Home Forces, General HQ, Defence of Certain Areas, Report on the Orkneys by Capt. W.B. Sallitt, 1940 July.
74. TNA WO 199/622 Home Forces, General HQ, Defence of Certain Areas, Report on the Orkneys by Capt. W.B. Sallitt, 1940 July.
75. TNA WO 199/2726 Home Forces, Scottish Command HQ, Orkney and Shetland Defences, Anti-invasion measures; Defence against seaborne landings, 1940 September – 1944 April.
76. TNA WO 199/2726 Home Forces, Scottish Command HQ, Orkney and Shetland Defences, Anti-invasion measures; Defence against seaborne landings, 1940 September – 1944 April; WO 199/618 Home Forces, General GHQ, Defence of certain areas: Shetlands [includes Orkney material], 1941 May – 1942 January; WO 199/622 Home Forces, General HQ, Defence of Certain Areas, Report on the Orkneys by Capt. W.B. Sallitt, 1940 July; WO 166/4303 Home Forces, War Diaries, 5/7 Gordon Highlanders, 1940 August – 1941 December.
77. TNA WO 199/2726 Home Forces, Scottish Command HQ, Orkney and Shetland Defences, Anti-invasion measures; Defence against seaborne landings, 1940 September – 1944 April.
78. TNA WO 199/2726 Home Forces, Scottish Command HQ, Orkney and Shetland Defences, Anti-invasion measures; Defence against seaborne landings, 1940 September – 1944 April.
79. TNA WO 199/2726 Home Forces, Scottish Command HQ, Orkney and Shetland Defences, Anti-invasion measures; Defence against seaborne landings, 1940 September – 1944 April; WO 199/618 Home Forces, General GHQ, Defence of certain areas: Shetlands [includes Orkney material], 1941 May – 1942 January.; WO 199/2668 Home Forces, Scottish Command HQ, Anti-invasion measures, Defence of beaches, obstacles including beach flame barrage, 1940 November – 1943 February.
80. TNA WO 166/1234 Home Forces, War Diaries, Orkney and Shetland Area, HQ, 1939 October – 1940 December.
81. TNA WO 199/618 Home Forces, General GHQ, Defence of certain areas: Shetlands [includes Orkney material], 1941 May – 1942 January.
82. TNA WO 199/2729 Home Forces, Scottish Command HQ, Orkney & Shetland Defences Island defence: Defence works Inganess–Scapa line, 1943 January – 1944 July. The file in fact contains papers from 1941 onwards.
83. TNA WO 199/2729 Home Forces, Scottish Command HQ, Orkney & Shetland Defences, Island defence: Defence works Inganess-Scapa line, 1943 January – 1944 July.
84. TNA WO 199/2729 Home Forces, Scottish Command HQ, Orkney & Shetland Defences, Island defence: Defence works Inganess-Scapa line, 1943 January – 1944 July.; WO 199/2668 Home Forces, Scottish Command HQ, Anti-invasion measures, Defence of beaches, obstacles including beach flame barrage, 1940 November – 1943 February.
85. TNA WO 199/2729 Home Forces, Scottish Command HQ, Orkney & Shetland Defences, Island defence: Defence works Inganess-Scapa line, 1943 January – 1944 July.
86. TNA WO 199/2729 Home Forces, Scottish Command HQ, Orkney & Shetland Defences, Island defence: Defence works Inganess-Scapa line, 1943 January – 1944 July.
87. TNA WO 199/618 Home Forces, General GHQ, Defence of certain areas: Shetlands [includes Orkney material], 1941 May – 1942 January.
88. TNA WO 166/1234 Home Forces, War Diaries, Orkney and Shetland Area, HQ, 1939 October – 1940 December.
89. TNA WO 166/1234 Home Forces, War Diaries, Orkney and Shetland Area, HQ, 1939 October – 1940 December.
90. TNA WO 199/618 Home Forces, General GHQ, Defence of certain areas: Shetlands [includes Orkney material], 1941 May – 1942 January.

11. Sutherland Sub-area

1. The National Archives, Kew (TNA) WO 166/1211 Home Forces, War Diaries, North Highland Area HQ, 1940 July – 1941 December.
2. TNA WO 166/128 Home Forces, War Diaries, Scottish Command HQ, General Staff, 1941 January–July.
3. TNA WO 192/112 Fort Record Books, Scottish Command, North Head (Wick) Battery, Caithness, 1940–1944.
4. TNA WO 166/1211 Home Forces, War Diaries, North Highland Area HQ, 1940 July – 1941 December.

5. TNA WO 166/6035 Home Forces, War Diaries, Scottish Command, General. Commands: Scottish Command: General, 1942 January – December.
6. TNA WO 192/112 Fort Fort Record Books, Scottish Command, North Head (Wick) Battery, Caithness, 1940–1944.
7. TNA WO 166/116 Home Forces, War Diaries, Scottish Command HQ, General, 1940 August – December.
8. TNA WO 166/931 Home Forces, War Diaries, 26th Infantry Brigade, HQ, 1939 September – 1940 July; WO 166/1211 Home Forces, War Diaries, North Highland Area HQ, 1940 July – 1941 December.
9. TNA WO 166/1211 Home Forces, War Diaries, North Highland Area HQ, 1940 July – 1941 December; WO 166/1322 Home Forces, War Diaries, Sutherland Sub-area, HQ. 1940 October – 1941 December.
10. TNA WO 166/1322 Home Forces, War Diaries, Sutherland Sub-area, HQ, 1940 October – 1941 December.
11. TNA WO 166/1322 Home Forces, War Diaries, Sutherland Sub-area, HQ, 1940 October – 1941 December.
12. TNA WO 166/1322 Home Forces, War Diaries, Sutherland Sub-area, HQ, 1940 October – 1941 December.
13. Polish Institute & Sikorski Museum (PISM) 3.2.XII.Sap Sc.C.C.R. S3/96963/31/G(Ops.) Defence Works.
14. TNA WO 166/1080 Home Forces, War Diaries, 227th Infantry Brigade, HQ, 1941 February–November.
15. TNA WO 166/1080 Home Forces, War Diaries, 227th Infantry Brigade, HQ, 1941 February–November.
16. TNA WO 166/1080 Home Forces, War Diaries, 227th Infantry Brigade, HQ, 1941 February–November. While the coast battery was referred to as 303rd Battery in Brigade papers and in coast artillery lists, it referred to itself as both 303rd and 307th Battery. Andrew Guttridge, who drew this to my attention, postulates a redesignation before December 1942.
17. TNA WO 166/1080 Home Forces, War Diaries, 227th Infantry Brigade, HQ, 1941 February–November.
18. TNA WO 166/1080 Home Forces, War Diaries, 227th Infantry Brigade, HQ, 1941 February–November.
19. TNA WO 166/1080 Home Forces, War Diaries, 227th Infantry Brigade, HQ, 1941 February–November.
20. TNA WO 166/4183 Home Forces, War Diaries, Second, 12 Cameronians (Scottish Rifles), 1940 June – 1941 December.
21. Ritchie, W. et al., *The Beaches of Caithness: A Survey of the Beach, Dune and Dune Pasture Areas of Caithness* (Dept. of Geography, University of Aberdeen, Aberdeen, 1970), p. 24.
22. TNA WO 166/5630 Home Forces, War Diaries, Royal Pioneer Companies, 146 Company, 1940 July – 1941 December.
23. Ritchie et al., *The Beaches of Caithness*, pp. 27–9.
24. TNA WO 199/103 Home Forces, General HQ, Beach Defences, Charting of obstacles on foreshore, 1943 February – 1945 January; WO 166/1080 Home Forces, War Diaries, 227th Infantry Brigade, HQ, 1941 February–November.
25. TNA WO 166/1080 Home Forces, War Diaries, 227th Infantry Brigade, HQ, 1941 February–November.
26. TNA WO 166/1080 Home Forces, War Diaries, 227th Infantry Brigade, HQ, 1941 February–November.
27. TNA WO 199/2668 Home Forces, Scottish Command HQ, Anti-invasion measures, Defence of beaches, obstacles including beach flame barrage. Home Forces, War Diaries, 227th Infantry Brigade, HQ, 1941 February–November.
28. TNA WO 166/3841 Home Forces, War Diaries, Royal Engineers, 656 General Construction Company, 1940 July – 1941 March.
29. TNA WO 166/4654 Home Forces, War Diaries, 8 Seaforth Highlanders (Ross-shire Buffs, The Duke of Albany's), 1939 September – 1941 December.
30. TNA WO 166/3876 Home Forces, War Diaries, Royal Engineers, 692 General Construction Company, 1940 July – 1941 December.
31. TNA WO 166/3876 Home Forces, War Diaries, Royal Engineers, 692 General Construction Company, 1940 July – 1941 December.
32. TNA WO 166/3876 692 Home Forces, War Diaries, Royal Engineers, 692 General Construction Company, 1940 July – 1941 December.
33. TNA WO 166/1080 Home Forces, War Diaries, 227th Infantry Brigade, HQ, 1941 February–November.
34. TNA WO 166/1080 Home Forces, War Diaries, 227th Infantry Brigade, HQ, 1941 February–November.
35. TNA WO 166/5630 Home Forces, War Diaries, Royal Pioneer Companies, 146 Company, 1940 July – 1941 December.
36. TNA WO 166/128 Home Forces, War Diaries, Scottish Command HQ, General Staff, 1941 January–July.
37. TNA WO 166/10362 Home Forces, War Diaries, Scottish Command, General, 1943 January–December.
38. TNA WO 166/128 Home Forces, War Diaries, Scottish Command HQ, General Staff, 1941 January–July; WO 166/10362 Home Forces, War Diaries, Scottish Command, General, 1943 January–December.
39. TNA WO 166/115 Home Forces, War Diaries, Scottish Command Headquarters, General, 1943 January–December.
40. TNA WO 166/129 Home Forces, War Diaries, Scottish Command HQ, General, 1941 July–December.
41. Fjaerli, E., *Den norske haer i Storbritannia, 1940–1945* (Tanum-Norli, Oslo, 1982), p. 44.
42. Roskill, S.W., *The War at Sea, 1939–1945* (HMSO, London, 1976), p. 68.
43. TNA WO 166/419 Home Forces, War Diaries, 5th Division: General Staff, 1939 August – 1941 December.
44. TNA WO 166/635 Home Forces, War Diaries, 52nd Division, General Staff, 1939 Sept – 1940 May, July–December.
45. TNA WO 166/128 Home Forces, War Diaries, Scottish Command HQ, General Staff, 1941 January–July; WO 166/10362 Home Forces, War Diaries, Scottish Command, General, 1943 January–December.
46. TNA WO 199/164 Home Forces, General HQ, Denial of resources, Immobilization of ports, Scottish Command, 1940 May – 1941 March.

12. Aberdeen Sub-area

1. Delve, K., *The Military Airfields of Britain: Scotland and Northern Ireland* (Crowood, Marlborough, 2010), pp. 222–3.
2. The National Archive, Kew (TNA) ADM 1/12607 Navy Department, Correspondence and Papers, Defences, United Kingdom, Defences of small ports in the Moray Firth: reports, 1940–1943.
3. ADM 1/12607 Navy Department, Correspondence and Papers, Defences, United Kingdom, Defences of small ports in the Moray Firth: reports, 1940–1943.

4. Balfour, G., *The Armoured Train: Its Development and Usage* (Batsford, London, 1981).

5. TNA WO 166/1449 Home Forces, War Diaries, Royal Armoured Corps, 4 Armoured Train Group, 11 Train Detachment, 1940 July – 1941 January.

6. TNA WO 166/4653 War Diaries, 7 Seaforth Highlanders (Ross-shire Buffs, The Duke of Albany's), 1939 August – 1941 December.

7. TNA WO 166/5634 Home Forces, War Diaries, Royal Pioneer Companies, 150 Company, 1940 July – 1941 December.

8. Polish Institute and Sikorski Museum, London (PISM) C.384 Kronika 1/11 Komp. Sap., 1940–41.

9. TNA WO 166/1211 Home Forces, War Diaries, North Highland Area: HQ, 1940 July – 1941 December.

10. TNA WO 166/1254 Home Forces, War Diaries, Aberdeen Sub-area HQ, 1940 October – 1941 December.

11. TNA WO 166/619 Home Forces, War Diaries, 51st Division, General Staff, 1939 September–October, 1940 August – 1941 March, May–December.

12. 'Stand To' was a GHQ codeword indicating conditions particularly favourable for an invasion. Troops would come to a complete state of readiness but the Home Guard would not be called out except for special purposes as ordered by General Officers in Chief. 'Action Stations' indicated an immediate threat of invasion, for which a full-scale state of readiness and calling out of the Home Guard was required. WO 166/1322 War Office, War Diaries, Sutherland Sub-area, HQ, 1940 October – 1941 December.

13. TNA WO 166/1254 Home Forces, War Diaries, Aberdeen Sub-area HQ, 1940 October – 1941 December. 490th Battery, RA, is an elusive unit in the records, which may have been part of 46th Division's artillery, detached from the Division, in the Borders Training Area.

14. TNA WO 166/4142 Home Forces, War Diaries, 1 Black Watch (Royal Highland Regiment), 1940 June – 1941 December.

15. TNA WO 199/2740 Home Forces, Scottish Command, North Highland District, Anti-invasion measures, Beach defence, 1941 November – 1944 December.

16. TNA WO 199/2739 Home Forces, Scottish Command, North Highland District, Anti-invasion measures, removal and salvage of obsolete defence works, 1942 December – 1944 September.

17. TNA WO 199/88 Home Forces, General HQ, Beach Defence Reconnaissance, Scottish Command, 1940 May–August; WO 199/103 Home Forces, General HQ, Beach Defence, charting of obstructions on foreshore. 1943 February – 1945 January.

18. Ritchie, W. et al., *Beaches of Northeast Scotland* (Countryside Commission for Scotland, Perth, 1978), pp. 146–7.

19. TNA WO 199/88 Home Forces, General HQ, Beach Defence Reconnaissance, Scottish Command, 1940 May–August.

20. TNA WO 199/2882 Home Forces, Aberdeen Sub-area, Anti-invasion measures: defence of aerodromes, 1941 May–December; TNA WO 166/4183 Home Forces, War Diaries, Second, 12 Cameronians (Scottish Rifles), 1940 June – 1941 December.

21. TNA WO 166/4142 Home Forces, War Diaries, 1 Black Watch (Royal Highland Regiment), 1940 June – 1941 December.

22. TNA WO 166/4142 Home Forces, War Diaries, 1 Black Watch (Royal Highland Regiment), 1940 June – 1941 December.

23. Cowley, D.C., Guy, J.A. and Henderson, D.M., 'The Sheriffmuir "Atlantic Wall": an archaeological survey on part of the Whitestone Military range', *Forth Naturalist and Historian*, 22 (1999), pp. 107–16.

24. TNA WO 166/4142 Home Forces, War Diaries, 1 Black Watch (Royal Highland Regiment), 1940 June – 1941 December.

25. TNA WO 199/2668 Home Forces, Scottish Command HQ, Anti-invasion measures, Defence of beaches, obstacles including beach flame barrage, 1940 November – 1943 February.

26. TNA WO 166/136 Home Forces, War Diaries, Scottish Command HQ, Royal Engineers, 1941 January–June, August–December.

27. TNA WO 166/1538 Home Forces, War Diaries, Royal Artillery, 126 Field Regiment, 1939 September – 1941 December.

28. TNA WO 166/4183 Home Forces, War Diaries, Second, 12 Cameronians (Scottish Rifles), 1940 June – 1941 December.

29. TNA WO 199/2882 Aberdeen Sub-area: Anti-invasion measures: defence of aerodromes. WO 166/4183 Infantry: 12 Cameronians (Scottish Rifles).

30. TNA WO 166/4183 Home Forces, War Diaries, Second, 12 Cameronians (Scottish Rifles), 1940 June – 1941 December.

31. Mark Keighley, personal communication.

32. TNA WO 166/1211 Home Forces, War Diaries, North Highland Area: HQ, 1940 July – 1941 December.

33. TNA WO 166/116 Home Forces, War Diaries, Scottish Command Headquarters, General, 1940 August – December.

34. TNA WO 166/1211 Home Forces, War Diaries, North Highland Area: HQ, 1940 July – 1941 December.

35. TNA WO 166/116 Home Forces, War Diaries, Scottish Command Headquarters, General, 1940 August – December; WO 166/129 Home Forces, War Diaries, Scottish Command HQ, General, 1941 July–December; WO 166/1211 Home Forces, War Diaries, North Highland Area, HQ, 1940 July – 1941 December.

36. TNA WO 199/103 Home Forces, General HQ, Beach Defence, Charting of obstructions on foreshore, 1943 February – 1945 January; WO 166/1211 Home Forces, War Diaries, North Highland Area, HQ, 1940 July – 1941 December; WO 166/1254 Home Forces, War Diaries, Aberdeen Sub-area HQ, 1940 October – 1941 December.

37. TNA WO 166/4183 Home Forces, War Diaries, 12 Cameronians (Scottish Rifles), 1940 June – 1941 December. The Banff Home Guard featured in the 1941 invasion thriller *The Black Milestone* by Catherine Gavin, foiling a large German landing in Cullykhan Bay.

38. TNA WO 166/1254 Home Forces, War Diaries, Aberdeen Sub-area HQ, 1940 October – 1941 December.

39. TNA WO 166/128 Home Forces, War Diaries, Scottish Command, General Staff, 1941 January–July.
40. TNA WO 199/568 Home Forces, Military Headquarters Papers, General HQ: Home defence, Defence against invasion, Scottish Command appreciation, 1940 June –1942 November.
41. TNA WO 166/1254 Home Forces, War Diaries, Aberdeen Sub-area HQ, 1940 October – 1941 December.
42. TNA WO 199/2882 Home Forces, Scottish Command, Aberdeen Sub-area: Anti-invasion measures: defence of aerodromes, 1941 May– December.
43. Osborne, M., *Defending Britain: Twentieth-Century Military Structures in the Landscape* (Tempus, Stroud, 2004), pp. 99–102.
44. TNA WO 166/1211 Home Forces, War Diaries, North Highland Area: HQ, 1940 July – 1941 December.
45. TNA WO 166/3866 Home Forces, War Diaries, Royal Engineers, 682 General Construction Company, 1940 July – 1941 December.
46. Miles, W., *The Life of a Regiment, Vol. 5, The Gordon Highlanders 1919–1945* (Warne, London, 1980), p. 114.
47. TNA WO 166/1069 Home Forces, War Diaries, 216th Infantry Brigade, HQ, 1940 October – 1941 December; WO 166/1254 Home Forces, War Diaries, Aberdeen Sub-area HQ, 1940 October – 1941 December.
48. TNA WO 166/1254 Home Forces, War Diaries, Aberdeen Sub-area HQ, 1940 October – 1941 December.
49. TNA WO 166/1254 Home Forces, War Diaries, Aberdeen Sub-area HQ, 1940 October – 1941 December.
50. TNA WO 166/1254 Home Forces, War Diaries, Aberdeen Sub-area HQ, 1940 October – 1941 December.
51. TNA WO 199/2672 Home Forces, War Diaries, Scottish Command HQ, Coastal Defence, General Policy, 1939 May – 1941 May.
52. TNA WO 166/619 Home Forces, War Diaries, 51st Division, General Staff, 1939 September–October, 1940 August – 1941 March, May–December.
53. TNA WO 166/619 Home Forces, War Diaries, 51st Division, General Staff, 1939 September–October, 1940 August – 1941 March, May–December.
54. TNA WO 166/619 Home Forces, War Diaries, 51st Division, General Staff, 1939 September–October, 1940 August – 1941 March, May–December.
55. TNA WO 166/619 Home Forces, War Diaries, 51st Division, General Staff, 1939 September–October, 1940 August – 1941 March, May–December.
56. TNA WO 166/4127 Home Forces, War Diaries, 15 Argyll & Sutherland Highlanders (Princess Louise's), 1940 October – 1941 December; WO 166/1069 Home Forces, War Diaries, 216th Infantry Brigade, HQ, 1940 October – 1941 December.
57. TNA WO 166/1254 Home Forces, War Diaries, Aberdeen Sub-area HQ, 1940 October – 1941 December.
58. TNA WO 166/1254 Home Forces, War Diaries, Aberdeen Sub-area HQ, 1940 October – 1941 December.
59. TNA WO 166/1254 Home Forces, War Diaries, Aberdeen Sub-area HQ, 1940 October – 1941 December.
60. TNA WO 199/2882 Home Forces, Scottish Command, Aberdeen Sub-area: Anti-invasion measures: defence of aerodromes, 1941 May–December.
61. TNA WO 199/2882 Home Forces, Scottish Command, Aberdeen Sub-area: Anti-invasion measures: defence of aerodromes, 1941 May–December.
62. TNA WO 166/1254 Home Forces, War Diaries, Aberdeen Sub-area HQ, 1940 October – 1941 December.
63. TNA WO 166/1254 Home Forces, War Diaries, Aberdeen Sub-area HQ, 1940 October – 1941 December.
64. TNA WO 166/128 Home Forces, War Diaries, Scottish Command, General Staff, 1941 January–July.
65. TNA WO 166/2032 Home Forces, War Diaries, Royal Artillery, Defence Batteries, 942 Defence Battery (Mobile), 1940 September – 1942 January.
66. TNA WO 166/1449 Home Forces, War Diaries, 4 Armoured Train Group, 11 Train Detachment, 1940 July – 1941 March.
67. TNA WO 166/5553 Home Forces, War Diaries, Royal Pioneer Corps, 67 Company, 1940 July – 1941 December.
68. TNA WO 166/5553 Home Forces, War Diaries, Royal Pioneer Corps, 67 Company, 1940 July – 1941 December.
69. TNA WO 199/2663 Home Forces, Scottish Command HQ, Anti-invasion measures, Obstruction of open water spaces, 1940 June – 1942 April.
70. TNA WO 166/1254 Home Forces, War Diaries, Aberdeen Sub-area HQ, 1940 October – 1941 December.
71. TNA WO 166/5559 Home Forces, War Diaries, Royal Pioneer Corps, 73 Company, 1940 January, July – 1941 December.
72. TNA WO 166/5553 Home Forces, War Diaries, Royal Pioneer Corps, 67 Company, 1940 July – 1941 December.
73. TNA WO 166/1254 Home Forces, War Diaries, Aberdeen Sub-area HQ, 1940 October – 1941 December.
74. TNA WO 166/1254 Home Forces, War Diaries, Aberdeen Sub-area HQ, 1940 October – 1941 December.
75. TNA WO 199/2740 Home Forces, Scottish Command, North Highland District, Anti-invasion measures, Beach defence, 1941 November – 1944 December.
76. TNA WO 166/5559 Home Forces, War Diaries, Royal Pioneer Corps, 73 Company, 1940 January, July – 1941 December.
77. TNA WO 166/4415 Home Forces, War Diaries, 11 Lancashire Fusiliers, 1940 October – 1941 June.
78. TNA WO 166/4415 Home Forces, War Diaries, 11 Lancashire Fusiliers, 1940 October – 1941 June.
79. TNA WO 166/4415 Home Forces, War Diaries, 11 Lancashire Fusiliers, 1940 October – 1941 June.
80. TNA WO 166/4415 Home Forces, War Diaries, 11 Lancashire Fusiliers, 1940 October – 1941 June.
81. TNA WO 199/2893 Home Forces, Scottish Command, Aberdeen Sub-area, Norwegian Brigade, Operational role, 1941 September – 1942 March.
82. TNA WO 199/103 Home Forces, General HQ, Beach Defences, Charting of obstacles on foreshore, 1943 February – 1945 January.
83. TNA WO 166/2032 Home Forces, War Diaries, Royal Artillery, Defence Batteries, 942 Defence Battery (Mobile), 1940 September – 1942 January.

84. TNA WO 166/619 Home Forces, War Diaries, 51st Division, General Staff, 1939 September–October, 1940 August – 1941 March, May–December.

85. Ritchie, W., Rose, N. and Smith, J.S., *Beaches of Northeast Scotland* (Countryside Commission for Scotland, Perth, 1978).

86. TNA WO 166/128 Home Forces, War Diaries, Scottish Command, General Staff, 1941 January–July; WO 166/129 Home Forces, War Diaries, Scottish Command HQ, General, 1941 July–December.

87. TNA WO 166/619 Home Forces, War Diary, 51st Division, General Staff. 1939 September–October, 1940 August – 1941 March, May–December.

88. TNA WO 166/5559 Home Forces, War Diaries, Royal Pioneer Corps, 73 Company, 1940 January, July – 1941 December.

89. TNA WO 166/1254 Home Forces, War Diaries, Aberdeen Sub-area HQ, 1940 October – 1941 December.

90. TNA WO 199/2672 Home Forces, Scottish Command HQ, Coast Defence, General Policy, 1939 May – 1941 May.

91. National Records of Scotland, Edinburgh (NRS) AF 83/1365 Department of Agriculture for Scotland, Land Scheme, Balmedie: Air Raid Precautions & Defence Works, Immobilisation of Landing Grounds, 1940–1944.

92. TNA WO 199/103 Home Forces, General HQ, Beach Defences, Charting of obstacles on foreshore, 1943 February – 1945 January.

93. TNA WO 166/5536 Home Forces, War Diaries, Royal Pioneer Corps, 50 Company, 1940 June – 1941 December.

94. TNA WO 199/2668 Home Forces, Scottish Command HQ, Anti-invasion measures, Defence of beaches, obstacles including beach flame barrage, 1940 November – 1943 February.

95. TNA WO 199/2668 Home Forces, Scottish Command HQ, Anti-invasion measures, Defence of beaches, obstacles including beach flame barrage, 1940 November – 1943 February.

96. TNA WO 166/1331 Home Forces, War Diaries, Aberdeen Garrison HQ, 1941 May–December.

97. TNA WO 166/5536 Home Forces, War Diaries, Royal Pioneer Corps, 50 Company, 1940 June – 1941 December.

98. TNA WO 199/103 Home Forces, General HQ, Beach Defences, Charting of obstacles on foreshore, 1943 February – 1945 January; TNA WO 199/2740 Home Forces, Scottish Command, North Highland District, Anti-invasion measures, Beach defence, 1941 November – 1944 December.

99. TNA ADM 1/11943 Navy, Defences, UK, Use of blockships as anti-invasion measures at home ports and harbours, 1940–1942.

100. TNA WO 166/1254 Home Forces, War Diaries, Aberdeen Sub-area HQ, 1940 October – 1941 December.

101. TNA WO 166/1254 Home Forces, War Diaries, Aberdeen Sub-area HQ, 1940 October – 1941 December.

102. TNA WO 166/5701 Home Forces, War Diaries, Royal Pioneer Corps, 217 Company, 1940 September – 1941 December.

103. TNA WO 166/5701 Home Forces, War Diaries, Royal Pioneer Corps, 217 Company, 1940 September – 1941 December.

104. TNA WO 166/5701 Home Forces, War Diaries, Royal Pioneer Corps, 217 Company, 1940 September – 1941 December.

105. TNA WO 166/1254 Home Forces, War Diaries, Aberdeen Sub-area HQ, 1940 October – 1941 December.

106. TNA WO 166/128 Home Forces, War Diaries, Scottish Command, General Staff, 1941 January–July.

107. TNA WO 166/1331 Home Forces, War Diaries, Aberdeen Garrison HQ, 1941 May-–December.

108. TNA WO 199/568 Home Forces, Military Headquarters Papers, General HQ: Home defence, Defence against invasion, Scottish Command appreciation, 1940 June –1942 November.

109. TNA WO 166/115 Home Forces, War Diaries, Scottish Command Headquarters, General, 1940 January – July; TNA WO 166/619 Home Forces, War Diaries, 51st Division, General Staff, 1939 September–October, 1940 August – 1941 March, May–December.

110. TNA WO 166/434 Home Forces, War Diaries, 9th Division: General Staff, 1939 September – 1940 August.

111. TNA WO 166/1254 Home Forces, War Diaries, Aberdeen Sub-area HQ, 1940 October – 1941 December.

112. TNA WO 166/1211 Home Forces, War Diaries, North Highland Area: HQ, 1940 July – 1941 December.

13. Angus Sub-area

1. The National Archives, Kew (TNA) WO 166/435 Home Forces, War Diaries, 9th Division, Commander Royal Artillery, 1939 January – 1940 December.

2. TNA WO 166/1811 Home Forces, War Diaries, Royal Artillery, 308 Coast Battery, 1940 May – 1941 March.

3. TNA WO 166/1259 Home Forces, War Diaries, Angus Sub-area, HQ, 1940 October – 1941 December.

4. TNA WO 199/164 Home Forces, War Diaries, General HQ, Denial of resources, Immobilization of ports, Scottish Command, 1940 May – 1941 March.

5. TNA WO 166/1259 Home Forces, War Diaries, Angus Sub-area, HQ, 1940 October – 1941 December.

6. Wright, R., *The Beaches of Tayside* (University of Aberdeen for Countryside Commission for Scotland, Aberdeen, 1981).

7. TNA WO 199/103 Home Forces, General HQ, Beach Defences, Charting of obstacles on foreshore, 1943 February – 1945 January; Polish Institute & Sikorski Museum, London (PISM) A.VI.1/74 Obrona odcinkow [Defence sector] Angus i Fife, 1941.

8. TNA WO 199/103 Home Forces, General HQ, Beach Defences, Charting of obstacles on foreshore, 1943 February – 1945 January

9. TNA WO 166/128 Home Forces, War Diaries, Scottish Command, General Staff, 1941 January–July.

10. TNA WO 199/2675 Home Forces, Scottish Command HQ, Defence of Fife and Angus ; appreciation of the situation, 1941 June. PISM A.VI.1/74 Obrona odcinkow [Defence sector] Angus i Fife, 1941.

11. TNA WO 166/4148 Home Forces, War Diaries, 9 Black Watch (Royal Highland Regiment), 1939 August – 1941 August.

12. TNA WO 166/1540 Home Forces, War Diaries, Royal Artillery, 128 Field Regiment, 1939 September – 1941 December.

13. TNA WO 166/1540 Home Forces, War Diaries, Royal Artillery, 128 Field Regiment, 1939 September – 1941 December.

14. TNA WO 166/1540 Home Forces, War Diaries, Royal Artillery, 128 Field Regiment, 1939 September – 1941 December.

15. TNA WO 166/1497 Home Forces, War Diaries, Royal Artillery71 Field Regiment, 1939 September – 1940 May, July – 1941 December.

16. TNA WO 166/1540 Home Forces, War Diaries, Royal Artillery, 128 Field Regiment, 1939 September – 1941 December.

17. TNA WO 166/4150 Home Forces, War Diaries, 10 Black Watch (Royal Highland Regiment), 1940 October – 1941 December.

18. TNA WO 166/1259 Home Forces, War Diaries, Angus Sub-area, HQ, 1940 October – 1941 December.

19. TNA WO 166/4150 Home Forces, War Diaries, 10 Black Watch (Royal Highland Regiment), 1940 October – 1941 December.

20. TNA WO 199/568 Home Forces, General HQ, Home defence, Defence against invasion: Scottish Command appreciation, 1940 June – 1942 November; PISM A.VI.1/74 Obrona odcinkow [Defence sector] Angus i Fife, 1941.

21. TNA WO 166/4150 Home Forces, War Diaries, 10 Black Watch (Royal Highland Regiment), 1940 October – 1941 December.

22. Smith, L., Paton, D., Betty, J. and Warren, L. *Learning to Fly at Montrose: The Story in Words & Pictures, 1913–1950* (Ian McIntosh Memorial Trust, Montrose, 2010), p. 103. 'Erk' was RAF slang for 'aircraftman'.

23. TNA WO 166/1259 Home Forces, War Diaries, Angus Sub-area, HQ, 1940 October – 1941 December.

24. TNA WO 166/1259 Home Forces, War Diaries, Angus Sub-area, HQ, 1940 October – 1941 December.

25. TNA WO 166/641 Home Forces, War Diaries, 52nd Division, Commander Royal Engineers 1941 January – December; WO 166/6035 Home Forces, War Diaries, Scottish Command, General. 1942 January – December.

26. TNA WO 166/5679 Home Forces, War Diaries, Royal Pioneer Corps, 195 Company, 1940 August – 1941 December.

27. TNA WO 199/2894 Home Forces, War Diaries, Scottish Command, Angus Sub-area, Defence Plans, 1942 April; PISM A.VI.1/73 Obrona odcinkow [Defence sector] Perth i Dundee, 1941–; A.VI.1/74 Obrona odcinkow [Defence sector] Angus i Fife, 1941.

28. Wright, R., *The Beaches of Tayside* (University of Aberdeen for Countryside Commission for Scotland, Aberdeen, 1981).

29. Polish Institute and Sikorski Museum, London (PISM) A.VI.1/74 Obrona odcinkow [Defence sector] Angus i Fife, 1941. TNA WO 199/103 Home Forces, General HQ, Beach Defence, charting of obstacles on foreshore, 1943 February – 1945 January

30. PISM A.VI.1/73 Obrona odcinkow [Defence sector] Perth i Dundee, 1941–.

31. TNA WO 166/1538 Home Forces, War Diaries, Royal Artillery, 126 Field Regiment, 1939 September, 1941 December.

32. TNA WO 166/1497 Home Forces, War Diaries, Royal Artillery, 71 Field Regiment, 1939 September – 1940 May, July – 1941 December.

33. TNA WO 166/4150 Home Forces, War Diaries, 10 Black Watch (Royal Highland Regiment), 1940 October – 1941 December.

34. TNA WO 166/5627 Home Forces, War Diaries, Royal Pioneer Corps, 143 Company, 1940 June – 1941 December.

35. TNA WO 166/1259 Home Forces, War Diaries, Angus Sub-area, HQ, 1940 October – 1941 December.

36. PISM A.VI.1/74 Obrona odcinkow [Defence sector] Angus i Fife, 1941. .VI.1/74 Obrona odcinkow [Defence sector] Angus i Fife, 1941.

37. PISM A.VI.1/74 Obrona odcinkow [Defence sector] Angus i Fife, 1941 A.VI.1/73 Obrona odcinkow [Defence sector] Perth i Dundee, 1941–.

38. Wright, R., *The Beaches of Tayside*, p. 58.

39. TNA WO 166/1538 Home Forces, War Diaries, Royal Artillery, 126 Field Regiment, 1939 September – 1941 December.

40. TNA WO 166/115 Home Forces, War Diaries, Scottish Command Headquarters, General, 1940 January–July.

41. TNA WO 166/116 Home Forces, War Diaries, Scottish Command Headquarters, General, 1940 August–December.

42. TNA WO 166/128 Home Forces, War Diaries, Scottish Command, General Staff, 1941 January–July.

43. TNA WO 166/129 Home Forces, War Diaries, Scottish Command HQ, General, 1941 July–December.

44. TNA WO 166/5514 Home Forces, War Diaries, Royal Pioneer Corps, 27 Company, 1940 July – 1941 December.

45. TNA WO 166/1259 Home Forces, War Diaries, Angus Sub-area, HQ, 1940 October – 1941 December.

46. PISM A.VI.1/74 Obrona odcinkow [Defence sector] Angus i Fife, 1941; A.VI.1/104 Plany obrony, instrukcje, 1940. A.VI.1/105Plan obrony odc. [Defence plans for area] Angus i Dundee, 1940–1.

47. TNA WO 166/2033 Home Forces, War Diaries, Royal Artillery, 943 Defence Battery (Mobile), 1940 August – 1941 September; WO 166/128 Home Forces, War Diaries, Scottish Command, General Staff, 1941 January–July.

48. TNA WO 199/2672 Home Forces, War Diaries, Scottish Command HQ, Coastal Defence, General Policy, 1939 May – 1941 May.

49. TNA WO 199/44 Home Forces, General HQ, Defence Works, Concrete defences, policy, 1941 July – 1941 September.

50. TNA WO 199/2672 Home Forces, General HQ, Scottish Command, Coast Defence, General Policy, 1939 May – 1941 May.

51. TNA WO 166/993 Home Forces, War Diaries, 137th Infantry Brigade, HQ, 1939 January – 1941 December; WO 166/552 Home Forces, War Diaries, 46th Division, General Staff, 1939 January – 1941 December.

52. TNA WO 166/1633 Royal Artillery: Anti-tank Regiments: 61 Anti-Tank Regiment 1939 September – 1941 December.
53. TNA WO 166/4691 Home Forces, War Diaries, 10 South Staffordshire Regt (Pioneer), 1940 March – 1941 December; WO 166/1497 Home Forces, War Diaries, Royal Artillery 71 Field Regiment, 1939 September – 1940 May, July – 1941 December.
54. PISM A.VI.1/104 Plany obrony, instrukcje, 1940.
55. TNA WO 166/128 Home Forces, War Diaries, Scottish Command, General Staff, 1941 January–July.
56. TNA WO 166/434 Home Forces, War Diaries, 9th Division: General Staff, 1939 September – 1940 August.
57. TNA WO 166/434 Home Forces, War Diaries, 9th Division: General Staff, 1939 September – 1940 August.
58. TNA WO 166/10362 Home Forces, War Diaries, Scottish Command, G, 1943 January–December.
59. National Library of Scotland (NLS) MS.3821, *Record of Scottish Home Guard 1940–1945: East Scotland District; Part two (Nos. 93–120)*. 1945.
60. TNA WO 166/434 Home Forces, War Diaries, 9th Division: General Staff, 1939 September – 1940 August.
61. TNA WO 166/1259 Home Forces, War Diaries, Angus Sub-area, HQ, 1940 October – 1941 December.
62. TNA WO 166/1 Home Forces, War Diaries, General HQ: General (G), 1939 September – 1940 December.
63. TNA WO 166/993 Home Forces, War Diaries, 137th Infantry Brigade, HQ, 1939 August – 1940 March, July – 1941 December.
64. PISM A.VI.1/77 Zalacznik do planu obrony Nr 1 [addendum to defence plan no 1], 1940–41
65. PISM A.VI.1/105 Plan obrony odc. [Defence plans for area] Angus i Dundee, 1940–41.

14. Fife Sub-area

1. The National Archives, Kew. WO 199/2668 Home Forces, Scottish Command HQ, Anti invasion measures, Defence of beaches, obstacles including beach flame barrage, 1940 November – 1943 February.
2. Polish Institute and Sikorski Museum, London. 1.28.XI.Sap Design of reinforcing works on sectors of 1, 2 and 4th Brigade, 1940.
3. TNA WO 199/2668 Home Forces, Scottish Command HQ, Anti-invasion measures, Defence of beaches, obstacles including beach flame barrage, 1940 November – 1943 February.
4. Ritchie, W., *The Beaches of Fife* (Countryside Commission for Scotland, Perth, 1979), p. 17.
5. Ritchie, *The Beaches of Fife*, p. 17.
6. Maps in files: PISM A.VI.1/61 Obrona odcinka [Defence sector] Fife, 1941–42; A.VI.1/73 Obrona odcinkow [Defence sector] Perth i Dundee, 1941–; A.VI.1/77 Zalacznik do planu obrony Nr 1 [addendum to defence plan no 1], 1940–41; A.VI.1/106 Plan obrony odcinkow [Defence plans sector] Dunfermline i Fife, 1940–41. C.384 Kronika 1/11 Komp. Sap, 1940–41.
7. TNA WO 166/2033 Home Forces, War Diaries, Royal Artillery, 943 Defence Battery (Mobile), 1940 August – 1941 September.
8. PISM A.VI.1/106 Plan obrony odcinkow [Defence plans sector] Dunfermline i Fife, 1940–41.
9. Lowry, B., *British Home Defences 1940–45* (Osprey, Oxford, 2004).
10. TNA WO 199/103 Home Forces, General HQ, Beach Defences, Charting of obstacles on foreshore, 1943 February – 1945 January.
11. PISM A.VI.1/77 Zalacznik do planu obrony Nr 1 [addendum to defence plan no 1], 1940–41.
12. A.VI.1/77 Zalacznik do planu obrony Nr 1 [addendum to defence plan no 1], 1940–41
13. TNA WO 166/122 Home Forces, War Diaries, Scottish Command Headquarters, Royal Engineers, 1939 November – 1940 December.
14. PISM A.VI.1/77 Zalacznik do planu obrony Nr 1 [addendum to defence plan no 1], 1940–41.
15. TNA WO 166/128 Home Forces, War Diaries, Scottish Command, General Staff, 1941 January–July; WO 166/129 Home Forces, War Diaries, Scottish Command HQ, General, 1941 July–December.
16. PISM A.VI.1/104 Plany obrony, instrukcje, 1940.
17. TNA WO 199/527 'Floodtide': reduction and reorganisation of coast artillery, 1943 May – 1944 August.
18. TNA WO 199/527 'Floodtide': reduction and reorganisation of coast artillery, 1943 May – 1944 August.

15. The Scottish Command Line

1. The National Archives, Kew (TNA) WO 166/122 Home Forces, War Diaries, Scottish Command Headquarters, Royal Engineers, 1939 November – 1940 December.
2. TNA WO 199/568 Home Forces, Military Headquarters Papers, General HQ: Home defence, Defence against invasion, Scottish Command appreciation, 1940 June –1942 November.
3. TNA WO 166/115 Home Forces, War Diaries, Scottish Command Headquarters, General, 1940 January – July.
4. TNA WO 166/115 Home Forces, War Diaries, Scottish Command Headquarters, General, 1940 January – July.
5. TNA WO 166/924 Home Forces, War Diaries, 17th Infantry Brigade, HQ, 1939 October; 1940 July – 1941 December.
6. TNA WO 166/115 Home Forces, War Diaries, Scottish Command Headquarters, General, 1940 January – July.
7. TNA WO 166/3443 Home Forces, War Diaries, Royal Engineers, No. 2 General Construction Battalion, 1940 June–December.
8. PISM A.VI.31/3 Os Dunkeld – Stanley, 1940–43; A.VI.31/4 Os Braemar – Perth, 1940–43; A.VI.31/5 Os przedmiescia [suburbs] Perth, 1940–43; A.VI.31/6 Os rzek [Rivers] Isla-Dean Water, 1940–43; A.VI.31/7 Os rzek [Rivers] Esk – West Water, 1940–43; A.VI.31/8(a/b) Odcinek [Sector] Angus, 1940–43.
9. Barclay, G., 'The Scottish Command Line: the archaeology and history of a 1940 anti-tank "stop-line"', *Tayside and Fife Archaeological Journal*, 17 (2011), pp. 114–56.

10. TNA WO 166/12 Home Forces, War Diaries, General HQ, Chief Engineer, 1940 June – 1941 December; WO 199/568 Home Forces, General HQ, Defence against invasion, Scottish Command appreciation, 1940 June – 1942 November.

11. TNA WO 166/122 Home Forces, War Diaries, Scottish Command Headquarters, Royal Engineers, 1939 November – 1940 December.

12. TNA WO 166/3699 Home Forces, War Diaries, Royal Engineers, 230 Army Field Company. June 1940–1941 December.

13. TNA WO 166/3443 Home Forces, War Diaries, Royal Engineers, No. 2 General Construction Battalion, 1940 June–December.

14. TNA WO 166/419 Home Forces, War Diaries, 5th Infantry Division, General Staff , 1939 August – 1941 December; WO 166/434 Home Forces, War Diaries, 9th Division: General Staff, 1939 September – 1940 August.

15. TNA WO 166/919 Home Forces, War Diaries, 13th Infantry Brigade; HQ, 1939 September, 1940 July–December, 1941 January–December.

16. TNA WO 166/3443 Home Forces, War Diaries, Royal Engineers, No. 2 General Construction Battalion, 1940 June–December.

17. TNA WO 166/3443 Home Forces, War Diaries, Royal Engineers, No. 2 General Construction Battalion, 1940 June–December.

18. PISM A.VI.1/73 Obrona odcinkow [Defence sector] Perth i Dundee, 1941–; A.VI.31/5 Os przedmiescia [suburbs] Perth, 1940–43.

19. PISM C.538/I 1 Bryg. Strz. [1st Rifle Brigade] (I Korpus) [I Corps], Kronika [Chronicle], 1940.

20. TNA WO 166/3609 Home Forces, War Diaries, Royal Engineers, 110 Army Troops Company, 1940 July – 1941 December.

16. Edinburgh Area

1. The National Archives, Kew (TNA) WO 166/641 Home Forces, War Diaries, 52nd Division, Commander Royal Engineers, 1941 January–December; WO 199/2743 Scottish Command, South Highland District, Defence scheme, McMerry [sic] Aerodrome, 1941 November; WO 199/2808 Home Forces, Edinburgh Sub-district, Home Guard, Defence scheme, 1st Battalion City of Edinburgh Zone, 1940 August – 1944 June.

2. TNA WO 166/1742 Royal Artillery, Coast Regiments, 542 Coast Regiment [No. 2 Group Coastal Artillery], 1940 October – 1941 December.

3. TNA WO 166/128 Home Forces, War Diaries, Scottish Command, General Staff, 1941 January–July; WO 166/2033 Home Forces, War Diaries, Royal Artillery, 943 Defence Battery (Mobile), 1940 August – 1941 September; WO 166/1496 Home Forces, War Diaries, Royal Artillery, 70 Field Regiment, 1939 January – 1941 December; WO 166/1567 Home Forces, War Diaries, Royal Artillery, 155 Field Regiment, 1939 September – 1941 March.; WO 166/552 Home Forces, War Diaries, 46th Division, General Staff, 1939 October – 1940 March, July – 1941 December.

4. TNA WO 166/6035 Home Forces, War Diaries, Scottish Command, General, 1942 January–December.

5. PISM A.VI.31/2 Odcinek [Sector] East Lothian, 1940–42.

6. TNA WO 166/122 Home Forces, War Diaries, Scottish Command Headquarters, Royal Engineers, 1939 November – 1940 December.

7. TNA WO 166/128 Home Forces, War Diaries, Scottish Command, General Staff, 1941 January–July.

8. TNA WO 166/641 Home Forces, War Diaries, 52nd Division, Commander Royal Engineers, 1941 January–December.

9. TNA WO 166/641 Home Forces, War Diaries, 52nd Division, Commander Royal Engineers, 1941 January–December.

10. Rose, N., *The Beaches of South East Scotland* (Countryside Commission for Scotland, Perth, 1980).

11. Rose, *The Beaches of South East Scotland*, p. 42.

12. TNA WO 166/122 Home Forces, War Diaries, Scottish Command Headquarters, Royal Engineers, 1939 November – 1940 December.

13. PISM A.VI.31/2 Odcinek [Sector] East Lothian, 1940–42.

14. TNA WO 199/2668 Home Forces, Scottish Command HQ, Anti-invasion measures, Defence of beaches, obstacles including beach flame barrage, 1940 November – 1943 February.

15. TNA WO 199/2668 Home Forces, Scottish Command HQ, Anti-invasion measures, Defence of beaches, obstacles including beach flame barrage, 1940 November – 1943 February.

16. TNA WO 199/2668 Home Forces, Scottish Command HQ, Anti-invasion measures, Defence of beaches, obstacles including beach flame barrage, 1940 November – 1943 February; PISM A.VI.31/2 Odcinek [Sector] East Lothian, 1940–42.

17. TNA WO 199/2668 Home Forces, Scottish Command HQ, Anti-invasion measures, Defence of beaches, obstacles including beach flame barrage, 1940 November – 1943 February.

18. TNA WO 199/2668 Home Forces, Scottish Command HQ, Anti-invasion measures, Defence of beaches, obstacles including beach flame barrage, 1940 November – 1943 February.

19. TNA WO 166/1567 Home Forces, War Diaries, Royal Artillery, 155 Field Regiment, 1939 September – 1941 March.

20. TNA WO 166/122 Home Forces, War Diaries, Scottish Command Headquarters, Royal Engineers, 1939 November – 1940 December.

21. I have used the position shown on the 1940 map.

22. TNA WO 199/2668 Home Forces, Scottish Command HQ, Anti-invasion measures, Defence of beaches, obstacles including beach flame barrage, 1940 November – 1943 February.

23. TNA WO 166/128 Home Forces, War Diaries, Scottish Command, General Staff, 1941 January–July.
24. TNA WO 166/641 Home Forces, War Diaries, 52nd Division, Commander Royal Engineers, 1941 January–December.
25. TNA WO 166/641 Divisions: 52nd Division: Commander Royal Engineers.
26. TNA WO 199/2662 HQ Scottish Command: Anti-invasion measures: Canadian pipe obstacles, 1941 July – 1942 March.
27. TNA WO 166/10362 Home Forces, War Diaries, Scottish Command, G, 1943 January–December.
28. TNA WO 199/2870 Home Forces, Scottish Command, Edinburgh Area, Defence Measures Forth and Tay Bridges, 1940 June – 1942 February.
29. Redfern, N., *Twentieth Century Fortifications in the United Kingdom: Vol. I, Introduction and Sources* (Council for British Archaeology, York, 1998), pp. 18–20.
30. TNA WO 199/2870 Scottish Command: Edinburgh Area: Defence Measures Forth and Tay Bridges, 1940 June–1942 February.
31. Redfern, N., *Twentieth Century Fortifications in the United Kingdom: Vol. V, Site Gazetteer: Scotland (ii)* (Council for British Archaeology, York, 1998).
32. TNA WO 166/998 Home Forces, War Diaries, 139th Infantry Brigade, HQ, 1939 January–1940 December.
33. TNA WO 166/4419 Home Forces, War Diaries, 2/5 Leicestershire Regiment, 1939 September – 1940 April, July–October, December – 1941 December.
34. Barclay, C.N., *The History of the Sherwood Foresters, Nottinghamshire and Derbyshire Regiment, 1919–1957* (William Clowes & Sons, London, 1959).
35. TNA WO 166/1496 Home Forces, War Diaries, Royal Artillery, 70 Field Regiment, 1939 January – 1941 December.
36. TNA WO 166/4668 Home Forces, War Diaries, 9 Sherwood Foresters (Nottinghamshire and Derbyshire Regiment), 1939 September – 1940 April, July – 1941 December.
37. TNA WO 73/146 Distribution of the Army; Monthly returns July to September 1940.
38. Rissik, D., *The DLI at War: The History of the Durham Light Infantry 1939–1945* (Durham Light Infantry, Durham, 1953).
39. Rissik, *The DLI at War*, p. 314.
40. TNA WO 166/1567 Home Forces, War Diaries, Royal Artillery, 155 Field Regiment, 1939 September – 1941 March.
41. TNA WO 166/1567 Home Forces, War Diaries, Royal Artillery, 155 Field Regiment, 1939 September – 1941 March.
42. TNA WO 166/4228 Home Forces, War Diaries, Second World War, Infantry: 14 Durham Light Infantry, 1940 July – 1941 December.
43. TNA WO 166/1450 Home Forces, War Diaries, Royal Armoured Corps: 4 Armoured Train Group, 12 Train Detachment, 1940 July – 1941 March.
44. Balfour, G., *The Armoured Train: Its Development and Usage* (Batsford, London, 1981).

INDEX